# Angela Carter's Pyrotechnics

# Angela Carter's Pyrotechnics

## *A Union of Contraries*

Edited by
Charlotte Crofts and Marie Mulvey-Roberts

BLOOMSBURY ACADEMIC
LONDON · NEW YORK · OXFORD · NEW DELHI · SYDNEY

BLOOMSBURY ACADEMIC
Bloomsbury Publishing Plc
50 Bedford Square, London, WC1B 3DP, UK
1385 Broadway, New York, NY 10018, USA
29 Earlsfort Terrace, Dublin 2, Ireland

BLOOMSBURY, BLOOMSBURY ACADEMIC and the Diana logo are trademarks of
Bloomsbury Publishing Plc

First published in Great Britain 2022
This paperback edition published 2023

Copyright © Charlotte Crofts, Marie Mulvey-Roberts and contributors, 2022

Charlotte Crofts, Marie Mulvey-Roberts and contributors have asserted their right under the
Copyright, Designs and Patents Act, 1988, to be identified as Authors of this work.

For legal purposes the Acknowledgements on p. xvi constitute
an extension of this copyright page.

Cover design: Namkwan Cho
Cover image © Fay Godwin/Alamy Stock Photo

All rights reserved. No part of this publication may be reproduced or transmitted
in any form or by any means, electronic or mechanical, including photocopying,
recording, or any information storage or retrieval system, without prior
permission in writing from the publishers.

Bloomsbury Publishing Plc does not have any control over, or responsibility for,
any third-party websites referred to or in this book. All internet addresses given in this
book were correct at the time of going to press. The author and publisher regret any
inconvenience caused if addresses have changed or sites have ceased to exist,
but can accept no responsibility for any such changes.

A catalogue record for this book is available from the British Library.

A catalog record for this book is available from the Library of Congress.

| ISBN: | HB: | 978-1-3501-8272-1 |
| --- | --- | --- |
| | PB: | 978-1-3501-8286-8 |
| | ePDF: | 978-1-3501-8273-8 |
| | eBook: | 978-1-3501-8274-5 |

Typeset by Integra Software Services Pvt. Ltd.

To find out more about our authors and books visit www.bloomsbury.com
and sign up for our newsletters.

*For Hannah, Nigel, Pushkin, Paula, Simon, Giorgio, Leonardo, Nonna, Angela and Ernie*

# Contents

| | |
|---|---|
| List of Illustrations | ix |
| Notes on Contributors | x |
| Foreword  *Gina Wisker* | xiv |
| Acknowledgements | xvi |
| | |
| Introduction   Fireworks: Angela Carter's incendiary imagination  *Charlotte Crofts and Marie Mulvey-Roberts* | 1 |

Part One   Signs and objects

| | | |
|---|---|---|
| 1 | Carter and Japanese signs: *Bunraku*, Mishima, *irezumi* and Sozo Araki  *Natsumi Ikoma* | 17 |
| 2 | Some kinds of love: Angela Carter, art and objects  *David Punter* | 31 |

Part Two   Music, performance and fairy tale

| | | |
|---|---|---|
| 3 | 'Down to the greenwood': Angela Carter and traditional folk singing  *Polly Paulusma* | 43 |
| 4 | From Griselda's patience to feminist grit: Angela Carter's 'The Patience of Grizelda' as a hidden intertext to 'The Bloody Chamber' and 'The Tiger's Bride'  *Martine Hennard Dutheil de la Rochère* | 71 |
| 5 | Of tales, tragic opera, transformation and 'tongues': *Tristan und Isolde* in Angela Carter's *The Bloody Chamber*  *Ashley Riggs* | 95 |

Part Three   Ways of seeing

| | | |
|---|---|---|
| 6 | Adapting Carter: *The Lady of the House of Love* and *The Bloody Chamber* on the Australian stage  *Belinda Locke* | 115 |
| 7 | 'What then?' Apocalypticism and Angela Carter's surrealist esthetics  *Scott A. Dimovitz* | 139 |
| 8 | Kaleidoscopes, stereoscopes and desire machines: Revolutions in vision in Angela Carter's *The Infernal Desire Machines of Doctor Hoffman*  *Caleb Sivyer* | 153 |

9  'The strangeness of the world made visible': Reading alignments between Angela Carter and Paula Rego  *Béatrice Bijon*   173

Part Four   Material bodies

10  Perceiving pleasures and appetites in *The Bloody Chamber*: 'Surprise me for dessert with every ice-cream in the ice box'  *Maria José Pires*   189
11  The skin that holds you in: States of dress and undress in Angela Carter's animal/human transformation stories  *Carys Crossen*   207
12  Angela Carter's questioning of 'age-appropriate' appearance and behaviour in *Wise Children*  *Zoe Brennan*   229

Index   244

# Illustrations

1. Some of the books in Paul and Angela Carter's Folk Music Archive. Reproduced with kind permission from Christine Molan — 45
2. Some of the vinyl in Paul and Angela Carter's Folk Music Archive. Reproduced with kind permission from Christine Molan — 46
3. Angela Carter's notation of 'Lucy Wan' in her notebook in Paul and Angela Carter's Folk Music Archive. Reproduced with kind permission from Christine Molan — 47
4. Angela Carter's notation of 'Higher Germany' in her notebook in Paul and Angela Carter's Folk Music Archive. Reproduced with kind permission from Christine Molan — 47
5. Detail of Angela Carter's notation of the key of E, from Paul and Angela Carter's Folk Music Archive. Reproduced with kind permission from Christine Molan — 47
6. Detail of Angela Carter's dedication to Paul inside their copy of James Reeves' *The Everlasting Circle* (1960). Paul and Angela Carter's Folk Music Archive. Reproduced with kind permission from Christine Molan — 48
7–9. The cover, reverse and disc of Peggy Seeger's EP 'Early in the Spring' (Topic Records TOP73, 1962) with Angela Carter's sleeve notes. Reproduced with kind permission from Topic Records — 50–51
10. *How Sir Tristram Drank of the Love Drink* (1893) by Aubrey Vincent Beardsley — 101
11. Promotional Image for *Lady of the House of Love* (2013) featuring Sandro Collarelli — 117
12. Production image from *The Bloody Chamber* (2013) featuring Alison Whyte — 119
13. Production image from *The Lady of the House of Love* (2013) featuring Sandro Colarelli — 126
14. Production image from *The Lady of the House of Love* (2013) featuring Sandro Colarelli — 126
15. Tables of character analysis of *The Lady of the House of Love* and *The Bloody Chamber* — 133

# Contributors

**Béatrice Bijon** is a Senior Lecturer at the Australian National University and a Senior Lecturer at the University of Saint-Etienne (France). She has published articles and chapters on Angela Carter as well as on British and Australian contemporary writers. She has edited several books on literature and travel, and is co-author of *Suffragistes et suffragettes: la conquête du droit de vote des femmes au Royaume-Uni et aux Etats-Unis* (2017). She has curated an exhibition on the British women's suffrage campaign for the National Library of Australia (2018) and co-directed and co-prodcued a film called *Etched in Bone* (2018).

**Zoe Brennan** is a Senior Lecturer in English at the University of the West of England, Bristol with a long-standing research and teaching focus on women's writing and representations of ageing. Regarding Angela Carter, a chapter in her book, 'The Older Woman in Recent Fiction', explores *Wise Children* and its framing of ageing sexuality. She has also contributed a chapter entitled 'Angela Carter's "Bristol Trilogy": A Gothic perspective on Bristol's 1960s Counterculture' to *Literary Bristol: Writers and the City* (2015), which is grounded in another of her interests: twentieth- and twenty-first-century Gothic.

**Charlotte Crofts** is an Associate Professor of Filmmaking at the University of the West of England, Bristol. She is an experienced editor (editor-in-chief of *Screenworks*, an online publication of screen media practice research (2006–present), on the editorial boards of *The Journal of Media Practice* (2006–17) and *Open Screens* (2017–present)). She has published a monograph on Angela Carter, *Anagrams of Desire: Angela Carter's Writing for Radio, Film and Television* (2003), a chapter 'Curiously Downbeat Hybrid or Radical Retelling? Neil Jordan's and Angela Carter's *The Company of Wolves*' in *Sisterhoods: Across the Literature/Media Divide* (1999) and written about her Japanese writings in '"The Other of the Other": Angela Carter's "New-Fangled" Orientalism' in *Re-Visiting Angela Carter: Texts, Contexts, Intertexts*, ed. Rebecca Munford (2006). She is currently developing a feature-film adaptation of Angela Carter's Japanese writings.

**Carys Crossen** was awarded her PhD in English and American studies from the University of Manchester in 2012. Since then she has spent her time researching and writing on vampires, gender, the Gothic and most particularly werewolves.

**Scott A. Dimovitz** received his PhD in modern and postmodern literature from New York University, and he is now an Associate Professor of English literature at Regis University in Denver, Colorado, where he specializes in postmodern literature, psychoanalysis and gender studies. He has written extensively on authors such as David Mitchell, Alison Bechdel and Paul Auster, and has published several works on Angela Carter, including *Angela Carter: Surrealist, Psychologist, Moral Pornographer*, which was released in 2016 from Routledge Press.

**Martine Hennard Dutheil de la Rochère** is Professor of English and comparative literature at the University of Lausanne. She has published on Dickens, Conrad, Nabokov, Rushdie, Carroll and Angela Carter, the international fairy tale tradition from Antiquity to the present and literary translation (theory, practice, reception). Her Carter-related work includes *Reading, Translating, Rewriting: Angela Carter's Translational Poetics* (2013), *Angela Carter traductrice – Angela Carter en traduction* (2014) and *Translation and Creativity – La traduction comme création* (2016), as well as several book chapters and articles for *EdL*, *CWW JSSE* and *Marvels & Tales*. She is currently pursuing her exploration of the interplay of translation and rewriting in Carter's fiction, notably in relation to Baudelaire.

**Natsumi Ikoma** received her PhD from the University of Durham and is a Professor of English and Japanese literature at International Christian University in Japan. Her research covers women's writing, representation of the body, monstrosity and grotesque, and gender performance and performativity, among others. She uses comparative and feminist methodology. Her recent publication includes the English translation of Sozo Araki's memoir of Angela Carter, *Seduced by Japan*. She writes extensively on Angela Carter and her current project deals with Japanese influences in Carter's writing.

**Maria José Pires** is a researcher at the University of Lisbon Centre for English Studies (ULICES/CEAUL), where she completed her MA in Angela Carter reading William Shakespeare in a postmodernity (2003) and her PhD 'Dealing with appetites: Angela Carter's fiction' (2013) in literature and culture studies/food studies. She co-coordinates the interdisciplinary project

Receiving|Perceiving English Literature in the Digital Age and coordinates the MSc in Innovation in Culinary Arts at Estoril Higher Institute for Tourism and Hotel Studies (ESHTE). She has been publishing since 2000 and her current research interests are literature, culture, tourism and food studies.

**Belinda Locke** is an independent researcher, theatre-maker and disability advocate. A graduate of Queensland University of Technology, her doctoral study focused on adaptations of Angela Carter's work for stage. Belinda's artistic practice brings to light hidden stories and experiences through performance. She has been awarded for her work as a young artist and leader as the inaugural recipient of the Rose Byrne Scholarship for an Emerging Female Leader in the Arts (2016) and was shortlisted for the Graham F. Smith Peace Award in 2019. Belinda serves as Chair of Arts Access Australia, the national peak body for arts and disability.

**Marie Mulvey-Roberts** is Professor of English Literature at the University of the West of England, Bristol and co-founder and Editor-in-Chief of *Women's Writing*. She is the author of *Dangerous Bodies: Historicising the Gothic Corporeal* (2016), winner of the Allan Lloyd Smith Memorial Prize and the editor of numerous books, including *The Arts of Angela Carter: A Cabinet of Curiosities* (2019) and *Strange Worlds: The Vision of Angela Carter* (2016), co-edited with Fiona Robinson, with whom she curated the 'Strange Worlds' exhibition on Angela Carter in Bristol. Her Massolit film on Carter's *The Bloody Chamber* has been widely shown in schools. She is one of the administrators of the website, getangelacarter.com, and a co-founder of the Angela Carter Society, https://angelacartersociety.com/. Currently, she is researching the influence of Old and Middle English on Angela Carter's work.

**Polly Paulusma** read English at Cambridge, graduating in 1997 with a first. In 2003 she signed to Björk's record label One Little Indian and toured internationally, supporting Bob Dylan, Jamie Cullum, Coldplay and Marianne Faithfull, among others. In 2012 she founded the Wild Sound label, now a folk imprint at newly named One Little Independent, and between them has to date released eight albums. She won a distinction for her MA from KCL in 2016 and in 2020 completed her PhD on Carter and folk song at UEA as a CHASE-funded scholar. She teaches at Cambridge University and ICMP specializing in practical criticism, musico-literary studies and songwriting. Her research has been published in *English: The Journal of the English Association* and *Contemporary*

*Women's Writing*, and her most recent album is 'Invisible Music: Folk Songs that Influenced Angela Carter'.

**David Punter** is an academic, writer and poet, currently professor of Poetry at the University of Bristol. He has published extensively as a literary critic, much of his work being on the Gothic, including *The Literature of Terror* (1980), *Gothic Pathologies* (1998) and *The Gothic Condition* (2016), but also on other themes and areas – *Writing the Passions* (2000), *Rapture: Literature, Addiction, Secrecy* (2009) and *The Literature of Pity* (2014). He has also published six books of poetry, *China and Glass* (1985), *Lost in the Supermarket* (1987), *Asleep at the Wheel* (1996), *Selected Short Stories* (1999), *Foreign Ministry* (2011) and *Bristol: 21 Poems* (2017). In 2014 he released a CD of his poetry, *Flashes in the Dark*, and he maintains a blog at www.davidpunter.wordpress.com.

**Ashley Riggs** is a Research and Teaching Fellow at the University of Geneva's Faculty of Translation and Interpreting. After completing her PhD, 'Thrice upon a Time: Feminist Fairy Tale Rewritings by Angela Carter and Emma Donoghue, and their French Translations' (University of Geneva, 2014), she contributed a chapter on Carter's rewritings of Little Red Riding Hood to *Angela Carter Traductrice – Angela Carter en traduction* (2014) and another on Donoghue's 'The Tale of the Shoe' to *Cinderella across Cultures* (2016). Ashley recently published *Stylistic Deceptions in Online News* (Bloomsbury, 2020). Her research and the Open Access publication were funded by the Swiss National Science Foundation.

**Caleb Sivyer** is a Senior Lecturer at the University of the West of England, Bristol, where he teaches a range of undergraduate and foundation year modules in the Humanities. He completed his doctoral thesis on gender and visuality in selected works by Virginia Woolf and Angela Carter at Cardiff University in 2016. His work focuses on women's writing, gender, visuality and twentieth-century English literature. He is also the founder and administrator of Angela Carter Online, as well as one of the founders of the Angela Carter Society.

# Foreword
## Gina Wisker

Prescient and vital, Angela Carter's statement in her 'Afterword' to *Fireworks* (1974) 'We live in Gothic times' (1995: 460) continues to haunt us today. Her voice and vision remind us how the insightful lens of the Gothic acts dutifully to enable us to shape the monstrous around us and within us, in order to respect and deal with it. This collection of wide-ranging, insightful chapters offers new, culturally inflected and critical views of Carter's writing. It ignites our fascination with her work and the rich insights with which she can still surprise us when we turn or return to it. Even the idea of pyrotechnics, the title of this collection with its rich, varied insights into Carter's work, is one which conjures up that brilliance, a colourful and critical explosion of the new, and edgy illumination of the commonplace, an exposure of the repressed and the repressive, which she brings to her fictions. Carter's writing is deliciously imaginative, generous and excessive in expression. History and literature are rich pickings for her, as are myths – those which repress freedoms and particularly the freedoms of women. It began by offering new perspectives on controlling myths of identity constructions, power relations and difference. Famously she announced in 'Notes from the Front Line': 'I'm in the demythologising business' and exposed 'what Blake called the "mind forg'd manacles"', with which we delude ourselves in internalizing and obeying dangerous and humiliating versions of self and human behaviour. A particular concern, as Carter points out, is 'How that social fiction of my "femininity" was created, by means outside my control, and palmed off on me as the real thing' (1997: 38).

An astute sense of literary and international cultural heritage infuses and is transmuted in Carter's critique of human folly, and her celebration of abundance, the carnivalesque richnesses of life. Carter's insightful, critical, comedic and Gothic work offers extraordinary insights into the repressive tales we publicly or secretly tell ourselves to maintain facades which hide the messiness and the excesses of both the physical and the imaginative life. She has given us a horde of expressive phrases which summon cutting imaginative insights, whilst her sense of the carnivalesque challenges small-minded constraints.

Carter's trajectory is focused on anew in this vital and lively collection of original work with fresh perspectives. Clearly there is so much more to discover about Carter's work, and many more ways of reading her, which even her fans and full-time literary critics have never imagined. This will, of course, continue. Her work and her insights are as hard to shut down as to put down. This is one of the important collections to re-open the gates to our future reading and understanding of her work. It was kindled by the successful 'Fireworks: The Visual Imagination of Angela Carter' conference (2017) hosted in Bristol by Marie Mulvey-Roberts and Charlotte Crofts (co-founders of the Angela Carter Society),[1] which took place during the exhibition, 'Strange Worlds: The Vision of Angela Carter', curated by Mulvey-Roberts and Fiona Robinson. This show formed a lively and creative relationship with the art which influenced Carter, her own artistic productions and art work either influenced by or running parallel to her own writing.

Angela Carter has always been responsive to difference, whether it be cultural, gendered or having blossomed from a worldview not of the ordinary, and her imagination travelling through time, space and the influences of the arts opens up and exposes and contests different views and values, behaviours and the acts of being and becoming. While Sarah Gamble (2005) commented on the absences and silences in her history, this collection gives us a sense of the creative responses of Carter, the alert, sensitive traveller and sojourner. She offers baroque versions of 1960s Bristol, and the strangenesses (to her) of Japan, in which she immersed herself in order to develop an appreciation of the culture, the artifice and restraint. Art, performance and the upsetting of divisive, oppressive binaries of gender and power run throughout the works of Carter as they do within the finely written chapters here. This book is truly pyrotechnic for, like Carter's own work, it is full of explosive new revelations lighting up darkened or hidden aspects of her work and reigniting our interest in all that she has written.

## Note

[1] The Angela Carter Society (www.angelacartersociety.com) was co-founded with Caleb Sivyer in 2017.

## Works cited

Carter, A. (1995), *Burning Your Boats: Collected Short Stories*, London: Chatto & Windus.

Carter, A. (1997), *Shaking a Leg: Collected Journalism and Writings*, London: Chatto & Windus.

# Acknowledgements

We would like to thank Ben Doyle for taking the project on in the first place and sustaining us with his enthusiasm, Laura Cope for copyediting and the rest of the Bloomsbury staff. Thanks are also due to Nigel Biggs for his astute eye and attention to detail in the indexing. Appreciation goes to the staff at Bauhaus, Bedminster. This collection was ignited by the 'Fireworks: Angela Carter's Visual Imagination' conference, hosted by the University of the West of England, Bristol, the Arnolfini and the Royal West of England Academy. We would also like to thank Christine Molan for permissions and keeping Angela Carter's musical heritage alive. A massive thanks to our contributors for their diligence and patience, to the Estate of Angela Carter for authors' permissions and also to members of the Angela Carter Society. The third-party copyrighted material displayed in the pages of this book are done so on the basis of 'fair dealing for the purposes of criticism and review' or 'fair use for the purposes of teaching, criticism, scholarship or research' only in accordance with international copyright laws, and is not intended to infringe upon the ownership rights of the original owners. Finally, thank you to Angela Carter for continuing to inspire us!

# Introduction
# Fireworks: Angela Carter's incendiary imagination

## Charlotte Crofts and Marie Mulvey-Roberts

Angela Carter's dazzling artistry can be seen to resemble a fireworks display, a myriad of radiant hues, bursting in different directions. We have set out to reflect her incendiary imagination in this explosive array of new scholarship on Carter's work, the title of which takes its point of inspiration from the etymology of the word 'pyrotechnics', which derives from the Greek nouns *pyr* ('fire') and *techne* ('art'). The term draws on the multi-valanced meanings and associations of the word 'pyrotechnics', which Angela Carter explores in her 1969 journal, written while she was living in Japan. She glosses the etymology of the word 'fireworks', translating it into different languages, including French: '*Feu d'artifice*, artificial fire' and Japanese: '*hana bi,* flower fire; Flowering fire'.[1] This also informs the title and themes of *Fireworks* (1974), her collection of short stories, written in Japan. The opening story is 'A Souvenir of Japan', in which Carter describes the sparks from sparklers falling down in 'beards of stars' and fireworks 'opening out like variegated parasols' (1995: 27). Whilst the lovers lay in the grass at night looking up at the sky, the narrator observes, 'Above our heads, the fireworks hung dissolving earrings on the night' (28). Here, fireworks form a series of metaphors which Carter utilizes to reveal the ephemeral and elusive nature of romantic love:

> [...] we were surrounded by the most moving images of evanescence, fireworks, morning glories, the old, children. But the most moving of these images were the intangible reflections of ourselves we saw in one another's eyes, reflections of nothing but appearances, in a city dedicated to seeming, and, try as we might to possess the essence of each other's otherness, we would inevitably fail.
> (1995: 34)

Carter had already explored the trope of the firework in an earlier 1961 journal, where she comments on the challenge of deploying it in a newly inventive way, lamenting:

> Too bad that so many writers have mucked around with fireworks. […] I don't know how to describe fireworks. 'See the sky is all in bloom,' nonsense. Whizz – a sparkling trail and a silent explosion into three dropping, dissolving trails. The cone of gunpowder that sent up a series of low, precise lights, tinted like fruit drops, red, blue, green, yellow boiled sweet colours.
> 
> (1961–62: Add. MS 88899/1/86, cited in Snaith 2018)

For Carter, fireworks were not just a source of aesthetic delight but also represented social and political disruption, which is, of course, the essence of Bonfire Night in Britain. In the Western tradition, firework displays often mark anniversaries of revolutionary activity. In the United States of America, they celebrate independence from Britain, on 4 July; in France, Bastille Day is marked by epic firework displays on 14 July. In Britain, fireworks have a very specific connotation used to commemorate Guy Fawkes' foiled revolutionary 'gunpowder plot', of 1605, celebrated on Bonfire Night every 5 November by burning a 'Guy' or effigy of Fawkes on communal bonfires across the nation. Carter sardonically observed 'Fireworks night; [is] celebrated today [Saturday 4 November] because one cannot profane the Lord's Day with such frivolities' (1961–62: Add. MS 88899/1/86). Quoting the same journal entry, her biographer Edmund Gordon describes how, after witnessing a fireworks display on Bonfire Night on the Downs, a green open space in Bristol, 'Angela noted the expressions of joy on faces lit by the flashing carousel of colours' (2016: 58). She and Paul then returned to their flat in Clifton and lit sparklers in the sitting room. Then they made love on the sofa – 'a new experience' (58).

The British version of national 'fireworks' celebrations, Bonfire Night, is used as a setting for the ending of Carter's second novel *The Magic Toyshop* (1967) when Uncle Philip sets fire to the house and Finn, Francie and Aunt Margaret (the 'red people') light a bonfire for Melanie 'to brighten away the wolves and tigers of this dreadful forest in which she lived' (122). This is rendered visually in the film adaptation (Wheatley 1987) which ends on Bonfire Night with Melanie lighting the pyre on which Uncle Philip is burnt as the Guy. The eponymous toyshop explodes dramatically, and as Angela Carter co-writes in the screenplay, 'the shop suddenly lights up with brilliant light and all the fireworks in the window go off, bursting through the glass' (1996: 293). Fittingly, the film adaptation was first broadcast on UK television on Bonfire Night in 1987.

This radical combustibility is re-enacted in the final short story of the *Fireworks* collection, 'Elegy for a Freelance', in which the protagonist finds herself living with aspiring terrorists plotting to blow up a member of the cabinet in a London on the brink of anarchy, paralleling Guy Fawkes' gunpowder plot. The heroine describes boys, in the basement of the house in which she lives, filling milk bottles with petrol to make explosions (1995: 96). This recalls Carter's oft-quoted line from 'Notes from The Frontline': 'I am all for putting new wine in old bottles, especially if the pressure of the new wine makes the old bottles explode' (1997: 37). The story is filled with allusions to incendiaries that foreshadow revolutionary upheaval:

> The sky opened like the clockwork Easter eggs the Tsars gave one another. The night would part, like two halves of a dark shell, and spill explosions. Because I lived in a house full of amateur terrorists, I felt I myself lit the fuses and caused these displays of pyrotechnics.
>
> (1995: 97)

In the story, the lover, known as X, is actually based on Carter's Japanese lover, Sozo Araki (Dimovitz 2016: 42), whose eyes she describes as 'lycanthropic', glowing in the dark 'like fuses' (1995: 99). She associates orgasmic love-making with 'a series of beautiful explosions' drawing on the image of an erupting volcano as 'an endless reduplication of ecstasy' (99). 'We were living on the crater of a volcano and felt the earth move beneath us. What stirring times! seismographic times!' (1996: 100). It is important to acknowledge that in 'Elegy for a Freelance' whilst the fireworks represent the thrill, the passion, the sex, there is also a nasty and sinister underside to this failed revolution, terrorist attacks and murders. What they had assumed was thunder turns out to be the 'gun and mortar fire' of a military coup, signalling the beginning of civil war (107). Writing in the 'Afterword' to *Fireworks*, Carter declared that on returning to England after living in Japan, she found herself in 'a new country. It was like waking up, it was a rude awakening' (1996: 459).

Like Carter we use both the Western and Eastern traditions of pyrotechnics as a conceptual framework for this re-appraisal of her work. This represents, paradoxically, a simultaneous clash and fusion of cultures. On the one hand, the Japanese *hanabi*, translated as 'fire-flowers', reflects the highly constructed artifice of her art and incendiary imagination. On the other, within the Western tradition, 'pyrotechnics' not only refers literally to firework displays but also has an extended figurative usage, embodying the idea of virtuosity, referring to any kind of 'brilliant or sensational performance' (OED). This original meaning has been deployed by literary critics to disparage overblown, ostentatious writing as in the following definition: 'A pyrotechnic performance is always impressive, but the word occasionally suggests something more like "flashy" or "flamboyant"' (Merriam-Webster). This latter use has been applied to Carter's virtuosic displays of literary technique. Carter's *The Bloody Chamber* was included in a review essay entitled 'Technics and Pyrotechnics' (Garrett 1980) and Merja Makinen refers to 'Carter's pyrotechnics of allusion' (2016: 297). As Helen Snaith points out, 'Robert Coover describes Carter's stories possessing a "fireworks-like tendency to fade a little at the end (a diminishing shower)", though he recognizes that they demonstrate, "very extraordinary pyrotechnics"'(2018: 23). Carter herself uses the word in this way in her short story, 'The Loves of Lady Purple' (1974): 'So foreclosed Lady Purple's pyrotechnical career, which ended as if it had been indeed a firework display, in ashes, desolation and silence' (1995: 47). Here, the imagery of burnt-out fireworks is used to bring to an end the virtuosic vocation of the cruel and deadly marionette. The spent firework, hollowed out or reduced to ashes, becomes *la petite mort*, contrasting with the sensory overload at the zenith of her debauchery. This is matched verbally in Carter's excessively florid and baroque writing style, through which she captures the cacophony of sound and silence and psychedelics of a pyrotechnical display. In a 1977 radio interview, Carter discusses her writing style in the *Fireworks* collection, suggesting that even she thought she was 'peaking a bit, stylistically', nevertheless she admits to having 'developed this highly decorative, very tightly structured prose that could almost fit anything', saying, 'I was quite consciously utilising it' and claiming, 'I mean it was lovely, it was beautiful, because I was in control of it' (1977b). Towards the end of her life, she defended this style of writing in her final interview, admitting: 'Okay, I write overblown, purple, self-indulgent prose. So fucking what?' (BBC 1992). Our use of the word 'pyrotechnics' in the main title seeks to reclaim the positive aspects, thereby corroborating Angela Carter's emphatic defense of her writing style.

Our subtitle relates to the Blakean notion of the 'union of contraries' taken from the poem, *The Marriage of Heaven and Hell* (1794), which Carter cites in her review of Christina Stead's book (1982), collected amongst her journalistic writings in *Shaking a Leg* (1997). Here she quotes Blake 'Without contraries is no progression. Attraction and repulsion, Reason and Energy, Love and Hate, are necessary to Human existence' (1997: 578). In Carter's hands, the 'union of contraries' is a way of breaking down binaries and embracing and exploding paradox. This is informed also by her attraction towards the surrealists, who she says were admirers of William Blake (1997: 512), such as Andre Breton who drew on the idea of the 'union of opposites' in 'The Manifesto of Surrealism' ([1924] 1969). This in turn informs Carter's development as a writer, which she described as 'various intellectual adventures in anarcho-surrealism' in 'Notes from The Front Line' (1997: 37). Although Carter 'got bored' (1997: 512) with the surrealists because they 'were not good with women', nevertheless she admits 'the old juices can still run, as in the mouths of Pavlov's dogs, when I hear the old *incendiary* slogans … "the marvellous alone is beautiful" (*First Manifesto of Surrealism*, 1924)' (our italics, 1997: 512).

Carter planned to write a surrealist allegorical trilogy, starting with *The Infernal Desire Machines of Doctor Hoffman*. The second novel, which was eventually published as *The Passion of New Eve*, started off life as *The Great Hermaphrodite* (Gordon 2016: 176), a title that represents a union of gender opposites and is also a culmination of the alchemical process. The figure of an alchemist appears in the novel, the Czech neighbour of the male protagonist, Evelyn who is later forcibly surgically transformed into the female Eve. For him/her this 'union of opposites' is a surrealist embodiment. In 'The Alchemy of the Word', Carter celebrates the surrealists' 'juxtapositions of objects, or people, or ideas, that arbitrarily extend our notion of the connections it is possible to make' (512).

Collectively the chapters in this book are disparate in topic and in their critical approach, yet they work together within the pyrotechnic conceptual framework and the notion of progressive paradox. Just as *Fireworks* is a seemingly diverse set of short stories, this collection can be seen as a bricolage, or patchwork of sorts. Indeed, in Carter's semi-autobiographical story called 'The Quilt Maker' (1995), she reveals the workings of a deliberate narrative strategy: 'With all patchwork, you must start in the middle and work outward, even on the kind they call "crazy patchwork", which is made of feather-stitching together arbitrary shapes scissored out at the maker's whim' (1995: 444). She goes on to say: 'The more I think about it, the more I like this metaphor. You can really make this image work for its living; it synthesizes perfectly both the miscellany of experience and the use we make of it' (444–5). We have therefore adopted this approach in this collection, analysing her eclectic output, buttressing multidisciplinary perspectives together and offering an explosion of new ideas which seeks to reinvigorate further Angela Carter scholarship.

The chapters are grouped in four parts, the first of which explores 'Signs and Objects' and foregrounds how the cross-cultural interpretation of signs and object-oriented ontology both informs and pervades Angela Carter's writings. The second part, 'Music, Performance and Fairy Tale', traces a direct line from

Angela Carter's early experience of folk music, through her translation of Perrault and engagement with Wagner's opera to contemporary stage adaptations of her work, emphasizing not only the performativity of her writing but also the musicality of her prose. The third part focuses on 'Ways of Seeing', with chapters focusing on Carter's visual acuity, and how her writing challenges the hegemony of vision and invites us to look anew. Finally, the closing part, 'Material Bodies', celebrates the sensual use of food, clothes and appearance in Carter's work. This section draws the collection together by interrogating the relationship between our senses, on the one hand, and material culture and lived experience, on the other. Implicated in this is the power of appearances, disguising and inventing the self.

In Chapter 1, 'Carter and Japanese signs: *Bunraku*, Mishima, *irezumi* and Sozo Araki', Natsumi Ikoma explores the influence of Carter's time in Japan and her relationship with Sozo Araki on her life and writing. Ikoma focuses on the ways in which Carter's Japan experience – and her attempts to decode the 'signs' she encountered in Japanese culture, including *bunraku* (puppetry), *irezumi* (tattoos) and the writings and suicide of Yukio Mishima – inform her developing consciousness as a postmodern, feminist writer. Carter experienced Japan through the lens of her Japanese lover, Araki, and Ikoma unpacks the complex nexus of power, race and gender underpinning their relationship, which forced Carter to confront her own Orientalist gaze towards Japan, whilst at the same time peeling back the layers of patriarchal power and desire.

David Punter explores Carter's allusion to art objects in her fifth novel, *Love* (1971) in Chapter 2, 'Some kinds of love: Angela Carter, art and objects', using the musty mise-en-scène of Annabel and Buzz's apartment as an aperture through which to offer a new reading of the novel, one that focuses less on the narrative love triangle between Annabel, Buzz and his brother Lee, and more on the expressionist textures and moments of the novel. Punter suggests that *Love* is steeped in the idea of collecting, not only in a descriptive sense – from the strange collection of objects Buzz hoards in his room, to Annabel's sketches – but also in a metaphoric and psychological sense. As Annabel's state of mind deteriorates, her relationship to the objects becomes more surreal, indicating not only her declining mental health but also that of the world around her.

Polly Paulusma investigates the relationship between Carter's involvement with folk singing and the themes and style of her writing in Chapter 3, '"Down to the greenwood": Angela Carter and traditional folk singing'. Paulusma identifies a gap in current scholarship, which, whilst it recognizes Carter's eclectic intertextual reference to folk tales, fairy tales and other arenas of popular culture, sets out to examine the lasting impact of Carter's experience as a singer, player and scholar of the traditional British folk song. During the 1960s, Carter not only supported her then husband, folk producer and field recordist Paul Carter in collecting British folk songs but also actively took part in the folk scene, singing live herself. Paulusma hones in on the theme of the greenwood in folk song – that site of danger, violence, aberration, magic and transformation – and how it is woven into Carter's oeuvre from 'The Erl-King' to *Nights at the Circus* and *Wise Children*, as part of her demythologizing project. Paulusma goes further to suggest that folk singing not only informs the themes of Carter's writing but its very structure – arguing for a somatic understanding of the rhythms and cadences of Carter's prose.

In Chapter 4, 'From Griselda's patience to feminist grit: Angela Carter's "The Patience of Grizelda" as a hidden intertext to "The Bloody Chamber" and "The Tiger's Bride"', Martine Hennard Dutheil de la Rochère argues that Carter's *The Bloody Chamber* collection needs to be read in tandem with her experience of translating the *Fairy Tales of Charles Perrault*, focusing particularly on the story of 'The Patience of Grizelda' as a hidden intertext to 'The Bloody Chamber' and 'The Tiger's Bride'. Hennard Dutheil analyses Carter's unpublished translation and argues that the story of an aristocratic husband's domination, manipulation and cruelty towards his young wife is a hidden (and heretofore unidentified) intertext that informs the feminist writer's take on 'Bluebeard' in 'The Bloody Chamber' as cautioning against the seductive dangers of submitting to a perverse husband. The argument is underpinned by an understanding of Angela Carter's 'translational poetics', which recognizes that the act of translation informs Carter's own reworking and rewriting of the original fairy tales.

Similarly, in Chapter 5, 'Of tales, tragic opera, transformation and "tongues": *Tristan und Isolde* in Angela Carter's *The Bloody Chamber*', Ashley Riggs identifies another neglected intertext, the story of Tristan und Isolde which is woven into three key stories in *The Bloody Chamber* collection, 'The Bloody Chamber', 'The Company of Wolves' and 'Wolf-Alice'. Riggs argues that Carter's demythologizing project relies in part on a 'critical dialogue' with Wagner's well-known opera, particularly in her rewriting of the *Verklärung* (German for 'transfiguration') motif that enabled her to posit a new era for gender relations and a complex understanding of female eroticism that informs her feminist project.

In Chapter 6, 'Adapting Carter: *The Lady of the House of Love* and *The Bloody Chamber* on the Australian stage', Belinda Locke undertakes a comparative analysis of two theatre adaptations of different stories from *The Bloody Chamber*.

Drawing on interviews with the creative practitioners and an analysis of the performances, Locke identifies the ways in which the two productions address the complexity of dramatizing Carter's highly wrought prose, her rich imagery and use of metaphor, through set design, costume and casting. Locke goes on to explore how both productions attempt to navigate the tensions involved in staging the gender and power dynamics at work in the original stories, using the same actor to play multiple characters, cutting across genders, and exploding narrative conventions.

Scott Dimovitz explores Carter's apocalyptic worlds in Chapter 7, '"What then?" Apocalypticism and Angela Carter's surrealist esthetics', arguing that the Cold War threat of nuclear annihilation informs her attraction to surrealist symbolism in *The Infernal Desire Machines of Doctor Hoffman* (1972), *The Passion of New Eve* (1977a) and *Nights at the Circus* (1984) – the triad of novels that she referred to in her journals as the *Manifesto for Year One*. Dimovitz unpacks Carter's sadistic apocalyptic vision, which takes pleasure in the end of the world because it offers the possibility to transform it, suggesting that she falls short of offering an alternative vision – leaving us only to speculate, like the reference to Keats' 'wild surmise' with which she ends *The Magic Toyshop* (1967: 200).

In Chapter 8, 'Kaleidoscopes, stereoscopes and desire machines: Revolutions in vision in Angela Carter's *The Infernal Desire Machines of Doctor Hoffman*', Caleb Sivyer explores, for the first time, Carter's use of pre-cinematic devices, including the kaleidoscope, daguerreotype, stereoscope and phantasmagoria, to challenge the hegemonic scopic regime. Sivyer argues that Carter's recourse to these optical devices in the novel enables her to explore the theme of visuality, troubling Desiderio's 'sardonic' masculine gaze and exploding the conventional patriarchal structures of looking.

In Chapter 9, '"The strangeness of the world made visible": Reading alignments between Angela Carter and Paula Rego', Béatrice Bijon offers a chiasmic reading of Carter's writing in relation to the surrealist artist Paula Rego. In comparative readings of Carter's short stories, 'The Courtship of Mr Lyon' and 'The Tiger's Bride' in *The Bloody Chamber* (1979) and 'The Executioner's Beautiful Daughter' in *Fireworks* (1974), with Rego's 'Girl and Dog' series and other works, Bijon suggests that both Carter and Rego draw on similar themes of violent fairy tale, dark sexuality and gender ambiguity and both artists confront disturbing issues around incest and familial dysfunction. Similarly, Bijon argues, both Carter and Rego are preoccupied with disrupting the gaze and ways of seeing. This builds on Sivyer's exploration of the way in which

Carter's work explodes traditional structures of looking. Both artists present horrific tableaux that invite us to reposition ourselves as readers/viewers in order to construct our own meanings.

In Chapter 10, 'Perceiving pleasures and appetites in *The Bloody Chamber*: "Surprise me for dessert with every ice-cream in the ice box"', Maria José Pires takes us on a culinary tour of Carter's fairy tale worlds through close textual analysis of stories from *The Bloody Chamber* collection, and a detailed discussion of two gastronomic experiences inspired by her writing. This interdisciplinary chapter is exciting in its combination of theory and practice, creating a dialogue between literary and food studies in this critical examination of food and its contexts of production, preparation and consumption. Two Angela Carter-inspired interactive tasting events both draw on and draw attention to the culinary grammar of her writing and invite the participants to indulge their appetites, not only of the imagination but also the physical, in a multi-sensory experience.

In Chapter 11, 'The skin that holds you in: States of dress and undress in Angela Carter's animal/human transformation stories', Carys Crossen examines the role of fashion, clothing and costume in the short stories from *The Bloody Chamber* and 'Peter and the Wolf' from the *Black Venus* collection. Crossen suggests that, in Carter's rewritten fairy tales, clothing plays an important role in differentiating between humans and animals, as well as contributing to the performance of identity. Drawing on the work of Joanna Trevenna, Crossen questions the 'Butlerification' of Carter, interrogating how closely Carter's work aligns with Judith Butler's idea of gender as performance. Crossen suggests instead that Carter is more interested in an exploration of identity beyond gender, as evident in the endings of both 'The Tiger's Bride' and 'Peter and the Wolf', where the female characters reject humanity itself.

Finally, Zoe Brennan explores Carter's representation of ageing in Chapter 12, 'Angela Carter's questioning of "age-appropriate" appearance and behaviour in *Wise Children*'. Brennan argues that the septuagenarian Chance sisters defy and trouble our expectations about their age in three ways: through their defiant application of make-up and wearing of 'age-inappropriate' lycra – rendering them visible in the public space; through Dora's active sexuality; and through the taking on of a post-menopausal, non-biological maternal role at the end of the novel. Situating the novel within emerging gerontological discourse, Brennan explores how the novel both draws attention to the mask of ageing and celebrates the usually invisible agency, subjectivity and interiority of the aged twins, through Dora's irreverent, life-affirming narration. Novels like *Wise Children* reveal how Carter was equally at home with low as well as high art.

Throughout all of these chapters, the various emanations of 'fireworks' are displayed. Several contributors explicitly draw on the firework trope to express intercultural clashes and convey the stylistic dazzle of Carter's work. The pyrotechnics of this collection cuts across cultures – not simply East and West but through various subcultures, from Japanese semiotics, high art and popular culture, scopic regimes, gendered performances and translational poetics, through which we encounter and shape the world. Every chapter is in critical dialogue with published work on Carter. The ever-mounting number of essay collections and critical works on Carter serve as a testimony to her enduring versatility and ability to address the present moment. The way in which the alchemy of Carter's art transforms different media is reflected in the various chapters of this new collection which foreground fresh perspectives, building on Crofts' work on Carter's writing for radio, film and television, which is discussed extensively in *Anagrams of Desire* (2003) and Mulvey-Roberts' exploration of Carter's interdisciplinarity in *The Arts of Angela Carter* (2019). Previous editors have included Joseph Bristow and Trev Lynn Broughton (1997), who take their cue from Carter's novel *The Infernal Desire Machines of Doctor Hoffman* for an engagement with Carter's 'infernal desires' in the context of feminism and femininity, while Rebecca Munford (2006) revisits Carter through her penchant for intertextuality. Yutaka Okuhata's *Angela Carter's Critique of Her Contemporary World: Politics, History and Mortality* (2021) is the most recent reminder that her world is also, in so many ways, still our world with many of the same unresolved issues and that her voice remains as relevant as ever. Stephen Hunt's book on Carter's contribution to the counterculture in the West Country in the 1960s and 1970s (2020) is yet another step away from the sanitized perception of Carter as a tame 'white witch' and spinner of other-worldly fairy tales (Rushdie 1992). This collection also highlights how Carter was a highly politicized and in many ways unruly writer. For example, one contributor reveals how Carter engaged with folk music, which was then a component of a radical subculture (see Paulusma), and another demonstrates how her apocalyptic vision fed into her anxieties about the Cold War (see Dimovitz).

It was a conference entitled 'Fireworks: The Visual Imagination of Angela Carter', organized by Crofts and Mulvey-Roberts, which lit the touchpaper for *Pyrotechnics: A Union of Contraries*. The conference coincided with the 'Strange Worlds: The Vision of Angela Carter' exhibition at the Royal West of England Academy in Bristol in 2016 (see Mulvey-Roberts and Robinson) and was timed to commemorate twenty-five years since her death. In contrast, for this book, it seemed appropriate to look forward, celebrating what would have been Carter's eightieth birthday. Our belated birthday present serves as yet another textual memorial though it can never pay full tribute to the soaring power of Carter's extraordinary imagination and literary gymnastics. For that, one need only look upwards to a night-sky, lit up by the kaleidoscopic, effervescent and anarchic choreography of cascading, exploding fireworks.

## Note

1  We are indebted to Martine Hennard Dutheil for this observation (see Hennard Dutheil de la Rochère, forthcoming).

## Works cited

*Angela Carter's Curious Room* (1992), [TV programme] Dir. Kim Evans, BBC1, 15 September, 22.10.
Breton, A. ([1924] 1969), 'Manifesto of Surrealism', in *Manifestoes of Surrealism*, trans. R. Seaver and H. R. Lane, Ann Arbor, MI: University of Michigan Press.
Bristow, J. and T. L. Broughton (1997), *The Infernal Desires of Angela Carter: Fiction, Femininity and Feminism*, London: Longman.
Butler, J. (2006), *Gender Trouble: Feminism and the Subversion of Identity*, London and New York: Routledge.
Carter, A. (1961–62), Unpublished Journal, Angela Carter Papers, London: British Library, Add. MS 88899/1/86.
Carter, A. (1967), *The Magic Toyshop*, London: Heinemann.
Carter, A. (1969–74), Unpublished Journal, Angela Carter Papers, London: British Library, Add. MS 88899/1/93.
Carter, A. (1971), *Love*, London: Rupert Hart-Davis.
Carter, A. (1972), *The Infernal Desire Machines of Doctor Hoffman*, London: Rupert Hart-Davis.
Carter, A. (1974), *Fireworks: Nine Profane Pieces*, London: Quartet.
Carter, A. (1977a), *The Passion of New Eve*, London: Victor Gollancz.
Carter, A. (1977b), Interview with Angela Carter (interviewer unidentified), The British Library Sound Archives, BLSA C1365/12.
Carter, A. (1979), *The Bloody Chamber*, London: Victor Gollancz.
Carter, A. ((1995) [1981]), 'The Quilt Maker', in *Burning Your Boats: Collected Short Stories*, 444–60, London: Chatto & Windus.
Carter, A. (1984), *Nights at the Circus*, London: Chatto & Windus.
Carter, A. (1991), *Wise Children*, London: Chatto & Windus.

Carter, A. (1995), *Burning Your Boats: Collected Short Stories*, London: Chatto & Windus.

Carter, A. (1996), *The Curious Room: Collected Dramatic Works*, London: Chatto & Windus.

Carter, A. (1997), *Shaking a Leg: Collected Writings*, London: Chatto & Windus.

Crofts, C. (2003), '*Anagrams of Desire*': *Angela Carter's Writing for Radio, Film and Television*, Manchester: Manchester University Press.

Dimovitz, S. (2016), *Angela Carter: Surrealist, Psychologist, Moral Pornographer*, London and New York: Routledge.

Garrett, G. (1980), 'Technics and Pyrotechnics', *The Sewanee Review*, 88 (3): 412–23.

Gordon, Ed. (2016), *The Invention of Angela Carter: A Biography*, London: Chatto & Windus.

Hennard Dutheil de la Rochère, M. (forthcoming), '"Morning Glories of the Night": Angela Carter's Translational Poetics in *Fireworks*', *Contemporary Women's Writing*, special issue on Angela Carter in Japan, ed. Charlotte Crofts and Natsumi Ikoma.

Hunt, S. (2020), *Angela Carter's 'Provincial Bohemia'; The Counterculture in 1960s and 1970s Bristol and Bath*, Bristol: Bristol Radical History Group.

Hunt, S., C. Crofts, and M. Mulvey-Roberts (2020), '"Truly It Felt Like Year One": A Tour of Angela Carter's 1960s Bristol'. Available at: http://getangelacarter.com/truly-it-felt-like-year-one-a-tour-of-angela-carters-1960s-bristol (accessed 21 December 2020).

Makinen, M. (2016), Review of *Erotic Infidelities: Love and Enchantment in Angela Carter's 'The Bloody Chamber'*, by Kimberly J. Lau. *Tulsa Studies in Women's Literature*, 35 (11): 296–7. https://doi.org/10.1353/tsw.2016.0009.

Merriam-Webster, 'Pyrotechnic', *Merriam-Webster*. Available at: https://www.merriam-webster.com/dictionary/pyrotechnic (accessed 14 December 2020).

Mulvey-Roberts, M. (2019), *The Arts of Angela Carter: A Cabinet of Curiosities*. Manchester: Manchester University Press.

Mulvey-Roberts, M. and F. Robinson (curators) (December 2016–March 2017), 'Strange Worlds: The Vision of Angela Carter' Exhibition, Royal West of England Academy, Bristol.

Mulvey-Roberts, M. and F. Robinson (eds) (2016), *Strange Worlds: The Vision of Angela Carter*, Bristol: Sansom & Company.

Munford, R. (2006), *Re-visiting Angela Carter: Texts, Contexts, Intertexts*, Basingstoke: Palgrave Macmillan.

OED 'Pyrotechnics', *Oxford English Dictionary*. Available at: https://www.lexico.com/definition/pyrotechnics (accessed 14 December 2020).

Okuhata, Y. (2021), *Angela Carter's Critique of Her Contemporary World: Politics, History and Mortality*, Bern, Switzerland: Peter Lang.

Paulusma, P. (2021), *Invisible Music: Folksongs that Influenced Angela Carter*, Online Concert. Available at: https://vimeo.com/417590661 (accessed 7 December 2020).

Rushdie, S. (1992), 'Angela Carter, 1940–92: A Very Good Wizard, a Very Dear Friend', *New York Times*, 8 March.
Smith, A. C. H. (2017), *Pussy*, Renato's Theatre Company, Alma Theatre, 10–13 October.
Smith, A. C. H. (2019), *The Ruby Choker*, Renato's Theatre Company, Improv Theatre, 26–28 January.
Snaith, H. (2018), 'Fictions Written in a Certain City': Representations of Japan in Angela Carter's work. PhD Thesis, Swansea University. Available at: http://cronfa.swan.ac.uk/Record/cronfa51160 (accessed 7 December 2020).
*The Magic Toyshop* (1987), [Film] Dir. David Wheatley, UK: Granada Television.
Trevenna, J. (2002), 'Gender as Performance: Questioning the "Butlerification" of Angela Carter's Fiction', *Journal of Gender Studies*, 11 (3): 267–76.

Part One

# Signs and objects

1

# Carter and Japanese signs: *Bunraku*, Mishima, *irezumi* and Sozo Araki

Natsumi Ikoma

Until the publication of Carter's official biography in 2016, how Angela Carter spent her years in Japan had been 'mysterious' to the public (Gamble 2006: 106), though it is shared knowledge that her literary style significantly changed post-Japan. Edmund Gordon's book sheds light on some part of it and reveals to the world the existence of her ex-boyfriend, Sozo Araki, with whom she cohabited, and how she had a devastating and intense relationship with him. I have the good fortune of knowing Sozo, and after interviewing him, I persuaded him to write a memoir of Angela Carter, which was translated and published in 2017.[1] Informed by Sozo, as well as by Carter's own writing, this chapter examines how Carter analysed Japanese signs – culture, social incidents and people – that made a huge impact on the pyrotechnics in Carter's later works.

Going against the easy temptation for a European to distance themselves from Japanese elements by treating them as an 'Other' and transferring anything alien onto the 'orientals', either positively or negatively, Carter chose instead to immerse herself in Japanese culture and to analyse it intimately. By doing so, and by being absorbed in Japan so as to call it 'home' (Carter [1974] 1988: 70), she managed to acquire a unique vantage point from which she examined things in Japan, such as *irezumi*, *bunraku* puppet theatre, *kabuki*, films, literature, Yukio Mishima and her ex-boyfriend Sozo, among others.

This unique vantage point originates in the fact she was deeply in love with Sozo. Her fascination with him was, in the beginning, largely aesthetic. When she met Sozo at a cafe in Shinjuku, in downtown Tokyo, she found him 'incredibly beautiful' (Gordon 2016: 140). Sozo himself remembers having been complimented on his beauty by Carter; she praised his smooth skin, slender physique and supple muscles (Araki 2017: 105). He was, to her, initially a work of art, whose beauty she appreciated. Like a beautiful object, he was easy to approach and make contact with. She found Japanese men in general very beautiful. In the interview with Ronald Bell, when asked what has given her the most pleasure while living in Japan, she replied, 'Japanese men… They're very beautiful!' (Bell 1973: 26).

As her love for Sozo grew more intense, however, going past the beautiful look became an issue for her. She may have wanted to read him like a book, if she could. But he was a complicated book, hard to decipher, and she could not read Japanese. Their relationship was not all bliss, as Sozo was an unreliable partner, and their relationship was turbulent. She had to rely on Sozo's translations, and it was not an ideal situation for her, receiving only what had been filtered through him. They argued often, though they had passionate as well as peaceful moments, too. Trying to understand him and Japan, Carter observed, dissected and analysed everything around her.

Asked what had been the least pleasant aspect of her stay, Carter gave the same response as before: 'Japanese men!' (Bell 1973: 27). The interview took place after Sozo had left her, and she talked about Sozo in the past tense:

> I lived with a Japanese national for a year. It is a great adventure to love a Japanese; much more so, maybe, than any of the other cross-cultural, cross-racial explorations, because of the peculiar severity of the Japanese idea of themselves. And one never knows where it will end because one becomes very much aware of one's own culture as one – well, at any rate, I – learned more and more about the sheer horror of being Japanese, of being a Japanese man, of the Procrustean bed of the traditional mores.
>
> (Bell 1973: 27)

By 'the Procrustean bed', Carter seems to suggest how Japanese society demands its citizens to fit in: to a certain concept, a style, a form. This insightful verdict on Japanese men may have been what she arrived at after she broke up with Sozo. But one of her earliest descriptions of Sozo in her journal around the time of their initial meeting compares him to a *samurai* (ADD Ms. 88899/1/93). This is quite discerning and prophetic, when read in conjunction with her published analysis of *samurai* in 'A Souvenir of Japan':

> To look at a samurai, you would not know him for a murderer, or a geisha for a whore. The magnificence of such objects hardly pertains to the human. They live only in a world of icons and there they participate in rituals which transmute life itself to a series of grand gestures, as moving as they are absurd.
>
> ([1974] 1988: 10)

In this entry, with the remarkable acuteness of a true artist, Carter noted that the extravagance of the Japanese performance of gender, which is epitomized in the stylized beauty of *samurai* and *geisha*, makes them 'objects hardly pertains to the human'. These constructions are dazzling, but underneath their layers of *kimono* is humanity obliterated and made irrelevant. From very early on in her stay in Japan, Carter somehow managed to grasp this principle in Japanese culture: the detachment of the surface from what is underneath. The frequently used Japanese expressions, '*tatemae*' and '*honne*', or 'what you express to others' and 'what you truly feel', might show the extent of how commonplace this principle is. What matters and is valued is the surface in the tradition of Japanese culture. From the very first time she met Sozo, Carter sensed something repressed and repressive underneath his friendly and beautiful smile, and this gap between the smooth and beautiful mask and repressed humanity is what could have fascinated Angela Carter.

## *Bunraku* puppet theatre and its performance of femininity

Carter could not read the Japanese language, though she tried to learn it from Sozo briefly. But perhaps because she was illiterate in Japanese, Carter had a peculiar ability to grasp the 'signs', including human performance, as pure visual 'signifiers' independent of their 'signified' meanings, as 'not speaking Japanese, and so having to interpret the culture entirely through its visual aspect, was an invaluable "apprenticeship in the language of signs"' (Gordon 2016: 157). Her use of the word 'signs' here is most certainly a nod to Roland Barthes' *Empire of Signs* published in 1970, overlapping Carter's stay in Japan.[2] This book exhibits a sensibility extraordinarily similar to the one expressed in Carter's writing. With regard to *bunraku* traditional puppet theatre, Barthes writes, 'In the West, the puppet (Punch, for instance) is supposed to offer the actor the mirror of his contrary... *Bunraku*, however, does not sign the actor, it gets rid of him for us' ([1970] 1983: 58). As explained by Barthes, a puppet in *bunraku* is controlled by three male masters: the leading master manipulates the head and the right hand, another the left hand, and the third one the legs. Only the headmaster shows his face, while the other two conceal their faces behind black covers. Puppets are voiced by a male chanter, even when the character is female. Importantly, the corporeality of these masters and chanters, even in the case of the headmaster who is not clad in inconspicuous black costume but in formal *kimono* for men, is erased in the stylized performance. The bodies of the puppet masters in *bunraku* theatre, as Barthes analyses, are reduced to mere functionality. Their masculine bodies and voices do not need to be hidden, because the theatrical codes bury them in the background as the fabled performance of 'ultimate femininity' comes to the fore.

Ultimate femininity, performed by a doll that is controlled and voiced by men, may attest to what is appreciated in the Japanese theatrical tradition: a constructed femininity, not a real woman. Indeed, not a single woman is allowed to take part in the traditional *bunraku* puppet theatre. Another theatre tradition in Japan, *kabuki*, is also an all-male endeavour in which no woman is allowed to perform, and *kabuki* actors playing female roles are praised for their performance of 'femininity' that is said to exceed that by real women.[3] Barthes analyses these *kabuki* male actors thus:

> The Oriental transvestite does not copy Woman but signifies her: not bogged down in the model, but detached from its signified; Femininity is presented to read, not to see: translation, not transgression; the sign shifts from the great female role to the fifty-year-old paterfamilias: he is the same man, but where does the metaphor begin?
>
> ([1970] 1983: 53)

Barthes seems to suggest here that the respect a male puppet master receives from society somehow paves the way for the detachment of the concept of femininity from women and supports the patriarchal structure of puppet theatre.

Barthes then continues to write how this tradition represses feminine reality and prioritizes the signifier:

> the refinement of the code, its precision, indifferent to any extended copy of an organic type (to provoke the real, physical body of a young woman), have as their effect – or justification – to absorb and eliminate all feminine reality in the subtle diffraction of the signifier: signified but not represented, Woman is an idea, not a nature.
>
> ([1970] 1983: 91)

His analysis of 'femininity' in the Japanese theatre tradition, of its being an idea, a concept quite detached from the feminine reality of a live woman, is shared by Carter, although Carter, as a feminist writer, seems to find the repression of female reality in Japanese theatre, as well as the everyday performance of gender in Japan, misogynistic and abhorrent. What differentiates Carter from Barthes is the fact that this repression of female reality mattered to Carter significantly more, because it was her body and her reality that were being repressed. She was not, therefore, taken in by the Orientalist exoticism when she observed the puppet theatre in Japan, raving about the sheer beauty of these dolls. Instead, she found in *bunraku* problems for women in Japanese society.

'The Loves of Lady Purple', a short story inspired by *bunraku*, can be read as Carter's remonstrance towards this Japanese tradition. In this story, the female puppet, Lady Purple, is manipulated by a male master, until one day she comes to life, breaks free from her bondage, devours him and leaves for town to become a whore. The story has triggered discussions among Carter scholars whether this ending is not entirely a success, because Lady Purple's total liberation is not achieved. To this discussion Rebecca Munford offers an insightful analysis, that 'Lady Purple materialises here as a creation of the male imagination', 'she is cast in a Sadeian mould' and 'is the machine itself' (2013: 121). As Munford rightly suggests, this story is not a story of liberation where a puppet breaking free from the control of a patriarchal puppet master, turns into a human being. Instead, the puppet turns into a killing machine, an automated whore, to reveal the nature of the 'femininity' which Japanese theatre tradition constructs. What Lady Purple represents is 'an idea' of femininity, fabricated solely from male fantasy, reflecting their desire and fear. Lady Purple cannot become a real woman precisely because she has no relation to her. After liberation, she can only become an automaton, a devouring monster born out of a misogynist fear for women.

## 'Femininity' in everyday life in Japan

Apart from in Japan's theatre tradition, Carter found a similar imposition of the constructed notion of 'femininity' upon real women in the form of the Japanese societal notion of 'the foreign woman'. In 'A Souvenir of Japan', the protagonist is keenly aware of the expected role she is supposed to play, that of the role of a 'foreign woman':

> I had never been so absolutely the mysterious other. I had become a kind of phoenix, a fabulous beast; I was an outlandish jewel. He found me, I think, inexpressibly exotic. But I often felt like a female impersonator.
> 
> (Carter [1974] 1988: 7)

What is described here is a doubly alienating experience of a non-Japanese woman in Japan: she needs to perform the concept of 'femininity' as well as that of 'a foreigner' – both epitomize a 'to-be-looked-at-ness' in Japanese society. Carter seems to connect both as a fundamentally 'female' experience here, when the narrator feels compelled to impersonate a 'foreign' 'woman', even when she already is one in either category. By performatively establishing her double otherness, she exerts the power of attracting the gaze, which paradoxically alienates her by turning her into a sign of otherness. The trouble is that the narrator, despite feeling self-conscious and awkward, seems to enjoy being an object of male gaze at the same time.

'Flesh and the Mirror' is another short story in which Carter uses the motif of performativity. The protagonist ends up performing a romantic female character, who is so unlike her self-definition, unwittingly conforming to, and supporting, this romanticized notion of 'femininity' ([1974] 1988: 61–70). Similarly, 'Poor Butterfly' describes Carter's experience as a part-time bar-hostess in the Ginza district, where the hostesses played mothers 'to feed their large infants food' (Carter [1982] 1993: 48), the 'large infants' being adult male customers. The women in these stories are expected to perform certain roles set out for them by Japanese society. These roles are for the convenience of men; they buy these women's services along with their compliance. The hostesses are there to please men, to attend to their needs, a 'masturbatory device' for men (Carter [1982] 1993: 50), with no need for reciprocity.

As these examples show, Carter found the principle of the Japanese theatre tradition to be permeating everyday life in Japanese society. A type, a style, an idea to perform is imposed on women and men both, and women especially suffer from it, because they are more objectified. Even though this 'femininity' is quite an alien notion – a male construct, after all – women are supposed to perform it 'naturally'. They inevitably fail, destined to fall short of expectation. The only other options available to women are to be categorized as wives and mothers. Carter said in an interview:

> In general, Japanese men seem to find women who cannot be easily categorized as either wives or mothers a great threat… Japanese men often treat women who can't be classified as mother or surrogate mother as ambulant sexual orifices and regard any manifestation of intellectual activity or even proper female pride in a woman with open amazement and ferocious derision, as if such a thing were a threat to the very fabric of the world.
>
> (Bell 1973: 28–9)

In such a society, it may be no wonder why a constructed notion of 'femininity' is more highly valued than a real woman, as the former never deviates from that idealized form to pose any threat. A *kabuki* actor's performance of femininity is therefore more artistic and 'feminine', and paradoxically more 'authentic', than that of a woman, precisely because it is not rooted in the body and sensibility of an actual woman.

## Carter on Mishima

Yukio Mishima, a renowned novelist in the early half of the twentieth century, is perhaps one of the clearest examples to demonstrate the misogynistic creation of 'femininity' in Japanese culture and is the subject of one of Carter's essays (Carter [1997] 1998: 238–44). He directly dealt with the concept of 'femininity' in *kabuki* theatre in his story, 'Onnagata'. In this story, Masuyama, the male protagonist, compares Mangiku, the *kabuki* actor he adores, with real women, and likens the latter disdainfully to 'animals in the zoo' (Mishima [1967] 1997: 298). Masuyama 'never felt so distinctly alien as in Mangiku's dressing room; nothing in these real women made him feel particularly masculine' (Mishima [1967] 1997: 298). Interestingly, as shown in this excerpt, Mangiku's performed 'femininity' helps Masuyama feel 'masculine'. 'Femininity' here supports the counterpart concept, 'masculinity', showing these two are interdependent.

Carter read Mishima's works, as her essay, 'Mishima's Toy Sword', testifies. She disapproved of Mishima's works, most probably detecting misogyny in them, and likened the reading of his novels to 'being on a train with someone very unpleasant' (Bell 1973: 34) and being forced to listen to 'adolescent' 'Angst' (Bell 1973: 35). Carter's analysis of Mishima reveals the constructed notion of 'masculinity' in Japan as she saw it, as well as the notion of 'the Japanese'.

Mishima committed suicide in *hara-kiri* style while Carter was in Japan in 1970. She was watching television with Sozo when it happened. Mishima, whom Carter calls 'a superlative showman' (Carter [1997] 1998: 240), took his life in front of the camera, as though it were a performance. He first stealthily infiltrated a Self-Defence Force base in Ichigaya with his group of young students, and then urged the officers to rise in military action. When this plan failed, he cut his belly open with a sword, and had his head cut off by a fellow member in the group. It was an imitation of a *samurai* act. Carter analyses this horrible event:

> the Mishima incident seems perfectly scrutable in terms of the man's own personality as revealed in his books, pronouncements and activities. He had made, and starred in, a film in which an army officer committed hara-kiri..after the 1936 insurrection. The connection of hara-kiri with a metaphysical notion of Japaneseness depends on what weight one gives such intangible nostra. Mishima's notion of Japaneseness seems as much a bookish stereotype as Enoch Powell's notion of Britishness. However, by the use of rhetorical gesture – which is particularly suited to a culture where appearance often assumes an abstract

importance – Mishima may have presented the Japanese with an idea that some remember seemed authentic, once.

(Carter [1997] 1998: 241)

Here Carter connects the performance of Mishima to an imaginary, masculinized notion of Japaneseness, something Mishima believed that all Japanese men shared, which commands death in *samurai*-style. Here again, the idea supersedes the body, the sign the signified, and a pure death is preferred to a compromised life. When Sozo showed some understanding of, and respect for, Mishima's act, Carter's initial description of Sozo as a *samurai* takes on an eerie ring. Mishima's act was not an odd, incomprehensible action but rather it hit the chord of something that was rooted firmly in the Japanese male psyche, and Sozo certainly shared it.

Carter saw that whatever that something was, it was oppressive for both women and men, and said, 'I think a society that systematically degrades and abuses women cripples men as well as women' (Bell 1973: 30).

Whereas a perfect and artificial 'femininity' is so highly valued that real women are to be detested, the counterpart 'masculinity' it supports also demands the sacrifice of real men. 'Masculinity', in this view, the kind that can be found in *Hagakure*, a book on the codes of conduct for *samurai* published in circa 1716, has to be a perfect, self-sacrificing, non-feeling entity, embodying the infallible 'Japan', the country of Gods. Carter said, commenting on the danger of suppressing the real body for the sake of art, 'I think that in Japan art becomes far more important than life. Because they make life an art, and once you do that you forget how to live' (Bell 1973: 26). She further pondered on the inevitable consequences of such a formation of identity:

> The Japanese, I think, have always wished to make themselves works of art. They have an urge towards self-destruction. They make themselves perfect – perfect on their own terms. The thing is, once you have a perfect work of art what do you do with it? You see, that is a moral problem.
>
> (Bell 1973: 35–6)

## *Irezumi*: Art on the body[4]

It is with the same sensibility that Carter was drawn to *irezumi*, the Japanese tattoos. She saw how *irezumi*, unlike the contemporary Western version of tattoos, supersedes the human body of the wearer. The contemporary Western tattoos, more or less, are bodily inscriptions of the wearer's artistic, political, familial or relationship statements, an outer expression of what he or she holds dear: 'statements of the self' or *individuation*' (Benson 2000: 244–5, italics original). Tattoos are often perceived as 'cool' in their defiant attitude towards normalized and polite society. These new tattoos derive a certain 'exotic' quality from non-Western tattooing practices, particularly Asian; among these are the Japanese tattoos. Susan Benson analyses the mentality behind contemporary Western tattoos as follows:

> [T]he identification with the primitive and the exotic is thus no longer abjected, but is reconfigured as identification with the authentic, the uncommodified, the pure, in opposition to the corruptions of mainstream society… for many, to inscribe upon the skin the marks of the primitive other is 'anti-repressive', a way of releasing the savage within or of returning to a corporeal authenticity occluded by the disciplines of contemporary conformity.
> (Benson 2000: 242)

In a way, Western tattooing practice has assimilated and appropriated the idea of the 'oriental other' in an idealized mode, which is, in fact, quite removed from actuality. These kinds of tattoos are considered as something one can buy and wear, something equivalent to a designer garment, the garment of 'the Other'. It exploits other cultures for service to Western culture in a capitalist and commodifying way.

Carter seems to have been aware of many contradictions in tattoo practice, even before her years in Japan. In *Heroes and Villains*, created pre-Japan and published in 1969, for instance, Carter depicts how tattoos can rob the wearer of his or her agency and subjectivity, transforming them into an object of art, their existence and value dependent upon the observer's judgement. Jewel, the young leader of the Barbarians in this novel, is extensively tattooed to assume the role of a savage, reinforcing the Professors' concept of an enemy. Through this heavy tattooing, however, Jewel is transformed into 'the savage', losing his original identity:

> Sometimes I dream I am an invention of the Professors; they project their fears outside on us so they won't stay in the villages, infecting them, and so, you understand, they can try to live peacefully there.
> (Carter [1969] 1981: 82)

By incorporating the image of savage Barbarians, fabricated by the Professors, Jewel is transformed into one, and thus unwittingly alienates himself from who he really is. He becomes dependent on Dr Donally, an ex-Professor who tattooed him. Jewel wonders, 'I think he'd like to flay me and hang me up on the wall, I think he'd really like that. He might even make me up into a ceremonial robe and wear me on special occasions' (ibid: 86). In the end, he loses his power to rebel against Dr Donally, having been reduced to a mere puppet, his *objet d'art*.

This transformative power of tattoos was explored more deeply once Carter moved to Japan. In the essay 'People as Pictures', she specifically deals with Japanese-style tattoos, those practiced by certain working-class men and *yakuza* members in the 1970s. The *irezumi* of the *yakuza* carry a specific historical legacy, originally being a branding upon criminals, and then of a working-class self-obtained mark of caste, showing pride in the dangerous work they performed in the premodern period. The latter especially generates a sense of masculinity connected to *irezumi*. In the modern era, the practice was banned by the government many times, but it survived mostly among underworld criminals and mafia. Perhaps because of the government's ban, it acquired additional meanings in modern Japanese society: that the wearers are not only brave and masculine but also rebellious and lawless.[5]

*Irezumi* tattoos are not random statements inscribed on the body, like some of the Western variations, but a full-body art, carefully designed. When Carter describes how it 'transforms its victim into a genre masterpiece' ([1982] 1993: 33), she had this kind of the *yakuza*'s *irezumi* in mind. The tattooist is an artist, and the tattooed is a mere canvas. The pain inflicted is enormous, as the process is lengthy. It is effectively an initiation rite, testing one's will, courage, loyalty and lifetime commitment to become a legitimate member of the mafia. It marks the repression of one's autonomy, prioritizing the clan's benefit. *Irezumi* separates the wearer from the rest of the law-abiding society by marking the person as a terrible member of the lawless mafia. But more importantly, by making the tattooed person endure extreme pain, the procedure creates a loyal member of a mafia clan, who can repress one's fear and emotion for the sake of the clan's activities, subsuming individual identity. *Irezumi* in *yakuza* society, therefore, is not an individualistic expression as conceptualized in the Western tattoo but a communal mask to erase the wearer's individuality. His own individuality, upon assuming the *irezumi*, is hidden, erased and overwritten.

Carter intuitively grasps this strange function of *irezumi*, when she writes, '[h]e is visually superb; he exudes the weird glamour of masochism; and he carries upon his flesh an immutable indication of caste. Bizarre beauties blossom in the programmed interstices of repression' ([1982] 1993: 33). The beauty of the *yakuza*'s *irezumi* comes from its various colours and designs of traditional motifs such as flowers, dragons and fish. I argue elsewhere that these almost feminine designs suggest a compensation for the 'femininity' they rigorously repress (Ikoma 2005: 32–40). Carter also sees this beautiful garment as protective clothes on a naked body, which traditionally has been considered distasteful in Japan:

> Traditionally, the Japanese have always felt a lack of interest, verging on repugnance, at the naked human body... Now, a man who has been comprehensively tattooed – and the *irezumi* artist is nothing if not comprehensive – can hardly be said to be naked, for he may never remove this most intimate and gaily coloured of garments. Stark he may be, but always decent, and therefore never ashamed. He will never look helplessly, defencelessly, indelicately, nude. This factor may or may not be important in the psychological bases of *irezumi* – which provides the potentially perhaps menacing human form with an absolute disguise. In Japan, the essence is often the appearance.
> 
> ([1982] 1993: 35–6)

An ugly naked body and vulnerable ego are, Carter analyses, successfully covered by the superb artwork of the *irezumi*, and so is the wearer's individuality. When Carter wrote, 'Masochism and sadism are different sides of the same coin, and perhaps a repressive culture can only be maintained by a strong masochistic element among the repressed' (ibid: 38), she was clearly aware of the difference between Japanese *irezumi* and the Western tattoos. There is something unpalatable in Japanese *irezumi* that demands the erasure of one's self, autonomy, agency and individuality. This prioritization of form, concept or idea to the real body can be identified in *irezumi*, as well as *bunraku* and *kabuki* as we have seen. This could be, most certainly, what Carter was initially drawn to, and ultimately repelled by, because, in this analysis of *irezumi*, it becomes more and more apparent that what is prioritized is 'masculinity', symbolized in emotional detachment, over 'femininity', taken as weakness and vulnerability. *Irezumi* is a symbolic art, a representation of perfect 'masculinity' in a bizarrely 'feminine' form: 'femininity', extracted and sacrificed, is put on show on the wearer's skin, supporting the uncontaminated 'masculinity' that can overcome pain and even death; although both concepts, Carter reckoned, are fabrications.

The narrator of 'A Souvenir of Japan', while enjoying the exotification of herself by her lover, realizes a disturbing possibility: 'If he valued me as an object of passion, he had reduced the word to its root, which derives from the Latin, *patior*, I suffer. He valued me as an instrument which would cause him pain' (Carter [1974] 1988: 11). The price of being appreciated as a foreign woman, an exotic Other, might be pain, suffering and repression, on his side as well as hers. It is revealed that, as she conforms to the notion of ideal 'femininity', she becomes an instrument of oppression.

## Conclusion

When Carter met Sozo, she enjoyed appreciating him as an exotic work of art. Yet she chose not to leave it there but to dissect the art and find the objectifying gaze within herself. She faced complex issues, revolving around the concepts of masculinity and femininity, of sadism and masochism, of ego and power, and of an orientalist tendency in herself:

> I suppose I do not know how he really looked and, in fact, I suppose I shall never know, now, for he was plainly an object created in the mode of fantasy… I created him solely in relation to myself, like a work of romantic art, an object corresponding to the ghost inside me.
>
> (Carter [1974] 1988: 67–8)

When they broke up, Sozo had his own reason for the split, but for Carter, I suspect, it was this imposition of a form, this prioritization of an idea over the real body, that might have become too much to bear. She stopped trying to be the woman he expected, just as she stopped imposing on him the concept of the ideal Other. Her conclusion was arrived at from in-depth research into Japan's history, culture and psychology, daily first-hand observations and self-reflection, and is quite distant from her initial fascination with the exotic.

During the interview, as a retort to the interviewer's comment on the frequently used notion of the 'inscrutability' of the Japanese, Carter says, 'I don't find them inscrutable; I'm afraid I find them terribly scrutable' (Bell 1973: 33). She used the phrase 'I'm afraid' as an ironic reaction to the stereotypical notion behind the interviewer's question, as if irritated by it. The interview was part of a book project, in which many famous artists from overseas were asked about their impression of Japan (Bell 1973: xi). Carter was one of the artists interviewed. One might suggest the inevitably orientalist nature of such a project as this one is being revealed in the interviewer's question about Japanese inscrutability. This is indicative of a desire to construct the Other as totally different and alien, and a wishful transference of whatever Westerners regard themselves as free from onto the 'orient', either to consume or to ridicule. Carter, who had previously held such assumptions herself, now reacted with a denial. By saying, 'I'm afraid I find them terribly scrutable', Carter tried to destroy the preconceived notion of 'extraordinary', 'exotic' or 'fantastic' Orientals as a mere fantasy. It is as if she is saying that they are not inscrutable at all; if you look into them, you will know them for who they are, and they are not unlike you.

What Carter did in Japan was to look at the signs she could not comprehend by observing them intensely as if to dissect them, until the deeper meaning came to her. It was an act of deciphering that can only be done by someone who knows the codes. What she found was a horrible obliteration of individuality, an erasure of humanity and repression of feminine corporeality. But what horrified her most was that they were not foreign in nature; they had been there in herself and in her culture all the time. In Japan, she discovered them in an extreme form, which she reclaimed and used as food for thought. This process prompted Carter to write, 'In Japan I learnt what it is to be a woman and became radicalised' ([1982] 1993: 28). What she experienced in Japan might have been uniquely Japanese but only in the sense that it was the Japanese mirror that did not reflect the image she wanted to see. But the mirror could be anywhere. And it was not the Other, the Japanese Other in this instance that she found in that mirror for her own critical analysis, but herself, her imagination and her universe. This allowed Carter to develop her discoveries into the theory of power struggle and of performativity that has had wider application, out of which were born her fantastic, feminist and postmodern stories, whose peculiar technique of mixing visual signs in her narrative continues to present readers the world at once made unfamiliar and extraordinary.

# Notes

The research for this article was supported by KAKENHI 24520307 (Grant-in-Aid for Scientific Research (C)) from the Japan Society for the Promotion of Science (JSPS).

1   See Araki (2017).
2   The compiled list of Angela Carter's library, archived at University of East Anglia, shows she owned a copy of this and many more books written by Roland Barthes.
3   Originally, *kabuki* was an all-female erotic performance, which was then taken up by young male performers. Both male and female *kabuki* performers in those days were partly engaged in prostitution. Their performance was banned by the Edo government around 1629. At the end of the seventeenth century, *kabuki* was reborn as a stylized all-male performance with the approval of the government. Today, there are some small troupes of female *kabuki* actors, but they remain minor

and unofficial. The connection of *kabuki* and prostitution is further investigated in Ikoma (2020).

4   For a more detailed analysis of *irezumi* and how Carter analyses it, see Ikoma (2005).

5   This notion of rebelliousness and lawlessness of *yakuza*'s *irezumi* seems to appeal to the fashionista tattoo wearers since around the beginning of the twenty-first century, and the kind of hybrid between Western-style tattoo and *irezumi* has become popular among not only the connoisseurs of foreign exoticism but also the Japanese youth. They wear this new tattoo to make a fashion statement, to set their individuality apart from the rest of the society. However, the connotations it carries are very different from the original *irezumi* for *yakuza*.

## Works cited

Araki, S. (2017), *Seduced by Japan: A Memoir of the Days Spent with Angela Carter*, trans. N. Ikoma, Tokyo: Eihosha.

Barthes, R. ([1970] 1983), *Empire of Signs*, trans. E. Howard, New York: Hill and Wang.

Bell, R. (1973), *The Japan Experience*, New York and Tokyo: Weatherhill.

Benson, S. (2000), 'Inscriptions of the Self: Reflections on Tattooing and Piercing in Contemporary Euro-America', in J. Caplan (ed), *Written on the Body: The Tattoo in European and American History*, 234–54, London: Reaktion Books Ltd.

Carter, A. (1969–1974), Unpublished Journal, Angela Carter Papers, London: British Library, ADD Ms. 88899/1/93.

Carter, A. ([1969] 1981), *Heroes and Villains*, London: Penguin Books.

Carter, A. ([1974] 1988), *Fireworks*, London: Virago.

Carter, A. ([1982] 1993), *Nothing Sacred: Selected Writings*, London: Virago.

Carter, A. ([1997] 1998), *Shaking a Leg: Collected Writings*, London: Penguin Books.

Gamble, S. (2006), *Angela Carter: A Literary Life*, Basingstoke: Palgrave Macmillan.

Gordon, E. (2016), *The Invention of Angela Carter*, London: Chatto & Windus.

Ikoma, N. (2005), 'Gender Masquerade: Reflections on Irezumi', *Asian Cultural Studies* (International Christian University Publications, 3-A), 31: 27–42.

Ikoma, N. (2020), 'Monstrous Marionette: The Tale of a Japanese Doll by Angela Carter', in M. Murai and L. Cardi (eds), *Re-Orienting the Fairy Tale: Contemporary Adaptations across Cultures*, 111–36, Detroit: Wayne State University Press.

Mishima, Y. ([1967] 1997), 'Onnagata', in T. W. Goossen (ed), *The Oxford Book of Japanese Short Stories*, 293–312, Oxford: Oxford University Press.

Munford, R. (2013), *Decadent Daughters and Monstrous Mothers: Angela Carter and European Gothic*, Manchester: Manchester University Press.

2

# Some kinds of love: Angela Carter, art and objects

## David Punter

In this chapter I want to focus on Angela Carter's fifth novel, *Love*, which was published in 1971 and is sometimes referred to, after *Shadow Dance* (1966) and *Several Perceptions* (1968), as the third of the 'Bristol trilogy'. It is an engaging, puzzling and alarming novel, which appears to tell the story of a disastrous triangle through the constantly shifting relationships between Annabel and the brothers Buzz and Lee, although this story is bedevilled throughout by the utter opacity of each character to the others. Each of them, as we would expect from Carter, is strange – strange in ways which only occasionally peep through the surface; but I am not concerned here with the narrative, such as it is. For it is, I believe, less the narrative that stands out to the reader than the place in which it is largely set, an apartment which is crammed with objects, a 'heterogeneous collection' which 'seemed to throb with a mute, inscrutable, symbolic life', as Carter puts it ([1971] 2006: 7). Buzz, for example, is a photographer, and 'cardboard crates of prints and negatives' (25) accumulate in his room. To Annabel, who draws and sketches incessantly, Lee is at one point no more 'than a collection of coloured surfaces' (30). We can gather from these kinds of remark that there is an emphasis throughout both on physical space and on the object, in many different senses, of art: the object as the 'thing in itself' but also the object as the purpose or end of the artistic process. What are all these things *for*? And do any of the characters have any understanding of what they are for, or are they simply following unconscious imperatives that cause them, *inter alia*, to externalize inner conflict? Is the 'art object' a provocation or a refuge, an attempt at perfection or a reflection of a shattered life – or, at any rate, of a life perpetually on the brink of shattering or of being shattered? In a manner we might consider reminiscent of Elizabeth Bowen in, for example, *The House in Paris* (1935), the things take on a life of their own, a life by which Annabel is pathologically drained so that she finds it increasingly difficult to hold her 'self' together in the face of the encroachments of the object.

In what follows, I have picked out eight different moments from the novel. In the first of them, we see Annabel in the first instance trying to find a way of dealing with the presence of Lee, her husband, a presence welcome at times but at others intrusive, but finding herself constantly impeded because any possible apprehension of a 'real' Lee is always already overlaid by a different set of images, images drawn from dream, and this, we learn, is typical of her peculiar apprehension of the wider world.

> She suffered from nightmares too terrible to reveal to him, especially since he himself was often the principal actor in them and appeared in many hideous dream disguises. Sometimes, during the day, she stopped, startled, before some familiar object because it seemed to have just changed its form back to the one she remembered after a brief, private period impersonating something quite strange, for she had the capacity for changing the appearance of the real world which is the price paid by those who take too subjective a view of it. All she apprehended through her senses she took only as objects for interpretation in the expressionist style and she saw, in everyday things, a world of mythic, fearful shapes.
>
> (3)

The objects around her, it seems, withdraw from her gaze, in a manner reminiscent of recent philosophical approaches to perception and the life of objects in the rhetoric of object-oriented ontology (see, e.g., Harman 2010). In the text itself, this is assimilated to an 'expressionist' mode of perception: Annabel's own mythic images, the images that populate the world in which she perforce has to live, however dysfunctional this renders her everyday behaviours, form a matrix within which the distinctions between actual people and the surroundings in which they are set constantly dissolve. In this series of stagings of desire, the set and the scenery are at least as significant as the human participants, and Annabel is constantly 'startled' by an apprehension of meaning that never quite appears, a kind of apophenia (the tendency to perceive meaningful connections between unrelated things) based on an elusive, endlessly withdrawing sense of pattern.

We see this process more fully at work in the second passage. Here we begin again with Lee, with a figure in a space, but Annabel's gaze is constantly distorted and tormented by her apprehension of the things around her, and the reference points here are from the world of art – or rather, from several competing worlds of art.

> In their room, Lee lay face down on the carpet in front of the fire, perhaps asleep. The walls round him were painted a very dark green and from this background emerged all the dreary paraphernalia of romanticism, landscapes of forests, jungles and ruins inhabited by gorillas, trees with breasts, winged men with pig faces and women whose heads were skulls. An enormous bedstead of dull since rarely polished brass, spread with figured Indian cotton, occupied the centre of the room which was large and high but so full of bulky furniture in dark woods (chairs, sofas, bookcases, sideboards, a round mahogany table covered with a fringed, red plush cloth, a screen covered with time-browned scraps) that one had to move around the room very carefully for fear of tripping over things.[...] On the mantelpiece stood the skull of a horse amongst a clutter of small objects such as clockwork toys, stones of many shapes and various bottles and jars.
>
> (6–7)

There is the *faux* romanticism of the jungles and ruins, reminiscent, of course, of a certain strain of high romanticism but here reduced, in common with the general mise-en-scène of the novel, to the worlds conjured by everyday reproductions of the kind to be found in a thousand student rooms. The trees with breasts and the women whose heads were skulls have, it seems to me, a more precise reference. Here, surely, is the imagistic repertoire of Max Ernst, from the all-too-well-known *The Robing of the Bride* (1940) to the less-well-known *The Antipope* of 1942. The 'skull of a horse' might take us forward to the contemporary master of fantasy M. John Harrison, and the figure in his novel *Light* (2002) of the Shrander, a being with a horse's skull for a head: the horse's skull, Harrison reminds us, has nothing of the familiarity of a horse's head but is a thing comprised entirely of large, snapping jaws – his own references seem to be back to the Mari Lwyd, a creature from Welsh legend (see, e.g., Owen 1987).

Everywhere in the apartment there are objects, but, as seen in the third passage, these are not objects from some collection that might enable us to make sense of the world around, or even of the collector.

> Buzz's room was packed full of his fetishes, which included knives, carcasses of engines salvaged from the scrapyard and all his tanks of chemicals. He had also boarded up the windows to keep the light out. If Lee's room was like a fresh sheet of paper, Buzz's was like a doodling pad but the many objects which filled it were so eclectic in nature and lay about so haphazardly where he had let them fall that it was just as difficult to gain any hints from it towards the nature of whoever lived there.
>
> (28)

Instead, it seems, they manifest the incoherence of inner life which marks the overall psychopathology of *Love* – the novel, that is; but it may also be seen here as the pathology of love itself as it, apparently inevitably, trips into obsession. Buzz's collection, we see, is an assemblage of fetishes, and, as we would expect from the history and function of the fetish, they are all linked to a semiotics of danger, the knives, the engines, the tanks of photographic chemicals. Yet there is, from another point of view, nothing to be read from these doodles; the objects remain resolutely themselves, refusing to comment on the world around them, and in them any semblance of the humane, the anthropomorphic, is lost – as it is also lost in the relatively antiseptic world that Lee inhabits, the 'fresh sheet of paper' which yields no meaning but is constantly waiting, waiting for a meaningful inscription which might also be a communication, a sign that the objects can be fitted into a version of the world rather than standing as constant obstructions. These objects shed no light, and neither, here, can light shed upon them through the boarded-up windows. If the apartment has any life of its own, then it is the life of a melodramatic chiaroscuro, perhaps something out of Caravaggio, hovering between blinding light and the darkness symbolized by Buzz's tottering crates of negatives.

When Annabel leaves the flat, which she does but rarely, the world of things shows similar tendencies to erase the distinction between the body and the work of art, symbolized in Carter's description of photographs in the window of a tattoo parlour. Here she can see 'Men turned into artificial peacocks displayed chests where ramped ferocious lions, tigers or voluptuous houris in all the coloured inks which issued from the needle.' There is one image of a man with the head of Christ crowned with thorns emblazoned on his chest and another sports the stripes of a zebra. The art of the tattooist is also evident from the array of flowers and memorial crosses and words such as 'MOTHER R.I.P' etched into skin:

> A young girl coyly raised her skirt to show a flock of butterflies tattooed along her thigh. In the centre of the window hung a very large photograph of a man upon whose entire back was described a writhing dragon in reds and blues; and every scale and fang of the beast, each flame it blew from its nostrils, was punctured into the skin for good and all unless he were unpeeled like an orange or pared like an apple.
>
> (66–7)

Transmutation is everywhere: these are not 'men like peacocks', but men 'turned into artificial peacocks', their humanity dissolved behind a facade which comes to be more real than the human scaffolding on which these tattoos and canvases are stretched. Yet the movement, the dissolution into an artistic realm is here doubled: these are not even men as peacocks, human/animal hybrids, but photographs of such physical anomalies. The head of Christ arising from a man's chest might remind us, at least in passing, of the curious geometry of Salvador Dalí's *Christ of St John of the Cross* (1951), especially when accompanied by the lurid colourings typical both of Dalí and of the tattoo; as to the dragon on the back, then, of course, the references are all too clear in a line stretching from Blake to the later Thomas Harris; indeed, Blake's 'The Great Red Dragon and the Woman Clothed with the Sun' (c. 1805) seems to hover behind *Love*, as Annabel attempts, fruitlessly, to throw off her own clothing of flesh and to find a different way of accommodating herself to the world.

Where, we might ask, did all this begin, the radical alienation that pervades all of Annabel's attempts to relate to the outside world? The novel does not really answer this question, but the nearest it comes to a sense of origins is in this fifth passage, where we are in the company of a young Annabel, only 'two or three years old' – the imprecision is significant, for almost any memory in *Love* may be a screen memory in Freud's sense (see Freud 1899).

> Carter describes how when Annabel's mother takes the two- or three-year-old girl shopping, she slips out of a grocer's shop while her mother is chatting. After playing in the gutter for a while, the child wanders dangerously in front of a car, which is forced to brake, crashing into a shop front. Annabel is disorientated, and watches the slivers of glass flash in the sunshine until a crowd of distraught giants broke upon her head, her mother, the grocer in his white coat, a blonde woman with dark glasses, a man with four arms and legs and two heads, one golden, the other black, and many other passers-by, all as agitated as could be imagined.
>
> (73)

In response to her mother's alarm that she might have been killed, she responds, "'But I wasn't killed, I was playing", said Annabel, no bigger than a blade of grass, who had caused this huge commotion all by herself just because she could play games with death'

(73).

The point here is that Annabel's childhood memory is also an aesthetic, or aestheticized, memory: what stands out as significant are the slivers of glass flashing in the sunshine and the giants – of course, any adult seen from the perspective of a toddler may well be construed as a giant, but here something monstrous is already fully in place with the 'man with four arms and legs and two heads, one golden, the other black', which may tell us something about the role of shadow in perception, since shadows are no less real to Annabel than the physical bodies to which they are, at least usually, attached. There is a curious but symptomatic inconsequentiality in Annabel's response to her mother's anxiety: 'But I wasn't killed, I was playing'; it is as if an almost fierce concentration on playing, on ignoring threats of physical violence, might be sufficient to save the adult Annabel from the potentially disastrous consequences of the games of life and death she seems forced (though by whom or what?) into playing with the brothers.

But we need to return from this glimpse of the outdoors to the apartment and to the things collected within it. Reminiscent of the extraordinary den of chaos which is the Pitt Rivers Museum in Oxford, where crocodile masks dangle from the darkened ceiling and fetish objects rub shoulders with unnamed things whose provenance and function have become increasingly mysterious over time, the scenario of the sixth passage may seem familiar, or more prosaically, it may be familiar from memories of student days or the horror that accompanies many parents when at last looking into the lives their cherished offspring are leading. Here is a world which is slowly returning to the primal slime, where objects are increasingly losing their distinctness in a reflection of the gradual deterioration in Annabel's always precarious mental health.

> All the shoulders of Annabel's collection of bottles were padded with the dust which ridged the picture frames and rose up in clouds from the rarely disturbed plush of chairs and tablecover if, by chance, they were touched. Images could no longer force their way through the grime on the mirror and the lion's-head handles on the sideboard wore soft, gritty deposits in each wooden eyeball and curl of mane. Dust hooded the glass case so thickly you could not see that the stuffed fox inside was now diseased; its muzzle was grey with mould and its hide sprouted with thriving fungi.... The pigments of her landscapes round the green walls were already beginning to fade so faces yellowed, flowers withered and leaves turned brown in a parody of autumn.
>
> (80–1)

The phrase 'Images could no longer force their way through the grime on the mirror' clearly has a wider resonance: the layers of imagery which have previously coloured Annabel's world and formed the basis of Buzz's photography are now themselves receding, becoming obscured, and this is in one sense a refraction of a kind of act of self-preservation: if the obscuring layers become thick enough, then it will be impossible to glimpse the terror that lies in wait, the diseased fox, its 'muzzle grey with mould'. As psychoanalysts have come increasingly to remind us, varieties of mental illness may be terrifying in themselves, but essentially, they are only baroque forms of protection against the worse terror, which is the dissolution of the self.

In the seventh passage, we are in Buzz's room, the sanctum where he can live entirely surrounded by images and obsessions, in a psychic retreat which simultaneously encapsulates what Didier Anzieu refers to as the envelope of the self (see Anzieu 1990).

> The windows of his room were pasted over with sheets of black paper and the meagre sticks of landladies' furniture were hidden by the detritus of his obsessions. The stained, brownish wallpaper was pinned everywhere with photographs of Lee and herself, of herself alone and of Lee alone. Lee had once possessed the rare knack of looking exactly like himself when photographed; his self-consciousness made it inevitable.
>
> ([1971] 2006: 89)

Here nothing of the shape of the outer world can be seen: no light can come through the windows, and such furniture as there is has entirely lost its shape and meaning as it becomes, like Annabel's collection of bottles, hidden by detritus. Yet there is a complex, even paradoxical, movement here: what is substituting, for Buzz, for human relationship is a series of photographs, a series of ways of bringing the other within his grasp, or at least to his attention, but even this withdrawal is thwarted by Lee's uncanny ability to look 'exactly like himself'. Neither the moment of relatedness nor the moment of withdrawal can ever work perfectly: the attempt to reduce the world to the shapes of art is forever accompanied by something that will break through that facade. Melanie Klein may be right in her claim that the motivation behind the creation of art is an attempt to recompense for childhood fantasies of parental destruction, to render broken things whole (see Klein 1975); but this recompense, this sense of having made something perfect that can stand on its own in the world and not betray inner disease, will always be relative, or perhaps fail completely, as the pigments of Annabel's own landscapes begin to fade.

And so, in my final passage, we see that Annabel's attempts to conjure life through drawing and sketching have come full circle: even as she has invested in them a version of living that is denied to her in any other form, so they will eventually betray her, the curious life they may have once possessed becoming dead matter.

> She took out her old sketchbooks and fingered wistfully through them for every stroke of crayon or pencil had once been alive to her; her pictures had never referred to the objects they might have seemed to represent but, to her, had been

palpable things themselves. But she could not draw anything any more and so was forced to make these imaginative experiments with her own body which were now about to culminate, finally, in erasure, for she had failed in the attempt to make herself the living portrait of a girl who had never existed. [...] She was irritated rather than disturbed to sense occasionally the almost inarticulate breathings and the infinitely subtle movements of the figures on the walls.

(100)

So this is all the more important because these works, we are told, are not mere representations; they are objects in themselves, and their disintegration threatens precisely the disintegration of the self against which art might protect. We might be reminded of the figure of Sufiya Zinobia in Salman Rushdie's novel *Shame* (1983), a deeply damaged girl who tries to cling on to the 'good images' she stores in her mental cupboard, but in the end to no avail as she is increasingly seen in herself as being a representation of the threatening monstrous. Under these circumstances, erasure seems the only possibility, the rubbing out of the intricate lines in which the self tries to etch its own presence on the world, no matter what the ostensible object of representation. The text, after all, as Carter says in her wry 1987 Afterword to the novel, is 'Annabel's coffin' (111), for, as it says in this passage, 'she had failed in the attempt to make herself the living portrait of a girl who had never existed'.

Moving aside, finally, from the intricacies and patternings of *Love*, we might find in this phrasing a whole series of refractions of Carter's thought and writings. For what, we might ask, is life except a series of attempts to forge a being, to imitate that which has gone before, even when such a mythical progenitor has always already disappeared, is absent from the shadows on the walls, from the bottles on the mantelpiece, from the fading, curling photographs that might seem to constitute the record of a life? But perhaps more to the point, what is the trajectory of the formation of a specifically female self, beset by image, manipulated time and time again by those patriarchal forces that seek only to force women into a mould from which there is no escape?

But it is perhaps interesting – and reminiscent of some of the arguments in *The Sadeian Woman* (1978) – that on this battleground, there are no winners or losers, and neither are there clear agents: Lee and Buzz are as bewildered by Annabel as she is by them, and they have no realistic resources on which to draw to bolster their fragile patriarchal claims. Neither is there any rescue or resolution through art here; the objects continue their implacable resistance. The sardonic humour of the novel is a skin tight-stretched over the skull – if it were not such a cliché, I would say a 'bracelet of bright hair about the bone' (Donne [1633] 1990: 130).

But the title of this chapter comes, of course, from a different register, from Lou Reed's 'Some Kinds of Love', recorded three years before the publication of Carter's *Love* but only a year before it was written – it was written, Carter tells us, in 1969 – in the emblematic year of 1968, following the Summer of Love, a year which could be seen as signifying the plenitude from which the action and scenario of *Love* might signify as a withdrawal, a retreat, as though the characters are living amid the bits and pieces, the shards, the incomprehensible detritus of the failed revolution. In conclusion, the final line from 'Some Kinds of Love' is pertinent for issues relating to Angela Carter and art since it prompts the question of whether it is really true that 'Some kinds of love/Are mistaken for vision'.

## Works cited

Anzieu, D. (1990), *Psychic Envelopes*, London: Karnac Books.
Bowen, E. (1935), *The House in Paris*, London: Gollancz.
Carter, A. ([1966] 1995), *Shadow Dance*, London: Virago.
Carter, A. ([1968] 1997), *Several Perceptions*, London: Virago.
Carter, A. ([1971] 2006), *Love*, introd. Audrey Niffenegger, London: Vintage.
Carter, A. (1978), *The Sadeian Woman*, London: Virago.
Donne, J. ([1633] 1990), 'The Relic', in J. Carey (ed), *John Donne*, 130, Oxford: Oxford University Press.
Freud, S. ([1899] 1953–74), 'Screen Memories', in J. Strachey et al. (eds), *The Standard Edition of the Complete Psychological Works of Sigmund Freud*, 24 vols, III, 301–22, London: Hogarth Press.
Harman, G. (2010), *Towards Speculative Realism: Essays and Lectures*, Ropley, Hants: Zero Books.
Harrison, M. J. (2002), *Light*, London: Gollancz.
Klein, M. (1975), *Love, Guilt and Reparation and Other Works 1921–1945*, introd. R. E. Money-Kyrle, London: Hogarth.
Owen, T. M. (1987), *Welsh Folk Customs*, Cardiff: Gomer.
Reed, L. (1969), 'Some Kinds of Love', on *The Velvet Underground* [LP], MGM.
Rushdie, S. (1983), *Shame*, London: Jonathan Cape.
Russell, J. (1967), *Max Ernst: Life and Work*, New York: Thames and Hudson.

Part Two

# Music, performance and fairy tale

3

# 'Down to the greenwood': Angela Carter and traditional folk singing

## Polly Paulusma

That Angela Carter was a practitioner and scholar of traditional folk song during the 1960s is a little-known fact bolstered by the discovery of a new archive (Carter and Carter n.d.), containing her folk song research notes and musical notations, folk records and books which she and her first husband, Paul Carter, shared and recordings of her singing and playing English concertina in a folk club (Carter 1967c). This recently unearthed archive, taken together with texts already in the public domain, confirms a suspicion I have long harboured that one of the reasons why Carter remains one of the English language's most exhilarating modern writers is that her peculiarly canorous prose betrays a somatic understanding of what it feels like to sing, and specifically, to sing folk songs.

I am not the first to observe musical qualities in her writing. Marina Warner celebrates her 'word-notes' (2012), and Salman Rushdie praises her 'smoky, opium-eater's cadences' (1996: x). Critics have touched on the role of folk song in Carter's early adulthood but not realized its significance: Warner nods cursorily to its influence, describing how Carter 'first began developing her interest in folklore, discovering with her husband the folk and jazz music scenes of the 1960s' (1992: xiii), but she frames it as a minor detour on a longer journey towards a seemingly more satisfying relationship with fairy tales. Susannah Clapp mentions Carter's 'Sixties days of folk music at Bristol University' (1997: x) but does not then connect Carter's early folk singing praxis with her desire 'to write works that could be performed' (1997: viii). Charlotte Crofts notes Carter's 'involvement with the folk movement in the early 1960s' (2003: 39) observing that her writing for radio enabled Carter to explore the processes at work in the transmission of oral narratives and their audiences – the active relationship between the teller of the tale and the listener – which foregrounds the potential for renegotiating the patriarchal structures of the literary versions.

(2003: 41)

Crofts' scholarly exploration of Carter's engagement, via radio, with the subjective 'inner voice' unpacks Carter's instinctive orality, but Crofts does not then forge links between Carter's interest in the 'atavistic' orality of radio and her deep prior investment in folk song, nor the relationship between Carter's phonocentric writing for radio, film and stage and her engagement with her own singing voice. Carter's biographer Edmund Gordon provides some detail about Carter's 'interest in the English folk revival' (2016: 65) and her admiration for what she described as 'our great and still living heritage of rough and ready poetry' (Carter 1962a: 4), but he does not then link Carter's singing experiences with her subsequent artistic development.

But the most silent participant of all in this discussion is Carter herself, who, after 1970, hardly mentions her involvement in the 1960s folk revival. There are a handful of exceptions: in her 1974 'Afterword' to *Fireworks*, she mentions the 'subliterary forms of pornography, ballad and dream' in a longer analysis of the tale ([1974c] 1996: 549–50), and in her 1983 essay 'Alison's Giggle', she uses folk song to illustrate a point about sex education:

> It is almost a cliché of orally transmitted poetry, that is, folksong, that one unprotected act of intercourse will lead inevitably to pregnancy [...] Such songs were, no doubt, intended to help proscribe extramarital sexual activity on the part of young village girls.
>
> ([1983a] 2013: 675–6)

Lastly, in 1990, she dedicates *The Virago Book of Fairy Tales* to A. L. Lloyd, one of the architects of the second-wave British folksong revival of the 1950s and 1960s:

> Years ago, the late A.L. Lloyd, ethnomusicologist, folklorist and singer, taught me that I needn't know an artist's name to recognize that one had been at work. This book is dedicated to that proposition, and therefore, to his memory.
>
> (1990: xxii)

Other than these sparse examples, after 1970 it is as if folk song were dead to her.

In stark contrast, in the 1960s Carter was an active participant in the Bristol folk scene, the co-founder with her first husband of a folk club and a regular folk singer and player. The private archive of Carter's folk song notes and research currently resides with Christine Molan, a Bristol-based artist and former friend of the Carters. Molan attended regular folk club nights with 'the Folk Singing Carters' (Gordon 2016: 104) in Bristol throughout the 1960s, and her accounts of those nights present Carter's participation in the folk scene as both frequent and long term:

> I have vivid recall of Angela singing solos because we sang fortnightly together at her Bristol club 'Folksong and Ballads'. She'd adopt a traditional singer's swagger with hands thrust into her pockets, eyes shut, maybe a grin. [...] Angela flowered. She experimented freely with narrative and the timing of beautiful, sinister ballads like 'Twa Sisters', whose female protagonists are rivals in love.
>
> (2016: 29, 32)

Molan also reveals the multi-medial nature of Carter's assimilation of the form (see Figures 1 and 2):

> Few of us knew that Angela was absorbing folksong on every level, in libraries, among singers, from Alan Lomax vinyl, and through listening to Paul's unique reel-to-reel tapes piled in boxes at her Bristol home.
>
> (2017: 21)

**Figure 1** Some of the books in Paul and Angela Carter's Folk Music Archive. Reproduced with kind permission from Christine Molan.

**Figure 2** Some of the vinyl in Paul and Angela Carter's Folk Music Archive. Reproduced with kind permission from Christine Molan.

When Paul Carter died in 2012, Molan inherited from him a box filled with the Carters' shared folk song research, their books and vinyl; Paul and Angela each had their own notebooks.

Angela Carter's notebook contains quotations from influential books such as Cecil Sharp's *English Folk Songs from the Southern Appalachians* (1932) and handwritten staves of musical notation of folk song tunes and lyrics. Some of these tunes were notated from textual sources, such as 'Lucy Wan' from *The Penguin Book of English Folk Songs* (Lloyd and Vaughan Williams 1959: 65) (see Figure 3).

But in other cases, she notated tunes orally, directly from records, such as Phoëbe Smith's singing of 'Higher Germany' (Smith 1970) (see Figure 4).

Carter also wrote out important features of musical keys, revealing evidence of a desire to master the mechanics of tunes and their key changes, perhaps in an effort to learn to master the concertina (see Figure 5).

Inside their copy of James Reeves' collection of folk songs *The Everlasting Circle* (1960), there survives a touching inscription from Angela to Paul,

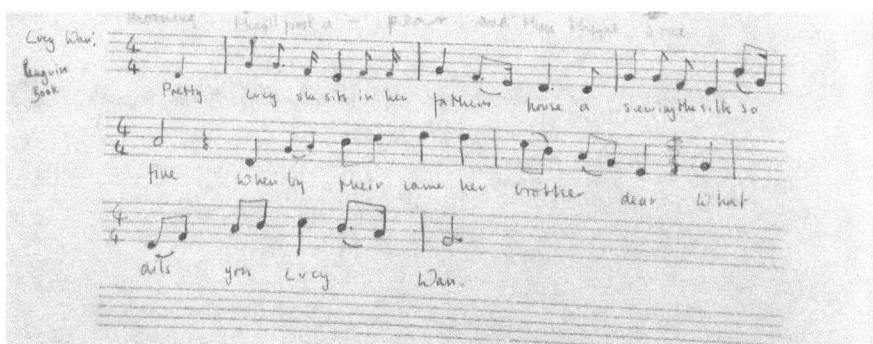

**Figure 3** Angela Carter's notation of 'Lucy Wan' in her notebook in Paul and Angela Carter's Folk Music Archive. Reproduced with kind permission from Christine Molan.

**Figure 4** Angela Carter's notation of 'Higher Germany' in her notebook in Paul and Angela Carter's Folk Music Archive. Reproduced with kind permission from Christine Molan.

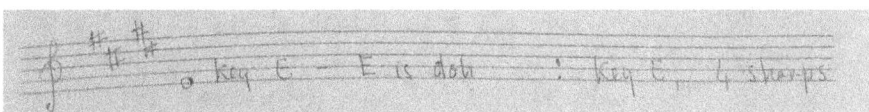

**Figure 5** Detail of Angela Carter's notation of the key of E, from Paul and Angela Carter's Folk Music Archive. Reproduced with kind permission from Christine Molan.

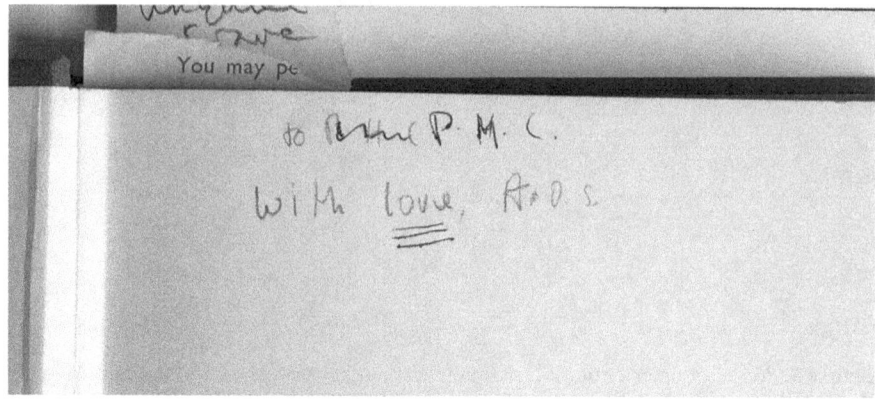

**Figure 6** Detail of Angela Carter's dedication to Paul inside their copy of James Reeves' *The Everlasting Circle* (1960). Paul and Angela Carter's Folk Music Archive. Reproduced with kind permission from Christine Molan.

presumably (because of the initials – and the uncertainty!) written before they were married (see Figure 6).

The archive also contains the co-authored manifesto for their club, which expresses the formation of an organization

> concerned exclusively with the promotion of a wider appreciation and deeper understanding of the great heritage of traditional folksong, ballad and music of the British Isles, and especially that of England. It also seeks to further the natural evolution of contemporary work within the framework described by tradition.
>
> (Carter and Carter n.d.: A01)

That the club was interested in folk song's 'natural evolution' suggests Carter was already thinking about how folk song might mutate.

Before this archive came to light, there was already evidence to suggest that, as a young woman, Angela Carter loved the folk song form. Lyrical song fragments litter her diaries like a private language: in her 1961 journal she writes out lines from 'The Unquiet Grave': 'I suppose, by true poetry, I mean, for example, "Cold is the wind tonight, my love, / And a few drops of rain; / I never had but one true love, / In cold earth he was lain"' (Carter 1961). In the same journal on the inside cover, she transcribes lines from 'The Twa Corbies': 'O'er his white bones, when they are bare, / The wind sall blow for evermair' (Carter 1961). In her 1963–4 journal, she quotes lines from 'The Cottage in the Wood': 'One moonlit night as I sat high, / Waiting for one, but two came by, / The bough did bend, my heart did quake / To see the hole the fox did make' (Carter 1963–64). She also collates a list of eighty folk song titles across a double-spread, one section tantalizingly titled 'To Learn'. This list includes songs of female agency such as 'Jackie Munroe' and 'The Female Highwayman', which might be seen as early evidence of her expressing a feminist agenda through curation.

Moreover, in her unpublished 1965 undergraduate dissertation, she discusses links she perceives between twentieth-century folk song and medieval poetry; one can see gestating preoccupations which were to reverberate throughout her oeuvre as she concludes:

> These songs survived the centuries, being continually re-moulded to suit each new generation of country singers, but often retaining ancient features; and newly written or adapted songs were often, new wine in old bottles, cast in ancient forms.
>
> (Carter 1965a: 98)

With her use of the wine-bottle metaphor from Matthew 9:17, recycled so memorably in her 1983 essay 'Notes from the Front Line' ([1983b] 2013: 46), this is an early example of Carter raising questions about the problematic yet creative tension between tradition and creation, which underpins so much of her subsequent work.

Carter also shows an extraordinary affinity with the figure of the folk singer. Her exegetic sleeve notes for records by Peggy Seeger (Carter 1962b, 1962c see Figures 7, 8 and 9) and Louis Killen (Carter 1965b) reveal both her intimate knowledge of folk songs and their contexts and her musicological appreciation of singer style and delivery. She praises Seeger's 'lively eclecticism' (Carter 1962b), and her 'deep respect for tradition […] her singing is always direct and alive, an act of creation not resuscitation' (Carter 1962c). Killen 'stamps each performance with his own musical individuality and dynamism through keeping to the disciplines of traditional singing, a paradox which is the basis of the serious folksong revival' (Carter 1965b). Carter reveals in these notes a practical understanding of somatic performance, voice and resonance, alongside an academic understanding of the song-texts, and she expresses a preoccupation with the singer and with singing as much as the song.

Carter engages further with the figure of the folk singer in other essays and articles. In a 1961 newspaper article (writing under her maiden name, Stalker),

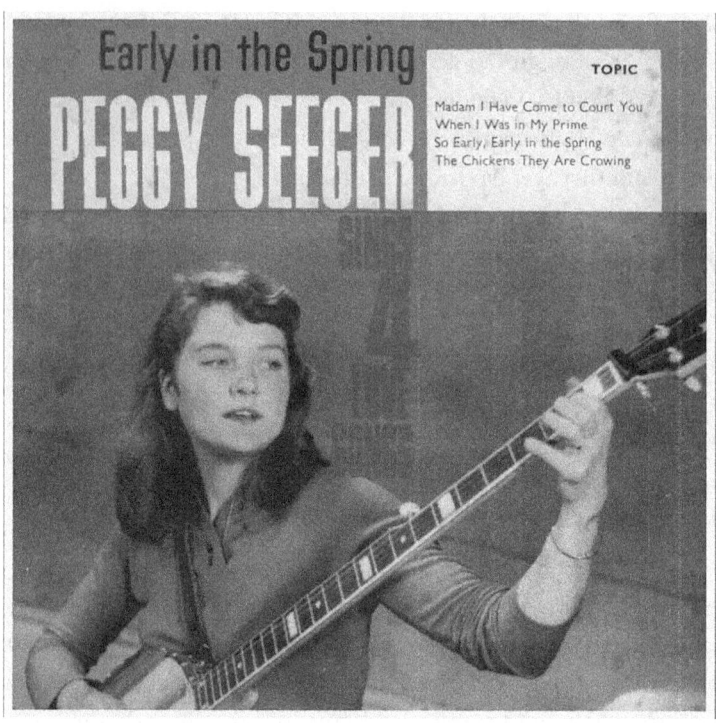

**EARLY IN THE SPRING**
Four Courting Songs
**PEGGY SEEGER**

An American visitor to this country recently observed that Peggy Seeger is developing " quite a strong British accent these days ". In spite of the time she has spent in England however, Peggy Seeger's style on the guitar and banjo remain as indigenously American—and as highly accomplished—as ever. And she has not forgotten any of the songs in her enormous repertoire. She describes herself as " a product of the folk music revival " but she has always closely studied and learned from traditional styles and material. She has a deep respect for tradition, but her singing is always direct and alive, an act of creation not resuscitation.

On this record there are four songs which are either directly or indirectly concerned with courting.

MADAM I HAVE COME TO COURT YOU. Peggy Seeger has based this comic courting song on *I'm Going Away To Texas* (Vance Randolph, *Ozark Folk Songs*, Vol. 3) with additional verses from other variants. The suitor is rejected very firmly several times until he mentions money.

WHEN I WAS IN MY PRIME. This is the first example available of Peggy Seeger's unaccompanied singing. The song's highly ornamented melody demands this treatment. It is a variant of the widely found *Sprig of Thyme* and *Seeds of Love* and follows the textual pattern of these songs. There is considerable symbolism in the imagery of the text, but this version is perhaps easier of interpretation than many, and could mean that a woman, no longer young, is regretting a youthful misadventure with a sexual opportunist. The gardener perhaps represents a fertility element.

SO EARLY, EARLY IN THE SPRING. A sailor leaves his love with many protests of affection and returns to find her married to a richer man. This song can be traced back to various nineteenth century British broadsides, and the theme is found in innumerable versions both in America and Britain.

THE CHICKENS THEY ARE CROWING. This courting song is a collation of two texts from Sharp's *English Folk Songs from the Southern Appalachians*. The verse sung here *I won't go home till morning* possibly refers to the old American courting custom of " bundling " when to conserve fuel, the couple would take themselves to bed with a board between them. The song is a favourite among banjo players.

ANGELA CARTER

Recording by Bill Leader    Photo by TECHET

**TOPIC RECORDS Ltd · 27 Nassington Road · London · N.W.3**

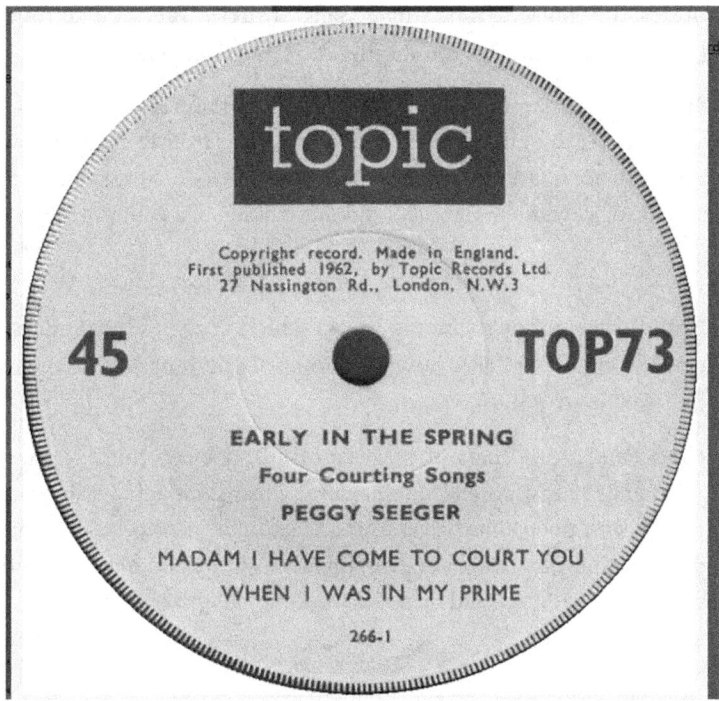

**Figures 7, 8 and 9** The cover, reverse and disc of Peggy Seeger's EP 'Early in the Spring' (Topic Records TOP73, 1962) with Angela Carter's sleeve notes. Reproduced with kind permission from Topic Records.

she describes in minute detail the stance, gesture and delivery of a folk song performer, fascinated with his singing body:

> Slinging his jacket nonchalantly over one shoulder and adopting a casual stance half-leaning against a chair – both traditional attitudes of the serious student of folk-song – Garry James eschewed accompaniment (very properly) to sing a selection of fairly esoteric and markedly attractive English and Irish folk-songs at *The Swan and Sugar Loaf* on Friday evening.
>
> (Stalker 1961: 4)

In her 1967 article on the Shropshire singer Fred Jordan, she recounts lovingly how he

> has a strong, ringing tenor and often uses a pronounced vibrato effect which sometimes disconcerts people who have never heard him before. His style is straightforward, sweet and dignified. […] When he sings old songs, it is an everyday, honest miracle, like bread.
>
> (Carter 1967a: 283)

She celebrates the Norfolk folk singer Sam Larner's 'spectacular timing and control' (1964: 12) and praises the singing of Harry Cox, whose

> style is a compound of subtle and beautiful rhythms; there is a marvellous pulse to his singing and he modulates the tune of a song from verse to verse and decorates, with great taste and economy, the basic melodic line so that it grows with organic logic, with the rightness and inevitability of a natural growth.
>
> (1964: 13)

But most of all, it is her own singing praxis which enriches her understanding of the form. She states explicitly how the somatic experience of her own singing informs her imaginative understanding:

> the richness and allusiveness of imagery in folk poetry, which reaches one through singing almost on a subliminal level, means one's appreciation of the mode grows with one's knowledge. And so, naturally, does one's imagination, one's ability to think in images oneself, one's sensibility and one's perceptions, because folk song is an art, and these are the things all the arts do.
>
> (1964: 15)

Through her own singing praxis, therefore, and from her proximity to the singers Paul was recording (A. L. Lloyd, Ewan MacColl, Anne Briggs, Seamus Ennis, Peggy Seeger, Joe Heaney, Louis Killen, Sarah Makem and many others), Carter witnesses first-hand what Milla Tiainen describes as 'open materiality', that awareness of the resonance of the singing body in a space and its capacity to influence its surroundings and be influenced in turn in an ever-spiralling dialogue. As Tiainen explains:

> the spatial character of vocal bodies is hence comprised of continuous foldings-in of physical and affective particles and simultaneously, unfoldings-out of sonic-bodily forces. […] Singing bodies are spatial formations that exist, emerge and change in time.
>
> (2007: 158)

Carter can be seen through her descriptions of singers and singing to be articulating her understanding of the intimate relationship between the singer and the song.

Vitally, Carter chooses to use this knowledge in her creative life. In a letter written in 1966, she states plainly that she is looking for ways to transcode her singing experience into her prose:

I believe in not wasting anything, and all these years' work on folk-song and traditional verse will be a waste of time unless I can assimilate it, somehow, into my writing.

(1966b)

Carter realizes this deliberate 'assimilation', I propose, in two discernible ways. Firstly, she is able to illuminate her writing with the explosive energy of folk song's symbols, figures and motifs – recurring figures and motifs such as the seductive music man or the penknife with indelible blood, or recognizable loci such as the greenwood – creating chains of association and circulations of signs, learned somatically from the singing of them. Secondly, and perhaps as a more direct consequence of her singing, she finds ways to infuse her writing with folk song's audial features – melodic shapes such as chiasmus, or evocative rhythmic patternings of dactyls and iambs – imbuing her writing with a distinctive musicality by transcoding the raw elements of folk song into her prose in what could be seen as multimodal processes of evolution. The evidence that she succeeds is clear when one examines the contemporary musicians who either cite her as a musical influence or who have the connection routinely made for them by others, such as Björk, Bat for Lashes, P. J. Harvey, Wolf Alice and Emily Portman, the contemporary folk artist, who through her own work has returned Carter's musicality specifically back to folk song.

Although in 1966 Carter stated her deliberate intention to 'assimilate' folk song into her writing in a private letter, she rarely discussed its influences publicly; sometimes this omission glares. For example, in 'Notes from the Front Line', she claims to use 'shifting structures derived from orally transmitted traditional tales' ([1983b] 2013: 47), but she does not mention the folk songs with which she is so familiar; in her *Virago Book of Fairy Tales* introduction (having simultaneously dedicated it to Lloyd), she states that 'fairy tales, folk tales, stories from the oral tradition, are all of them the most vital connection we have with the imaginations of the ordinary men and women whose labour created our world' (1990: ix); folk song is notably absent from her list – why? Edmund Gordon suggests that Carter associated folk song with her first husband; the Carters' mutual love of folk song was a bond between them; she may have wanted to distance herself from the folk revival scene once her marriage to him had ended. But, although it was Carter's grandmother who first sang folk songs to her: 'songs that celebrated the wily fox, the poacher's comrade, and his depredations of bourgeois farmyards' (Carter [1976] 2013: 6), by the time Carter arrived in Bath in the mid-1970s, she was expressing publicly feelings of unease about the folk singing tradition. Christopher Frayling remembers how a Shirley Collins song

> became a standing joke by the time she came to Bath. Whenever she wanted to take the piss out of folk music, she'd say, 'the larks are singing melodious'.
>
> (Paulusma 2014a)

Another possible explanation for the omissions may have been ideological: perhaps Carter came to associate folk song revival on some levels with the 'mind-forg'd manacles' (Carter [1983b] 2013: 47) of oppressive patriarchy she perceived to be at work in wider society, broader patriarchal hegemonic structures which, post-1968, she was in the business of dismantling. The cornerstone folk song collector practices of 'carefully and accurately gathering what of [the] wreck we can yet find floating around us' (Motherwell 1827: v), the preservation of precious oral artefacts endangered by the encroachment of modernity through collecting, field-recording and archiving may at first appear to be an admirable ethnomusicological occupation in keeping with more left-wing political agendas, performed by those keen to celebrate the voice of Sharp's 'Common People' (1907: 3). But such activities become problematized under closer scrutiny. The collectors' fixing in text of 'living', evanescent, oral artefacts has been seen by some as fatally invasive; the source singer Mrs. Hogg warned Sir Walter Scott that her songs 'were made for singin' an' no for readin'; but ye hae broke the charm noo, an' they'll never be sung mair' (Harker 1985: 70). Transcription becomes an intrusion which 'inexorably changes' (Carter 1990: x) the orally transmitted artefacts these collectors are seeking to salvage.

Secondly, the folk song collectors' tendencies to select, omit, edit, 'improve' and sometimes even fabricate folk song material, based on their own personal prejudices, political agendas and notions of 'correctness', have more recently been critiqued by musicologists such as Georgina Boyes (1993), Dave Harker (1985) and Trish Winter and Simon Keegan-Phipps (2013). Boyes accuses the collector Percy Grainger, who once hid under a bed to secure a recording of a reluctant source singer, of 'ruthless expropriation' (1993: 49); Harker claims that folk songs in the hands of collectors such as Frank Kidson and Lucy Broadwood 'represented the highly-mediated product of the dominant cultural values acting through even the more enlightened collectors' (1985: 207). Winter and Keegan-Phipps criticize Sharp for promoting his fantasy of Romantic nationalism through his collecting: 'Sharp's "folk" were […] a whimsical ideal that was both symptomatic and a perpetuating construct of the essentialising nationalism to which he and his numerous followers subscribed' (2013: 6). Even Paul Carter himself, who made important recordings of source singers such as Tom Willett and Sarah Makem in the field, may have grown uncomfortable with the idea of recording folk songs. Reg Hall, a folk activist and friend of the Carters, remembers how during a conversation with Paul in later years, 'I got the feeling he was in some way wanting to cut his links from recording traditional music, as if he felt that recording it had somehow been not in the spirit of the music' (Paulusma 2014b). Angela Carter may have arrived independently at similar conclusions about the uncomfortable power politics of revival, but it does not mean that she grew to dislike the form itself.

For Carter to identify folk song with patriarchal constructs would be contradictory to both her own experiences and wider cultural reception. She remembers her granny singing 'The Fox' to her when she was a child:

> Old Mother Flipperty-flop jumped out of bed,
> Out of the window she stuck out 'er 'ead —
> 'John, John, the grey goose is gone
> And the fox is off to his den, oh!'

([1976] 2013: 6)

If anything, folk song as cultural practice occupies matriarchal spaces in Carter's personal history. Folk song is more often widely aligned with femino-cultural practices: as Catherine Kerrigan explains:

> women played such a significant role as tradition-bearers and transmitters that it can be claimed that the ballad tradition is one of the most readily identifiable areas of literary performance by women. [...] the ballad presents a vital and sustained women's tradition.

(1991: 2)

If anything, it might rather have been the more venatic practices of revival itself – collecting, recording, transcribing, 'improving', archiving, databasing – which may have grown unpalatable to her. But I posit her love of the form itself continued unabated.

For while Carter's own omissions of folk song's influence in her self-reflexive writing may have thrown critics off the trail, authors can 'speak' in other ways. Folk song's influence on Carter's fiction-writing becomes wildly apparent when one starts to listen for it in her fiction writing. From my vantage point as a singer-songwriter and a singer of traditional folk songs as well as a philologist, I have grown increasingly aware of the immanent corporeal resonance of folk song threaded into the thematic and prosodic warp of Carter's fiction. From the opening lines of her debut novel *Shadow Dance* (1966) to the closing pages of *Wise Children* (1991), a reader with a canorous bent can perceive the musical 'assimilation' of folk song's prosodic, thematic and structural features into Carter's writing.

Folk song's melodies, rhythms, images and motifs infuse Carter's prose; through her syntactic and prosodic choices, Carter 'sings' – and invites us to 'sing' – the patterns of British folk song. Her prose demands that we 'form', 'perform', acoustic events every time we read her, reconstructing acoustic shapes in our minds; she is continually enacting through us a spiralling mediation of forms, an interfusion, a 'folding-in' and 'unfolding-out' of the song form in and out of prose. What's more, this process can be seen as entirely consistent with the mediational folk processes of 'continuity, variation and selection' (1907: 16) first propounded by Sharp, of which Carter, through her folk scholarship, was well aware.

The presence of such features in Carter's prose challenges the argument that Carter distanced herself from folk song at the end of the 1960s simply because of the collapse of her marriage. Rather, I propose that, as an intellectual response to some of the more problematic aspects of folk song revival she may have perceived, Carter developed ways to variegate the form, keep it alive, liberate it, by migrating it into her prose – evolving it onwards as she stated she intended to do in her club manifesto – burying it like treasure in a place where the musicians of the future might find it, in the very music of her prose.

## The rhythms of the greenwood

I propose in this chapter to explore just one aspect of Carter's folk song assimilation: her appropriation of the greenwood locus, that dangerous peripheral site in folk song where maids are raped, babies murdered, knights abducted and where society 'turns a blind eye' to its own necessary disgorgements. The manifestation of Carter's folk singing voice in her prose can be located in her careful prosodic choices, in which specific rhythms of folk song are evoked via syntax to create an undulating 'invisible music' (Carter [1968] 1995: 1). Carter was drawn to the idea that literature is audial; in her 1962–3 journal, she enthuses about Northrop Frye's concept of 'melos' ([1957] 1973: 262–3) which Carter identifies as

> a musical quality; and by musical he means rhythmic, language following an elaborate internal scheme of balances, chords and discords, with meter and relations of harsh consonants very pronounced, also speeds.
>
> (Carter 1962–63)

Carter blended Frye's ideas of 'melos' with her singing praxis in her early literary experiments, and the result was music-in-prose. When Carter wanted to conjure the atmosphere of the greenwood space in her fictive universes, she used the musical features of the locus such as its intoxicating rhythm, which she had learnt from singing, to create a 'melody of letters' (Stevenson ([1885] 1905: 40), a songful landscape, a sonic cartography.

English folk songs can share closely related sets of metrical variations, perhaps partly due to the way the tunes and words can be interchangeable depending on regional or familial bias. Folk songs which depict the greenwood, adventure, galloping horses, danger and flight are often presented within a dactylic rhythmic framework; the lines of these ballads can be acephalous in nature, which can make them harder to spot (and become mistakenly labelled anapaestic), but the drive and excitement incited by the dactylic canter transports one during a close analysis. In folk songs set in the greenwood, such as 'Lady Isabel and the Elf-Knight' and 'Babes in the Wood', dactylic tetrameter is a compelling ingredient in the overall semantic recipe, creating the danger and excitement the greenwood locus demands.

The dactylic gallop in 'Lady Isabel and the Elf-Knight' is best discerned using the musical scansion techniques proposed by Geoffrey Leech, which acknowledge 'silent beats' (2008: 76). The song depicts a young lady's seduction by a dangerous magical music-man, their elopement into the greenwood and her cunning escape from his murderous clutches – a folk song which contributes in more ways than one to Carter's 'Erl-King', as we shall discuss further. Leech's methodology requires us to 'hear' the text musically with its associated 'rests'. Try reading this verse from 'Lady Isabel and the Elf-Knight' aloud, following the schema of stressed (´), unstressed (˘) and silent (x) syllables as indicated. Strike your finger on a table wherever you see a silent beat (x) to get the feel of it:

| | | | He |
|---|---|---|---|
| ´ ˇ ˇ | \| ´ ˇ ˇ | \| ´ ˇ ˇ | \| ´ ˇ ˇ |
| leapt on a | \| horse, (x) and | \| she on a- | \| -nother, (x) |
| ´ ˇ ˇ | \| ´ ˇ ˇ | \| ´ ˇ ˇ | \| ´ ˇ ˇ |
| Aye, as the | \| go-wans grow | \| gay (x) (x) | \| (x) And they |
| ´ ˇ ˇ | ´ ˇ ˇ | ´ ˇ ˇ | ´ ˇ ˇ |
| rode (x) (x) | \| on to the | \| greenwood to – | \| -gether (x) |
| ´ ˇ ˇ | \| ´ ˇ ˇ | \| ´ ˇ ˇ | \| ´ ˇ ˇ |
| On the first | \| mor- ning in | \| May (x) (x) | \| (x) (x) (x) |

(Child 1882: 55; Theriot 2001)

Another folk song to use the hypnotic, driving dactylic rhythm to draw us into the horror of the greenwood is the murderous 'Babes in the Wood':

| | | | \| ˇ ˇ |
|---|---|---|---|
| | | | \| Pretty |
| ´ ˇ ˇ | \| ´ ˇ ˇ | \| ´ ˇ ˇ | \| ´ ˇ ˇ |
| babes in the | \| wood prett-y | \| babes in the | \| wood, (x) oh, |
| ´ ˇ ˇ | \| ´ ˇ ˇ | \| ´ ˇ ˇ | \| ´ ˇ ˇ |
| don't you re- | \| -mem-ber those | \| babes in the | \| wood (x) (x) |

(Copper and Copper 1963)

Molan remembers Paul singing 'Babes in the Wood' at their folk club; for Molan the song

> is linked indelibly for me with the verdant woodland scene of a flat-pack Victorian toy theatre which Angela bought for Paul's birthday in 1966, one of her jokey gifts. [...] the woodland dell when side-lit, was so enchanting that I went to Pollock's Toy Shop in London and bought one for myself.
>
> (2016: 31)

Carter borrows the claustrophobic dactylic rhythms of 'Lady Isabel and the Elf-Knight' and 'Babes in the Wood' to conjure the greenwood space across her oeuvre. In her alter-Edenic short story 'Penetrating to the Heart of the Forest', twins Emile and Madeline lose themselves and their innocence in the transformative 'enchanted forest':

| |′ ˘ ˘ | |′ ˘ ′ | |˘ ˘ ˘ | |′ ˘ ˘ | |′ ˘ ˘ ˘ |
|---|---|---|---|---|
| \| Here, they walked | \| hand in hand | \| be-neath the | \| vault-ed (x) | \| arch- i-traves of |

| |′ ˘ ˘ | |′ ˘ ˘ |′ ˘ ˘ | |′ ˘ ˘ | |′ ˘ ˘ |
|---|---|---|---|---|
| \| pines in a | \| hushed (x) in- \| ter – ior like | \| that of a | \| sen-tient cath- |

| |′ ˘ ˘ |
|---|
| \| e- dral (x) |

| |′ ˘ ˘ | |′ ˘ ˘ | |′ |
|---|---|---|
| \| Ferns (x) un- | \| curled as they | \| watched |

| ˘ ˘ | |′ ˘ ˘ | |′ ˘ ˘ | |′ ˘ ˘ | |′ |
|---|---|---|---|---|
| there were | \| trees that bore | \| brown speckled | \| plum – age of | \| birds |
| | […] | | | |

| ˘ | |′ ˘ ˘ | |′ ˘ ˘ | |′ ˘ |
|---|---|---|---|
| And | \| when they had | \| grown ve-ry | \| hun-gry |

| ˘ | |′ ˘ ˘ | |′ ˘ ˘ | |′ ˘ ˘ | |′ ˘ ˘ |
|---|---|---|---|---|
| They | \| came to a | \| clump of low | \| trees (x) with | \| trunks scaled like |
| \|′ | | | | |
| \| trout | | | | |

(Carter [1974b] 1996: 71, 76)

The relentless dactylic feel embodies in rhythmic terms the irresistible draw of the greenwood, and the dialectic at the heart of our greenwood imaginings which oscillates between attraction and repulsion, wonder and horror, excitement and danger, a dialectic which lies at the very heart of the greenwood's allure and at the heart of the human condition. Carter was attuned to this rhythm of concupiscence and transposed it into the assonant interplay of her prosody.

This is apparent when the following example from 'The Erl-King' is read aloud:

> There was a little tangled mist in the thickets, mimicking the tufts of old man's beard that flossed the lower branches of the trees and bushes; heavy bunches of red berries as ripe and delicious as goblin or enchanted fruit hung on the hawthorns but the old grass withers, retreats. One by one, the ferns have curled up their hundred eyes and curled back into the earth.
>
> (Carter [1979] 1996: 222)

In the rich description of the Erl-King's home, one can map in the assonant word-play and dactylic rhythm the rising and falling of the seasons and the potential for corruption in the height of ripeness, with the oscillation of the heroine's enthralment and repulsion. Carter simultaneously disturbs and attracts with the passage's prosodic beauty, just as the Erl-King's music both seduces and admonishes the heroine. The asphyxiating short /ɪ/ sounds – 'little', 'mist', 'thickets', 'mimicking' – wind tightly round us, strangle us; the /e/ sounds of 'heavy', 'red' and 'berries' suggest an opening, a wideness, a sexual fecundity. Immediately this ripeness is negated by 'old grass' which 'withers, retreats'; the ferns have 'curled up their hundred eyes' – they don't want to bear witness – 'and curled back into the earth': the repetitive /ɜː/ sound suggests collapse, a return, a cyclic closure – 'the year, in turning, turns in on itself.' This phonetic cycle echoes itself in the /ɜː/ and /ɪ/ of the Erl-King's very name. Dactyls once more summon the greenwood:

| ˘ | \| ′ ˘ ˘ | \| ′ ˘ ˘ | \| ′ ˘ ˘ |
|---|---|---|---|
| the | \| ferns have curled | \| up (x) their | \| hun (x) dred |

| \| ′ ˘ ˘ | \| ′ ˘ ˘ | \| ′ ˘ ˘ | \| ′ ˘ ˘ |
|---|---|---|---|
| \| eyes (x) and | \| curled (x) back | \| in- to the | \| earth (x) (x) |

This innate musicality, drawing on folk song's rich store of resonances through its prosody and rhythm, intensifies the Erl-King's melodious seduction, and draws a line through our collective memory back to folk song's dangerous, wonderful greenwood.

Moreover, Carter learns that through rhythm she can form the greenwood locus in urban spaces: artificial forests assume the greenwood's transformative attributes in *Wise Children*:

| ˘ | \|ˊ ˘ ˘ | \|ˊ ˘ ˘ | \|ˊ ˘ ˘ |
|---|---|---|---|
| The | \| leg- end- ary | \| For- est of | \| Ard- en, the |
| \|ˊ ˘ | \|ˊ ˘ ˘ | \|ˊ ˘ ˘ | \|ˊ |
| \| res- i | \| dent- ial mo- | \| tel of the | \| stars |

alongside the overblown film set supposedly depicting the woods near Athens with

| \|ˊ ˘ ˘ | \|ˊ ˘ ˘ | \|ˊ ˘ |
|---|---|---|
| \| Bind- weed in | \| stream- ers and | \| con- kers |

where

| \|ˊ ˘ ˘ | \|ˊ ˘ ˘ | \|ˊ ˘ |
|---|---|---|
| \| What I missed | \| most was il- | \| -lusion. |

(Carter [1991] 1992: 120–5)

In Genghis Khan's office, the 'Grünewald crucifixion' ([1991] 1992: 145) – presumably a reproduction of the famous Isenheim Altarpiece by Matthias Grünewald, which through name-association evokes the dangerous locus of the anglicized 'greenwood' – oversees the action in the –

| \|ˊ ˘ ˘ | \|ˊ ˘ ˘ | \|ˊ ˘ | \|ˊ ˘ |
|---|---|---|---|
| \| ho- ly of | \| ho- lies, the | \| or-chid | \| ar- bour |

all are transformative greenwood spaces which, as Dora confesses, 'changed me for good and all' (1991: 121).

Once attuned, we can feel the rhythm of the greenwood wherever Carter is alerting us to its presence. Morris' unassuming bric-a-brac shop in *Shadow Dance*, for example, is a locus for transformation: here Ghislaine will succumb to her masochistic desires, whereas Emily will assume control of her destiny. Carter tunes us into the space's transformative possibilities through the cadences of her similes, describing:

| ˘ | \| ′  ˘  ˘ | \| ′  ˘  ˘ | \| ′     ′ \| |
|---|---|---|---|
| a | \| sort of sub- | \| aqu - e- ous | \| deep sea \| |
| \| ′  ˘  ˘ | \| ′  ˘  ˘ | \| ′  ˘  ˘ | \| ′     ˘  ˘ \| |
| \| at- mos- phere | \| (x) in which | \| piles (x) of | \| furn- i- ture \| |
| \| ˘  ′  ˘ | \| ′  ′ | \| ′  ˘  ˘ | \| ′  ˘  ′ \| |
| \| and rags and | \| tea chests | \| seemed the en- | \| crust- ed, drowned \| |
| \| ′  ˘  ˘ | \| ′     ′ | \| ′  ˘  ˘ | \| ′  ˘     ˘ \| |
| \| car- goes of | \| long-dead | \| ships. (x) There | \| should have been \| |
| \| ′  ˘  ˘ | \| ′  ˘ |   |   |
| \| lim- pets and | \| sea- weed. |   |   |

([1966] 2014: 68)

Ghislaine is raped by Honeybuzzard in another urban greenwood, a 'padlocked and deserted' (12) city cemetery; her dactylic acquiescence to his will is irradiated with greenwood rhythms:

| ˘ \| ′  ˘  ˘ | \| ′  ˘  ˘ | \| ′  ˘  ˘ | \| ′     ˘  ˘ |
|---|---|---|---|
| I \| can't live with- | \| -out you, (x) | \| you are my | \| mast- er (x) |
| \| ′  ˘  ˘ | \| ′  ˘  ˘ |   |   |
| \| do what you | \| like with me.' |   |   |

([1966] 2014: 166)

Ghislaine is sickeningly complicit in her own suffering, and her lethal 'transformation' in the urban 'greenwood' of *Shadow Dance* is unequivocal. But by the time Carter writes 'The Erl-King', she has developed subtler and more complex ideas of victimhood and power viewed through the lens of her intervening work on *The Sadeian Woman*. The narrator-heroine of 'Erl-King' wanders into a greenwood complicated by Sado-Lacanian concepts of the split subject and the passive role of the executioner willed to inflict pain by the 'obscene jouissance' (Žižek 1998) of the situated other; her protagonist's complicity with her executioner is therefore far more nuanced. But while the greenwood's repeated evocation across Carter's oeuvre may develop and mature, its menacing, enticing, intoxicating rhythmic force is constant. No matter where it appears, through syntax Carter transcodes the pulse of the greenwood from folk song into prose, and its driving force sends us into the greenwood ourselves, where the prosodic manifestation of the dynamic paradox of attraction and repulsion, wonder and horror lurking at the heart of the greenwood works to estrange us from ourselves.

## The figures of the greenwood

Carter does not just transcode the rhythmic features of the greenwood into her creations; she also borrows recognizable figures and motifs to evoke its terror and excitement. The magical music-man, who seduces his female victims with supernatural melodies, is familiar from folk song. His music is potent in the greenwood, where verbal language, along with rationality and law, is ineffective: as J. R. R. Tolkien observed, faërie 'cannot be caught in a net of words; for it is one of its qualities to be indescribable, though not imperceptible' ([1939] 2008: 32). The language of music in the greenwood communicates where words fail. In 'Lady Isabel and the Elf-Knight' (Child 1882: 55), for example, a dangerous music-man uses irresistible music to lure his victims. Lady Isabel hears the 'elf-knight blawing his horn', whom she longs 'to sleep in my bosom'; instantly he appears at her window. They elope but their adventure ends abruptly when the Elf-Knight announces his true intention to murder her, as he has seven (/ten/twelve) girls before her. Having willingly abandoned the safety of her father's house, and now beyond the jurisdiction of the known world, Isabel appears to be at the Elf-Knight's mercy. But rather than yielding, she formulates a plan:

> 'O sit down a while, lay your head on my knee,
> That we may hae some rest before that I die.'

She sings to him, lulling him to sleep on her lap to disarm him:

> She stroakd him sae fast, the nearer he did creep,
> Wi a sma charm she lulld him fast asleep.

And then she stabs him with his own dagger:

> Wi his ain sword-belt sae fast as she ban him,
> Wi his ain dag-durk sae sair as she dang him.

Isabel is saved by her cunning, a 'dauntless heroine' (Carter 1965b) amongst a plethora of brave, quick-thinking clever lasses in the folk songs Carter so admired.

While Carter may have borrowed certain elements for her short story 'The Erl-King' ([1979] 1996: 221–9) from Goethe's 1782 'Erlkönig' poem (the name, and the boy's cry, 'Erlkönig hat mir ein Leids getan!' meaning 'The Erlking has done me harm!') as critics such as Marion May Campbell have suggested (2013: 119–32), there are many displeasing inconsistencies; to my mind the story owes so much more to the ballad 'Lady Isabel and the Elf-Knight' which Carter knew well (Carter 1984, 1992, n.d.: 57–78). Just like Lady Isabel in the song, Carter's narrator-heroine succumbs to the Erl-King's 'magic lasso of inhuman music' ([1979] 1996: 226), she has a choice whether to avenge other victims and escape or become incarcerated (228) and she lulls her assailant to sleep (228). Her murderous intentions, however, hang ambiguously in the future tense:

> I shall take two huge handfuls of his rustling hair as he lies half dreaming, half waking, and wind them into ropes, very softly, so he will not wake up, and softly, with hands as gentle as rain, I will strangle him with them.
>
> (228)

Carter's narrator oscillates between desire and despair: one minute she is overjoyed ('how pleasing, how lovely' (226)) and enthralled ('He knows all about the wood and the creatures in it' (224)) by the Erl-King, and the next repulsed ('his flesh is of the same substance as those leaves that are slowly turning into earth' (225)) and panic-stricken ('I was shaken with a terrible fear' (228)). Like Isabel, the narrator-heroine alternates between feelings of attraction and repulsion for her abductor; he is a sexualized being for whom she feels unmitigated desire – 'he has stiff, russet nipples ripe as berries' (226) – and yet he is 'gaunt' (226). She recognizes this oxymoron: 'His touch both consoles and devastates me' (227). This is the true nature of their destructive love: 'His embraces were his enticements and yet, oh yet! they were the branches of which the trap itself was woven' (228). Carter transcodes the greenwood oscillation of attraction/repulsion into the actions of her narrator-heroine, who concludes that Erl-King really will 'do you grievous harm' in time to aspire to extricate herself from his devastating embraces. But escape is only a potentiality for our narrator-heroine, suspended in the future tense.

The singing fiddle strung with his hair – 'Mother, mother, you have murdered me!' – resonates with imagery from folk tales such as 'The Juniper Tree', from Ovid's tale of Procne and Philomela, and from the 'singing bone' song 'The Twa Sisters', which Molan remembers Carter singing. In this sinister song of sororicide, a musical instrument is made from a dead sister's body parts and strung with hair to sing out in grisly witness against the murderer: 'Woe to my sister, false Helen!' (Child 1882: 128). Carter weaves this powerful trope into the warp of 'The Erl-King' to summon up ancient collective memories of horror, entrapment and transgression.

Another folk song figure who creeps around Carter's stories is the devilishly vulpine Reynardine. Among the 'leaves of green', the mysterious Reynardine with his shining teeth lures a young girl after him over the mountain to his castle. 'Reynardine' was on Carter's 1964 journal list of folk songs and Molan remembers Bert Lloyd performing it (in conjunction with the folk tale 'Mr. Fox') at the Carters' folk club. He

> took the club by storm one night with his meandering tale of *Mr Fox*. In a masterstroke, he ran the blood-soaked finale into a short song, 'Reynardine'. Pure theatre.
>
> (2017: 21)

Lloyd questions whether 'Reynardine' is an 'ordinary man, or an outlaw maybe, or some supernatural lover?' (1956). He highlights the bestial undertones of his charactonym: 'A vulpine name for a crafty hero. [...] The dread uncertainty is whether he is man or animal. [...] Reynardine, the "little fox", [may] be a supernatural, lycanthropic lover' (1966). Lloyd instinctively recognizes the unease inspired by our uncertainty surrounding Reynardine's ontology; because we cannot be sure what Reynardine is, we are drawn after him like the girl, led over the mountain by our oscillating horror and attraction, our disgust and our fascination.

Debates rage about the true provenance of the 'Reynardine' folk song itself (Winick 2004: 286–308) but, whether authentic or fabricated, this vulpine antihero stalked into Carter's creative imagination. Carter's male lovers have a tendency to display unsettling, vaguely threatening, simultaneously seductive yet animalistic features. Honeybuzzard's 'inexpressible carnivorous mouth', with its 'tearing teeth, small, brilliantly white' ([1966a] 2014: 56), evokes Reynardine's shining teeth; Finn's 'wild beast's mouth', his grin 'like Pan in a wood' and his words of comfort to Melanie, '"It is only poor Finn, who will do you no harm"' ([1967b] 1992: 105), foreshadow the Erl-King's threat couched in a promise. The Erl-King's murine teeth form part of his repulsion, part of his charm; his den in the woods, full of incarcerated girl-birds, could be a fox's lair. Mary S. Pollock observes that in both form and content 'The Erl-King' displays metamorphic attributes, like the song:

> Everything in this story shifts its shape. The plants are transformed into food [...] But the plants and animals are also friends and companions, who flock around the Erlking of their own free will. [...] The larks and linnets are birds and girls. The Erlking's cottage is a vortex of tenderness, violence, and change.
>
> (2000: 49)

The Erl-King shares ambiguities of nature with Reynardine: 'The Erlking may be a sexual predator, he may be an innocent, or he may be an innocent predator; there is no way for the narrator to know, and the reader is no wiser' (2000: 51). He also shares ambiguities of form – like the authorial uncertainties surrounding 'Reynardine', in 'The Erl-King' tense and pronoun fluctuations unsettle us. We are both fascinated and repulsed, which is the nature of the greenwood.

Carter knew folk song's greenwood from singing these songs. She knew it as an ancient locus of 'grave, hideous and elemental beings' (Carter [1985a] 1996: 330), and in more motivic terms as a dangerous space on the perimeter of civilized society, culture and legislature, a place just out of the corner of one's eye, where transformations, corruptions, mutations and violations may be quietly ignored. It is a place for 'things that can live only on the margin of the mind' (Lewis [1964] 2012: 9), where the hegemonic rules of society, law, propriety, reality, even time are diluted because of their distance from 'the centre'. The greenwood exists at once outside civilization and yet is constructed by it, a sort of controlled liminal explosion where culture attempts to manage its own deviations and desires. Carter was well aware of its potency.

The greenwood, Carter knew, is always with us. In contemporary culture, the Allies' post-9/11 political practice of 'extraordinary rendition' (Cobain and Ball 2013), the reported rapes in New Orleans following Hurricane Katrina in 2005 (Burnett 2005) or the 'Jungle' refugee camp in Calais (Harker 2016) could all be seen as contemporary expressions of the greenwood. It shares some features of Giorgio Agamben's 'state of exception', an ambiguous governmental paradigm triggered in times of emergency which posits itself as a 'no-man's land between public law and political fact' (Agamben 2005: 1). Agamben uses the concentration camp to illustrate problematic juridical ambiguities surrounding necessity and sovereignty, as a place 'being-outside, and yet belonging' (2005: 35) like the greenwood. But Agamben's state of exception is 'provisional and exceptional' (even though its potentiality is 'always'), whereas the greenwood is permanent, and whereas the state of exception is bureaucratically secured within documentary discourses of domination – ledgers, registers, spreadsheets – the greenwood is illiterate; nothing is recorded except via protean oral narratives. The greenwood is para-linguistic, para-juridical and blind to class; anyone's daughter is in danger; it is a place of unprejudiced peril, where rapes and murders are routinely perpetrated, where unwanted babies are dumped and lovers slain, a Castle Silling against which society discreetly and conveniently blocks its ears and averts its gaze.

This is why Carter loved the greenwood locus so much, and why its activation in our collective memory – not just through folk song's rhythms and figures but through other aspects such as melody, lyric, voice and performance for which there is no space here – is so intrinsic to Carter's transcoding project. Here in the greenwood gravity is suspended; the moral compass spins. Fantasy as a genre has 'a subversive function in attempting to depict a reversal of the subject's cultural formation' (Jackson 1981: 177) – it has the power to estrange us from our own reality. In Japan, Carter felt like 'the mysterious other. I had become a kind of phoenix, a fabulous beast' (Carter [1974a: 35–6]); her cultural estrangement allowed for new perspectives and the song-inspired greenwood became just one of a number of fictive spaces where she found she could play. In the greenwood where she transports us, we all become phoenixes and we are all estranged and transformed, so that we might see what we could not see before, immersed in 'the centre'. That is precisely why she wants to take us there.

## Works cited

Agamben, G. (2005), *State of Exception*, trans. Kevin Attell, Chicago: University of Chicago Press.

Boyes, G. (1993), *The Imagined Village: Culture, Ideology and the English Folk Revival*, Manchester: Manchester University Press.

Burnett, J. (2005), 'More Stories Emerge of Rapes in Post-Katrina Chaos', *NPR*, 21 December. Available online: http://www.npr.org/templates/story/story.php?storyId=5063796 (accessed 16 June 2020).

Campbell, M. M. (2013), *Poetic Revolutionaries: Intertextuality and Subversion*, London: Rodopi.

Carter, A. (1961), Unpublished Journal, Angela Carter Papers, London: British Library, MS 88899/1/86.
Carter, A. (1962a), 'Rich life behind the cool mask', *Western Daily Press*, 19 March: 4.
Carter, A. (1962b), sleeve notes for Peggy Seeger, *Troubled Love*, [EP] Topic Records TOP72.
Carter, A. (1962c), sleeve notes for Peggy Seeger, *Early in the Spring*, [EP] Topic Records TOP73.
Carter, A. (1962–3), Unpublished Journal, Angela Carter Papers, London: British Library, MS 88899/1/88.
Carter, A. (1963–4), Unpublished Journal, Angela Carter Papers, London: British Library, MS 88899/1/89.
Carter, A. (1964), 'Now Is the Time for Singing', *Nonesuch*, 122 (Autumn): 11–15.
Carter, A. (1965a), 'Some Speculations on Possible Relationships between the Medieval Period and 20th Century Folk Song Poetry', BA diss., Bristol University, London: British Library, MS 88899/1/116.
Carter, A. (1965b), sleeve notes for Louis Killen, *Ballads and Broadsides*, [LP] Topic Records 12T126.
Carter, A. ([1966a] 2014), *Shadow Dance*, London: Virago.
Carter, A. (1966b), 'Letter to Father Brocard Sewell', Unpublished Letter, 11 January, Aylesford Mss., Lilly Library, Indiana University.
Carter, A. (1967a), 'Fred Jordan – singer', *New Society*, 23 February: 283.
Carter, A. ([1967b] 1992), *The Magic Toyshop*, London: Virago.
Carter, A. (1967c), 'The Flower of Sweet Strabane' and 'St Mary's/Church Street Medley', recorded live at the Cheltenham Folk Song Club, copyright Denis Olding, 15 January.
Carter, A. ([1968] 1995), *Several Perceptions*, London: Virago.
Carter, A. ([1974a] 1996), 'A Souvenir of Japan', repr. in *Burning Your Boats: Collected Stories*, 31–9, London: Vintage.
Carter, A. ([1974b] 1996), 'Penetrating to the Heart of the Forest', repr. in *Burning Your Boats: Collected Stories*, 67–78, London: Vintage.
Carter, A. ([1974c] 1996), 'Afterword to *Fireworks*', repr. in *Burning Your Boats: Collected Stories*, 549–50, London: Vintage.
Carter, A. ([1976] 2013) 'The Mother Lode', repr. in *Shaking a Leg: Collected Writings and Journalism*, 3–19, London: Vintage.
Carter, A. ([1979] 1996), 'The Erl-King', repr. in *Burning Your Boats: Collected Stories*, London: Vintage.
Carter, A. ([1983a] 2013) 'Alison's Giggle', repr. in *Shaking a Leg: Collected Journalism and Writings*, 662–76, London: Vintage.
Carter, A. ([1983b] 2013), 'Notes from the Front Line', repr. in *Shaking a Leg: Collected Journalism and Writings*, 45–53, London: Vintage.
Carter, A. (1984, 1992, n.d.), 'Angela Carter Papers: Miscellaneous Fairy Tale Material (1984, 1992, n.d.) Notes on Virago Fairy Tales Vol. 2', Unpublished Notes, London: British Library, MS 88899/1/82.

Carter, A. ([1985a] 1996), 'Overture and Incidental Music for *A Midsummer Night's Dream*', repr. in *Burning Your Boats: Collected Stories*, 326–38, London: Vintage.

Carter, A. (1990), 'Introduction', in A. Carter (ed), *The Virago Book of Fairy Tales*, ix–xxii, London: Virago.

Carter, A. ([1991] 1992), *Wise Children*, London: Vintage.

Carter, A. and P. Carter (n.d.), *Paul and Angela Carter's Folk Music Archive*, unpublished.

Child, F. J. (1882), *The English and Scottish Popular Ballads*, Vol. 1 Part 1, Boston: Houghton Mifflin.

Clapp, S. (1997), 'Introduction', in A. Carter, *The Curious Room: Plays, Film Scripts and an Opera*, vii–x, London: Vintage.

Cobain, I., and J. Ball (2013), 'New light shed on US government's extraordinary rendition programme', *Guardian*, 22 May. Available online: https://www.theguardian.com/world/2013/may/22/us-extraordinary-rendition-programme (accessed 16 June 2020).

Copper, B. and Copper, R. (1963), *Traditional Songs from Rottingdean* [LP] EFDSS LP1002.

Crofts, C. (2003), '*Anagrams of Desire*': *Angela Carter's Writing for Radio, Film and Television*, Manchester: Manchester University Press.

Frye, N. ([1957] 1973), *The Anatomy of Criticism: Four Essays*, Princeton, NJ: Princeton University Press.

Gordon, E. (2016), *The Invention of Angela Carter*, London: Chatto & Windus.

Harker, D. (1985), *Fakesong: The Manufacture of British 'Folksong' 1700 to the Present Day*, Milton Keynes: Open University Press.

Harker, J. (2016), 'Stop calling the Calais refugee camp the "Jungle"', *Guardian*, 7 March. Available online: http://www.theguardian.com/commentisfree/2016/mar/07/stop-calling-calais-refugee-camp-jungle-migrants-dehumanising-scare-stories (accessed 17 June 2020).

Jackson, R. (1981), *Fantasy: The Literature of Subversion*, London: Methuen.

Kerrigan, C. (1991), 'Introduction', in C. Kerrigan (ed), *An Anthology of Scottish Women Poets*, 1–11, Edinburgh: Edinburgh University Press.

Leech, G. (2008), 'Music in Metre: Sprung Rhyme in Victorian Poetry', in G. Leech, *Language in Literature: Style and Foregrounding*, 70–86, London: Pearson.

Lewis, C. S. ([1964] 2012), *The Discarded Image*, Cambridge: Cambridge University Press.

Lloyd, A. L. (1956), *The Foggy Dew and Other Traditional English Love Songs*, [LP] Tradition Records TLP 1016.

Lloyd, A. L. (1966), *First Person*, [LP] Topic Records 12T118.

Lloyd, A. L. and Ralph Vaughan Williams (1959), *The Penguin Book of English Folk Songs*, Harmondsworth: Penguin.

Molan, C. (2016), 'Authentic Magic: Angela, Folksong and Bristol', in M. Mulvey-Roberts and F. Robinson (eds), *Strange Worlds: The Vision of Angela Carter*, 29–32, Bristol: Sansom.

Molan, C. (2017), 'Angela Carter', *fROOTS*, 409 (July): 21.

Motherwell, W. (1827), *Minstrelsy Ancient and Modern*, Glasgow: John Wylie.
Paulusma, P. (2014a), Interview with Edward Horesh and Christopher Frayling, 8 March.
Paulusma, P. (2014b), Interview with Reg Hall, 5 December.
Pollock, M. S. (2000), 'Angela Carter's Animal Tales: Constructing the non-human', *Literature Interpretation Theory*, 11 (1): 35–57.
Reeves, J. (1960), *The Everlasting Circle*, London: Heinemann.
Rushdie, S. (1996), 'Introduction', in A. Carter, *Burning Your Boats: Collected Stories*, ix–xvi, London: Vintage.
Seeger, P. (1962a), *Troubled Love*, [EP] Topic Records TOP72.
Seeger, P. (1962b), *Early in the Spring*, [EP] Topic Records TOP73.
Sharp, C. (1907), *English Folk Song: Some Conclusions*, London: Novello.
Smith, P. (1970), 'Higher Germany', on Phoebe Smith, *Once I Had a True Love*, recorded by P. Carter and F. Purslow in 1969, [LP] Topic 12T193.
Stalker, A. (1961), 'Come in, take a chair, lean on it, and sing', *Croydon Advertiser*, 31 March: 4.
Stevenson, R. L. ([1885] 1905), 'On Some Technical Elements of Style in Literature', in *Essays in the Art of Writing*, 3–46, London: Chatto & Windus.
Theriot, L. (2001), 'Lady Isabel and the Elf-Knight', on *A Turning of Seasons* [LP], Raven Boy Music.
Tiainen, M. (2007), 'Corporeal Voices, Sexual Differentiations: New Materialist Perspectives on Music, Singing and Subjectivity', in S. Mieszkowski, J. Smith and M. De Valck (eds), *Sonic Interventions*, 147–68, New York: Rodopi.
Tolkien, J. R. R. ([1939] 2008) *On Fairy-Stories*, V. Flieger and D. A. Anderson (eds), London: HarperCollins.
Warner, M. (1992), 'Introduction', in A. Carter (ed), *The Second Virago Book of Fairy Tales*, ix–xvi, London: Virago.
Warner, M. (2012), 'Why Angela Carter's *The Bloody Chamber* Still Bites', *Scotsman*, 15 September.
Winick, S. (2004), 'A. L. Lloyd and Reynardine: Authenticity and Authorship in the Afterlife of a British Broadside Ballad', *Folklore*, 115 (3): 286–308.
Winter, T. and S. Keegan-Phipps (2013), *Performing Englishness: Identity and Politics in a Contemporary Folk Resurgence*, Manchester: Manchester University Press.
Žižek, S. (1998), 'Kant with Sade: The Ideal Couple', *Lacanian Ink*, 13. Available online: http://www.lacan.com/zizlacan4.htm (accessed 17 June 2020).

# 4

# From Griselda's patience to feminist grit: Angela Carter's 'The Patience of Grizelda' as a hidden intertext to 'The Bloody Chamber' and 'The Tiger's Bride'

Martine Hennard Dutheil de la Rochère

## The interplay of translation and rewriting in Angela Carter's fiction

As her lifelong interest in the fairy tale tradition testifies, Angela Carter was a born comparatist whose taste for languages and literatures materialized in her activity as a translator from French, which stimulated her extraordinary creativity, sparking ideas and inspiring new writing.[1] In her early twenties already, she used fireworks as a metaphor for artistic creation and sexual pleasure, capturing an essential aspect of her visual imagination, working method and aesthetics.

> Catherine wheels sunflowers – symbol of the female orgasm. Sexual imagery of fireworks, light the blue touch paper & retine.
> 
> I want to make images that are personal, sensuous, tender & funny; like the sculpture of Arp, for example, or the paintings of Chagall. I may not be very good yet, but am young & work very hard. Or fairly hard.
> 
> (MS 88899/1/89: 1963–4)

From her early translations/adaptations of medieval poetry (Carter 2015) to surrealist texts and criticism (Watz 2017), from fairy tales (Hennard Dutheil de la Rochère 2013, 2016) to Baudelaire (Hennard Dutheil de la Rochère 2019), Carter used translation as a source of images and ideas grounded in verbal wonder. In her journal of the Japan years, she defines *pyrotechnics* and muses on the Japanese word for fireworks, *hanabi*, before translating it into French and English, playing with its constitutive elements and associations and making it the emblem of her eponymous short story collection (Hennard Dutheil de la Rochère forthcoming). A few years later, her translations of Charles Perrault's *contes* paved the way for *The Bloody Chamber and Other Stories* (1979a), an innovative, baroque and sensuous collection of woman-centred 'stories about fairy stories', as she calls them in 'Notes from the Front Line' (Carter 1998b: 38), which not only marked a turning point in her career but were truly genre-bending. To quote Marina Warner (2014: 141), 'the fairy tale grew up in 1979' with the publication of this little book, whose deep and lasting impact is perceptible in literature but also visual art, film, music, opera, drama and puppet theatre today (see Get Angela Carter website).

Commissioned by Victor Gollancz, Carter's translation of *The Fairy Tales of Charles Perrault* (Perrault 1977) was published with illustrations by Martin Ware a couple of years before Carter's famous collection of fairy tale rewritings, and when studied together as a coherent, twofold project, these two books shed light on her working method. Through Perrault, Carter discovered the familiar stories of Sleeping Beauty, Cinderella and Bluebeard anew, and her translation strives to capture the specific nature and purpose of Perrault's tales away from Disneyfied clichés and received ideas about the genre.[2] Reading Perrault's *contes* in the original language and context as 'fables of the politics of experience' (1998a: 452) chimed in with Carter's '*committed materialism*' (1998a: 452). The translation thus prompted her to retell the stories for an older audience (Gordon 2016: 267–8), unpacking hidden aspects of the texts to explore 'the shifting structures of reality and sexuality' (1998a: 452), and freely experimenting with the language, imagery, plot, themes and message (or 'moral') of the tales from a feminist perspective alert to the complex interactions of cultural myths and ideology. Dismissing 'myth' in favour of 'folklore', she famously added:

> I believe that all myths are products of the human mind and reflect only aspects of material human practice. I'm in the demythologising business. I'm interested in myths – though I'm much more interested in folklore – just because they *are* extraordinary lies designed to make people unfree.
> (Carter 1998a: 38)

Besides being an act of individual re-creation, the practice of translation sensitizes the reader to the intricate fabric of literary texts where aspects of language, form and style all contribute to produce meaning. Furthermore, it draws attention to their dialogic and multilayered nature through allusions, irony, parody and intertextual echoes. As such, it brings an awareness of textual, paratextual and material aspects, anchoring texts in a broader milieu that they both reflect and comment on, all of which requires a close reading of the sources in context. Against widespread ideas about fairy tale types and stereotypes, Carter became alert to the changing significance of these stories, their editorial history and reception. A voracious reader who aspired to become a published translator, a self-styled bookish writer driven by intellectual curiosity as well as a university-trained teacher of literature, Carter was well aware of the need to consult reliable scholarly editions and critical studies. Her 'Select Bibliography' of *The Fairy Tales of Charles Perrault* lists Jacques Barchilon's reference edition of Perrault's prose tales published by the Pierpont Morgan Library in 1956, including a facsimile of the 1695 manuscript and a volume of critical commentary. The bibliography also mentions Barchilon's ground-breaking study *Le Conte merveilleux français de 1690 à 1760* (sic; the actual date is 1790) (Paris, 1975); Iona and Peter Opie's lavishly illustrated *The Classic Fairy Tales* (Oxford, 1974); and Andrew Lang's edition of *Perrault's Popular Tales* (Oxford, 1888), including the *contes en vers*. It is probable that Carter also consulted the Lamy edition of *Contes des fées* (1781), which includes 'Griselidis' along with an anonymous prose version of Perrault's 'Donkey-Skin', and the first volume of Charles-Joseph de Mayer's *Le Cabinet des fées* (1751).

Based on an in-depth knowledge of her source, a good command of French and a writer's literary sensibility, Carter's translation renders Perrault's *contes* in modern English in a fluid, lively and fresh manner that Barchilon himself praised for its 'accuracy and imagination' (2001: 26). The translator-writer-scholar could indeed appreciate their artfulness, mock-naive tone and style, subtle humour and irony, hidden political critique, literary echoes and even potential for feminist retellings, which already inflects her translation. As she explains in the article 'The Better to Eat You With' (1976), Carter's prime aim as a translator in *The Fairy Tales* is to convey the 'politics of experience' contained in Perrault's tales, and she pays homage more fully to the French academician as a gifted writer, father and educator, enlightened spirit and proto-folklorist in the eleven page foreword to *The Fairy Tales of Charles Perrault* (1977). As it turns out, her perception of the author and the nature of his texts is largely indebted to Andrew Lang's *Perrault's Popular Tales* (1888), where she also found the lesser-known verse tales.

Carter's rediscovery of the French fairy tale tradition as a crossover genre is perceptible not only in the interplay of translation and rewriting but also in her decision to translate Perrault's *contes en vers*, 'Peau d'Âne' and 'Les Souhaits ridicules', and even his earlier *nouvelle en vers* 'La Marquise de Salusses ou la Patience de Griselidis' (henceforth 'Griselidis'). Historically, the verse tales were published before the prose tales collected in the *Histoires ou Contes du temps passé* (1697) (*Histories or Tales of Past Times*, aka *Contes de ma mère l'Oye*) – neither of which were originally intended for children.[3] Carter nevertheless chose to include a prose translation of 'Donkey-Skin' and 'The Foolish Wishes' in *The Fairy Tales*. Her translation of 'Griselidis' as 'The Patience of Grizelda', a self-styled *nouvelle* that significantly departs from the genre and does not belong to the fairy tale canon (except from the point of view of editorial history), however, is not included in the published book.[4] Neither did Carter go on to retell the tale as such in *The Bloody Chamber*, unlike the more familiar stories of Bluebeard, Little Red Riding Hood, The Sleeping Beauty in the Wood and Puss in Boots. And yet, the story of Griselda – a staple feature of late medieval and Renaissance literature and religious exemplum extolling female submissiveness and absolute obedience to male authority – unsurprisingly caught her eye.

Significantly, Carter refers to Griselda in 'Alison's Giggle' (1983), an essay centred on the heroine of Chaucer's bawdy 'The Miller's Tale', whose laughter is associated with female sexual pleasure and playful transgression. Here Carter pits Alison's laughter against Griselda's tears in an argument that echoes her vindication of Juliette in *The Sadeian Woman: An Exercise in Cultural History* (1979b).[5] She observes that '"Patient Griselda" is the idealisation of one type of medieval wife as Alison is the crystallisation of a more down-to-earth variety' (Carter 1979b: 199). The stereotype, she argues, is even perpetuated in twentieth-century fiction by female writers, as in Doris Lessing's *The Golden Notebook* or Jean Rhys's fiction, where 'sexuality is no laughing matter and good women… gain treasure in heaven by letting men behave badly to them' (201). In this sense, they are no more than 'recycled Patient Griseldas' who, ironically, are 'now idealised by women themselves, rather than by men' (201). Baffling as this may be, women's repression of sexuality may have to do with a fear of getting pregnant, which is alluded to in unofficial culture such as 'orally transmitted songs and stories' (204) that are therefore well worth studying in Carter's opinion.

## Lang's *Perrault's Popular Tales* and the *contes en vers*

Andrew Lang's edition of *Perrault's Popular Tales* (1888) is framed by a preface, an introduction presenting Perrault's life and work in context, a short essay on the origin of fairies and ogres in antiquity and a section devoted to individual tales and their variants. Lang explains in the preface that the book is intended 'as an introduction to the study of Popular Tales in general' (Perrault 1888: v), which would subsequently lead to the publication of the twelve volumes of the famous Rainbow Fairy Books series extending from 1899 to 1913, starting with *The Blue Fairy Book* (1889).

The scrupulous editor presents his textual sources and working method to restore the original prose and verse texts based on volumes held by the British Museum, along with André Lefèvre's annotated edition of the *Contes de Perrault* and Charles Deulin's *Contes de Ma Mère l'Oye avant Charles Perrault*. As a folklorist interested in traditional stories and children's lore, Lang pays limited attention to Perrault's verse tales, which is probably why they are reproduced *after* the prose tales (though complete with Perrault's dedicatory preface and *envoi*), in conformity with his project of editing Perrault's popular tales, in the double sense of allegedly stemming from the people and well known to his readers.

The introduction begins with a lively biographical portrait of Charles Perrault based on his memoirs, which Carter manifestly draws upon in her own foreword to *The Fairy Tales*.[6] Lang presents the French academician somewhat anachronistically as a romantic rebel, self-taught 'truant from school', 'man of letters by inclination' and folklorist *avant la lettre* (Perrault 1888: vii). This portrait, peppered with humorous anecdotes, ends with the assertion that Perrault's fame resulted from his 'publishing versions of old traditional Fairy Tales'. Warming to his subject, Lang concludes that:

> Charles Perrault was a good man, a good father, a good Christian and a good fellow. He was astonishingly clever and versatile in little things, honest, courteous, and witty, and an undaunted amateur. The little thing in which he excelled most was telling fairy tales. Every generation listens in its turn to this old family friend of all the world.
>
> (xvi)

The next section, entitled 'Perrault's Popular Tales', is devoted to the history of the tales following the chronological order of their publication, and so starting with the earlier verse tales. Lang situates Perrault's endeavour within the broader context of the fashion for fairy tales in French courtly circles, and rightly insists on the 'spirit of sham simplicity' (xviii) in which the tales were written. He mentions the circumstances of the publication of 'Griselidis' during the Battle of the Books, adding that: 'Griselidis is not precisely a popular tale, as Perrault openly borrowed his matter from Boccaccio, and his manner (as far as in him lay) from La Fontaine' (xx). He then compares Perrault's and Giovanni Boccaccio's versions, underlining how Perrault 'greatly softened the brutality of the narrative' and praising his proto-romantic description of the woods: 'there is a certain simple poetry and sentiment of Nature, in Griselidis' (xx). He also notes that Perrault 'added an amusing little essay on the vanity of Criticism' where he claims to have found Boccaccio's story in its blue paper cover in a Troyes bookshop, and so 'in the popular form of the chap-books called La Bibliothèque Bleue' (xxi). This detail testifies to the circulation of literary texts in cheap print format and hence to the close intermeshing of elite and popular culture, although Lang uses it to support the idea that Perrault drew on popular sources. He points out that the verse tales reignited the famous quarrel with Boileau about 'Peau d'Âne' (xxii), with Perrault being likened to the donkey of the tale by his opponent. If Perrault had authored only the verse tales, Lang surmises, 'it is probable that he would now be known chiefly as an imitator of La Fontaine' (xxiv). His abundant notes presenting the stories along with 'analogous *contes*... found among most peoples, ancient and modern' (cxi) certainly contributed to Angela Carter's perception of the genre, and provided her with a wealth of material for her own rewritings in *The Bloody Chamber*.

## Carter's *The Fairy Tales of Charles Perrault* and 'Donkey-Skin' as a pivotal tale

Clearly indebted to Lang, Angela Carter's foreword to *The Fairy Tales* (1977) introduces Charles Perrault's stories as 'Mother Goose Tales' (9), followed by a biographical sketch of the French author that includes the famous anecdotes of Perrault quitting school after an argument with his philosophy teacher, his many talents and interest in children's education and the aesthetic debates and controversies in which his *contes* played a part, together with information about their circulation, reception and anthologization in *Le Cabinet des fées*. Carter also comments on Perrault's narrative style to underline that his misleadingly simple tales, in fact, reflect 'a great deal of literary art... that conceals art' (15) and 'consummate craftsmanship' (19), contrasts Madame d'Aulnoy, Straparola and Grimm and presents her own project of (re)translating ten tales as 'little parables of experience from which children can learn' (17). In other words, she explicitly follows in the footsteps of Perrault's modern, secular and down-to-earth world view consistent with early Enlightenment values: 'From the work of this humane, tolerant and kind-hearted Frenchman' (19), 'children can learn enlightened self-interest from Puss; resourcefulness and courage from Hop o' my Thumb; the advantages of patronage from Cinderella; the benefits of long engagements from the Sleeping Beauty; the dangers of heedlessness from Red

Riding Hood; and gain much pleasure, besides' (19). Carter therefore seeks to emulate Perrault's project by freshening up the stories for today's children, including 'prose translations of the two tales in verse, "The Foolish Wishes" and "Donkey-Skin"' (19).

Carter describes 'The Marquise de Salusses, or the Patience of Griselda' (11) as an early attempt at writing verse tales based on Boccaccio's literary version, and gives her reasons for dismissing it as follows: 'The style is that of La Fontaine and the subject matter the abuse of his wife by a psychopathic aristocrat' (11), and she adds parenthetically: '(I have not included a translation of it here because it is neither a popular tale nor a folk tale, clearly bearing the marks of its derivation, virtually a versified translation of Boccaccio)' (11–12). Besides the fact that Perrault's self-styled *nouvelle* is of literary origin, she must have deemed it unsuitable as a children's story, as Griselda is a poor shepherdess married to a tyrannical prince who tests her obedience, forbearance and fidelity through increasingly cruel trials. The tale ends with a contrived happy ending and praise of wifely patience.

Perrault's framing of the tale reproduced in Lang's edition, however, tells a somewhat different story: the dedication to an aristocratic lady wittily twists the moral in the *galant* spirit by contrasting the barbaric past incarnated by the cruel Marquis de Salusses with contemporary courtly culture, where women are said to lead their husbands by the nose. Moreover, the tale is followed by an amusing piece questioning its literary merits and proposing various improvements in the *envoi*, a letter addressed to *Monsieur\*\**, which further contributes to distancing the reader from the allegedly pious message. Even though Carter does not allude to the frame, she seems to follow the advice of the critical reader in her translation when she trims the text of all superfluous stylistic ornaments, cuts the lengthy descriptions and ironic asides. No wonder that the religious exemplum subtly mocked by Perrault irked the feminist translator, who went on to respond to it in her own rewritings, especially in 'The Bloody Chamber', where the bride takes revenge on her powerful, cruel and manipulative husband on the model of the Bluebeard tale.

Carter points out that Perrault's ironic and sophisticated *contes en vers* contrast markedly with 'the simplicity of form and the narrative directness' of the prose tales, and she translates them accordingly. Perrault's 'Peau d'Âne' is rendered into prose as 'Donkey-Skin', drastically shortened, simplified (syntax, lexis, narrative point of view), streamlined (characters, plot) and even bowdlerized for young readers. The highly rhetorical style and pointed social critique are altogether eliminated in conformity with modern-day expectations about the genre.

The main changes introduced in 'Donkey-Skin' include a complete reworking of the beginning of the tale in keeping with fairy tale conventions, a removal of the poetic persona's sarcastic side comments on the tyrannical, twisted and perverse king, hypocritical courtiers and corrupt representatives of the Church ready to legitimize the king's incestuous union on the basis of pseudo-doctrinal evidence. It is interesting to note that Carter mentions the Lilac Fairy among Perrault's worldly fairy godmothers, which signals that she was also familiar with the softened anonymous prose version of the tale anthologized in *Le Cabinet des fées*.

After Lang, who compares the magical helpers of Cinderella and Donkey-Skin in his introduction to *Perrault's Popular Tales*, Carter links the two tales in her working notes ('Cinderella is a folkloristic cousin of Donkey-Skin', MS 88899/1/82), and this colours her translation choices.[7] More importantly, she retains Perrault's mock-naive moral but updates it for a modern audience:

> Le Conte de Peau d'Âne est difficile à croire,/Mais tant que dans le Monde on aura des Enfants,/Des Mères et des Mères-grands,/On en gardera la mémoire.
>
> (Perrault [ed. Lang] 1888: 115)

> The story of Donkey-Skin is not something you might read every day in the morning papers. But as long as there are children, mothers, grandmothers and Mother Goose, it will always seem new.
>
> (Perrault [trans. Carter] 1977: 157)

Perrault's moral draws attention to the popular origin and transmission of the story of Donkey-Skin in oral female culture, as well as its ambiguous status (fiction or fact?). The story of Donkey-Skin is hard to believe because it is either too fanciful or too shocking, and Carter unsurprisingly chooses to stress its truth-value: even though incest is taboo and seldom talked about openly in the daily papers, an alternative, unofficial tradition of stories passed on by older women to the younger generations keeps alive unpalatable stories of the real-enough threat of sexual abuse at home and, with a little luck and some help (this being a fairy tale), of narrow escape.[8]

Carter's decision to end *The Fairy Tales* with 'Donkey-Skin' pays tribute to the mythical figure of Mother Goose, which symbolizes an anonymous female story-telling tradition that the feminist author, after Perrault, sought to perpetuate and revisit in her own collection of 'New Mother Goose tales' (MS 88899/1/34). Ending with a story about incest also broaches the theme of deviant sexuality that Carter would centrally address in *The Bloody Chamber* and beyond.[9]

*The Bloody Chamber* thus pursues a dialogue with Perrault initiated in *The Fairy Tales*, Carter using what she had found in the French texts as well as in

Lang's critical edition, but inevitably had to leave out in her translation for children: subtle allusions to the writer's own time and milieu; sexual subtext and social critique; adult humour and pointed irony; dense intertextuality; complex treatment of beastliness versus humanity; as well as a self-conscious play with kindred genres and conventions (including the fable and the more realistic *nouvelle*/short story). Though moral tales were not in fashion in the late 1970s, as Carter notes at the beginning of 'The Better to Eat You With' (1976), she rehabilitated Perrault's tales as stories to think with, work through and act upon because they convey important lessons and useful practical advice to ward off dangers both inside and outside the home. It is to be noted that the themes of domestic violence, sexual abuse and incest appear not only in *The Bloody Chamber* but also in unpublished short stories collected in the same file as her translation of 'Griselidis' (which the librarian probably mistook for an original story); namely, 'The Events of a Night' (on incest among siblings), and 'Misery City' about an abusive husband and his long-suffering wife and daughter, whose topical moral is that the religious and sociocultural tabooing of sexuality serves as a cover for female abuse: 'Sex was a sin and you didn't talk about it. Instead, you got raped' (MS 88899/1/43).

## Carter's unpublished translation of 'Griselidis' in context

Probably around the time of her Perrault translations, although included in the file of unpublished (and undated) short stories in the Angela Carter Papers (MS 88899/1/43), Carter drafted an English version of 'Griselidis'. This unpublished translation is in line with the simplifying and modernizing strategies adopted in *The Fairy Tales*, especially in 'Donkey-Skin'. The story is pared down to its core elements in order to highlight the dismal fate of women under patriarchy, as if to expose the cultural myth behind Perrault's literary treatment: Carter shows how a feudal system sustained by religious dogma and a misogynistic culture breeds oppression and misery in women, who go so far as to endorse their inhuman treatment and that of their daughter in the name of wifely submission, piety and virtue. In this respect, the story provides ample material for a creative and critical response from a feminist standpoint.

Carter opts for a short title, 'The Patience of Grizelda', which anglicizes the name of the heroine in keeping with the reception of the tale in literature and opera, and stresses her outstanding 'patience' in the double sense of suffering and bearing pain or hardship without complaint. Unsurprisingly, the tale lends itself to contradictory interpretations and uses, although its ubiquity in the medieval and early modern period as a 'choice piece' is telling: the story of Griselda was long used to educate women into submission in keeping with religious doctrine, teaching them to be virtuous and obey their husband and master. With the gradual secularization of European culture, however, it also served to counter negative stereotypes of woman's sinful nature and rebelliousness against masculine authority, with patristic misogynistic discourse being subjected to increasingly openly ironic treatment. In this respect, Perrault's reframing of the tale and deliberate departures from Boccaccio's and especially Petrarch's Latinate versions are telling.

In Boccaccio's version of the story written around 1350 (*Decameron*, day X, novella 10) Griselda marries the Marquis of Saluzzo, who tests her by pretending that their two children must be killed (he secretly sends them to Bologna instead). A few years later he declares that he wants to remarry, and so repudiates his wife. As a last humiliation he asks her to get his young bride ready for the wedding, who turns out to be their own daughter: he finally admits that all this was to test the patience of his wife. Throughout the years, Griselda submits to the cruel humiliations devised for her by her tyrannical husband without complaining or rebelling until she is ultimately restored to her role as wife and mother. The story of Griselda was well known throughout Europe, especially in Petrarch's *Historia Griseldis* (1375), which was even more widespread than Boccaccio's version and probably known to Perrault (Bottigheimer 2008). It is also found in Chaucer's 'The Clerk's Tale' in *The Canterbury Tales* (1387–1400) as a kind of anti-Wife of Bath figure.

Charles Perrault's 'La Marquise de Salusses ou La Patience de Griselidis' (1691) was penned as part of the aesthetic debates during Louis XIV's reign and its significance must be understood in context. Perrault's 'Griselidis' exemplifies female virtue and endurance *against* stereotypes of feminine fickleness, immodesty and unfaithfulness targeted in Nicolas Boileau's 'Satire X' (1692/1694) mocking women's alleged vices. Originally presented to the Académie française as a rhetorical exercise in 1691, Perrault's *nouvelle en vers* was subsequently printed along with other verse tales in *Griselidis, Nouvelle, avec le conte de Peau d'Âne et celui des Souhaits ridicules* in 1694. Perrault's take on the familiar story unsurprisingly reignited the famous 'Quarrel Between the Ancients and the Moderns', which had started in 1687, as Lang had noted, when Perrault's praise for the Moderns in *Le Siècle de Louis le Grand* provoked the fury of Boileau, who championed the Ancients, along with the 'Quarrel About

Women' raging in Europe on women's role and place in society. Promoting modern French literature during the reign of Louis XIV, Perrault sided with female authors of literary *contes de fées*, and his pointed response to Boileau in *L'Apologie des femmes* (1694) is self-consciously echoed in 'Griselidis' as a vindication of women, even though the verse tale remains wittily ambiguous and double-edged in the *galant* style, as it makes gentle fun of Parisian women ruling over their husbands in humorous (*enjoué*, i.e. tongue-in-cheek and burlesque) fashion. The verse form mixes the classic alexandrine metre with shorter lines and an irregular rhyme scheme. A self-conscious imitation of La Fontaine's verse, 'Griselidis' is therefore part of a complex, ironic and polemical dialogue that Perrault engages with his contemporaries. Despite his allegiance to the Classics, La Fontaine had indeed expressed his delight in hearing old stories such as 'Peau d'Âne' in *Le Pouvoir des Fables*: Perrault took him at his word, as it were, by writing his own version of the familiar story and asserting the superiority of the 'modern' tales against the 'old' fables of the Ancients.[10] As Christine A. Jones convincingly argues, Perrault's 'Griselidis' was designed to 'celebrate the French language and the ways it could change writing and ideas themselves' (2016: 52), as a companion piece to *L'Apologie des femmes* and illustration of the superiority of a modern aesthetics and ethics. Indeed, the prince's morbid obsession with female virtue and self-sacrificial types like Lucretia (his model mythical woman), which he invokes to justify his infliction of psychological and emotional suffering on Griselda, eventually gives way to a very different vision of marriage in the subplot introduced by Perrault:

> The daughter has been read as a pawn in the relationship between husband and wife: her removal from the home the ultimate atrocity to commit against a mother, and her return the sign of the prince's conversion. But there is more to her than that. Offstage, she has grown into a woman capable of falling in love of her own accord with a man who loves her and choosing him as her husband; this is a model of behavior completely unlike that of the mother figure.
> 
> (Jones 2016: 58)

The presence of the girl forced to accept an arranged marriage with a man she does not love (her own father!) even provokes the ever-patient Griselda to make a plea on her behalf, and her daughter is made to embody modernity against a brutal, archaic, barbaric past: 'In that sense, the future plot of the daughter's happy marriage is crucial to the story's success, as Perrault tells it' (Jones 2016: 59). As Jones aptly sums it up:

> The daughter's right to leave the old master/servant world behind occasions a rebirth of the genre in the form of a new plotline for balanced gender relations.
>   In the intense wish Griselidis expresses to love and protect her daughter and in the ability of the daughter to choose, Perrault's verse tale models, for the next generation, a forward-thinking approach to marriage that breaks with a patriarchal vision of women as objects of exchange or prizes for hunting men. Marrying for love is the lifeline Perrault gives the daughter of 'Patient Griselda,' one not afforded her in Boccaccio's tale, which is focused wholly on a married woman and her punishing fate.
>
> (62)

In that sense, Perrault's translation-adaptation of Boccaccio's Italian tale (and, more obliquely, his response to Petrarch's Latinate version) in order to tell a *different* story anticipates Carter's own method of translating and rewriting in counterpoint.

## From Perrault's *nouvelle en vers* to Carter's *conte en prose*: Comparative analysis

'Griselidis' is not only an occasion for Perrault to position himself within contemporary literary debates but also for *ad personam* piques and subtle social critique: the old topos of the patient wife serves as a pretext to insert comic vignettes satirizing a vain orator, scheming courtiers and hypocritical female bigots hoping to catch the prince's attention. It also serves to uphold the long-suffering wife of a despotic husband whose virtue will shine and be recognized ultimately. Through Griselidis as emblematic of modern poetics in the famous quarrel, Perrault praises rural simplicity, virtue, modesty, patience and even breastfeeding as embodying native culture against the feudal tyranny of noble lineage (the Classics?). Interestingly, 'Griselidis' also contains some themes, scenes and motifs that are found again in Perrault's prose tales, such as the chance encounter and romance of a kind and beautiful peasant girl with a young prince in 'The Fairies', the threat of father–daughter incest in 'Donkey-Skin', the comedy of the ladies' dressing up to attract the prince's attention and his choice of a low-class bride in 'Cinderella' as well as domestic violence in 'Bluebeard'.

  In her translation of Perrault's tale that embodies her own reading of the story from a contemporary, woman-centred, vantage point, Carter retains the specific setting in northern Italy, but greatly simplifies the text as follows: 'In a country at the foot of the mountains, at the mouth of the River Po, once lived a young prince.' Similarly, she summarizes the detailed portrait of the Marquis de Salusses, celebrating his physical qualities and moral virtues as a ruler in an ornate, periphrastic and elevated diction. Perrault's flattering portrait draws on the official imagery of Louis XIV, but his dark moods target Boileau's bile and misogyny, in marked contrast with the sensuous king, who was married twice and had countless mistresses. Carter sums up Perrault's twenty lines of verse in one single sentence and only selects the qualities of the prince that are consistent with the story ('a young prince who was handsome, strong, clever, a fine soldier and a wise governor'), omitting the reference to his tender and generous heart. She also marks a clear break in her text to heighten the contrast between his qualities as a statesman and his misogyny: 'But he had one flaw – he was a sombre & gloomy man who hated women.' Introduced by a strong conjunction, the sentence focuses on the darker side of the young man, and the long dash further underlines his hatred of women. While the lengthy and more allusive French text hints at the negative influence of the courtly milieu and cultural context as aggravating factors in the prince's temperament, Carter pits the prince's qualities against his 'fear of women' in light of Freudian theory.[11] Carter also drops the enumeration of alleged female vices, the influence of the climate on the prince's character and the allusions to antiquity that are so many jibes at Boileau. She cuts the passage where Perrault mocks the conceited orator who recycles hackneyed clichés and stilted rhetoric to flatter the prince into producing an heir, as well as the prince's response justifying his decision by invoking female duplicity and listing various female types such as the sour and bad-tempered bigot, the coquettish and vain blabbermouth, the art-loving, arrogant, pedantic and opinionated *précieuse*, the obsessive player who loses a fortune and even her clothes, and finally the domineering types. The prince declares that he will only marry a young and beautiful woman: 'Sans orgueil et sans vanité,/D'une obéissance achevée,/D'une patience éprouvée,/Et qui n'ait point de volonté' (Perrault 1980: 62). Unsurprisingly, Carter gets rid of this discourse in praise of submissive, passive and selfless women with no will of their own in her translation, before arguing that Griselda-like behaviour only fuels cruelty and sadism in *The Bloody Chamber*.

Of the lengthy hunting scene that follows, she retains the 'wild beasts'' 'trembl[ing]' in fear of the hunter and his pack of hounds, and the prince losing his way in the forest. While the prince's love of hunting and putting animals to death foreshadows his cruelty towards his wife, it also echoes Carter's 'The Tiger's Bride', which explicitly draws a parallel between the condition of animals and of women that are used, exploited and traded like 'beasts in bondage' (Carter 1979a: 62):

> I was a young girl, a virgin, and therefore men denied me rationality just as they denied it to all those who were not exactly like themselves, in all their unreason.... since all the best religions in the world state categorically that not beasts nor women were equipped with the flimsy, insubstantial things when the good Lord opened the gates of Eden.
>
> (63)[12]

Generally, Carter shifts the narrative focus from the prince to Griselda, and she trims the tale of its ornaments and literary flourishes to avoid a jarring discrepancy between the obfuscating rhetoric of love (the girl's beauty taming the wild beasts, the hunter wounded by the arrow of love etc.) and *locus amoenus* of the beautiful shepherdess surprised by a handsome hunter, on the one hand, and the prince's subsequent cruel behaviour, on the other: matching words and action, style and subject matter, Carter sticks to the bare facts. She refrains from describing the young woman's beauty and modesty in the *galant* style, and conveys her reaction to being watched unawares in very simple terms: 'she blushed & he saw how innocent, how sweet, how simple she was'. The erotic topos, however, raises the issue of voyeurism that will be explored more fully in 'The Bloody Chamber'. The girl addresses the prince directly and the long journey through a dangerous landscape of rocks and rivers back to the prince's castle (which evokes Perrault's 'La Belle au bois dormant', down to the detail of the towers visible above the woods) is shortened. Once again, Carter cuts to the chase, and removes all digressions from the plot, including the prince's speech and the comic asides and repetitions (the vain orator again), except for the amusing and topical vignette about women who pretend to be pious and chaste and dress modestly to seduce him (since he is obsessed with female purity and virtue), though Carter tones down the sarcastic tone somewhat:

> Le plaisir fut de voir le travail inutile
> Des Belles de toute la Ville
> Pour s'attirer et mériter le choix
> Du Prince leur Seigneur qu'un air chaste et modeste
> Charmait uniquement et plus que tout le reste,
> Ainsi qu'il l'avait dit cent fois.
> D'habit et de maintien toutes elles changèrent,
> D'un ton dévot elles toussèrent,
> Elles radoucirent leurs voix,

> De demi-pied les coiffures baissèrent,
> La gorge se couvrit, les manches s'allongèrent,
> À peine on leur voyait le petit bout des doigts.
>
> (Perrault 1980: 68)

> All the ladies of the court went to great pains to please the prince when they heard of his marriage plans, just in case she might be the lucky one; they knew he liked modest and submissive women & all talked in very low voices, even coughed as though they were in church. They stopped piling their hair high on their heads; they buttoned their necks up to their chin & wore dresses with long, concealing sleeves.
>
> (MS 88899/1/43)

Further on, the young shepherdess addresses the prince in a familiar tone and modern diction that reflects her simple nature and spontaneity: 'Oh, my lord, you're joking!' When the prince proposes to her, he makes her promise that she will obey him in all things, which she agrees to on the grounds that a woman has to obey her husband in keeping with customary law and religious teachings enshrined in marriage vows:

> Mais afin qu'entre nous une solide paix
> Éternellement se maintienne,
> Il faudrait me jurer que vous n'aurez jamais
> D'autre volonté que la mienne.
> Je le jure, dit-elle, et je vous le promets;
> Si j'avais épousé le moindre du Village,
> J'obéirais, son joug me serait doux;
> Hélas! combien donc davantage,
> Si je viens à trouver en vous
> Et mon Seigneur et mon Époux
>
> (Perrault 1980: 71)

> But before we marry, I must ask you to promise me that you will obey me in everything once we are man & wife. 'Oh, yes,' she said. 'If I were to marry the poorest man in the village, I know it would be my duty to obey him; but I would much rather obey a prince.'
>
> (MS 88899/1/43)

This promise, which is punctuated by the word 'alas' in French (from the Latin word for weary and unfortunate), suggests that Griselidis somehow anticipates her miserable fate, even though she cannot refuse the prince's marriage proposal. Her English counterpart, however, seems to be flattered to marry a prince and accepts without a second thought (not unlike the heroine of 'The Bloody Chamber').

The wedding ceremony is described at length, based on Louis XIV's own lavish ceremony and festivities that Perrault had celebrated in an earlier poem, down to the realistic detail of the horses being frightened by the cheering crowds. A year later, Griselda gives birth to a girl, to the disappointment of her husband, according to Carter, who accounts for his behaviour in psychological terms – unlike Perrault, who insists on the king's subjects or ministers expecting a male heir for political reasons. When the prince is no longer infatuated with his bride and when his dark moods return, he starts persecuting the young woman, a word used by Carter instead of the more euphemistic phrasing in the French text. The lengthy description of the prince's increasingly cruel behaviour towards his wife and daughter stems from his misogyny disguised as a test of her virtue: the translation unpacks the metaphor of 'obscurci ses sens et corrompu son cœur' (Perrault 1980: 74) in 'It was as though a dark cloud descended on him, & he could no longer see clearly or think rationally or love trustfully' (MS 88899/1/43), and conveys 'il aime à la troubler' (74) (whose sexual undertones Carter unpacks in her rewriting) more explicitly and forcefully as 'I must persecute her' (MS 88899/1/43). The prince locks her up, and the bride interprets his jealous and tyrannical behaviour as a test of virtue (in Perrault), and as a token of tough love in Carter's translation (like the foolish bride in 'The Bloody Chamber'):

> Pour m'éprouver mon Époux me tourmente,
> Dit-elle, et je vois bien qu'il ne me fait souffrir
> Qu'afin de réveiller ma vertu languissante,
> Qu'un doux et long repos pourrait faire périr
>
> (Perrault 1980: 75)

> I am like his beloved child, whom he wishes to punish, & I shall love his harsh treatment – I shall be happy to suffer at the hands of his goodness.
> (MS 88899/1/43)

But Griselda's patience only makes him more furious and whets his appetite for cruelty. When he takes away her baby, he assumes that she is going to rebel, in the belief that a true mother would fight for her cub 'like a tigress' ('Comme on craint de revoir une fière Tigresse/A qui son faon vient d'être ôté',

Perrault 1980: 78). And yet, the wife does not react and they go on to live happily for some years. But the dark moods return and the prince devises yet another trial by repudiating his wife on the grounds that he needs an heir and wants to remarry. She meekly submits, leaves the castle and returns to live in poverty with her father. The prince orders her back to prepare the young bride for the wedding as a final humiliation. After a recognition scene and some tears, Griselda is finally restored to her role as wife and mother. The story ends with the wedding of the daughter and the young nobleman who loved her, a romantic subplot added by Perrault to distract from the main dire plot, but also to make a point about love marriages being happier than arranged ones. This double plot foreshadows the Bluebeard tale, which condemns forced unions and cruel husbands even more openly, and concludes happily with the bride marrying a man after her heart. 'Griselidis', for its part, ends on *people* praising her wifely patience as a saintly exemplum to be emulated, as distinct from the *poetic persona* who underlines their complacency for their capricious prince:

> Où sur Griselidis se tournent tous les yeux,
> Où sa patience éprouvée
> Jusque au Ciel est élevée
> Par mille éloges glorieux
> Des Peuples réjouis la complaisance est telle
> Pour leur Prince capricieux,
> Qu'ils vont jusqu'à louer son épreuve cruelle,
> À qui d'une vertu si belle,
> Si séante au beau sexe, et si rare en tous lieux,
> On doit un si parfait modèle
>
> (Perrault 1980: 89)

Carter translates the lines in a matter-of-fact, straightforward fashion:

> And even the prince's cruelties were forgiven, because they had given Grizelda the opportunity to be so very, very patient and understanding, and become a model wife for all women, everywhere, to copy.
>
> (MS 88899/1/43)

Perrault's ironic undertones therefore pave the way for Carter's subsequent reflections on female submission and virtue leading to ever more bitter persecution (as theorized by Sade), and it is no wonder that the feminist author felt the need to respond to it and radically critique the religiously sanctioned praise of wifely 'patience' and martyrdom in 'The Bloody Chamber'.

## 'Griselidis' as a hidden intertext to 'The Bloody Chamber'

It is tempting to see in the moody prince's persecution of his young wife a blueprint for Carter's perverse Marquis in 'The Bloody Chamber'. 'Griselidis' may therefore be a hidden intertext to her retelling of the Bluebeard story that pits religious myth against the fairy tale tradition to explore sadomasochism and the danger of internalizing patriarchal dictates exalting self-sacrifice and martyrdom.

It is a critical commonplace that 'The Bloody Chamber' revisits Perrault's 'La Barbe bleue', as well as related folktales, and that it echoes Carter's reflections in *The Sadeian Woman*. Carter's Marquis dominates and manipulates his young and pliant wife (who married for money, status and prestige), and trains her to do his bidding to the point that she consents to her submission, oppression and punishment. The relationship between the bride and her husband is marked by significant differences in social class, age and experience, and his symbolic authority is also grounded in cultural myths subordinating women that the bride has integrated until she remembers the old fairy tale where the monstrous husband is gotten rid of at the end, unlike the religious exemplum that rewards female patience as supreme virtue.

As in 'Griselidis', the cruel husband is a Marquis, and the story is set in France (Brittany), which echoes Bluebeard-like stories and legends, but can also be read as homage to Perrault's *nouvelle* (as Perrault himself points out, the difference between the *conte* and the *nouvelle* lies in the latter's verisimilitude). *The Bloody Chamber* raises the issue of voyeurism, in response to the prince stumbling across the shepherdess unobserved in 'Griselidis', and it elaborates on the Marquis treating his wife like a child (even suggesting incest in remarrying). Not only does Carter's Marquis eroticize his bride's innocence and ignorance but this enables him to condition her to do his bidding and participate in the sadomasochistic scenario he has prepared for her. His perverse inflicting of pain in the name of 'love' is present in both stories, though Carter's surviving bride reflects on the perverse psychological mechanism that makes the victim willingly submit to a sexual predator: 'My dear one, my little love, my child, did it hurt her? He's so sorry for it, such impetuousness, he could not help himself; you see, he loves her so… I clung to him as though only the one who had inflicted the pain could comfort me for suffering it' (Carter 1979a: 18). The bride entirely depends on her husband financially, psychologically and emotionally, besides being trapped in a castle, where she is conditioned to endorse the role of a saintly martyr, as is clear from the Marquis gift of a painting of Saint Cecilia. Similarly,

Griselda's 'patience' is condoned by religious teachings and sermonizing. In the Bluebeard tale, however, the promise made by the wife to her evil husband is broken, unlike Griselda, who submits to his will until the bitter end, and the manipulation is revealed for what it is by Carter's bride: "'You disobeyed him,' he said. "That is sufficient reason for him to punish you,'" to which she replies: "'I only did what he knew I would'" (37).

Even the style of Perrault's highly literary *contes en vers* chimes with Carter's own unfashionably ornate style in *The Bloody Chamber*. The title story is told from the perspective of the surviving bride, like the heroine of 'The Tiger's Bride', a story which also borrows some elements from 'Griselidis', even though it is based on Beauty and the Beast tales, including Beaumont's version that Carter had also translated. While the classical fairy tale suggests that true love can turn a beast-like husband into a Prince Charming, 'Griselidis' is not so hopeful (or naive): the 'bestial madness' which characterizes the cruel Marquis de Salusses is not tamed by his patient wife, but keeps returning despite her obedience and submission to his will, and knows no bounds until the end the tale. Carter herself seems to have made the rapprochement between the two stories when she locates 'The Tiger's Bride' in the very region where Perrault (and Boccaccio before him) set his *nouvelle*. As she confirmed in an interview with Anna Katsavos, 'The Tiger's Bride' is set in northern Italy, where lives a 'grand seigneur' (Katsavos 1994: 52) who buys a bride from an irresponsible, gambling father, and lives in a ruined palazzo in the self-same Po valley, where the cruel story of Griselda is set.[13] Moreover, Carter uses as a starting point for her woman-focused rewriting the simile of the tigress becoming wild with fury when her cub is taken away from her in Perrault's text ('une fière Tigresse', Perrault 1980: 78), an image that she literalizes in 'The Tiger's Bride' as the young bride chooses to embrace the animal condition in recognition of her own beastly nature.

Charles Perrault's 'Griselidis' thus contains themes and motifs that are echoed in two of Carter's most famous fairy tale rewritings, one responding to the conditioning of women into submission, the other proposing a way out of patriarchal oppression. Using translation as a creative method, Carter pursued in *The Bloody Chamber* an exploration of the tale's complex literary and generic affiliations, and even potentialities for retelling and radical critique, as she unpacked their social, sexual and psychological implications from a feminist perspective alert to the impact of the Griselda myth which, filtered through the Bluebeard tale, served as the basis to tell a more empowering story, while providing a key image, 'personal, sensuous, tender' (if not 'funny', unless we think of Carter's heroine as a 'Donkey-Skin' gone wild) for 'The Tiger's Bride'.

Emulating Perrault's 'little parables of experience' as an early Enlightenment figure promoting 'sweet reason' (*Fairy Tales*, 17) against blind submission to religious doctrine and authority, Carter in turn exposed the lies that 'make people unfree' for her own times. Because she was familiar with several versions of the Griselda story, she knew that the 'same' tale can be retold for different purposes and audiences in ever-changing circumstances and contexts that renew its significance, 'moral' and implications. Having taken the trouble to translate Perrault's densely allusive and subtly ironic take on the tale based on Lang's scholarly edition, she could not ignore its textual complexity and paratextual frame, and so recognized the importance of treatment, form, language and tone manifesting new authorial intentions and unique creativity. Fashioning a complex, multi-layered reading experience for her older readers in the manner of Perrault, she challenged received ideas about the genre (including in feminist criticism), and sparked new (fire)works as she exploded cultural myths and critical commonplaces alike by making the fairy tale tradition anew.

## Acknowledgements

The Agreed Upon 621 Words from Angela Carter's Papers by Angela Carter (The British Library): Copyright © The Estate of Angela Carter. Quotations reproduced by permission of the Estate, c/o Rogers, Coleridge & White Ltd., 20 Powis Mews, London W11 1JN.

## Notes

1   For Pascal, as always – for his patience, support, love and humour. I extend my gratefulness to Jean-Paul Sermain and Sue Bottigheimer for offering perceptive comments on this chapter.
2   See Hennard Dutheil de la Rochère (2013: 175). The translation also highlights significant differences from Joseph Jacobs's *English Fairy Tales* (1895) and Jacob and Wilhelm Grimm's versions of the 'same' stories that Carter was familiar with from childhood. Carter took notes on the *Kinder- und Hausmärchen* in her journal for 1960 (MS 88899/1/100). Her extensive knowledge of the fairy tale would subsequently feed into her fiction, editorial work and academic teaching. *The Bloody Chamber* reflects Carter's familiarity with the international fairy tale tradition, which informed the classes she taught at Sheffield as a Fellow in Creative

Writing between 1976 and 1978. Her detailed notes provide ample evidence of her solid background as a folklorist and literary scholar as well as her interest in formalist and anthropological approaches to the genre.

3  See Bottigheimer (2008) and Leclerc (2020). Petrarch's free Latin translation turned Boccaccio's story of Griselda into an edifying tale in which the persecuted heroine was cast as an archetype of female virtue, obedience and submission to her husband, exalting her suffering in conformity with religious teachings and aspiration to a cult of martyrdom. Unsurprisingly, Petrarch's Christian allegory became the canonical version which almost altogether eclipsed Boccaccio's for centuries. The tale was widely circulating in Perrault's time, notably in chapbook versions in the *Bibliothèque Bleue*. See also the introduction in Jones (2016: 53–63). On the (*post hoc*) generic labelling, aesthetic implications and editorial history of Perrault's *contes en vers* vs. *contes en prose*, see Sermain (2017). See also Sermain's '*Griselidis* de Perrault: l'anti-Baudelaire' (2008: 209–16), which argues that as a defender of modern aesthetics and politics Perrault defends a historicizing mode of reading against the timeless authority of the Ancients. In this sense, *mutatis mutandis*, Carter shared Perrault's early Enlightenment rationalism, his questioning of the authorities of the past, his sense of the critical role of literature and, last but not least, his wry sense of humour.

4  Carter's translation of the story of Griselidis is grouped with unpublished short stories in the Angela Carter Papers (MS 88899/1/43). It is to be noted that the translation is titled 'The Patience of Grizelda', although Carter refers to her as Griselidis in the essay. Both spellings are kept in the present essay.

5  On Carter's Chaucerian intertexts, see Pireddu (1997).

6  See Hennard Dutheil de la Rochère (2013: 51, 78–80).

7  In the same file (MS 88899/1/82), Carter jots down the following notes on 'Donkey-Skin':

Donkey-Sking [*sic*] (Peau d'Ane).

There is a donkey whose dung is gold in a story in Basile's Pentamerone and in another of Basile's stories, not only does the dying queen extract the same vow from her husband as Donkey-Skin's father makes, but the heroine actually transforms herself into a bear to evade her father's incestuous advances.

Donkey-Skin has an English cousin, Catskin, whose story – 'Catskin, or the Wandering Gentlewoman,' exists in a couple of chapbook ballads. Catskin in her fur coat looks very much as though she, too, was originally transformed into a real cat; when a bad-tempered cook throws a basin of water over her, she 'shakes her ears' just as a cat would do. She, too, bathes in a pool before she puts on her magic dresses and a dip in water, or sometimes, in milk, is always necessary before a transformation from non-human back to human can take place. The Scots ballad hero, Tamlane, turns in succession into ice, into fire, into an adder, a doe, a swan and at last into a red-hot glaive [sword] before his true love, Burd Ellen, throws the glaive into a well and he becomes a mother-naked man again. So, at some primitive stage of the story, the beautiful princess may have actually become a donkey herself, in order to run away from home. Donkey-Skin's magic wardrobe is usually transported inside three nuts (for preference, a walnut, a hazelnut and an almond) in traditional versions of the story.

The story itself is distantly related to the sources of Shakespeare's 'King Lear', another king who asked his daughters to love him too much.

8   See Warner (1994).
9   Carter's interest in 'Gothic tales, cruel tales, tales of wonder, tales of terror', and her aim 'to extract the latent content from the traditional stories and to use it as the beginnings of new stories', is voiced in her often-quoted interview with John Haffenden (1985: 84).
10  All French quotations are from Collinet's critical edition (Perrault 1980), and their English translation from Carter's translation (Perrault 1977) unless specified otherwise. Lang's edition reproduces the old spelling, capitals and typography.
11  See Dimovitz (2016: 81–103).
12  See Hennard Dutheil de la Rochère (2013: 227–62).
13  In her interview with Katsavos (1994), Carter states that the tale is set in Mantua: '"The Tiger's Bride" landscape, admittedly, is touristic, but it's one of the palaces in Mantua that has the most wonderful jewels, and that city is set in the Po Valley, which is very flat and very far out'.

## Works cited

Barchilon, J. (2001), 'Remembering Angela Carter', in D. M. Roemer and C. Bacchilega (eds), *Angela Carter and the Fairy Tale*, 26–9, Detroit: Wayne State University Press.

Bottigheimer, R. (2008), 'Before *Contes du Temps Passé* (1697): Charles Perrault's "Grisélidis" (1691), "Souhaits Ridicules" (1693), and "Peau d'Asne" (1694)"', *The Romantic Review*, 99 (3–4): 175–89.

Carter, A. [created 1987–2002], Angela Carter Papers, British Library Manuscript Collections, GB 58 Add. MS 88899:

- Add. MS 88899/1: Notebook, 1963–4
- Add. MS 88899/1/34: 'The Bloody Chamber and Other Short Stories', pt. 2, 1975–7
- Add. MS 88899/1/43: Unpublished short stories, 1962–77
- Add. MS 88899/1/82: Miscellaneous fairy tale material, 1984, 1992 (including 'Roots of Narrative' notes for 'Class One')
- Add. MS 88899/1/100: Journal, 1960

Carter, A. (1979a), *The Bloody Chamber and Other Stories*, London: Victor Gollancz.

Carter, A. (1979b), *The Sadeian Woman: An Exercise in Cultural History*, London: Virago Press.

Carter, A. (1992), 'Alison's Giggle' (1983), in *Nothing Sacred: Selected Writings*, 189–204, London: Virago Press.

Carter, A. (1998a), 'The Better to Eat You With' (1976), in J. Uglow (ed), *Shaking a Leg: Collected Journalism and Writings*, 333–5, London: Vintage.

Carter, A. (1998b), 'Notes from the Front Line' (1983), in J. Uglow (ed), *Shaking a Leg: Collected Journalism and Writings*, 36–43, London: Vintage.

Carter, A. (2015), *Unicorn: The Poetry of Angela Carter*. With an essay by Rosemary Hill, London: Profile.

Dimovitz, S. A. (2016), *Angela Carter: Surrealist, Psychologist, Pornographer*, London: Routledge.

Gordon, E. (2016), *The Invention of Angela Carter: A Biography*, London: Chatto & Windus.

Get Angela Carter, http://getangelacarter.com, curated by C. Crofts and M. Mulvey-Roberts, supported by University of the West of England.

Haffenden, J. (1985), 'Angela Carter', in J. Haffenden (ed), *Novelists in Interview*, 76–96, New York: Methuen Press.

Hennard Dutheil de la Rochère, M. (2013), *Reading, Translating, Rewriting: Angela Carter's Translational Poetics*, Detroit: Wayne State University Press.

Hennard Dutheil de la Rochère, M. (2016), 'From the Bloody Chamber to the *cabinet de curiosités*: Angela Carter's Curious Alices through the Looking-Glass of Languages', *Marvels & Tales*, 30 (2): 284–308.

Hennard Dutheil de la Rochère, M. (2019), 'Angela Carter's *objets trouvés* in Translation: From Baudelaire to *Black Venus*', in M. Mulvey-Roberts (ed), *The Arts of Angela Carter: A Cabinet of Curiosities*, 98–126, Manchester: Manchester University Press.

Hennard Dutheil de la Rochère, M. (forthcoming), '"Morning Glories of the Night": Angela Carter's Translational Poetics in *Fireworks*', in *Contemporary Women's Writing*, special issue on Angela Carter in Japan, ed. Natsumi Ikoma.

Jones, C. A. (2016), *Mother Goose Refigured: A Critical Translation of Charles Perrault's Fairy Tales*, Detroit: Wayne State University Press.

Katsavos, A. (1994), 'A Conversation with Angela Carter', *Review of Contemporary Fiction*, 14 (3). Available online: https://www.dalkeyarchive.com/a-conversation-with-angela-carter-by-anna-katsavos/ (accessed 9 August 2019).

Leclerc, Marie-Dominique. (2020), 'Grisélidis, ou le mythe de la femme parfaite', *Grandes et petites mythologies I: Monts et abîmes: des dieux et des hommes*. Sous la direction de Karin Ueltschi et Flore Verdon, Reims: Editions et Presses Universitaires de Reims: 139–64.

Perrault, C. (1888), *Perrault's Popular Tales*, ed. A. Lang, London: Clarendon Press.

Perrault, C. (1977), *The Fairy Tales of Charles Perrault*, trans. A. Carter, illustr. M. Ware, London: Victor Gollancz.

Perrault, C. (1980), *Contes*, ed. Jean-Pierre Collinet, Paris: Folio Gallimard.

Pireddu, N. (1997), 'CaRterbury Tales: Romances of Disenchantment in Geoffrey Chaucer and Angela Carter', *The Comparatist*, 21 (May): 117–48.

Sermain, J.-P. (2005), *Le Conte de fées du classicisme aux Lumières*, Paris: Desjonquères.

Sermain, J.-P. (2008), '*Griselidis* de Perrault: l'anti-Baudelaire', in *Cahiers Parisiens*, Paris: University of Chicago, 209–16.

Sermain, J.-P. (2017), 'Perrault, conteur en vers', *Féeries*, 31 July. Available online: http://journals.openedition.org/feeries/1041 (accessed 9 August 2019).

Warner, M. (1994), 'Angela Carter: Bottle Blonde, Double Drag', in L. Sage (ed), *Flesh and the Mirror: Essays on the Art of Angela Carter*, 243–56, London: Virago Press.

Warner, M. (2014), *Once Upon a Time: A Short History of Fairy Tale*, Oxford: Oxford University Press.

Watz, A. (2017), *Angela Carter and Surrealism: 'A Feminist Libertarian Aesthetic'*, London: Routledge.

# 5

# Of tales, tragic opera, transformation and 'tongues': *Tristan und Isolde* in Angela Carter's *The Bloody Chamber*

## Ashley Riggs

Angela Carter was a prolific, provocative and talented author, translator, essayist, literary and cultural critic and editor, and she wrote at the crossroads of different genres, languages, cultures and art forms. Carter constantly played with and deconstructed – or used and abused – all kinds of literary and artistic references. Her use of the Tristan and Isolde motif in her collection of radically transformed fairy tales, *The Bloody Chamber*, is just one small example of how her fiction crosses linguistic, cultural, genre and even media boundaries. Importantly for this chapter, Carter's own work was thrillingly operatic, as well as highly sensual, as Marina Warner (2012) observes:

> Open any page and a full score rises from its word-notes, of winds howling, teardrops falling, diamond earrings tinkling, snapping teeth, sneezing, and wheezing. Storytelling for Angela Carter was an island full of noises and sweet airs, and like Caliban, who heard a thousand twangling instruments hum about his ears, she was tuned to an ethereal universe packed with sensations, to which she was alive with every organ.

Among the many unexpected and subversive characteristics of the stories in Carter's collection, the tales engage in 'a complex dialogue with the long history of pictorial and literary' – and, one must add, musical – 'representations of women in Western art and culture' (Hennard Dutheil de la Rochère 2006: 183–4). While Hennard Dutheil de la Rochère and others have explored allusions to, and criticism of, such representations in Carter's collection, the references to Richard Wagner's celebrated opera have not, to my knowledge, been examined in detail. Therefore, in this chapter I will discuss how Carter's dialogue with

Wagner's *Tristan und Isolde* contributes to her goal of deconstructing myth: 'demythologizing', as she called it, for emancipatory purposes. As she famously put it, 'I am all for putting new wine in old bottles, especially if the pressure of the new wine makes the old bottles explode' (Carter 1997: 37). Her use of the opera in her fairy tale rewritings is one of the ingredients of that 'new wine' with which she explodes certain 'old bottles', including the distinction between 'high' and 'low' art; decadent art that fetishizes (female) death; rigid gender power structures; or the form and messages of well-known fairy tales, to name a few. For this analysis,[1] I will focus on Carter's opening tale, 'The Bloody Chamber', which is a rewriting of Bluebeard, and two of the three Red Riding Hood rewritings which close the collection: 'The Company of Wolves', and 'Wolf-Alice'.

## Explosive influences: From Sade to Wagner

When Carter wrote *The Bloody Chamber*, she was also preparing a translation of Charles Perrault's fairy tales and a volume on the Marquis de Sade, *The Sadeian Woman*; her collection participates in a critical dialogue not only with the French and other fairy tale traditions but also with both her own non-fictional work, and Wagner's opera. While detailed discussion of the interplay between *The Sadeian Woman* and Carter's collection is beyond the scope of this chapter, it is worth noting that they elicited negative reactions (see, for instance, Clark 1987; Duncker 1984; or Lewallen 1988) not unlike common responses to *Tristan*. Huebner (2011: 157) observes that 'criticism of the opera has often revolved around its particular paradox of pain and pleasure'. The ways in which Carter tried to work through this paradox in *The Sadeian Woman* and explored gender, female sexuality and the representation of women in part through the prism of pornography in *The Bloody Chamber* were extremely unpalatable to a number of contemporary feminists and critics (also see Dworkin 1981, 1982, or Kappeler 1986, for example) as the texts seemed to redeem, in a sense, both Sade and pornography. As we will see below, the *raison d'être* and messages of the collection are, in fact, much more complex.

Given that the *Tristan und Isolde* opera may be less familiar to readers than Carter's *Bloody Chamber*, I will introduce it briefly here. Wagner wrote both the libretto and the opera, basing the story on Gottfried von Strassburg's *Tristan* (c. 1210), which was in turn based on Thomas von Britanje's *Roman de Tristan* (c. 1150) and Eilhart von Oberge's *Tristrant und Isolde* (c. 1170) (Rosenthal and Warrack 1990). Wagner was inspired by the legend of Tristan and Isolde because, as he put it, 'the all-pervading tragedy of the legend impressed me so deeply that I felt convinced it should stand out in bold relief, regardless of minor details' (Wagner [1911] 1963: 617). Wagner was a lover and would-be inventor of myths (Deathridge 2011: 29), and intent on producing high art; like Schopenhauer, he believed music to be the very highest form of art. He was also inspired by his own love affair, writing *Tristan* at a time when he was making amorous claims on the wife of one of his own most generous benefactors, Otto Wesendonck (Deathridge 2011).

The three-act opera tells the following story: In Act I, Tristan is escorting Princess Isolde of Ireland by ship to be wedded to his uncle King Marke in Cornwall. She is enraged with Tristan because he killed her previous fiancé. We learn that she had planned to avenge her fiancé's death by killing Tristan with his own sword but that when he gazed upon her, she could not. She demands that he drink a deadly poison to atone for his betrayal. They both drink it, but her attendant has substituted a love potion for the lethal mixture. Pleasure and pain are already poignantly intertwined.

Act I opens with the Prelude and the so-called 'Tristan chord', famous because its move away from traditional tonal harmony and the resulting 'tonal indeterminacy' marked a radical innovation in music. The chord has often been interpreted as conveying extreme longing and desire (Kerman 2011; Maehder 2011; Meyer 1989). These overpowering emotions continue to be emphasized in the music through evolving but constantly unresolved chords, an effect also called harmonic suspension. In this way, the musical and dramatic tension is maintained throughout the opera until the very end, when tension and desire are finally resolved – or reach their climax – through final resolution of the salient, striking and heretofore unresolved harmony introduced in the overture and echoed throughout the opera. Various passages and examples discussed by Daverio (2008: 125) 'establish the *Tristan* chord as a primary vehicle of *harmonic magic and mutability*' (emphasis in original). These powerful characteristics certainly found resonance with Carter, whose use of *Tristan* contributes to demonstrating the magic and the mutability of the fairy tale form. Moreover, like the Prelude, 'The Bloody Chamber' is programmatic, opening the dialogue with Sade through its truly Sadeian Bluebeard figure (the heroine indeed refers to him as 'my Marquis' on page 4), and introducing motifs and themes (such as the pain/pleasure, human/beast, man/woman, victim/oppressor, innocence/knowledge, power/weakness, submission/transgression and old/new oppositions) which, as dramatic – and also, sexual – tension similarly builds throughout the collection, will be repeated, examined, played with and dismantled.

In Act II of *Tristan*, the tension continues to build. Although Isolde has married Marke, Tristan and Isolde declare their mutual passion. During this Act, their faith in the night, the time of their romantic tryst, is emphasized. Indeed, the scene in which they meet and celebrate the night, when they cannot be *seen*, is a key moment in Act II. For them, night is the realm of truth and reality, and they believe that only by escaping the physical day world of falsehood and unreality through death can they achieve transcendence and release and be united forever. However, they are discovered by Marke and his hunting party, and Tristan allows one of Marke's knights to wound him. Both pleasure and pain are again foregrounded in moments of extreme dramatic and harmonic tension.

In Act III, Tristan is taken to his ancestral castle in Brittany to die. Isolde is summoned because she is a skilled healer. Just after she arrives at Tristan's side, he dies. Isolde collapses. Then King Marke and his knights appear; Marke, having heard the story of the love potion and the lovers' passion, has come to give his blessing and unite them. Isolde sings a final aria describing her vision of Tristan transfigured, resurrected, and then she also dies. This ending has often been read as a union in death which exalts the pair, transporting them from the paltry real world to a kind of metaphysical ecstasy. According to Maehder (2011: 98), this 'mystical fusion of love and death' was a theme which fascinated Wagner. As we will see, in *The Bloody Chamber* and in particular its closing tale, 'Wolf-Alice', Carter appears to celebrate, instead, a sensual, but also rational, fusion of love and life.

Despite Wagner's own somewhat macabre fascination, surely fuelled in part by his impossible love affair, the final scene of the opera has been read in a number of other ways, as we will see below. Its capacity to generate multiple interpretations is certainly something that would have appealed to Carter, characterizes her own work and undoubtedly motivated her use of the opera. For the present analysis, it is important to know that when the Prelude and Isolde's aria were performed alone, the final piece, traditionally called the *Liebestod*, or Love-death, was re-named the *Verklärung*, or Transfiguration, by Wagner, and the Prelude was referred to as the *Liebestod* (Nattiez 1990). As mentioned above, the music's marked lack of chord resolution parallels the longing and agony suffered by Tristan and Isolde over the course of the opera. Carter uses the term *Liebestod* to refer to the ending of the opera but *already references it* in her opening tale to imply that a love-death ending is to come. However, as suggested above, she proposes a different kind of transfiguration to close her collection.

## *Tristan* and/in 'The Bloody Chamber': Deconstructing the male gaze

It is in the programmatic opening tale of Carter's collection, also entitled 'The Bloody Chamber', that we first encounter *Tristan*. According to Grey (2011), the *Tristan und Isolde* 'drama... is structured to a significant degree by a dialectic of vision and hearing' (70), with 'looking', and in particular Tristan's gaze, playing a 'predominant role... throughout Act I' (83). The male gaze is a key feature of 'The Bloody Chamber' as well. How does Carter link *Tristan* and this tale? In its use of various works of art and literature that objectify and fetishize women, the rewriting of Bluebeard exposes the power of the male gaze to shape women's identities and self-perception. In Carter's version of Bluebeard, not only does the Marquis aim to make his wife correspond to paintings that are pornographic or martyrize women (Hennard Dutheil de la Rochère 2006), but it is *at the opera*, in the mirrors, that the bride-narrator first sees her flesh objectified in the Marquis' eyes: 'I saw him watching me in the gilded mirrors with the assessing eye of a connoisseur inspecting horseflesh' (Carter [1979] 2006: 6). A later undressing scene 'is [e]xplicitly associated by the narrator with the scene at the opera' (Hennard Dutheil de la Rochère 2006: 192) through a quotation of the Decadent poet Baudelaire: 'Of her apparel she retains/Only her sonorous jewellery.'[2] In the meantime, the objectifying male gaze is emphasized throughout the story, from the 'monocled lecher who examined her, limb by limb' (Carter [1979] 2006: 11) to the 'chauffeur' who 'eyed' her: 'was he comparing me, invidiously, to the countess, the artist's model, the opera singer?' (8) The latest bride is meant to meet a tragic end like Isolde – and like all the previous wives, as she progressively realizes.

There are also multiple *direct* references to the *Liebestod* and *Tristan und Isolde* in 'The Bloody Chamber' which maintain a critical dialogue between the two works. For example, in Carter's tale, we learn that the first of the Marquis' wives was an opera singer. His soon-to-be new wife, an accomplished pianist, 'had heard her sing Isolde' when, as a child, she went to the opera with her father. From an early age, she was thrilled by Isolde's 'white-hot passion', and even though the scene and music suggested the heroine 'would die young', 'all' the little girl 'heard was the glory of her voice' (Carter [1979] 2006: 5). From an early age, then, she learns to admire tragic heroines and subscribe to 'the model narrative of martyrdom for women' (Bacchilega 1995: 83) so often conveyed by Decadent art. Later, the young wife-to-be also allows the passion she feels when hearing the *Liebestod* to convince her that she loves the

Marquis: '[H]e took my mother and me, curious coincidence, to see *Tristan*. And, do you know, my heart swelled and ached so during the Liebestod that I thought I must truly love him. Yes. I did' (5). It is the emotion and melodrama of the performances – and the dangerously attractive association of love with death – which define her own feelings. Later, she discovers in the Marquis personal papers a note from that previous opera-singer wife, written on the score of the *Liebestod*. Its cryptic message evokes their union or love-death, and probably also predicts her own end. In addition, the heroine discovers a postcard which makes two significant connections: it links pleasure and pain, again through a quotation of Baudelaire, and it features a scene that we will in fact encounter in the final tale in the collection, 'Wolf-Alice'. This internal textual echo foreshadows the transformation that is to come.

So far, we have observed the presence and influence of the Tristan motif in Carter's rewriting of Bluebeard. The ending of 'The Bloody Chamber' self-consciously mocks both the Tristan drama and the stereotypical 'happily ever after' so often expected of fairy tales. As the Marquis prepares to kill his young bride, her mother arrives to save the day. The description is ironic, almost a parody:

> The Marquis stood transfixed, utterly dazed, at a loss. It must have been as if he had been watching his beloved *Tristan* for the twelfth, the thirteenth time and Tristan stirred, then leapt from his bier in the last act, announced in a jaunty aria interposed from Verdi that bygones were bygones, crying over spilt milk did nobody any good and, as for himself, he proposed to live happily ever after.
>
> (Carter [1979] 2006: 40)

The traditional tale and the girl have been freed from the confines of their tragic endings; the Marquis, stuck in the past, must go. Significantly, he is replaced as the heroine's lover by a blind piano tuner; while music may reign, the objectifying male gaze, too, must go.

The exaggerated portrayal of the mother's bravery is also a subtle mockery; it is in part accomplished through a comparison to Medusa. This mythical figure resonated with nineteenth-century thinkers as a fearsome and dangerous *femme fatale* but has also been appropriated by feminism as a symbol of female agency (see the discussion of Hélène Cixous, for example, below). In light of the connections Carter self-consciously highlights between the Medusa myth, the Bluebeard tale and *Tristan*, it is interesting to consider this illustration by Aubrey Beardsley.

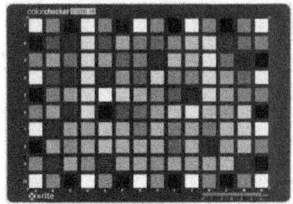

**Figure 10** *How Sir Tristram Drank of the Love Drink* (1893) by Aubrey Vincent Beardsley. © President and Fellows of Harvard College. Original on display at Harvard Art Museums. Accession number: 1986.681. Credit: Harvard Art Museums/Fogg Museum, Bequest of Scofield Thayer.

In his chapter 'Tristan's Traces', Steven Huebner (2011: 151) observes that Beardsley,

> [i]n his drawing *How Sir Tristram Drank of the Love Drink,...* depicts an Isolde with a Medusa-like crop of hair and prominent vaginal flower who towers over an effeminate Tristan. Such illustrations of Wagner's heroine as a *femme fatale*, an extension of interpretations that see her [as] in control of the action, seem echoed in later feminist descriptions [of Isolde].

Whereas Beardsley conflates Isolde and Medusa, Carter re-appropriates the Medusa role for the mother. This allows her to not only evoke nineteenth-century artistic references to the mythical figure but also to highlight ironically, in her extreme descriptions of the mother's heroism, the reclaiming of Medusa by second-wave feminism. Indeed, the connection drawn by Carter brings to mind Hélène Cixous's 1975 essay 'Le Rire de la Méduse' ('The Laugh of the Medusa'). Cixous exemplified a brand of feminism that Carter found to be over mythologizing, but she shared with Carter – and with Wagner – a focus on drives and desire and, like Carter, emphasized the female *eros*. By giving the narrative voice to the young heroine, Carter transforms Bluebeard into a tale of female agency, intellectual and sexual development and the acquisition of 'survival skills and useful knowledge to resist' subjugation by men, by culture, and by 'the power of images' (Hennard Dutheil de la Rochère 2006: 206). In addition, 'The Bloody Chamber' and the final tale 'Wolf-Alice', discussed below, may be read as 'call[ing] into question the primacy of vision' (207), 'privileging... different sensory paradigms' (Lau 2014: 36), and proposing 'an alternative erotics' (60). According to some interpretations, this is not at all at odds with Wagner's *Tristan* and its celebration of the interior, non-visual, otherwise sensual realm of music. However, Carter's 'plotting of the Bluebeard tale... raises the possibility of female emancipation from decadent images' (Hennard Dutheil de la Rochère 2006: 190) that fetishize 'the violent death of women' (Bacchilega 1995: 80) by laying bare 'the seductive power of martyrdom' (recall the heroine's fascination, even as a little girl) but also demonstrating convincingly 'the need to resist it' (82). Moreover, in stark contrast to Wagner, Carter refuses any notion of the divinely sublime, constantly desacralizing religious themes and images in her fiction.

## In the company of (tender) werewolves

References to *Tristan* continue to appear throughout the collection and play a particularly important role in the last two tales of *The Bloody Chamber*, 'The

Company of Wolves' and 'Wolf-Alice', two of three rewritings of Red Riding Hood.[3] Let us now explore the way these references are incorporated at the end of Carter's collection.

'The Company of Wolves' is a complex and stylistically rich tale. The main plot features a young girl, the Red Riding Hood figure, who is approaching puberty. Defying her parents, she goes off into the forest and meets a charming hunter (who is actually the wolf). They decide to compete – the prize will be a kiss – to see who can reach Grandmother's house first. She lets him win. After he has devoured Granny, the girl arrives; as wolves howl (or, rather, sing) outside, the two protagonists engage in the traditional 'all the better to see/eat you with' exchange, but the girl laughs, undaunted by the supposed threat of the wolf's 'big teeth'. Confident rather than fearful, she undresses[4] and they lie down together, she 'between the paws of the' now '*tender*' wolf (Carter [1979] 2006: 139; my emphasis). Importantly for this analysis, not only does 'The Company of Wolves' 'foreground … the musical aspect of the text through a highly alliterative style' (Hennard Dutheil de la Rochère 2013: 99), it also abounds in musical references. Indeed, the undressing scene – so unlike that earlier one in 'The Bloody Chamber' in which the young bride was objectified, assessed as if she were 'horseflesh' – is accompanied by a series of surprising and poetic musical terms: the wolves' howling is described as a 'threnody' (defined by the *OED* as a 'lament for the dead, dirge') and then a 'prothalamion' (*OED*: '[a] song or poem written in celebration of a (forthcoming) wedding'), and it culminates in 'the clamour of the forest's Liebestod' (Carter [1979] 2006: 138). The final Wagnerian term combines the previous two, evoking 'death', union and the impending *sexual* union of the two protagonists (sexual climax is sometimes called the 'little death'). At the same time, the chain of musical references can be seen to mock its own content because it is both so erudite and so melodramatic. Furthermore, Carter immediately deflates the *Liebestod* reference, as the girl bursts out laughing at the wolf's familiar refrain, 'all the better to eat you with' because now, 'she knew she was nobody's meat' (138). In this penultimate tale of the collection, the transformed Red Riding Hood figure echoes the 'jaunty' version of Tristan that Carter introduced to poke fun at both the Marquis and Wagner's glamorization of the tragic (Carter [1979] 2006: 40), in line with her 'demythologizing' enterprise.

These comical depictions, the forest's *Liebestod*, the girl's merry dismissal of the wolf's threat and her tender care for the gentle wolf in 'The Company of Wolves' completely disrupt the gender power structures which so often characterize both nineteenth-century art and the plots of the classic tales. Moreover, with

Carter's comparison of the love scene to 'a savage marriage ceremony' (138–9), the kind of exalted union envisioned by Wagner becomes a wild, animal one; the 'carnivore incarnate' (Carter uses the phrase multiple times in *The Bloody Chamber*) becomes a loving, even submissive beast. In blatant counterpoint to the sophistication and cultivation of opera (recall that it is 'high art' for Wagner), Carter proposes the beastly pair as a legitimate alternative to both the romantic and tragic tale of *Tristan und Isolde*, and to the rags-to-riches, happily-ever-after endings of popularized fairy tales.

## Alternative arias, or a new politics of representation

Carter does something quite similar in the final scene of 'Wolf-Alice', which can be read as a rewriting of Isolde's final aria. This tale presents us with two characters, both hybrid, or wolf-human – and therefore neither animal nor human. The first, Wolf-Alice, is a utopian figure for Carter, as she learns a sense of self while remaining unfettered by culturally and religiously inculcated values. I think Carter subtly references Tristan and Isolde's celebration of the night as the realm of truth and reality in this text, as she highlights the role of the moon and the 'metamorphic' (Carter [1979] 2006: 142) night in Wolf-Alice's evolution. In addition, I believe that Carter's reference to a 'seed' initiating Wolf-Alice's intellectual development alludes to Wagner's musings on the process of creativity and inspiration or, put otherwise, on the germination of art. For Wolf-Alice, '[t]he shape of this theory was blurred yet, out of it, there took root a kind of wild reasoning, as it might have from a seed dropped in her brain off the foot of a flying bird' (144). The seed recalls Wagner's *Opera and Drama* in which he discusses his theory of (musical) art. To put it very simply, 'poetic intent' plants itself like a seed[5] within a receiving element (which is, significantly, both 'female' and 'primitive') (Nattiez 1990: 115, referencing Wagner's *Opera and Drama*; my translations). The resulting germination leads to a capacity for understanding (seen as 'male') and a new and 'liberating' language (the 'melody') (115) to express, experience and allow the representation of emotion. Wagner celebrates the creative (and, for him, masculine) power of culture; 'the poet of the future, as both poet and musician, will be the poet-redeemer' (Nattiez 1990: 61; my translation).

Carter, of course, puts a twist on this in order to deconstruct it, and at the end of *The Bloody Chamber*, we encounter an alternative, and female, poet-redeemer. Carter's 'primal' and hybrid female figure achieves understanding not through anything civilized, cultural or poetic but through a budding awareness of the physical and sensual workings of her own body; the seed planted in her brain marks the germination of her sexuality. Moreover, in her newfound primitive wisdom she will be a (resolutely irreligious) saviour, a 'wise child who leads them all and her silence and her howling' an alternative aria, 'a language as authentic as any language of nature' (Carter [1979] 2006: 143). She will also redeem that other hybrid figure, the now fragile and outmoded male, through her tender, gentle and sensual 'ministrations' (149).

That other figure is the Duke. A textual echo of the Marquis – and also, surely, of both Sade and the dying Tristan at home in Brittany in Act III – he is portrayed as a decrepit, pitiful version of the proverbial werewolf, described as 'the lord of cobweb castle' (148) and therefore not very lordly after all. He is nevertheless otherworldly in that '[h]is mirror faithfully reflects his bed but never the meager shape within the disordered covers' (146). He will be brought (back) into the real-world realm of representation and (re)united with humanity by the wolf-girl.

I believe that in the final scene of this closing tale, Carter essentially rewrites Wagner's Transfiguration. There is no dramatic flight from the visible world, rife with the kinds of religious implications which Carter constantly criticized through desacralizing moves in her fiction. There is no ascension of a male Tristan figure or accompanying female death. In fact, there is neither man nor woman. Instead, we watch the 'bringing into being', the redemption through a kind of 'pure' eroticism and entry into the realm of representation, of a previously damned, misunderstood, imagined, mythical figure. Consider the final lines of 'Wolf-Alice' in *The Bloody Chamber*:

> The lucidity of the moonlight lit the mirror propped against the red wall; the rational glass, the master of the visible, impartially recorded the crooning girl.
>
> As she continued her ministrations, this glass, with infinite slowness, yielded to the reflexive strength of its own material construction. Little by little, there appeared within it, like the image on photographic paper that emerges, first, a formless web of tracery, the prey caught in its own fishing net, then in firmer yet still shadowed outline until at last as vivid as real life itself, as if brought into being by her soft, moist, gentle tongue, finally, the face of the Duke.
>
> (149)

Wolf-Alice is no martyr; there are no exoticized corpses or tragic endings here, nor any escape from or transcendence of the earthly such as that which marked the end of Wagner's *Tristan*. Instead, Wolf-Alice exercises a new form of redemptive power. Not by force nor through an objectifying gaze, not as a strident *femme fatale*, but rather by literally *licking* the Duke into existence with her tongue.

And yet, '*Wolf-Alice never speaks*' (Lau 2008: 89; my emphasis). Whereas Isolde closes the opera as a 'disembodied voice' (Groos 2011: 52), the two figures at the end of Carter's collection evolve and transform into what I would like to call 'dis-voiced bodies'. By highlighting this tongue which does not speak but fundamentally transforms, Carter succeeds in creating 'a subjectivity that does not rely on visualization and language *to the exclusion of the body*' (Bacchilega 1997: 163, fn 134; my emphasis). At the same time, this is also all *written*, so that Carter may be seen to propose a new language for conceptualizing desire, gender relations and, more generally, what it is to be human.

Moreover, Carter's transfiguration is not the clear-cut yet final 'happily ever after' often associated with fairy tales and lightheartedly referred to in 'The Bloody Chamber'. A closing chapter to a series of transformations, it nevertheless subtly suggests new beginnings. Instead of that 'mystical fusion of love and death' (Maehder 2011: 98), we witness the corporeal fusion of sensuality and life. In addition, by virtue of all the mirror imagery, this re-imagined Transfiguration constitutes a reflection (in both senses of the word) on the constructedness of religious and cultural myths of love, origin and identity, and on language itself as inevitably implicated in myth-making. (Warner (2012) has described the mirror as Wolf-Alice's (and by extrapolation, Carter's) 'rational glass, a glass which is love and knowledge, faith and doubt all combined'.) As a result, the reader's perceptions of familiar fairy tales and of celebrated art are also transformed. Carter's ending links desire, corporeal being and visual representation, but without the asymmetrical power structures which that representation often carries in art and culture. Bacchilega has highlighted the pervasive and magical presence of the mirror throughout the collection and the dramatic and far-reaching evolution it represents: '[T]he transformation of the mirror in *The Bloody Chamber* is positively magic: from inorganic speculum serving the masculine gaze in "The Bloody Chamber", to dream-like but porous matter in which to envision our futures, in "Wolf-Alice"' (Bacchilega 1997: 141).

Emil Preetorius, who designed sets for early twentieth-century productions of *Tristan*, described Wagner as 'a man for whom the ultimate authority was not the eye, but the ear' (qtd. in Spencer 2011: 132). Carter, however, provocatively suggests it is the tongue. Indeed, it is as if in promoting female agency and (primal) desire, she subtly proposes a variation on the famous Cartesian formula: the message of her hybrid heroine is, instead, 'I lick, therefore I am.'

## Creative conjuring for the twenty-first century

Carter's dialogue with *Tristan* in part recognizes, in part prefigures, later reinterpretations of Wagner's opera. Both her collection and these new readings of Wagner speak, in turn, to current trends in feminist and queer theory – in particular, their emphasis on the constructedness of gender roles and norms, and the fluidity of (sexual) identity. Just as Carter demonstrates the mutability of the fairy tale and, by extrapolation, other cultural myths, novel interpretations of *Tristan* demonstrate the continuing mutability both of the musical form which Wagner himself so radically demonstrated and perpetuated, and of the signification of his famous opera. To cite just a few examples, '[r]epresentation of desire in *Tristan* has resonated with different sexualities. George Bernard Shaw heard a style that exuded virility… Ferruccio Busoni, on the other hand, interpreted the style as feminine' (Huebner 2011: 151). As we saw above, illustrations like Beardsley's which depict Isolde as a *femme fatale* informed later feminist interpretations which emphasize the heroine's agency: she is also seen as powerful because she 'befuddle[s] and seduce[s] poor Tristan by means of her chromatic excess' (McClary 1991: 100). The Tristan chord has often been interpreted as an androgynous one, as a 'metaphor of the fusion of the two sexes in a work of art which is complete' (Nattiez 1990: 322; my translations), and even as exemplifying 'the androgyny of equality' (330). A homosexual interpretation by Polish composer Szymanowski in his 1917 novel *Efebos*, also based on androgyny, is particularly reminiscent of Carter's closing scene,

> appear[ing] to position the *Liebestod* as a mere stepping-stone to same-sex love embodying an even purer union of the physical with the aesthetic. Whether one pursues homosexual implications or not, this line of criticism obviously moves in a different direction from the excesses of Isolde as *femme fatale* towards a critical construction of desire disassociated from gender, a view of the opera where, in Lawrence Kramer's words, 'as desiring subjects, Tristan and Isolde are indistinguishable'.
> 
> (Huebner 2011: 152; quotes Kramer 1990)

Yet Carter resented the annihilation of the female, including the female body, in the Decadent and Symbolist art that was roughly contemporaneous with Wagner's work. She posits instead a utopian scenario in which a resolutely sensual self can be constructed outside of the constraints of culture and its myths, although she complicates her own proposition by self-reflexively showing it as constructed at the end. This means, however, that her transfiguration and the collection as a whole call on readers to read critically and to interrogate their culturally constructed assumptions. It is true that Wagner's radically innovative use of musical strategies throughout the opera 'directs our attention beyond *the visible frame* of the stage' (Grey 2011: 71; my emphasis). However, while he proposes to move us 'towards some higher, deeper or wider dimension of the imaginary space of the drama' (71), Carter, on the other hand, specifically, self-reflexively reminds us of the frame.

As we have seen, both Carter and Wagner appropriate the 'old', 'contemporary poetic motifs and dramatic structures' (Groos 2011: 38) in order to reinterpret them in new, creative and mutable forms which in turn lend themselves to reinterpretation. Daverio (2008: 126) has described Wagner as 'a musical conjuror who reveled in unleashing the magic latent in the tonal harmonic system'. In an interesting parallel, Carter revelled in, as she put it, unleashing 'the latent content of the traditional stories', which she saw as 'violently sexual'. 'I read it that way', she insisted in an interview, 'because I am a woman' (Goldsworthy 1985: 10). This strategy of extracting and emphasizing previously latent content is, in fact, closely linked to queer approaches to fairy tales, and more generally to queer theory. Turner and Greenhill (2012), for example, concur with Carter that fairy tales include latent sexual content, especially where the female protagonists are concerned. Such content constitutes a 'faultline', to use Alan Sinfield's (1992) term, a crack or entry point in the traditional version that allows a writer to question the belief system represented, to turn the marginal into the central, to deconstruct the classic tale and to reconstruct it anew. The age-old polarities which are so central to the works discussed here constitute another faultline, a 'source of dramatic tension' that can be refashioned to 'allow for a deeper look at transformations and projections along social and sexual lines' (Turner and Greenhill 2012: 15). Sade's writings were yet another faultline for Carter since, as Keenan (2000: 40) put it, they 'provided a speculative starting point' for her interrogation of gender power relations and female eroticism.

The strategy of bringing to the fore what was only covert in previous artistic and literary forms, the diverse interpretations of *Tristan* discussed above, and Carter's decision to include three radically different versions of the Red Riding Hood tale in her collection all demonstrate the performativity of both artists' works.[6] According to Judith Butler ([1990] 1999), gender norms are in fact socially and culturally, rather than biologically, constructed, but become accepted and fixed, and achieve legitimacy, through repeated performance. According to queer theory, it follows that if one enacts new, subversive performances of gender, one can expose the constructed nature of the concept. Carter's mobilization of the fairy tale form in general and of Wagner's *Tristan* in particular accomplishes exactly that.

## Conclusions

Given the material that Carter and Wagner chose to re-vision and the strategies they used, both the collection and the opera address such age-old conflicts as pleasure versus pain, nature versus culture, the physical versus the spiritual, and of course the old versus the new. With Carter, though, the long history of dichotomies allegedly reconcilable only in death is debunked, along with the melodramatic, 'martyrific' artistic and cultural apparatus that inculcates and preserves those dichotomies. To achieve this meant abandoning the tragic, moving beyond male-female antagonism and the subjection of women, and reclaiming a space within the realm of the visible rather than fleeing it for some supposedly higher existence. It also meant challenging the supposed superiority of 'high' art, unmasking myths, and critically highlighting the cultural constructions which determine our view of the world and of ourselves. Finally, it meant recognizing the power of the tongue – the tongue as words, as writing, as literature and as singing, but also as purveyor of sensual pleasure. Indeed, for Carter, sensual and sexual drives are an important, legitimate part of our essence as animal beings.

It is true that through their re-appropriation of existing art forms, both Wagner and Carter realized transformations that were radical for their time and that continue to shape music, visual art and literature today. However, Wagner intimated a future which Carter may well have seen as useless religious nonsense – she famously declared that 'this world is all that there is' (Carter 1997: 38). Through her creative, unconventional and often explosive rewriting of fairy tales which relies in part on critical dialogue with Wagner's famous opera, Carter succeeded in positing a new era for gender relations and moved the reader towards a new understanding of the complex workings of female eroticism. While we may never know the full extent of Carter's knowledge of Wagner's opera or of its many and diverse interpretations, it is clear that her critical dialogue with *Tristan und Isolde* played an essential role in her 'demythologizing' use of fairy tale and her feminist project in *The Bloody Chamber*.

## Notes

1. This chapter builds upon a paper given at the 'Reading the Fantastic: Tales Beyond Borders' conference held at the University of Leeds in April 2015 and also draws inspiration from my doctoral thesis (Riggs 2014). I am grateful to Lance Hewson and L. and S. Riggs for re-reading earlier versions of this chapter.
2. ' Elle n'avait gardé que ses bijoux sonores', from the once-banned poem 'Les Bijoux', published in *Les Fleurs du mal*.
3. The other, 'The Werewolf', precedes them.
4. 'She [...] took off her scarlet shawl, the colour of poppies, the colour of sacrifices, the colour of her menses... The thin muslin went flaring up the chimney like a magic bird and now off came her skirt, her woolen stockings, her shoes' (138).
5. For more on this, see Frank Glass's *The Fertilizing Seed, Wagner's Concept of the Poetic Intent?* (1983).
6. Carter achieves a similar effect with her three versions of 'Ashputtle *or* the Mother's Ghost'. For in-depth analyses of this tripartite tale, see Michelle Ryan-Sautour's article (2011), Martine Hennard Dutheil de la Rochère's book (2013) and my doctoral thesis (Riggs 2014).

## Works cited

Bacchilega, C. (1995), 'Sex Slaves and Saints? Resisting Masochism in Angela Carter's "The Bloody Chamber"', in I. Rauch and C. Moore (eds), *Across the Oceans: Studies from East to West in Honor of Richard K. Seymour*, 77–86, Honolulu: University of Hawai'i Press.

Bacchilega, C. (1997), *Postmodern Fairy Tales: Gender and Narrative Strategies*, Philadelphia: University of Pennsylvania Press.

Butler, J. ([1990] 1999), *Gender Trouble: Feminism and the Subversion of Identity*, New York/London: Routledge.

Carter, A. (1997), 'Notes from the Front Line', in *Shaking a Leg: Collected Journalism and Writings*, 36–43, London: Chatto & Windus.

Carter, A. ([1979] 2006), *The Bloody Chamber and Other Stories*, London: Vintage.

Clark, R. (1987), 'Angela Carter's Desire Machine', *Women's Studies*, 14: 147–61.

Daverio, J. (2008), '*Tristan und Isolde*: Essence and Appearance', in T. S. Grey (ed), *The Cambridge Companion to Wagner*, 115–33, Cambridge: Cambridge University Press.

Deathridge, J. (2011), 'Public and Private Life: On the Genesis of *Tristan und Isolde* and the *Wesendonck Lieder*', in A. Groos (ed), *Richard Wagner: Tristan und Isolde*, 19–35, Cambridge/New York: Cambridge University Press.

Duncker, P. (1984), 'Re-Imagining the Fairy Tales: Angela Carter's Bloody Chambers', *Literature and History*, 10 (1): 3–14.

Dworkin, A. (1981), *Pornography: Men Possessing Women*, London: The Women's Press.
Dworkin, A. (1982), 'The Sexual Politics of Fear and Courage', in *Our Blood: Prophecies and Discourses on Sexual Politics*, 50–65, London: The Women's Press.
Glass, F. W. (1983), *The Fertilizing Seed, Wagner's Concept of the Poetic Intent?*, Ann Arbor, MI: UMI Research Press.
Goldsworthy, K. (1985), 'Angela Carter', *meanjin*, 44 (1), 4–13.
Grey, T. S. (2011), 'In the Realm of the Senses: Sight, Sound and the Music of Desire in *Tristan und Isolde*', in A. Groos (ed), *Richard Wagner: Tristan und Isolde*, 69–94, Cambridge: Cambridge University Press.
Groos, A. (2011), 'Between Memory and Desire: Wagner's Libretto and Late Romantic Subjectivity', in A. Groos (ed), *Richard Wagner: Tristan und Isolde*, 36–52, Cambridge: Cambridge University Press.
Hennard Dutheil de la Rochère, M. (2006), 'Modelling for Bluebeard: Visual and Narrative Art in Angela Carter's "The Bloody Chamber"', in B. Maeder, J. Schwyter, I. Sigrist, and B. Vejdovsky (eds), *The Seeming and the Seen: Essays in Modern Visual and Literary Culture*, 183–208, Bern: Peter Lang.
Hennard Dutheil de la Rochère, M. (2013), *Reading, Translating, Rewriting: Angela Carter's Translational Poetics*, Detroit: Wayne State University Press.
Huebner, S. (2011), '*Tristan*'s traces', in A. Groos (ed), *Richard Wagner: Tristan und Isolde*, 142–66, Cambridge: Cambridge University Press.
Kappeler, S. (1986), *The Pornography of Representation*, Ser. Feminist Perspectives, Cambridge: Polity Press.
Keenan, S. (2000), 'Angela Carter's *The Sadeian Woman*: Feminism as Treason', in A. Easton (ed), *Angela Carter*, 37–57, London/New York: Macmillan/St. Martin's.
Kerman, J. (2011), 'The Prelude and the Play', in A. Groos (ed), *Richard Wagner: Tristan und Isolde*, 53–68, Cambridge/New York: Cambridge University Press.
Kramer, L. (1990), *Music as Cultural Practice, 1800–1900*, Berkeley/Los Angeles/Oxford: University of California Press.
Lau, K. J. (2008), 'Erotic Infidelities: Angela Carter's Wolf Trilogy', *Marvels & Tales*, 22 (1), 77–94. doi:10.1353/mat.0.0058.
Lau, K. J. (2014), *Erotic Infidelities: Love and Enchantment in Angela Carter's* The Bloody Chamber, Detroit: Wayne State University Press.
Lewallen, A. (1988), '"Wayward Girls but Wicked Women?" Female Sexuality in Angela Carter's *The Bloody Chamber*', in G. Day and C. Bloom (eds), *Perspectives on Pornography: Sexuality in Film and Literature*, 144–57, New York: St. Martin's.
Maehder, J. (2011), 'A Mantle of Sound for the Night: Timbre in Wagner's *Tristan und Isolde*', in A. Groos (ed), *Richard Wagner: Tristan und Isolde*, 95–119, Cambridge/New York: Cambridge University Press.
McClary, S. (1991), *Feminine Endings: Music, Gender and Sexuality*, Minneapolis, MN: University of Minnesota Press.
Meyer, L. (1989), *Style and Music: Theory, History and Ideology*, Philadelphia: University of Pennsylvania Press.

Nattiez, J.-J. (1990), *Wagner androgyne: Essai sur l'interprétation*, Paris: C. Bourgois.

Riggs, A. (2014), 'Thrice Upon a Time: Feminist Fairy Tale Rewritings by Angela Carter and Emma Donoghue, and Their French Translations', doctoral diss., Faculty of Translation and Interpreting, University of Geneva.

Rosenthal, H. and Warrack, J. (1990), *The Concise Oxford Dictionary of Opera*, 2nd edn, Oxford/New York: Oxford University Press.

Ryan-Sautour, M. (2011), 'Authorial Ghosts and Maternal Identity in Angela Carter's "Ashputtle or the Mother's Ghost: Three Versions of One Story" (1987)', *Marvels & Tales*, 25 (1), 33–50.

Sinfield, A. (1992), *Faultlines: Cultural Materialism and the Politics of Dissident Reading*, Oxford: Clarendon Press.

Spencer, S. (2011), 'Staging *Tristan und Isolde*', in A. Groos (ed), *Richard Wagner: Tristan und Isolde*, 120–41, Cambridge: Cambridge University Press.

Turner, K. and P. Greenhill, eds (2012), *Transgressive Tales: Queering the Grimms*, Detroit: Wayne State University Press.

Wagner, R. ([1911] 1963), *My Life*, authorized translation from the German, vol. 2, London: Constable.

Warner, M. (2012), 'Chamber of Secrets: The Sorcery of Angela Carter', *The Paris Review*, 17 October. Available online: https://www.theparisreview.org/blog/2012/10/17/chamber-of-secrets-the-sorcery-of-angela-carter/ (accessed 21 April 2021).

Part Three

# Ways of seeing

# 6

# Adapting Carter: *The Lady of the House of Love* and *The Bloody Chamber* on the Australian stage

Belinda Locke

Angela Carter's wide-ranging and scintillating creative output includes publications of nine novels, short stories, anthologies of fairy tales, journalism, non-fiction, radio plays, film adaptations of her own work, children's books and poetry. Although there is now a groundswell of critical literature deconstructing Carter's work utilizing an array of theoretical lenses, the analyses are predominantly located within the field of English Literature. The interdisciplinarity of Carter's practice is clearly demonstrated when examining her complete works, and to privilege Carter's fictional writing ahead of her engagement in other mediums suggests a hierarchical bias towards literature. Charlotte Crofts' 2003 publication *Anagrams of Desire: Angela Carter's Writing for Radio, Film and Television* is one exception that addresses the lack of critical attention paid to Carter's writing for media. Crofts argues, 'By ignoring her work in media, traditional English studies is in danger of missing the opportunity that her interdisciplinarity presents to challenge and expand the boundaries of the academy' (2003: 198).

Carter's interest in theatre is evident from both her engagement with the form and the references to live performance prevalent in her novels and short stories. Her own writing for stage consisted of an adaptation of Benjamin Franklin Wedekind's *Lulu*, commissioned by the National Theatre in London, and a libretto for opera *Orlando: The Enigma of the Sexes*; neither of which was realized during her lifetime. The theatricality of Carter's writing, intertextual references and use of performance venues as settings in her fictional works are documented by Peach (2009), Gamble (1997), Lee (1997), Stoddart (2007), Gruss (2014) and Tonkin (2019), amongst others. Lee affirms, 'All manner of performances pervade her work, from the individual character with a flair for dressing up to vaudeville, pantomime, and the circus to film and Shakespeare. Her writing itself is spectacle' (1997: 13). However, theorists have seldom made links between Carter's theatricality and the impetus this may provide to adapt her work for stage.

The interdisciplinary, intertextual nature of Carter's work lends itself to multiple interpretations, and artists across the world have been inspired to adapt Carter's writing for different mediums. UK company Kneehigh Theatre's production of *Nights at the Circus* (2005), directed by Emma Rice and adapted by Rice and Tom Morris, has to date generated the most in depth discussion of any singular theatrical adaptation of Carter's work. Rice states, 'The amazing thing is that nobody has adapted this text before. It's one of the seminal books of the twentieth century… It's about theatre and show business. It's also about women in that world' (cited in Taylor 2005: 3). Here Rice identifies from a theatre practitioner's perspective what academics in the field of English literature have alluded to: the inherent theatricality of Carter's writing as the source text.

Rice later launched Bristol-based company Wise Children, the namesake of Carter's 1991 novel, with a theatrical adaptation of Carter's tale in 2018. Interviewed for *The Observer* in anticipation of Wise Children's debut and upcoming UK tour, Rice claims Carter had 'a love/hate relationship with acting. [Carter] shuddered at "that dreadful spectacle of painted loons in the middle distance making fools of themselves"' (cited in Kellaway 2018). Nevertheless, Rice considers the novel *Wise Children* to be Carter's 'love letter to the theatre' (Kellaway 2018). The theatrical potential of Carter's 'Puss-in-Boots' and 'The Bloody Chamber' was gleaned by playwright A. C. H. Smith and composer Christopher Northam, who teamed together to produce musicals *Pussy: An Angela Carter Musical Extravaganza* (2017) and *The Ruby Choker* (2019) both staged in Bristol by Renato's Theatre Company ('Angela Carter Show' 2019). While there is clearly evidence of creative practice in this area, and journalistic reviews of some productions, little academic writing is available on the topic.

This chapter therefore seeks to examine the unique processes and considerations involved in adapting Carter's writing for stage and comprises a comparative case study of two Australian theatrical adaptations of Carter's short stories. Theatre productions *The Lady of the House of Love*, directed by David Fenton and adapted by Daniel Evans (Metro Arts, Brisbane), and *The Bloody Chamber*, directed by Matthew Lutton and adapted by Van Badham (Malthouse Theatre, Melbourne), were both presented in 2013 and derive from short stories of the same names published in Carter's 1979 collection *The Bloody Chamber*.

Key creatives participated in semi-structured interviews, an analysis of which is detailed in this chapter alongside relevant data from the performances. While this case study reinforces more widely applicable challenges of adapting literature to a theatrical context, it also reveals central, reoccurring concerns pertaining to the adaptation of Carter's writing for stage, namely: the poetics and complexity of Carter's use of language, integration of music, the rich imagery and its verbal as well as physical depiction, the historical and cultural positioning of the work, the relationship/balance between the characters and the representation of gender onstage.

## The process begins – *The Lady of the House of Love*

Performer Sandro Colarelli (see Figure 11) spawned the idea to adapt 'The Lady of the House of Love' for stage and that he, a male actor, would play the part of a female vampire, as well as that of the male soldier. Colarelli had a long-standing fascination with Angela Carter's writing, having first encountered her tale 'The Lady of the House of Love' at a book sale in his early teens (Colarelli 2015: Line 47–8). An opportunity arose with Queensland Cabaret Festival in 2005 for Colarelli to present a one-person show, and he decided to marry his theatrical experience with his musical experience by bringing together a team

**Figure 11** Promotional image for *The Lady of the House of Love* featuring Sandro Collarelli (Nat Lynn 2013).

to adapt the story of 'The Lady of the House of Love' and combine it with songs by Tori Amos (Colarelli 2015). Writer Daniel Evans was approached by Colarelli to be part of the project and describes his role in this preliminary development as being to adapt the short story into 'textual snippets' to exist around the music (Evans 2015: Line 8–10).

*The Lady of the House of Love* was Evans' first dramatic adaptation, and he faced the added complexity of melding literary and lyrical authorial voices of Carter and Amos. He states, 'It was quite a surreal experience. Taking I guess someone else's words and funneling them in around *someone else's* words' (Evans 2015: 12–13). Director David Fenton recalls the first showing of the performance coming together quickly, with his engagement commencing part way through the process almost as a 'directorial *consultant*' for a few rehearsals before it hit the stage (2013a: Line 36). Fenton was less taken by the assemblage of Carter's words and Amos' songs explaining, 'it had a narrative, it had this story, it had this complexity, and Sandro [Colarelli] was weaving through it. But the Tori Amos stuff… felt as if it was confusing the issue. Felt as if it was just *using* the story as some type of lever, or platform, to be able to rise up into these musical moments' (2013a: Line 40–46). Fenton describes the work as a kind of 'Frankenstein's monster' at the time of the first public presentation (2013a: Line 48–53).

All of the interviewees agreed that the work became more cohesive and gained clarity dramaturgically as the production was redeveloped for seasons in 2008 and 2013 at Metro Arts (Brisbane, Australia). Jacob Diefenbach was commissioned to write original music that superseded the Tori Amos songs, and the dramatic adaptation was reconsidered and given focused attention by Evans, Fenton and Colarelli. Giving credit to the combined effort of the creative practitioners involved in the project Evans states, 'What you had was really five brains on the project. David's directorially, Sandro's performatively, mine writing-wise, Jacob's head and Angela's head were still very much in the room. You know, the weight of her. All kind of like feeding this one mythical story. Her story about Sleeping Beauty' (2015: Line 119–23). The script Evans wrote was significantly reworked with rounds of feedback from the rest of the creative team. Fenton as the director was 'much more involved dramaturgically at that point' (2013a: Line 80), having previously felt that the adaptation had not, '*dramatised* the short story in such a way that it revealed itself very well for the complexity that the short story was' (2013a: Line 66–7).

By all accounts Diefenbach's compositions had a profound impact upon the maturity of the work and the interpretation of Carter's short story. Fenton recalls, 'Diefenbach came in and the whole thing started to gel, musically it started to gel, so all of a sudden there was something that cracked open in Sandro's engagement with the work' (2013a: Line 114–16). Evans could see the effect of Diefanbach's work upon the complex process of adaptation, stating, 'It *actually* felt like it honoured the story *more*. Because it, in quite crass terms, went from being a bit of a jukebox cabaret to something that felt much more nuanced and serious... he really used Angela's writing in another light' (2015: Line 114–16). Here it is evident that music played an integral role in revisioning 'The Lady of the House of Love' for the stage.

## The process begins – *The Bloody Chamber*

Director Matthew Lutton initiated the concept for a performance of *The Bloody Chamber* whilst he and writer Van Badham were both working as Artistic Associates at Malthouse Theatre in Melbourne. The genesis for the project was Lutton's interest in the opera *Bluebeard's Castle* by Béla Bartók, with Carter's version of the Bluebeard story in the back of his mind from reading 'The Bloody Chamber' seven or eight years prior (2014: Line 8–12). When

**Figure 12** Production image from *The Bloody Chamber* featuring Alison Whyte (Jeff Busby 2013).

someone suggested Lutton should revisit Carter's telling of the story he states that he 'became instantly obsessed with how sort of rich and subversive *her* work was... and then when it evolved the Bartók really started to slip away, and it just became more and more about the Carter. But initially it was going to be the two together' (2014: Line 14–19). Lutton then built the primary creative team, which consisted of writer Van Badham, composer David Chisholm and Alison Whyte as the performer. Similar to Carter, Badham has a varied writing practice as a novelist, journalist, dramatist and dramaturg, specializing in 'the way stories change meaning and form' (Badham 2014: Line 125–9).

After a concept meeting with Lutton and Chisholm, Badham was 'given some latitude to test out some ideas with an adaptation' and formulated several different scenarios in a theatrical context. There was a version, Badham elaborates, 'where the narrator was played by Angela Carter as like a chain-smoking, crazy in an armchair. And I also did one where Bluebeard's wives from the Bartók opera, the dead wives, walked through with the music. And it became quite meta-opera with the minor characters claiming their place in the narrative' (2014: Line 32–6). Theorist Linda Hutcheon's assertion in *A Theory of Adaptation* that 'Adaptation is repetition, but repetition without replication' (2014: 7) is apparent in Badham's approach to adapting 'The Bloody Chamber' for stage. Badham stresses that replication in the form of reading the short story aloud is not drama (2014: Line 54–5). Adapting to a dramatic text requires a maintenance of tone and a consistent stylistic 'using dramatic vocabularies to communicate literary vocabularies' (2014: Line 51–3).

As with the adaptation of 'The Lady of the House of Love', Badham was in the first instance reticent to engage in the processes of deconstruction and reconstruction or reconfiguration required to adapt the text due to her respect for Carter and the beauty of her writing; raising issues of fidelity with a desire to be faithful or loyal to Carter as the author as much as her writing. However, as Stam illuminates, 'it is questionable whether strict fidelity is even possible. A counter view would insist that an adaptation is automatically different and original due to the change of medium' (2000: 55). When the first experiments with theatrical scenarios were unfruitful a rereading of the short story gave Badham the confidence to pursue a strong narrative and 'strip and change' the text (2014: Line 41–2). This process of stripping and changing occurred on a macro and a micro scale, with over forty drafts of the script exchanged between Lutton and Badham by the time the performance premiered. The adaptation process involved one creative development period with actor Alyson Whyte, followed by many rewrites prior to the rehearsal period and performance of *The Bloody Chamber*.

## Poetics and complexity of Carter's use of language

The poetics and complexity of Carter's use of language consistently pose a challenge for theatrical adaptations, as experienced by the creative teams behind *The Lady of the House of Love* and *The Bloody Chamber*. Janis Balodis (2012) asserts in his doctoral thesis *The Practice of Adaptation: Turning Fact and Fiction into Theatre* that the additional time it takes to speak or sing a line of text than to read one necessitates that:

> There has to be a radical process of distillation of the narrative of the novel. Compression involves cutting plot lines, removal of sub-plots, omitting events and characters, removal of psychological analysis of and by characters, conflating events and characters, transferring action to a smaller number of locations, simplifying language and cutting dialogue. Yet sometimes there is the need to add events and or dialogue to bridge narrative gaps.
>
> (39)

Simplification of language and dialogue was at the forefront of Evans' mind when adapting 'The Lady of the House of Love'. He concurs, 'the hardest thing was editing. Because as you know, [Carter's] so poetic. And she's *dense*' (2015: Line 74–5). The interviews conducted for this case study reveal that there were extensive conversations between all parties involved regarding word choices and the removal or reintroduction of Carter's finely crafted phrases. The decision was made to return more closely to Carter's words in the second development of *The Lady of the House of Love*. Evans advises, 'You've got to be very careful to keep the alchemy of *her* world and her words very much at the centre of what you're doing' (2015: Line 29–31). Fenton indicates that the process involved cycles of both compression and expansion of narrative content, recalling that in the second development, 'There was something about bringing gestures back, and bringing words back, and bringing images back' which at the same time 'reduced the work poetically, symbolically, as far as its narrative tendrils… that simply made a more cohesive work' (2013a: Line 83–87). We may also consider this to be what Balodis (2012: 39) refers to as distillation, as although some gestures, words and images were re-introduced, other characters, events and subplots were omitted in their entirety.

The exclusion of one character in particular, the 'crone', was mentioned by Colarelli and Fenton during interviews for this case study. The crone appears in Carter's short story and Colarelli describes her function in the original draft of the script as the Countess' 'nanny, her housekeeper, her maid, her handmaiden, her protector' (2015: Line 56–7). The choice to adapt the short story as a one-person show inherently placed certain limitations upon the representation of the characters. Colarelli speaks to the need he felt as the sole performer to inhabit each of the characters when he explains that, 'Once you mention her [the crone], you then have to kind of *be* her, become her… And so we actually took her out. Even of the story all together, because it then just complicated it a little bit too much' (2015: Line 54–9).

The creative team ultimately decided to resist the temptation to explore even more characters in the adaptation of *The Lady of the House of Love*. Fenton notes, 'of course there are other smaller characters in there, but we've *downplayed* them' (2013a: Line 128–9). At one point during earlier phases of script development the narrator was conceptualized as a bird-like character, and Evans envisaged a forest of rounded antique bird cages hanging at different levels to set the scene (Colarelli 2015: Line 68–75). This interpretation required additional dialogue to be written by Evans; however, Colarelli says, 'When we went from Dan [Evan]'s words into Angela Carter's words it was not a match. It was clearly two different voices that belonged to the one narrative that weren't gelling' (2015: Line 87–9). The role of the narrator was subsequently reimagined, and the language was stripped back to more closely resemble that of the short story.

Badham and Lutton developed specific techniques to reduce the text and distil the language of 'The Bloody Chamber' for stage. Lutton states that when Badham started drafting the script he realized, 'for every three adjectives Angela Carter uses we have to use one' and that this 'almost became a rule of thumb the rest of the time' (2014: Line 117–20). For Lutton it was important they pursued an active voice in the adaptation and reduced the text in such a way that it retains the 'baroqueness of language' (2014: Line 55) whilst being speakable for the actor. A prominent example is the transformation of Carter's opening line from the short story:

> I remember how, that night, I lay awake in the wagon – lit in a tender, delicious ecstasy of excitement, my burning cheek pressed against the impeccable linen of the pillow and the pounding of my heart mimicking that of the great pistons ceaselessly thrusting the train that bore me through the night, away from Paris, away from girlhood, away from the white, enclosed quietude of my mother's apartment, into the unguessable country of marriage.
>
> (Carter 1996: 131)

Badham reconfigures this sentence at the opening of the second scene of the theatrical script:

I'm in a sleeper carriage,
wide awake.
My burning cheek is
pressed into a linen pillow.
My heart mimics ceaseless pistons
thrusting me away from Paris,
away from girlhood,
away from the quietude of my mother's apartment –
into the unguessable country
… of marriage.

(2013: 7)

In this example, Badham stripped the majority of the adjectives from the source text and reformatted the sentence into sizeable parts to be fit for purpose as lines that exist in the mouth rather than the mind. While there has been a 42 per cent reduction in the number of words used, and descriptors such as 'tender', 'delicious' and 'impeccable' are excluded, the essence of the phrasing is maintained in the new arrangement. Lutton argues that, 'an actor can say one adjective and play it with the qualities of the other. They don't need all three or four… it was about reducing it into the most penetrating words' (2014: Line 122–36). In the aforementioned scene, actor Alison Whyte communicates her character's excitement through the increased tempo of her speech and movement pacing across the stage, although the phrase 'the ecstasy of excitement' has not been included in the spoken text. Badham demonstrates the boldness required to fulfil this brief when she explains, 'I worked out that I cut about 80% of the text, and half of the text in the actual show was my work and not hers. But written in such a way that if you weren't obsessed with the story and knew it word by word you wouldn't be able to tell' (2014: Line 55–8).

## Integration of music

The productions of *The Lady of the House of Love* and *The Bloody Chamber* both utilize live music in their adaptations of Carter's tales, although the music fulfils a different purpose in each of the productions. Carter's knowledge of music, particularly classical music, is apparent in her writing given the many references to composers and specific pieces of music. The protagonist in 'The Bloody Chamber' describes how she was 'lost in a Debussy prelude' when her suitor lay a bouquet on the keys of her piano (Carter 1996: Line 133). She later recalls their visit to the opera and how, 'my heart swelled and ached so during the *Liebestod* that I thought I must truly love him' (Carter 1996: 135), perhaps foreshadowing their own relationship's dire end. Carter's musical references summon the knowledge of the reader to convey not only the mood and emotions of her characters but layers to the narrative beyond the words on the page. The theatrical adaptations in this study resist the temptation to perform these pieces and instead incorporate original musical worlds of their own. In the production of *The Lady of the House of Love* the narrator interchanges between spoken text and song accompanied by a pianist, whereas *The Bloody Chamber* features a layering of atmospheric, haunting sound design, interspersed by percussion and melody from the three harpists on stage as Whyte's voice carves out the narrative.

In the production programme for *The Bloody Chamber*, Lutton discusses how their intention was to create 'a musical framework that could expand the aural tapestry of storytelling' and to 'conjure Carter's erotic and horrific symbols in the mind of a listener through words and sound' (Malthouse Theatre 2013, 3). Lutton elaborates in the interview for this study that as he never wanted to create Bluebeard's castle literally, the aura of the castle was represented through music and voice (2014: Line 40–1). In the performance of *The Lady of the House of Love*, the music serves a more narrative-based function with songs from the perspectives of the narrator, the Countess and the soldier. Evans therefore faced another challenge in his endeavour to honour the magnificence of Carter's writing: how to transition between spoken text and song lyrics? Evans states, 'I'd kind of keyed myself into her voice. If there was anything I needed to get us to a song, or get us out of a song. I would try and bleed my words with her words, and then towards the end I was really trying to adapt her voice to create the ending. And I think that worked' (2015: Line 130–3).

Composer Jacob Diefenbach penned the lyrics of the songs, which feature key words, phrases, events and themes from the original story. Carter's repeated phrase 'now you are at the place of annihilation, now you are at the place of annihilation' (1996: 232 and 245) is spoken as part of the scripted text in this adaptation of 'Lady of the House of Love'. The first of Diefenbach's songs for the performance, titled *The Place of Annihilation*, provides alternative wordings in the last three lines of the lyrics:

> *Now, is the time of annihilation*
> *Come to the place of annihilation*
> *Now is the time of – now is the time of – annihilation.*
>
> (Evans 2013: 2)

Diefanbach's rephrasing of Carter's sentence becomes an active beckoning that Colarelli utilizes in direct address to the audience to draw them in as the Countess would her prey. If Evans distils Carter's language, Diefanbach takes the process even further with his lyrics to express the essence of the story and shifts in mood through music.

Although the production of *The Bloody Chamber* did not include song lyrics, voice manipulation became a key device in the communication of character. This required careful orchestration by Badham as the writer, sound designer Jethro Woodward and composer David Chisholm. Whyte shifted between the character of The Wife to that of her husband Bluebeard through the aid of voice manipulation, whereby a system of microphones and amplification enabled her voice to drop two octaves. Badham explains how the physical limitations of the actor impacted the development of the script and she had to 'structure the text in such a way that it was speech by speech, not second by second' (2014: Line 95–7). The music composition by Chisholm subsequently 'had to not only enhance the tonality and work with the narrative, but also to create gaps and silences for Alison [Whyte] to rest her voice' (Line 98–100). Directorially 'it was a way to conjure without visualizing' the actor's transformation into Bluebeard, and Lutton describes this deliberate manipulation as a 'mask' that 'became part of that aural world' (2014: Line 211–17). Hence the sound design and music played a key role in supporting Whyte's characterizations, as distinctively suited to the performative mode of reception.

## Rich imagery – Physical and verbal languages

Carter's rich use of imagery in 'The Lady of the House of Love' takes life in the verbal and physical language of the adaptation. The minimalist set design, consisting of a bent-wood chair and an upright section of custom-made trellis constructed by Josh McIntosh (see Figures 13 & 14), provides a simple framework from which Colarelli entrances the audience. Fenton describes the set as impressionistic: 'It is the *impression* of a lattice. The lattice gives us the *impression* of a chateaux. The rose motif gives you an impression. And so it's both functional, but an impression. And that impression is enough for us to then create the rest of the world poetically, with just a chair' (2013a: Line 437–41). The physicality of Colarelli's performance draws upon key images or motifs from Carter's text and, true to the form of theatre, embodiment of the characters he portrays. As Ingham suggests, the adaptation of literature provides the opportunity for stories, 'to come vibrantly to life again on the stage in a multi-levelled totally theatrical experience combining physicality and presence with narrative, music, and spatio-temporal freedom in order to stimulate the mind and senses' (cited in Balodis 2012: 21).

**Figures 13 and 14** Production images from *The Lady of the House of Love* featuring Sandro Colarelli (Sean Young 2013).

Fenton identifies an explosion of light, blooming of a monstrous rose and a rectilinear image of the boy on the bicycle as prime examples of images from the source text that were represented in the performance (2013a: Line 348–51). The rose is particularly emblematic of the association between Carter's text and fairy tale Sleeping Beauty, and it features heavily in the script, song lyrics and physical action of this dramatic adaptation. Carter first mentions roses in the short story when describing the Countess' residence: 'This garden, an exceedingly sombre place, bears a strong resemblance to a burial ground and all the roses her dead mother planted have grown up into a huge, spiked wall that incarcerates her in the castle of her inheritance' (1996: 234). In the performance adaptation we witness Colarelli's arms weave through a thorn-like lattice work wall with the motif or *impression* of a rose as part of the design (see Figures 13 and 14). Fenton asserts, 'She has to be trapped. There has to be a barrier' and that the trellis and Colarelli's ability to 'act in, around and through' it fulfils this function (2013a: Line 403–10). Here we also see echoes of Carter's deconstruction of *The Sleeping Beauty*, in which the barriers Fenton refers to are the castle walls, moat and the 'supernatural ring that surrounds it, the protective nature connection' (Fenton 2013a: Line 723–5). The creative team have therefore transformed physical and poetic elements of the imagery in the story, and its deep-rooted intertextual references, to suit the dynamics of theatrical space and storytelling.

The imagery expressed in speech and song is as crucial to the adaptation of 'The Lady of the House of Love' as the physical representations through gesture, movement and design. Fenton points to the role of the audience in the meaning-making process when he explains, 'Fundamentally, this is a piece of textual storytelling, wherein we all create the world with him [Colarelli]. And we have to see all of those images. So the density of the poetry and the text has to be rested into and acknowledged' (2013a: Line 240–3). The word 'see' in this context implicates Colarelli's capacity as the performer to ignite the imagination of each audience member to visualize the text he delivers. The rose motif is 'seen' or experienced by the audience through the repeated phrase 'too many roses' (Evans 2013), in the lyrics of the song 'too many roses growing on the vine' (Diefenbach cited in Evans 2013), the impression of roses in the scenic design and Colarelli's supporting gestures. A multitude of images deemed to hold less significance to the narrative or unsuited to visual/physical representations on stage have either been cut during the process of adaptation or are communicated primarily via spoken or sung text. Colarelli's oral descriptions of the village and the chateaux are evocative and are arguably more effectively expressed verbally than through any other means in a theatrical context.

This adaptation of 'The Lady of the House of Love' expertly harnesses the symbolism of theatre and its capacity to imply, suggest or allude in the faith that the audience will, through their interpretation, complete what is presented. As Murphy elucidates in *Page to Stage: The Craft of Adaptation*:

> We let the theatre imply all the realistic environments that film depicts or fiction describes. We trust the audience to be as imaginative, intelligent and open-minded as the company creating the work. Although the adapter and collaborators must till the soil to seed a well-told story, the crops are harvested in the mind, emotions, and personal experience of each audience member.
>
> (2013: 79–80)

In the case of the adaptation of 'The Lady of the House of Love' the environments implied are not just realistic but *magical* realist. Theatre critic Sonny Clarke (2013) captures the effect of Colarelli's performance on the audience when he states, 'the story is not acted out but rather *vocalised* but it is so much more than that. Colarelli is a captivating minstrel who holds court with velvet-tongued tales of a far away time'. Clarke clearly communicates the success of the adaptation in its connection with the audience, but also its positioning outside the margins of dramatic realism.

Lutton's comments regarding *The Bloody Chamber* synchronize with Fenton's approach to tackling the rich imagery in Carter's tales as an 'impression' in dramatic space. Lutton aimed to create a space on stage that 'hoped that you could *imagine* the castle, you could *imagine* this room, you could imagine lilies, you could imagine mirrors. So that the suggestion is there, but we don't have to *do* it. And trying to find that middle space' (2014: Line 137–42). Here too Lutton carefully crafts the audience's experience of the imagery by taking advantage of their imaginations as a resource. He continues, 'you need to allow everything in [the production] to be incomplete so that the audience can meet it. If you show the image, and speak the image, and illustrate it with music, there's nothing left to do for an audience's imagination' (2014: Line 143–6). Lutton states that what he loves about working from prose is that you can look at a section and decide whether it wants to be spoken, explored visually or explored sonically (2014: Line 22–4). The resulting production expertly translates the narrative in a manner that deftly navigates between the potential of the scenic design, lighting, gesture, music, physical and verbal languages to bestow Carter's imagery upon the audience.

The visual language of the work was key to Lutton's vision for the adaptation from an early stage. Badham notes that Set and Costume

Designer Anna Cordlingley was brought on board particularly early as Lutton's process is to lock in the design idea before he starts directing, and because Cordlingley 'had the right sort of gothic and feminine aesthetic that really matches Carter; where you have this inversion of the feminine, and the pulpy feminine' (2014: Line 103–5). Carter's telling of the tale of Bluebeard's castle begins with the young bride on a train journey to her new husband's ominous abode. However, the intention to follow Carter's lead proved to be a stumbling block in the development of the theatrical work. According to Badham, Lutton 'deals in spectacle' directorially, and 'he was *convinced* that the opening image had to be the train. Had to be the train. Because that's how the story starts' (2014: Line 177–9). The desire to adhere to the chronology of the source text when adapting is not unusual; however, the team behind the production of *The Bloody Chamber* were able to surpass the restrictions of 'faithfulness' to better serve the medium at hand. Theorist Márta Minier endorses this kind of action, stating, 'Adapting something implies adjusting it, making it suitable for a certain receiving community, even if that involves the possibility of changes that break away from the "source text", while still fulfilling a duty of care towards it' (2014: 16). Similarly, Ilse Feinauer and Amanda Lorens (2017) describe processes of translation that aspire to strike 'a balance between loyalty to the source text author and to the target text readers' (97).

Badham calls the opening image they settled on for *The Bloody Chamber* 'the wedding dress', which is not *visually* the first image experienced by the audience but is the first image described by The Wife:

The wedding dress
– that he'd picked out –
Was delivered to me in a massive box
Wrapped in cellophane and red ribbon like a bag of Christmas fruit.
(Badham 2013: 2)

Whyte's entrance to deliver this opening address is preceded by a visual prologue that makes use of the mechanics of Cordlingley's set design. A pool of cool light fades up on a stained floor, and with a creaking sound a large black box or room stage right lifts up around half a meter to reveal the legs of the three musicians and their instruments starkly lit. The harpists play discordant, percussive noises as a young woman walks across the stage before disappearing into darkness upstage centre. A stage manager enters and operates a pulley system that lifts a second large black box upstage, and as it rises, we see the now bloodied feet of the young woman dangling from the bottom of the box, dripping red blood onto the ground. Lutton describes this as 'the image of a young woman being devoured; being eaten' (2014: Line 276–7), and although he says no one on the creative team ever thought they should show the contents of the chamber as 'the description of it will be more horrific' (2014: Line 181–2), this opening foreshadows the gory truth of the 'bloody chamber'. The production diverges from the chronology of the source text yet still, as Minier suggests, 'fulfils a duty of care towards it' (2014: 16) both in terms of capturing the essence of the events and the use of foreshadowing – a technique also used by Carter. In Carter's short story the dead wives are gradually revealed to Bluebeard's new wife; using a series of lighted matches she sees snapshots of the bodies and blood. Similarly, Lutton reveals the bodies of the musicians and the young woman one at a time.

The mechanisms to 'hide' parts of the stage space in the production of *The Bloody Chamber* echo the hidden corners of Bluebeard's vast castle, including the chamber itself. As the performance proceeds, a large industrial window is uncovered and a third black box is lifted stage left, unveiling the gothic marital bed. Some items such as the bed are physically present in the space, and others are described by Whyte, who indicates their imaginary placement with her gaze. Once again, the dynamics of presentation shift between what is seen and what is delivered via speech. The timing within the performance has undoubtedly been meticulously considered and is accentuated by moments that are almost devoid of content: pauses, silence, darkness – moments that are paradoxically poignant as they highlight the *absence of* something. The lighting design is characterized by darkness, Whyte's movement is characterized by stillness, the music is as discordant as it is lyrical. Each element encapsulates its antithesis. While Badham asserts that 'every line has got to be a playable action' (2014: Line 64), Whyte seldom duplicates the verbal text with her physical enactment. The reoccurring gestures in the performance are highly symbolic and include Whyte's hands clasping at her throat, and movement reminiscent of depictions of the Virgin Mary with arms outstretched by her sides and palms open. However, when Whyte delivers the lines implying The Wife's imminent decapitation by Bluebeard she is motionless, with Lutton's earlier direction of Whyte clutching at her neck imprinted in the mind's eye of the audience.

## Historical and cultural positioning of the work

Carter's ability to appropriate fairy tales, folklore, eighteenth-century gothic, romanticism, nineteenth-century fantasy, 'aesthetics of camp' (Gamble 1997: 66) and many other influences are examples of what Magali Cornier Michael describes as a 'postmodern strategy' (1996, 6). The multiplicity of these influences that spans centuries of art and history contributes to the unconventional or unsettled placement of her narratives in time. Colarelli (2015) and Fenton (2013a) agree that 'The Lady of the House of Love' is set pre–First World War around 1914 due to the references to the young soldier being summoned to France to join his regiment after the lady has met her death. As already established, the performance does not have a realistic or fully representative mise-en-scène, so the time period is indicated to a greater degree through the spoken text and song lyrics. 'Song Three: Racing into Springtime' introduces the character of the soldier and clearly indicates his positioning in history:

> One hot ripe spring, in the pubescent years of the last century, a young officer in the British army – blond, blue-eyed and heavy-muscled – visiting friends in Vienna, decided to spend the remainder of his vacation exploring the little-know uplands of Romania.
>
> (Diefanbach cited in Evans 2013)

Fenton notes that 'placing it in that period seems to say we're in a period of transition between two paradigms, two world views. And that's where the slipperiness happens. So this is the best place to deconstruct that into something that is not just modernist, it's a postmodern gesture that she's using' (2013a: Line 682–5). Evans similarly described feeling that it was 'a world on the edge of something' (2015: Line 332). However, this time period is only one thread in the complex, postmodernist tapestry of Carter's text, and subsequently the adaptation. Colarelli elaborates that Carter is 'able to layer these different times so it's *all* time; it's *now* and it's all time, weaved together. So even though it is set in a specific time… it's kind of like the equivalent of going into say, a home in England, which is maybe a medieval castle, which is being built on by subsequent generations' (2015: Line 479–84). Lutton and Badham did not directly discuss the time period of 'The Bloody Chamber', but relatedly Badham credits Carter with 're-narrativizing *ten thousand years* of literature in order to posit a feminist politic' (2014: Line 380–1).

## Relationship/balance between the characters

One of the primary considerations in adapting literature to the stage is how to represent the characters of the story, and in the case of the productions of *The Bloody Chamber* and *The Lady of the House of Love*, how to convey these characters with limited human resources. Both adaptations were influenced in their decision-making by financial constraints that impacted the number of actors they could employ. Colarelli notes that 'we decided budget-wise it was easier to do it as a one-person show and probably more interesting' (2015: Line 71–2). Malthouse Theatre's *The Bloody Chamber* is also driven by one lead performer, but with the support of a second actor, Shelly Lauman, who performs the roles of the young woman and the piano tuner Jean-Yves, as well as appearances by the assistant stage manager. Lutton clarifies, 'I thought that it was important to allow the show to feel like it's got one actor, and then for the one person in the narrative that releases her to be a second actor that suddenly joins' (2014: Line 280–2). Unable to afford the wages of a third actor to fulfil this role, Lauman was also cast as Jean-Yves (2014: Line 282–4). There were artistic reasons behind these decisions too: Badham explains the concept that any characters not played by Whyte as the lead actor were 'played by technicians in order to remind everybody that Alison is the centre of attention, and she is storytelling' (2014: Line 112–14). Unfortunately, this was not well received by critics, with Kate Herbert (2013) writing for the *Herald Sun* that the introduction of a second speaking actor was 'intrusive', and the technicians on stage made the production less impactful.

The storytelling technique of narration binds together the portrayal of characters in the performances of *The Bloody Chamber* and *The Lady of the House of Love*. The lead actors in each production embody multiple characters, a total of three apiece (see Figure 15), maintaining direct address to the audience with no changes in costume. While both performers narrate the stories, Colarelli does so from a third person perspective whereas Whyte narrates in first person alternating between past and present tense. In Badham's script for *The Bloody Chamber*, character names 'The Wife' and 'The Bride' are used to assist with the demarcation of the changes in tense. The Bride speaks in present tense and The Wife in past tense in order to represent the same woman at two different stages in her life: the young bride experiencing what occurs in Bluebeard's castle for the first time, and the now older women reflecting back and sharing this story. Colarelli's narration of

**The Lady of the House of Love**

| Character | Actor | Narrative Perspective | Tense |
|---|---|---|---|
| Narrator | Sandro Colarelli | Third Person – Subjective & Omniscient | Present & Past |
| The Countess | Sandro Colarelli | First Person | Present |
| The Soldier | Sandro Colarelli | First Person | Present |

**The Bloody Chamber**

| Character | Actor | Narrative Perspective | Tense |
|---|---|---|---|
| The Wife | Alison Whyte | First person | Past |
| The Bride | Alison Whyte | First person | Present |
| Bluebeard | Alison Whyte | First person | Present |
| Young Woman | Shelly Lauman | N/A – non-speaking role | N/A |
| Jean-Yves | Shelly Lauman | First person | Present |

**Figure 15** Tables of character analysis of *The Lady of the House of Love* and *The Bloody Chamber*.

*The Lady of the House of Love* more closely aligns with traditions of fairy tale, where use of non-personal voice is common.

## Representation of gender onstage

All of the performers in the stage adaptations of *The Bloody Chamber* and *The Lady of the House of Love* play male and female characters, with the storyteller in *The Lady of the House of Love* considered to be androgynous (Colarelli 2015: Line 94). Fenton comments with regards to *The Lady of the House of Love* that 'the *de*construction of the masculine and the feminine' strengthened as the physical representation developed with costuming (2013a: Line 174–6). Colarelli's costume is a postmodernist layering of historical and aesthetic influences featuring black lace, corsetry, Victorian-esque riding boots, jodhpurs, a silver-buttoned jacket, heavy gothic eye make-up and black-painted fingernails. The ensemble enables Colarelli to transition seamlessly between his triptych of roles as the narrator, the Countess and the soldier. Fenton states that 'you could follow the gender story up through his body' (2013a: Line 137), and according to Colarelli, 'each bit of the costume had an element of both male and female to it, which contributed to the subversiveness of the whole imagery' (2015: Line 110–11). Fenton (2013a) and Colarelli (2015) noted independently that the characterization was not intended to be viewed as drag but rather the aim was to achieve a sense of balance between the masculine and the feminine.

Whyte's union of roles as The Bride, The Wife and Bluebeard are less physically apparent than Colarelli's. As mentioned earlier in this chapter, Whyte achieves the portrayal of Bluebeard through voice manipulation and remains clothed in an elegant black full-length dress throughout the performance of *The Bloody Chamber*. Earlier in the process the creative team discussed the idea of physically representing Bluebeard onstage as a monstrous, dream-like figure of hair situated in the corner; however, 'it only became an image of shutting something down, as opposed to opening something out' (Lutton 2014). Lutton was keen for Whyte to 'embody all roles. And all genders. I think it was really important that it was a woman who could be a wolf and a lamb, to use Carter's imagery. [Who] can transform into both and has the potential for both within the body' (2014: Line 208–10). Badham speaks of the work's connection to the body in metaphorical terms, outlining how Carter has located a fairy tale that is about innocence to experience within the visceral maturation of the female body, the title 'The Bloody Chamber' being a reference to menstruation 'and the understanding of maturity' (2014: Line 315–22). Day asserts, 'Carter's tales go deeper than Perrault's kind of moralising about experience: they look at the way in which experience is fundamentally structured in gendered terms' (1998: 134). The depth of Carter's reflection on gendered experience appears to have provided an opportunity through adaptation that resists singularity of gender in the depictions on stage.

Fenton claims that the creative team for *The Lady of the House of Love* 'didn't really talk about the way [they] gendered the work' (2013a: Line 203–4) until the development in 2013 when there were more rigorous conversations concerning the positioning and identity of the narrator (2013a: Line 253–5). While it was recognized that the Countess and the soldier were two separate characters with a sense of balance between them with regard to the storytelling, themes and gender politics of the piece, the question remained, 'who is this *third* persona in the space?' (2013a: Line 274–7). They came to identify the narrator as another performative version of actor Sandro Colarelli: 'As a *persona* embedded in the work' (2013a: Line 267–8) with the effect of enabling Colarelli to form a more intimate, personalized connection with all of the characters he inhabits (2013a: Line 277–83).

Dialogue regarding the representation of gender and feminist politics in the production of *The Bloody Chamber* began at an earlier stage and was deeply ingrained in the process, although Badham (2014) emphasizes that there were tensions and barriers to understanding that had to be negotiated. She explains that 'communicating… what the semiotics of feminist representation are really about was an enormous part of the process' (2014: Line 268–70). The area of greatest contention was how to interpret the consummation of Bluebeard and The Bride's marriage, which Badham refers to as 'the rape scene'. Badham opposed the suggestion that there could be an element of arousal for The Bride in this section, arguing that an image of a woman on the line between violence and eroticism would participate in a narrative that goes against the text (2014: Line 192–8) and 'participates in a hostile depiction of women' (2014: Line 270–1). The resulting scene evidently benefited from these difficult conversations as Whyte chillingly rapes herself, her voice communicating as Bluebeard and her body reacting as The Bride. The problem solving by the entire artistic team, spurred by a refusal to compromise on the ethics of presentation, produced an exceptionally unique and complex response to the source text that creatively departs from the structure but reinscribes the feminist principles of Carter's telling.

## Conclusion

This case study has identified key issues in terms of the process of adapting Angela Carter's work for stage based upon interviews with creatives who were instrumental to Australian adaptations of Carter's short stories 'The Lady of the House of Love' and 'The Bloody Chamber', and viewings of the performances during their respective seasons at Metro Arts and Malthouse Theatre in 2013. The interviewees demonstrated that well-documented concerns pertaining to adaptation such as tensions between fidelity to the source text, authorial hierarchy and the need for medium specificity were accompanied by challenges more unique to Carter's prose. Playwrights Evans and Badham addressed the pyrotechnic quality of Carter's tales and her sensational, often complex use of language by paring it back to its essence. Both productions integrated original live music and vocal techniques with explicit narrative-based functions such as Colarelli's narration through song or composition that is more symbolically representative in the tapestry of storytelling in terms of the aura of Bluebeard's castle. Carter's incandescent imagery led to considered decision-making from the creative teams regarding the physical and verbal languages of the theatrical work and where to give space in what is seen or told for the audience's imagination to complete the picture. The postmodernist appropriation and layering of influences in Carter's tales imbued the historical and cultural positioning of the adaptations with a sense of timelessness or, in Fenton's words, 'a period of transition between two paradigms' (2013a: Line 682). Actors represented multiple characters onstage and a balance was sought in the physical delivery of their performance of these roles and the politics of the representation of gender. Given the continued interest by creative practitioners and fertile theatrical possibilities presented by Carter's work, the knowledge gained from this case study and the central concerns highlighted may serve as a practical tool for practitioners and as a basis for further research into theatrical adaptations of Carter's short stories.

# Works cited

'Angela Carter Show' (2019), *Bristol Post*, 15 January: 48. Available online: https://www.pressreader.com/uk/bristol-post/20190115/282127817641502 (accessed 3 September 2020).
Badham, V. (2013), [Playscript] *The Bloody Chamber*, Unpublished.
Badham, V. (2014), Personal Interview, interviewed by Belinda Locke, Unpublished.
Balodis, J.M. (2012), 'The Practice of Adaptation: Turning Fact and Fiction into Theatre', PhD diss., Queensland University of Technology: Brisbane. Available online: https://eprints-qut-edu-au.ezp01.library.qut.edu.au/60917/ (accessed 3 August 2013).
Carter, A. (1996), *Burning Your Boats: Collected Stories*, London: Vintage Books.
Clarke, S. (2013), Reviews: *The Lady of the House of Love*. Available online: https://aussietheatre.com.au/reviews/the-lady-of-the-house-of-love (accessed 3 August 2013).
Colarelli, S. (2015), Personal Interview, interviewed by Belinda Locke, Unpublished.
Crofts, C. (2003), *'Anagrams of Desire': Angela Carter's Writing for Radio, Film and Television*, Manchester: Manchester University Press.
Day, A. (1998), *Angela Carter: The Rational Glass*, Manchester: Manchester University Press.
Evans, D. (2013) [Playscript], *The Lady of the House of Love*, Unpublished.
Evans, D. (2015), Personal Interview, interviewed by Belinda Locke, Unpublished.
Feinauer, I and A. Lorens (2017), 'The Loyalty of the Literary Reviser: Author, Source Text, Target Text or Reader?' *Linguistics Plus*, 53: 97–118. Available online: https://api.semanticscholar.org/CorpusID:158776567 (accessed 14 September 2020).
Fenton, D. (2013a), Personal Interview, interviewed by Belinda Locke, Unpublished.

Gamble, S. (1997), *Angela Carter: Writing from the Front Line*, Edinburgh: Edinburgh University Press.

Gruss, S. (2014), 'Angela Carter's Excessive Stagings of the Canon: Psychoanalytic Closets, Hermaphroditic Dreams and Jacobean Westerns', in S. Andermahr and L. Phillips (eds), *Angela Carter: New Critical Perspectives*, 54–66, London: Bloomsbury. Available online: http://ebookcentral.proquest.com/lib/qut/reader.action?docID=1014740&ppg=54 (accessed 19 July 2017).

Herbert, K. (2013), 'Theatre Review: *The Bloody Chamber*, Malthouse Theatre', *Herald Sun*, 7 August. Available online: http://www.heraldsun.com.au/entertainment/arts/theatre-review-the-bloody-chamber-malthouse-theatre/news-story/d7c94d4fb61bc4128e512950a1f017d0 (accessed 10 August 2013).

Kellaway, K. (2018), 'Interview Emma Rice: "I Don't Know How I Got to Be so Controversial"', *The Observer*, 1 July. Available online: https://www.theguardian.com/stage/2018/jul/01/emma-rice-controversial-shakespeares-globe-wise-children (accessed 3 September 2020).

Lee, A. (1997), *Angela Carter*, New York: Twayne Publishers.

Lutton, M. (2014), Personal Interview, interviewed by Belinda Locke, Unpublished.

Malthouse Theatre (2013), [Theatre program] *The Bloody Chamber*, Melbourne: Malthouse Theatre.

Michael, M. C. (1996), *Feminism and the Postmodern Impulse: Post-World War II Fiction*, Albany: State University of New York Press.

Minier, M. (2014), 'Definitions, Dyads, Triads and Other Points of Connection', in K. Krebs (ed), *Translation and Adaptation in Theatre and Film*, 13–35. Available online: https://www-taylorfrancis-com.ezp01.library.qut.edu.au/books/e/9781134114108 (accessed 12 May 2017).

Murphy, V. (2013), 'Building Block Four: Choose an Evocative Stageable Image', *Page to Stage: The Craft of Adaptation*, 75–89. Ann Arbor: University of Michigan Press. Available online: www.jstor.org/stable/10.3998/mpub.4353160.8 (accessed 20 November 2016).

Peach, L. (2009), *Angela Carter*, 2nd edn, New York: Palgrave Macmillan.

Stan, R. (2000), 'Beyond Fidelity: The Dialogics of Adaptation', in J. Naremore (ed), *Film Adaptation*, 54–76, New Brunswick: Rutgers University Press.

Stoddart, H. (2007), *Angela Carter's Nights at the Circus*, Oxon and New York: Routledge.

Taylor, T. (2005), *Nights at the Circus Teacher's Resource Pack*, London: Kneehigh Theatre. Available online: www.kneehigh.co.uk/userfiles/files/Nights%20circus_Ed%20Pack1.pdf (accessed 10 August 2013).

*The Bloody Chamber* (2013), [Theatre production] Malthouse Theatre, 3 August.

*The Lady of the House of Love* (2013), [Theatre production] Metro Arts, 1 August.

Tonkin, M. (2019), 'The Rough and the Holy: Angela Carter's Marionette Theatre', in M. Mulvey-Roberts (ed), *The Arts of Angela Carter: A Cabinet of Curiosities*, 246–62, Manchester: Manchester University Press.

7

# 'What then?' Apocalypticism and Angela Carter's surrealist esthetics

Scott A. Dimovitz

> *Yet somehow the hideous poetry of the* terminal nature *of nuclear warfare can exist almost in a dimension of its own.*
> (Angela Carter, 'Anger in a Black Landscape' 1997: 45)

In his classic 1935 analysis of modernist aesthetics, 'The Work of Art in the Age of Mechanical Reproduction', Walter Benjamin claimed that humanity's 'self-alienation has reached such a degree that it can experience its own destruction as aesthetic pleasure of the first order' (2003: 527). Clearly, disaster narratives evoke a certain paradoxical pleasure, as the nearly 16 million viewers of *The Walking Dead*'s season 5 finale would attest. From the beginning of her writing career, Angela Carter's fiction played with the 'hideous poetry' of this alienated pleasure even while she personally feared the growing possibility of a literal annihilation of the planet from a nuclear war. This use of pyrotechnically apocalyptic motifs as allegorical symbol systems would continue through most of her work, most directly in her 1969 post-nuclear war allegory, *Heroes and Villains*, although they changed in form and function at a transformative moment in her career. Around 1970, Carter began the triad of novels that make up what she initially referred to in her journals as the *Manifesto for Year One* (1969-1974: Add MS 88899/1/93). These novels would eventually become *The Infernal Desire Machines of Doctor Hoffman*, *The Passion of New Eve* and *Nights at the Circus*, and they employ an almost sadistic pleasure in imagining and depicting destruction with a strikingly visual symbolic vocabulary that she developed partly from Freud and partly from the surrealist artists who dominated her thinking in her twenties and thirties.

Surrealist art significantly informed Carter's apocalypticism. In a 1978 essay about surrealism that she wrote for *Harper's and Queen*, 'The Alchemy of the Word', Carter gave a critical background of the movement as context for those seeing an exhibit at London's Hayward Gallery, called 'Dada and Surrealism Reviewed'. In this essay, she discussed the apocalyptic tone she saw everywhere in early surrealist art, explaining that a 'premonition of the imminent end of the world is always a shot in the arm for the arts; if the world has, in fact, just ended, what then?' (1997: 507). This essay examines how Angela Carter's aesthetics merged her deep interest in surrealism and psychoanalysis with an uneasy interest in the apocalyptic themes and motifs of postmodern fragmentation. At first, this approach suggests an early alliance with a Dadaist aesthetic that may seem to have celebrated annihilation (of patriarchy, of institutional power, of signification) as an end in itself. Yet Carter's works always had its allegiance towards transformation of what she saw as the patriarchal order of the capitalist West. For Carter, as with the surrealists' break with the Dadaists, this transformation always served as 'the creative negation of destruction', because nihilism 'can never be an end in itself' (1997: 511). In Carter's surrealistic novels of the End, the apocalypse always points to a hope for a new world order – a demythologized socialist world of gendered equals, who face each other in a wild surmise.[1]

In her 1983 essay, 'Anger in a Black Landscape', Carter traces her darkly satirical destruction narratives to her being a 'child of the nuclear age', and thereby 'a child of irony and the absurd; of black humour, of guilt and of anger' (1997: 44). This ironic and satiric attitude functioned as a mechanism to cope with the deep existential fear of annihilation that she inherited from the postwar zeitgeist, and also to cope with personal fears that stemmed from her upbringing. In Edmund Gordon's biography, one of Carter's relatives recalled her various phobias and obsessions in her youth, suggesting that she 'worried fervently about illness and – not unreasonably in the context of the Cold War – nuclear catastrophe' (2016: 20). Later, Carter sublimated this childhood fear in a positive direction by protesting with resistance movements during the early years of her marriage to her first husband, when she participated rather heavily with the Campaign for Nuclear Disarmament (CND). Yet even in her journals, the gallows humour prevails, and she cannot help but ironically thinking of writing 'a CND novel' called *And Tomorrow's Doomsday*, which would end as 'a black joke', with a '4-minute warning in [Trafalgar] Square one Easter Day' (Gordon 2016: 46).

Carter's apocalypses incubated not from piety, as she was an atheist from a rather young age, but from more philosophically materialistic concerns of existential threat. This points to an apparently contradictory feature of Carter's atheistic apocalypticism, which was not inherently eschatological – exploring the traditional theological doctrines of the four Last Things: Death, Judgment, Heaven and Hell; rather, it functions as a moment of the self or society's fundamental structural transformation. These concerns paralleled those of the postmodern science fiction writings of J. G. Ballard, whose works, including his first four disaster novels, greatly influenced Carter in the 1960s. In Ballard's *The Drowned World*, for example, set in 2145 in a post-apocalyptic future, the heating of the planet has regressively led to a flooded age, where time slows to the pulses of a neo-Triassic rhythm, outside of humans and their civilizations. Unlike the case of *The Drowned World*'s protagonist, Dr. Robert Kerans, who regresses to a pre-civilized consciousness that rejects the thin patina of civilization for an atavistic state of being, Carter's use of apocalyptic motifs does not embrace or acquiescence to the coming catastrophe, nor does it elegiacally depict the world's devolution. Like many postmodern apocalyptic narratives, Carter's works figure the rupture not as prefiguring an eschatological Rapture but rather as a cataclysmic transformation of society, thereby highlighting a beginning that reshapes and inverts the temporal trajectory of popular fantasies of the End Times into parables about the origin of the (always new) beginning.

This seemingly paradoxical relation to time actually more closely reflects the forms of apocalypse in the biblical prophetic traditions. As Elizabeth Rosen (2008) argues, the original function of apocalyptic narratives, from Old Testament prophecies such as Isaiah and Daniel, to the New Testament vision in John of Patmos's Revelation, was not to depict the ultimate End, but to give hope to then currently suffering Hebrews and later Jewish proto-Christians that their suffering would end soon and their oppressors would perish. People sometimes forget that for all the surreal fire and brimstone imagery, even the Book of Revelation does not depict complete annihilation. As Elaine Pagels reminds us, John of Patmos's 'vision' allegorically depicts the final triumph over the Roman empire at the battle at Armageddon, which will destroy those who currently oppressed the implied audience, imprisoning Satan for a thousand years before the final battle, after which Yahweh would establish a New Jerusalem on earth (2012: 1–35).[2] Rosen sees this hope for the saved as the true importance of apocalypse, and not the complete obliteration of the whole of humanity. Rosen terms these ultimate disaster narratives 'neo-apocalyptic' literature, which 'is a literature of pessimism' that 'functions as a cautionary tale, positing potential means of extinction and predicting the gloomy probability of such ends' (2008: xv). Such neo-apocalyptic literature has several functions, and they usually are sadistically or masochistically hortatory, warning audiences that they are about to get what they deserve.

This slippage in genre definition affects most theorizations about how these narratives work and why. In his 1984 essay on the threat of nuclear war, 'No Apocalypse. Not Now', Jacques Derrida makes the claim that by definition, the apocalypse can never be *now*, as an apocalypse entails the irreversible destruction of humanity. For Derrida, the apocalypse serves as a metaphor for the centre, the 'absolute referent, the horizon and condition of all the others' (1984: 30); it is the perpetual endpoint beyond the act of communication, of being, which by definition cannot not be decoded. Therefore, it can never exist, as such. The apocalypse exists only in the realm of discourse before catastrophe, and is, therefore, 'fabulously textual' (1984: 23). Derrida here puns on the idea that these textual apocalypses are necessarily *fabulations*, existing in a fantasy realm of speculation that can have no real-world referent. From this point of view, the pleasures of the apocalypse, therefore, are inherently the pleasures of speculation and fabulation – the pleasures of narrative possibility, plurality and plentitude. To luxuriate in the possibilities of humanity's destruction is to delight in narrative construction. This pleasure operates both on the side of the artist's constructing ever more elaborate Rube Goldberg fantasies of our annihilation but also on the prophylactic fantasies of narrative anticipation: Just how is *this* nuclear annihilation novel going to depict the cause of our obliteration?

*Heroes and Villains*, published in 1969, is Carter's one truly post-apocalyptic novel, and it begins Carter's process of fabulous textualization. The novel arose, in part, out of her ecstatic engagement with the works of both J. G. Ballard and Michael Moorcock, whose editorship of *New Worlds* magazine in the mid-1960s helped Carter to jettison her anxieties about embracing speculative fiction as her primary aesthetic approach, although she still hedged at embracing purely surrealist apocalyptic ontologies. As Anna Watz (2017), Katie Garner (2012), and others have explored, Carter began using surrealist imagery in her first novel, *Shadow Dance* (1966). The novel's apocalyptic tone, however, comes through in metaphor and fantasy, such as when Morris Grey sadistically fantasizes about a 'second deluge' that would come and make him a second Noah, 'resolutely pushing underwater the swimming faces imploring him to take them aboard' ([1966] 1996: 79). Similarly, *The Magic Toyshop*'s Melanie imagines that her new life takes place 'in an empty space at the end of the world', under the oppressive control of Uncle Philip, 'the Beast of the Apocalypse' ([1969] 1993: 77). In these early texts, Carter avoided fully disrupting a diegetic naturalism to present a completely surreal world that violated the laws of physics, one that merged 'dream and reality, which are seemingly so contradictory, into a kind of absolute reality, a surreality' ([1924] 1969: 14), as Andre Breton described it in *The Manifesto of Surrealism* ([1924] 1969).

In *Heroes and Villains*, the post-apocalyptic world still exists in the real. Sixteen-year-old Marianne grows up in a white tower in the stiflingly enclosed world of the Soldiers, Workers and Professors, who barely survived a worldwide nuclear war.[3] Outside Marianne's small, heavily guarded society roam the Out People, a group of deformed and devolved monsters, and the Barbarians, a slightly more organized series of nomadic tribes. One of these tribes is led by a former professor, Donally, who has plans to groom a young Barbarian, Jewel Lee Bradley, into an embodiment of myth to rule his people. Donally prepares for this mystification by studying an array of anthropological sources – Claude Lévi-Strauss, among others – and by a cross-cultural study of world myths, including those of the Bible. The narrator and other characters constantly describe Jewel in terms of a prelapsarian state of humanity, and the narrator once bluntly states that he looked like 'an Antediluvian king or a pre-Adamite sultan' ([1969] 1993: 71). Donally has encouraged this mythologizing, and as part of his plan he has literally inscribed Jewel with a full-back tattoo of Eve offering the Fruit of the Tree of Knowledge of Good and Evil to Adam. As Donally pedantically explains, 'Tattooing is the first of the post-apocalyptic arts' ([1969] 1993: 125), and his artwork freezes the world in an ahistorical pastoral. Static temporality in Carter's work usually points to a mythic mystification that reinforces patriarchal power, and this stasis operates both inside and outside the Professors' walls: 'If time was frozen among the Professors, here she lost the very idea of time, for the Barbarians did not segment their existence into hours nor even morning, afternoon and evening but left it raw in the original shapes of light and darkness so the day was a featureless block of action and night of oblivion' ([1969] 1993: 41). Jewel parallels Adam, yet this world is hardly as simple as that depicted in the book of Genesis.

In a 1984 interview with John Haffenden, Carter claimed that she used this wilderness of the 'pre-Adamite' worlds in *Heroes and Villains* and *Nights at the Circus* to 'get characters into [a space] where they could discuss things' (1984: 95), and part of what they discuss and embody is how the apocalypse might disrupt industrialized patriarchy. What the novel depicts portends an ominous outcome. Jewel's violent murders and his unceremonious rape of Marianne certainly problematize any fetishization of Jean-Jacques Rousseau's 'noble savagery.'[4] As Carter explained to Haffenden, '*Heroes and Villains* is a discussion of the theories of Jean-Jacques Rousseau, and strangely enough it finds them wanting' (1984: 95). That Carter would not approve of Rousseau is evident from a very young age. In a journal entry from when she was 21, Carter refuted an unnamed debater: 'Why do they talk so much crap about innocence? As if lack of knowledge could ever be a good thing? I hate innocence' (1960: Add MS 88899/1/100), a point she emphasized in an interview in the 1970s, 'Eden is always evil… states of grace always are' (Gordon 2016: 32). For Carter, Rousseau's ideals were, in fact, incredibly dangerous.

Carter's apocalypticism, therefore, partly arose, like Ballard's, out of a critique of this popular Rousseauian branch of postwar nuclear apocalypses from the fifties and sixties. She described these narratives as 'post-apocalyptic novels as a sort of pastoral' (Haffenden 1985: 95) that depicted, as she stated in a later essay, 'the blissfully anarchic, tribal lives the lucky fifteen million survivors' who will 'lead in a Britain miraculously free of corpses, in which the Man with the Biggest Shot-Gun holes up in some barbed-wire enclave and picks off all comers' (1997: 44). *Heroes and Villains* shows the dark side of this pastoral, yet also critiques apocalyptic literatures that saw the development of the capability of nuclear warfare as an index of our essential fallenness. 'The Bomb', she wrote in 1983, had become 'a very potent, perhaps the most potent, symbol of Original Sin' (1997: 45), where social destruction is the fruit of the tree of knowledge of good and evil, casting humanity from the Garden into the temporal cycle of pain, suffering and death. Carter believed that these narratives erroneously embraced a view of humanity as a priori Fallen, thereby leading them masochistically to embrace civilization's destruction in the hopes of a return to 'innocence'. For Carter, such a state would push humanity into a timeless zone that destroyed an active engagement with the real historical world, always anathema to her staunch socialist worldview.

Carter's work undoes this symbolism by incorporating extraordinarily violent imagery in order to disrupt such complacent fantasies of a nostalgic pastoral. *Heroes and Villains* begins with such a world, where Professors surviving a nuclear holocaust hide from the primitive Barbarian others in a walled-in space the novel describes as a 'secluded place where a pastoral quiet possessed everything' ([1969] 1993: 1) – all before Marianne escapes with the Barbarian Jewel to her ultimate fate. In the end, after Jewel's death, Marianne suggests that she may assume power over the Barbarians and embody a symbolic 'tiger lady' archetype who will 'rule them with a rod of iron' ([1969] 1993: 150) – an identification with the phallic aggressor that will invert power relations among genders, yet will perpetuate the system's structure.[5] In a letter to a friend from the 1980s, she looks back on that ending as pointing to the beginning of a communist revolution, equating Marianne with the Chairman of the Communist Party and Paramount leader of China (and Mao Zedong's wife); Jewel is dead, she claimed, so Marianne 'can get on with her real task of becoming the Chiang Ching of the post-holocaust world' (no date: Add MS 88899/1/85). The evidence, however, of the final descent into primal patriarchal power relations outside of the strict, but tedious, world of the Soldiers and Professors, suggests Carter's early anxiety over losing the thin line between civilization, with all its discontents, and a primitive world of sheer male aggression.

Soon after the publication of *Heroes and Villains*, Carter left her husband and lived in Japan, which she saw as an overt patriarchal culture that laid bare the gender relations she had intuited back in England. She became radicalized, and her aesthetics merged her interest in surrealism with the real historical events that surrounded her. Surrealist apocalypticism became the best mode to explore what felt like 'Year One' – her recurring phrase in her journals and her journalism, along with the next three novels, for the state of the world after a socialist revolution would overthrow both patriarchy and its related capitalist economic system. She awaited this destructive transformation with great excitement. Gordon recounts an undated letter she wrote to Carole Roffe around this time, in which Carter describes her rapturous feelings that the patriarchal End Times were nigh when news reached her of terror campaigns by 'the Provisional IRA, the anarchist Angry Brigade, the Palestinian group Black September': 'This feverish, hysterical feeling of being In At The End is very exhilarating' except one doesn't know how if one is going to survive. 'I really do feel excited, this is history and one is living right in it', she wrote, while entertaining 'the most apocalyptic fantasies' (Gordon 2016). In another letter in 1972, she parenthetically embraced *The Omega Man*, Boris Sagal's 1971 film adaptation of Richard Matheson novel, *I Am Legend*: 'Saw THE OMEGA MAN the other night; made me v. exhilarated. Mankind is indeed in love with apocalypses!' (Add MS 89102/2/2). This glee at the possibilities of transformation by way of destruction partly derives from what she described in her journals as her 'anal-sadism', Freud's term for the group of personality traits that include a desire for control, aggressiveness, destructiveness and rage at others – both literal and metaphorical (see Dimovitz 2016: 23–48). This sadistic tendency crosses into her aesthetics, and she would even later characterize her early novels as a form of authorial sadism over the reader, with which, she told Les Bedford, she attempted to 'seduce, and perhaps to rape, my readers' (in Gamble 2006: 142). Even this quote demonstrates the very anal sadistic need to shock her audience with imagery she knew would make them uncomfortable.

While the early novels used apocalyptic and surrealist imagery and metaphors, 1972's *The Infernal Desire Machines of Doctor Hoffman* is the first novel that breaks the laws of physics into a fully surrealist post-apocalyptic space that merged dream and reality. The novel technically depicts a dystopia, since no apocalyptic event transforms Desiderio's world into the highly structured society that the novel wants to disrupt. Hoffman, the scientist who develops machines that can concretize the unconscious dreams of the city's inhabitants, embodies several prominent surrealists, especially Andre Breton, who was, for Carter, 'the Pope of surrealism, its theoretician, propagandist, and mage' (1997: 510). She underscored this connection often by using phrases from *The Infernal Desire Machines of Doctor Hoffman* in interviews and essays, such as saying that surrealism described 'a world transformed by imagination and desire', creating a world which was 'the dream made flesh' ([1972] 1994: 509). This latter phrase was Desiderio's exact term for Albertina, the Doctor's hermaphroditic offspring and ultimate creation, and when Desiderio murders both Hoffman and Albertina in the end, the novel implies a rejection of all that the Doctor symbolized in terms of the surrealist movement. The surrealist *aesthetic*, however, drives the entire endeavour, and the novel suggests more a rejection of a certain kind of surrealism – the masculine-dominated version that would not allow her own version of what she described in a letter as a 'feminist libertarian aesthetic'.[6] As Carter described this feeling of alienation from the surrealist tradition: 'I knew I wanted my fair share of the imagination, too. Not an excessive amount, mind; I wasn't greedy. Just an equal share in the right of vision' (1997: 512).

Carter's attempt to appropriate the surrealist aesthetic for feminist ends continued through her next two novels, and the apocalyptic unease permeated her worldview. By around 1975, during the time she was writing *The Passion of New Eve*, her anxiety about the possibility of nuclear warfare shifted from fearful hypothesis to resigned inevitability. In a handwritten manuscript from 1975, 'The Story that needs Re-writing', she reviewed a novel by the British New Wave science fiction writer, Josephine Saxton. In a footnote, she writes that thermonuclear weapons offered 'a great gift to science fiction, because, though we can guess, we do not really know what might happen were their fury to be unleashed' (1964–1992: Add MS 88899/1/62-68: 13). She scribbled over the next part of the manuscript, perhaps from a later time: '(I think it will be, actually, in about five or ten years time; this isn't pessimism, it's economics. The only thing that pulled capitalism out of its last doldrums in the 30s was a world war.) When the unemployment figures top the five million mark'. The paragraph ends ominously in mid-sentence. While she later undoes this prediction by scribbling over the passage, it does seem that she resigned herself at this point to humanity's inevitable self-destruction as a function of economic causality – a despondent Marxist's vision of apocalypse as a perhaps unforeseen final stage of dialectical materialism.

The surreal quasi-apocalyptic imagery of 1977's *The Passion of New Eve* arose partly from this resigned anticipation and partly from a Greyhound bus trip across America that she made in 1969, which she claimed gave her the imagery in only a slightly less exaggerated form. She drew, for example, the imagery of Mother's synthetic desert womb-world and Zero's ranch from the desolation she saw throughout the American West. As she recounted in her 1977 essay, 'That Arizona Home', the only life she saw was 'an old, lean dog nosing in the garbage' and 'an Indian child chucking stones at a wrecked Chevvy [*sic*] with a certain indifferent, apathetic hostility' (1997: 275). She recalled the failed Ghost Dance movement of the Native Americans, saying that the 'Apocalyptic religions had let them down' (1997: 275) and the landscape became a metaphor for, among other things, the death throes of capitalism and Western patriarchy (along with the Native American culture that this patriarchy had all-but-obliterated). Carter's transformation of this desolation into the gleeful delirium of the revolutionary apocalypse comes through more strongly in an early draft of *The Passion of New Eve*, in which an earthquake strikes, as Lilith describes it to Eve, setting in motion a chain of catastrophes, none of which make it to the final draft:

> the world presented an entirely altered picture… a piece of its face had fallen off, taking with it homes, surf-boards, power installations, rocket sites, automobiles, hamburger stands, men, women, children & dogs, trees, flowers, restoring swimming pools & reservoirs to a fundamental connection with water & setting off a chain reaction of nuclear explosions in missile [bases] all over the continent which had activated all the early warning systems, woken the delicately sleeping missiles in the plains of Central Asia & the ice-flos [*sic*] of the Arctic Circle, provoked a global nuclear holocaust that lasted 10 minutes & had brought down the phallic towers forever.
>
> (1973: Add MS 88899/1/5: 100)

This much clearer nuclear cataclysm creates another Year One, 'the first day of the first year', yet unlike *Heroes and Villains*' nuclear war, this war has crossed into surrealist metaphor. Lilith describes the events of this Year One as 'Orgasmic annihilation' (1973: Add MS 88899/1/5: 100), which sounds far closer to *The Infernal Desire Machines of Doctor Hoffman*'s Albertina than to the eventual character that Lilith becomes in the final published work, in which the civil wars in California lead to a demythologized transformation, but a far more ambivalently psychological one.

One of the major differences between *The Infernal Desire Machines of Doctor Hoffman* and *The Passion of New Eve* is the change of tone in the conclusion. *Hoffman* ends with the pyrrhic triumph of desireless reason over surrealist ideals; *The Passion of New Eve*, in contrast, has a sense of hope that human nature may change. In her 1972 journal, when she still referred to the novel as *The Great Hermaphrodite*, she called it a form of 'surrealist sociology' and described how she planned to end it 'on a note of, however bizarre, affirmation...' (1969–1974: Add MS 88899/1/93). America served as a potent critique of a kind of imperialist nostalgia for the passing of a capitalist patriarchy. In a letter to Carole Roffe in 1972, Carter wondered about what she called the 'New American Spiritual Apocalypse', which she speculated may have arisen as a 'reaction against the horrid realisation that, inch by hazardous inch, more & more of the world is embracing intransigent Marxian materialism day by day' (Add MS 89102/2/2) – an embrace she would have wholeheartedly endorsed.

Carter used apocalyptic science fiction as a way to explore this hope instead of other genres because science fiction had the unique potential to explore the possibilities of transformation. In another unpublished manuscript on Josephine Saxton's work, 'Addenda: to [*sic*] The Story that needs Re-writing', Carter critiques William Burroughs's appropriation of science fiction forms, since he predominantly wrote satire, a form she equates with traditional pornography, which assumes that 'whatever else changes, human nature will not do so' (1964–1992: Add MS 88899/1/62-68: 1–2). The science fiction writer, in contrast, 'accepts the theory that circumstances change human nature or, which is the same thing, that human nature modifies under changing circumstances' (1964–1992: Add MS 88899/1/62-68: 1–2). Satire and pornography rely on the immutability of human folly and sexuality, respectively, but speculative fiction – especially in the apocalyptic forms that *The Passion of New Eve* employs – can make the case that by changing our circumstances, we can change who we are. Unlike the anxiety expressed in the world of *Heroes and Villains*, Year One becomes entirely hopeful, even if what the world will look like after the apocalypse is never depicted in the text.

By 1984, Carter told Haffenden that she would no longer dream of setting a novel after a nuclear catastrophe, suggesting that 'it would be too much like tempting providence' (1984: 95), yet this gets her to the horns of her dilemma. On the one hand, people should not use the bomb for simplistic pastoral fantasies; paradoxically, the apocalyptically surrealist imagery of *The Manifesto for Year One* triad of novels provided her most effective mode of disrupting patriarchy.

What aesthetic was left for this disruption? Unsurprisingly, perhaps, this claim came on the eve of the publication of her great comic novel, *Nights at the Circus*, which revisits the surrealist imagery and ontology of the previous two novels, but with a much more tempered apocalyptic imagery in the scenes with Buffo and the Clowns of Chaos. The clowns dance 'the dance of Old Adam' (1984: 243), Carter's recurring term for the Oedipal structure of patriarchy and its arbitrarily nihilistic foundation, and thereby wipe themselves off the face of the earth in much the same way as *The Infernal Desire Machines of Doctor Hoffman's* Acrobats of Desire do. Patriarchy autodestructs, leaving the heroes to wander in Siberia before settling on the Year One of an apparently conventional heterosexual relationship (if 'conventional' can be used when one of the partners has wings), yet one in which there is an implied demythologized equality of the sexes.

For most of Carter's writing, surrealist apocalypticism served as the very condition for the symbolic rejection of the capitalist patriarchal system, leaving her characters in the rubble of Year One, pondering the question every socialist fantasized about the future: 'if the world has, in fact, just ended, what then?' Ironically enough, her apocalyptic surrealist works never quite answer this question. Instead, her novels often end with imagery drawn from Milton's *Paradise Lost*, right on the cusp of Adam and Eve's expulsion from the Garden. From *The Magic Toyshop*'s Melanie and Finn, who hold hands in a garden and face 'each other in a wild surmise' ([1967] 1996: 200); to *Heroes and Villains*' Marianne, whom Jewel sarcastically suggests should play 'Eve at the end of the world' ([1969] 1993: 46);[7] to *Love* (1971), which she sometimes referred to as *The Gates of Paradise* (Gordon 2016: 168); to *The Passion of New Eve*'s protagonist in a boat, sailing off to the amniotic sea; Carter ends her narratives with characters cast from the Garden, east of Eden, with the world all before them, yet never quite depicts what that world would look like. This leaves Carter's works in a quandary. In *Angela Carter: Writing from the Front Line*, Sarah Gamble underscores 'the danger' her works run 'in engaging in this process of deconstruction, for at the other end of change lies… what?' (2005: 69). Perhaps she did not bother to depict the socialist vision of society she had hoped for in her journals, essays and letters because such an imagining would make for rather dull stories, which usually depend on conflict. Ironically, this would seem to be opposite of what she thought she was doing. In a letter to Lorna Sage, after claiming that she continued to hope for the 'red dawn' to 'break over Clapham', Carter added that she was 'more interested in socialist reconstruction after the revolution than the revolution itself, which seems to mark me out from my peers' (1994: 22–3). Yet while Carter may have been interested in what the reconstruction might look like, her novels were not. Apocalypticism only pointed to the hopeful future, and beyond that, the novels that made up the exuberantly pyrotechnic and surreal worlds of *The Manifesto for Year One* remained silent.

## Notes

1. I here paraphrase the last line from *The Magic Toyshop*, after Melanie and Finn have escaped Uncle Phillip's flaming house: 'At night, in the garden, they faced each other in a wild surmise.' The novel's line references Keats's 1860 poem, 'On First Looking into Chapman's Homer', where an explorer's subordinates did not share his actual vision, even though they will be transformed by what he sees: 'and all his men / Look'd at each other with a wild surmise' (1970: 12–13). This seems to me an apt metaphor for Carter's apocalyptic fiction's characters at the end of their stories.
2. For this reason, D. H. Lawrence argues in his little-read and posthumously published 1931 work, *Apocalypse*, that all of Revelation was born of what Nietzsche, in *On the Genealogy of Morality* ([1887] 2006), referred to as *ressentiment* – a deep-seated resentment by an individual or an entire culture that is accompanied by a profound feeling of powerlessness, which leads to fantasies of vengeance against the dominant culture in the form of immediate annihilation ([1887] 2006: 20–2).
3. Heidi Yeandle sees *Heroes and Villains* as a critique of the superfluity of the Professors' knowledge, although she rightly notes that this portrayal ironically contradicts Carter's entire erudite worldview (2016: 72).
4. 'Noble savage' is a term that, as Heidi Yeandle has reminded us, does not actually appear in Rousseau's writings (2016: 62–3), although it has become synonymous with his philosophy. For more on the novel's critique of Rousseau, see Eva Karpinski (2000: 139–40).
5. See also Hope Jennings (2008: 72–3) and Geraldine Meaney (2000: 96).
6. Anna Watz (2017) has treated this aspect of her rejection thoroughly in her recent book, *Angela Carter and Surrealism: 'A Feminist Libertarian Aesthetic'*.
7. For a while, she considered calling the novel *Adam and Eve at the End of the World* (Gordon 2016: 119).

## Works cited

Ballard, J. G. ([1962] 2012), *The Drowned World*, New York: Liveright.
Benjamin, W. ([1935] 2003), 'The Work of Art in the Age of Mechanical Reproduction', in C. Harrison and P. Wood (eds), *Art in Theory: 1900–2000*, trans. H. Zohn, 520–6, Malden, Massachusetts: Blackwell Publishing.
Breton, A. ([1924] 1969), 'Manifesto of Surrealism', in *Manifestoes of Surrealism*, trans. R. Seaver and H. R. Lane, Ann Arbor, MI: University of Michigan Press.

Carter, A. (no date), Unidentified Works, Angela Carter Papers, London: British Library, Add MS 88899/1/85.
Carter, A. (1960), Unpublished Journal, Angela Carter Papers, London: British Library, Add MS 88899/1/100.
Carter, A. (1964–1992), Unpublished Journalism, Essays, Reviews, Angela Carter Papers, London: British Library, Add MS 88899/1/62-68: 13.
Carter, A. ([1966] 1996), *Shadow Dance*, New York: Penguin.
Carter, A. ([1967] 1996), *The Magic Toyshop*, New York: Penguin.
Carter, A. ([1969] 1993), *Heroes and Villains*, New York: Penguin.
Carter, A. (1969–1974), Unpublished Journal, Angela Carter Papers, London: British Library, Add MS 88899/1/93.
Carter, A. ([1971] 1997), *The Infernal Desire Machines of Doctor Hoffman*, New York: Penguin.
Carter, A. (1973), Unpublished Manuscript: 'The Passion of New Eve' 1, Angela Carter Papers, London: British Library, Add MS 88899/1/5: 100.
Carter, A. ([1977] 1996), *The Passion of New Eve*, London: Virago.
Carter, A. (1997), *Shaking a Leg*, ed. J. Uglow, New York: Penguin.
Derrida, J. (1984), 'No Apocalypse. Not Now', trans. C. Porter and P. Lewis, *Diacritics*, 14 (1): 20–31.
Dimovitz, S. A. (2016), *Angela Carter: Surrealist, Psychologist, Moral Pornographer*, Abingdon, Oxon: Routledge.
Gamble, S. (1997), *Angela Carter: Writing from the Front Line*, Edinburgh: Edinburgh University Press.
Gamble, S. (2006), *Angela Carter: A Literary Life*, New York: Palgrave Macmillan.
Garner, K. (2012), 'Blending the Pre-Raphaelite with the Surreal in Angela Carter's *Shadow Dance* (1966) and *Love* (1971)', in S. Andermahr and L. Phillips (eds), *Angela Carter: New Critical Readings*, 147–61, London: Bloomsbury Academic.
Gordon, E. (2016), *The Invention of Angela Carter: A Biography*, London: Chatto & Windus.
Haffenden, J. (1985), *Novelists in Interview*, 76–96, London: Methuen.
Jennings, H. (2008), 'Dystopian Matriarchies: Deconstructing the Womb in Angela Carter's *Heroes and Villains* and *The Passion of New Eve*.' *Michigan Feminist Studies*, 21: 63–84.
Karpinski, E. (2000), 'Signifying Passions: Angela Carter's *Heroes and Villains* as a Dystopian Romance', *Utopian Studies*, 11 (2): 137–51.
Keats, J. (1970), *The Poems of John Keats*, edited by Miriam Allott, London: Longman Group Ltd.
Lawrence, D. H. ([1931] 1995), *Apocalypse*, New York: Penguin.
Meaney, G. (2000), 'History and Women's Time: *Heroes and Villains*', in A. Easton (ed), *Angela Carter: Contemporary Critical Essays*, 84–106, London: Macmillan Press LTD.
Nietzsche, F. ([1887] 2006), On The Genealogy of Morality, edited by Keith Ansell-Pearson, translated by Carol Diethe. Cambridge: Cambridge University Press.

Pagels, E. (2012), *Revelations: Visions, Prophecy, & Politics in the Book of Revelation*, New York: Penguin.
Rosen, E. (2008), *Apocalyptic Transformation: Apocalypse and the Postmodern Imagination*, Lanham, MD: Lexington Books.
Sage, L. (1994), *Angela Carter*, Plymouth: Northcote House Publishers Ltd.
Watz, A. (2017), *Angela Carter and Surrealism: 'A Feminist Libertarian Aesthetic'*, New York: Routledge.
Yeandle, H. (2016), *Angela Carter and Western Philosophy*, New York: Palgrave Macmillan.

8

# Kaleidoscopes, stereoscopes and desire machines: Revolutions in vision in Angela Carter's *The Infernal Desire Machines of Doctor Hoffman*

Caleb Sivyer

## Introduction

A veritable cornucopia of visual delights, Angela Carter's body of work is saturated with references and allusions to the history of visual culture, from painterly motifs to Hollywood movie goddesses, and from pornographic tableaux to surveillance techniques. Much of the scholarly work on Carter has concentrated on her engagement with pornography and the politics of the male gaze. Some studies have examined her passion for twentieth-century popular visual culture, including Charlotte Crofts' (2003) analysis of Carter's interest in film and television and Sarah Gamble's examination of the influence of Jean-Luc Godard on Carter's novels from the 1960s (2006: 42–63). More recent work has begun to unpick the influence of various artistic traditions, from Anna Watz's (2017) comprehensive monograph on Carter and surrealism to Katie Garner's (2014) insightful chapter on the mingling of surrealist and pre-Raphaelite Brotherhood artistic motifs and concerns in Carter's early fiction. However, in this chapter I want to contribute to this rich body of work by considering an aspect of Carter's interest in the visual that has thus far been little studied: the plentiful presence of pre-cinematic optical devices in her writing. Of all her literary works, *The Infernal Desire Machines of Doctor Hoffman* (1972) contains the largest number of references and allusions to optical devices, including the daguerreotype, the kaleidoscope and the phantasmagoria. The titular desire machines themselves constitute a kind of visual technology, albeit a fantastical one, which transforms unconscious desires into hologram-like beings, or 'mirages' as the narrator calls them, thereby fundamentally reorganizing visual experience. Furthermore, the structure of the narrative is reminiscent of a magic lantern show as Desiderio, the protagonist and narrator, travels from one seemingly self-contained and picturesque 'world' to another in search of the diabolical Doctor Hoffman. It is for these and other reasons that this chapter will focus on this particular novel. I will demonstrate that the plethora of optical devices in this text dramatizes a number of concerns about visuality, including the conventional patriarchal conception of woman as an object to be seen, the threats (imagined or real) to the male sovereign spectator triggered by a reorganization of vision and finally both the hopes and fears associated with a revolution in visual experience, such as was witnessed in the nineteenth century with the invention of mechanically reproduced images on a mass scale.

## Kaleidoscopes, daguerreotypes and phantasmagoria

I want to begin by analysing a series of metaphors that appear early on in the text and which Desiderio as narrator uses to describe himself, the object of his desire, and his environment. All of these metaphors employ pre-cinematic optical devices invented in the nineteenth century and they serve several purposes: they reveal that in a patriarchal society woman exists to be seen by the male spectator but that her ephemerality is often experienced by men as troubling or threatening;[1] they also register an anxiety about the changes to visual experience in modernity, with the rise of new visual technologies; and finally they are evidence of Desiderio's efforts both to protect his status as a sovereign spectator and to contain the object of his desire by metaphorically turning her into an image.

The first of these metaphors appears in the opening section of the narrative, where Desiderio, now old and alone, wistfully recalls the days of the war with Doctor Hoffman and in particular the now lost object of his desire: Hoffman's marvellous and elusive daughter, Albertina. In a distinctly Proustian act of reminiscence, Desiderio sees Albertina through the lens of an optical device, picturing her in his memory as 'a series of marvellous shapes formed at random in the kaleidoscope of desire' (6).[2] The choice of visual instrument in this metaphor is significant given its frequent association with both femininity and the ephemeral epoch that is modernity. Charles Baudelaire, for example, famously described the modern, urban man, or *flâneur*, as like 'a kaleidoscope gifted with consciousness', and noted that one of the most arresting sights for this kaleidoscopic-man was what he called 'the passing woman', a fugitive figure who catches his gaze for the briefest of moments only to disappear into the crowd (1964: 12). In this analogy, although a certain type of masculinity is being associated with an optical device, what is important here is that the figure of woman is positioned as a passive image while the kaleidoscopic-man is in the position of active spectator. Indeed, the women seen by the *flâneur* are lacking in terms of having ontological substance. As Rachel Bowlby puts it, the passing woman is not so much a real and autonomous being as 'a mere projection from the spectator' (1997: 202). This description fits the way in which Desiderio sees Albertina both in the opening chapter and at various points throughout his narrative. As he observes, 'if Albertina has become for me, now, such a woman as only memory and imagination could devise, well, such is always at least partially the case with the beloved' (6). Strengthening this is the fact that, after associating Albertina with the images in a kaleidoscope, Desiderio then adds that she was 'her father's daughter, no doubt about that!' Desiderio thus aligns his beloved not only with the figures of femininity contained in the male visual imagination but with Hoffman's desire machines, as if she were merely another of the strange mirages produced by this fictional device. This ephemeral figure of woman is thereby contained within both the tube of the kaleidoscope, with its many reflecting surfaces and male eye at the opposite end, and within Hoffman's desire machines which, appropriately, turn out to be fuelled by imprisoned lovers. Indeed, containing the figure of woman is imperative for this typically male voyeur and narrator. As Bowlby argues, whilst the *flâneur*'s gaze positions woman as part of the ephemera of modernity, the way that she is written about by figures such as Baudelaire and Proust, that is, as a beautiful object, 'substantialises her fragmentariness', which in turn 'keeps her, fits her to him, in the image of his imagination' (1997: 202). Similarly, Desiderio attempts to trap his beloved within the bounds of his narrative as a desperate ploy to assuage his anxiety at not possessing her body. At the end of his introduction, Desiderio also positions Albertina as a kind of muse, dedicating his memories to her – a flattering if further example of the masculine desire to assuage his anxiety about femininity.

In a second metaphor, Desiderio pictures himself within the bounds of another optical device, though one markedly different to that which frames Albertina. Forever separated from her, Desiderio laments that he is 'condemned to live in a drab, colourless world, as though... living in a faded daguerreotype' (7). This contrast sets up an interesting divide between masculine and feminine images, for whilst Albertina is associated with the multiple mirrors of the kaleidoscope, which produce a series of fluctuating, colourful images, Desiderio is linked with a static and colourless image produced by the single mirror of the daguerreotype.[3] Added to this is the difference in the position of the observer's eye with respect to each device: whereas the daguerreotype produces an image that can be regarded at a distance from the observer's eye and thus surveyed in its totality, the kaleidoscope requires the observer to place his/her eye close to the lens in order to see the images produced and prevents him/her from seeing the whole image. In the latter case, then, the optical device and the eye become, in Jonathan Crary's words, 'contiguous instruments on the same plane of operation' (1990: 129). The implication of this is that Albertina appears more strongly as a troubling emanation of Desiderio's desire and gaze, and hence his status as a detached and masterful observer is put in question. With this initial opposition then, Carter quickly establishes a set of gender differences which structure the visual, showing how the male desiring gaze is strongly implicated in the production of a version of femininity which signifies visual pleasure, proximity and flux, and which produces both pleasure and anxiety.

A world in flux is also an appropriate description of the war with Hoffman, which Desiderio recalls throughout his narrative. As he observes, during the time of the war 'the city was full of mirages' and 'nothing… was identical with itself' (3–4). Wandering through the streets, Desiderio says that he 'saw only reflections in broken mirrors', which, he goes on to explain, is 'only natural because all the mirrors had been broken' (4). As Hoffman's desire machines unleashed an army of mirages on the world, mirrors became dangerous portals: 'Since mirrors offer alternatives, the mirrors had all turned into fissures or crannies in the hitherto hard-edged world of here and now and through these fissures came slithering sideways all manner of amorphous spooks' (4). In another linking of gender and the visual, Desiderio suggests that the city before Hoffman's attack was a 'thickly, obtusely masculine' place, 'solid, drab' and unchanging (10).[4] By implication, Hoffman's invasion of mirages has feminized the city. In fact, Desiderio claims that cities are either 'women and must be loved' or 'men and can only be admired or bargained with' (10). In a third metaphor involving a popular pre-cinematic visual device, Hoffman's attack is also described by Desiderio as effecting a '*phantasmagoric* redefinition' of the city, turning it into 'the kingdom of the instantaneous' in which everything fluctuates endlessly (12; emphasis added). As Crary explains, '[p]hantasmagoria was a name for a specific type of magic-lantern performance in the 1790s and early 1800s, one that used back projection to keep an audience unaware of the lanterns' (132).⁵ On the one hand, Hoffman's phantasmagoric transformation is clearly an allusion to nineteenth-century Paris through the lens of Walter Benjamin's account. In Benjamin's Marxist-Freudian reading, modern Paris is a phantasmagoria of fetishized commodities, elaborate window displays and arcades (2006: 30–45). On the other hand, given that Carter wrote this novel in the early 1970s in Japan, Hoffman's reorganization of vision is also a convincing portrait of the postmodern metropolis, the latter characterized by, in David Harvey's words, '[f]iction, fragmentation, collage, and eclecticism, all suffused with a sense of ephemerality and chaos' (1990: 98).⁶ In response to Hoffman's attack, the Minister, who rules the city 'single-handed', desperately attempts to maintain social order with his army of fascist-like Determination Police by destroying mirrors and incinerating any suspicious objects or people (11). His plan is thus associated with masculine, rational order, closer to the modernist ideals of urban planning than to those of the postmodernists. As potentially diverting as this might sound, Desiderio is unmoved by Hoffman's magic: 'I felt as if I was watching a film in which the Minister was the hero and the unseen Doctor certainly the villain; but it was an endless film and I found it boring for none of the characters engaged my sympathy' (21). Desiderio is here styled as the typical detached and angst-ridden spectator, seemingly unaffected by the spectacle surrounding him. Indeed, he even explains that he survived Hoffman's optical war because '[he] could not surrender to the flux of mirages' due to his being 'too sardonic' and 'disaffected' (4).

Desiderio's first encounters with Albertina take place amidst Hoffman's phantasmagoric spectacle and so she is aligned with this optical device too. She is, to use Christina Britzolakis's words, the 'chief emblem and embodiment of this phantasmagoric landscape' (1997: 47).⁷ She initially appears to him as a 'curious, persistent hallucination' on the 'borders of … sleep', making her a troublingly liminal figure poised between Hoffman's surreal world of mirages and the imaginary world of dreams (22). Whilst the daytime mirages are the work of 'an inefficient phantasist' and bore Desiderio, Albertina's appearances unsettle him 'obscurely' because 'nothing about [them] was familiar' (21–2). At first, Albertina appears before Desiderio in 'flesh [made] of glass', the 'exquisite filigree of her skeleton' visible beneath this 'transparent' body – a morbid parody of male voyeurism (22). On another occasion, she comes to him in the form of a black swan, evoking in him the 'fear of the unknown' and making him '[shudder] with dread' (27).⁸ In addition to these nightly apparitions, Albertina makes a physical appearance, but one which is much more ambiguously gendered. Playing an ambassador role to her 'phantasist' father, Albertina appropriately appears as a strange mixture of costumes, cosmetics and adornments, and is thus 'extravagantly oversignified' in Maggie Tonkin's helpful phrase (2012: 82).[9] Albertina is described as having 'skin like polished brass', 'glossy hair so black it was purplish', a 'blunt-lipped, sensual mouth', eyes like those painted on Ancient Egyptian sarcophagi, and dark crimson finger nails (30). Furthermore, she is dressed flamboyantly in 'gold thongs', 'flared trousers of purple suede' with a belt consisting of 'several ropes of pearls' (30). Albertina's eclectic style is reminiscent of 1960s fashion, which Carter once described as 'superdrag' and 'a fragment of a kaleidoscope' ([1967] 2013: 113).[10] This gender ambiguity is compounded by Albertina's bestial-like qualities for, as Desiderio notes, her gestures are 'all instinct with a self-conscious but extraordinary reptilian liquidity', and she 'move[s] in soft coils' (30). In this last image, Albertina appears in the guise of the *femme fatale* and Desiderio responds with a combination of desire and fear: while she is 'the most beautiful human being [he has] ever seen', Desiderio gushes, Albertina's appearance also hints at a kind of 'savagery' that both frightens and excites him (30).

Albertina's performance of gender mutability is also significant because it produces 'a fine tracery of cracks' in the 'surface of [Desiderio's] indifference' (38). Her enigmatic appearances arouse in Desiderio a desire to gaze at her sexually (scopophilia) and a desire to know the truth about her identity (epistemophilia).[11] In a final metaphor that appears in the early part of his narrative, Desiderio aligns Albertina with the trickery and deception of magic shows and phantasmagoria: she is, he suggests, like a magic trick which disguises 'a living being beneath' because 'such tricks imply the presence of a conjurer' (40). His ultimate ambition, he confesses, is 'to rip away the ruffled shirt and find out whether the breasts of an authentic woman swelled beneath it' (40). Relevant here is Peter Brooks' observation that '[w]hen the body becomes more secret, hidden, covered, it becomes all the more intensely the object of curiosity' (1993: 15). However, what I want to emphasize here is that this entire introduction to Albertina is, in the terms of my argument, an attempt to contain her enigmatic and arousing identity. Desiderio associates her with the images produced by pre-cinematic devices such as the kaleidoscope and phantasmagoria not just because he finds her bewildering and ephemeral but because it functions, wittingly or not, as an attempt to contain her within the technology of these optical devices, in this case aligned with a male gaze. As troubling as the ever-changing and potentially deceptive images of the kaleidoscope and phantasmagoria respectively might be, images can be (at least potentially) surveyed, possessed and manipulated by the spectator at will.

Towards the end of the text, Desiderio receives confirmation from Albertina herself that her existence is purely visual and that she is indeed one of the mirages produced by her father's desire machines. After encountering her in a number of different guises, including the Madame of a brothel and a Count's valet, she explains to him that she 'projected herself upon the available flesh' of the various people, describing one role in particular as 'a real but ephemeral show' (197). Albertina is thus able to shift and change her appearance at will, like some kind of holographic figure. Through Albertina, then, Carter literalizes the idea of woman as image for the male gaze. Indeed, Albertina even tells Desiderio that all the time he has known her, she has been '"maintained in [her] various appearances only by the power of [his] desire"' (243). In the final chapter, Albertina tells Desiderio that they are two 'disseminating mirrors' reflecting images which are 'multiplied without end' (241). Furthermore, she explains that her father has discovered that enormous amounts of energy could be harnessed from their 'supreme encounter' (241). In this final association between femininity and an optical device, this time a simple mirror, Albertina is not so much pictured as a visual object but as a mirror-image of Desiderio. The radical suggestion here is that the male spectator is himself a part of the spectacle rather than surveying it from above in a detached and masterful manner.

## Peep-shows, stereoscopes and the sovereign subject of vision

I want to turn now to another optical device that appears in the text, but one that appears not as a metaphor in Desiderio's narrative but as an actual device that he encounters on his journey: the pornographic peep-show. This optical device is significant because it functions as both a precursor to Hoffman's desire machines and as a tool in his arsenal, for much of what Desiderio encounters in the so-called real world appears to exist first in nascent form in the peep-show. It is for this reason that Ali Smith argues that each of the novel's chapters 'functions as its own seductive and terrifying peep-show "desire machine"' (2010: x).[12] Furthermore, Beate Neumeier argues that the parallels between the images in the peep-show and Desiderio's experiences in the so-called real world suggest that '[i]mage and experience' are 'inseparable' (1996: 143).

Given all of this, it is essential to understand how the peep-show functions.[13] At the level of representation, the peep-show pictures the gendered body in what Carter refers to in *The Sadeian Woman* as the 'elementary iconography' of pornography, whereby identity is reduced to the body's 'formal elements'. Woman, for example, is reduced to the image of the 'fringed hole', signifying that she is 'open, an inert space, like a mouth waiting to be filled' ([1979] 2011: 4). Carter concludes that '[f]rom this elementary iconography may be derived the whole metaphysic of sexual differences – man aspires; woman has no other function but to exist, waiting' ([1979] 2011: 4). Most of the exhibits inside the peep-show feature highly sexualized and mutilated wax figures of women. However, rather than addressing the pornographic iconography of these exhibits, which has been discussed in the vast majority of critical assessments of this novel, I want to focus on the peep-show as optical device and, more specifically, how it functions in relation to Desiderio's embodied gaze. Early on we learn that a prototype of the peep-show 'offered moving views in three dimensions' and that instead of projecting images onto a screen held at a distance from the audience, it featured 'slots … in which [the latter] could insert themselves and so become part of the shadow show they witnessed' (24). As with the kaleidoscope, this optical device requires that the body of the spectator be contiguous with its operation, thereby removing the distance separating spectator from spectacle. This operation therefore threatens '[t]he pleasure of watching the spectacle', which 'derives from the knowledge one is dissociated from [it]' ([1979] 2011: 162). In a similar fashion to its prototype, the peep-show that Desiderio visits consists of 'a pair of glass eye-pieces [which jut] out on long, hollow stalks' through which the spectator observes each exhibit (44). Once again, the observer inserts him or herself into the spectacle through the stalks which connect the body to it like nodes or corporeal appendages.[14]

This mode of observation is partly an allusion to Marcel Duchamp's *Étant donnés*, which, as Susan Rubin Suleiman notes, not only displays a similarly mutilated female figure but also 'requires that the viewer glue an eye to a peephole in order to see the scene' (130). However, Carter takes things further and creates a distinctively surreal picture of the notion of woman *as* optical device. In one exhibit, uncannily entitled 'I HAVE BEEN HERE BEFORE', a woman's vagina acts as 'a frame for a perfectly round hole through which the viewer glimpsed the moist, luxuriant landscape of the interior', including a model of Hoffman's castle (44). Here, woman is not (only) seen through the visual device but acts as part of its mechanism, her genital hole acting as a mechanical aperture.[15] Additionally, the peep-show also challenges Desiderio's position as a sovereign and voyeuristic spectator – Desiderio's official job title is 'Inspector of Veracity' – through another exhibit, which consists of 'two eyes looking back' at him (30, 45). The eyes function as mirrors, reflecting '[his] own eyes, very greatly magnified by the lenses of the machine' (46). This produces a *mise-en-abyme* effect as each pair of eyes reflects the other, creating 'a model of eternal regression' (46). By thus returning and fracturing his gaze, this exhibit problematizes the opposition between spectator and spectacle, the dizzying mirror effect undoing the stability of the subject as spectator.

When Desiderio visits the peep-show on a second occasion, the models inside each exhibit have been replaced by 'actual pictures painted with luscious oils on rectangular plates in such a way that the twin eye-pieces of the machine created a *stereoscopic* effect' (62, emphasis added). Another significant optical device invented in the nineteenth century, the stereoscope, according to Crary, emerged from 'research ... on *subjective* vision' and contributed to the transformation of the idea and function of the observer (1990: 118; emphasis added). The stereoscope created the illusion of a three-dimensional image by 'reconciling disparity, [by] making two distinct views appear as one', for it featured the same image but seen from slightly different angles so that the combination created the illusion of depth (1990: 120). Significantly, the 'desired effect of the stereoscope was not simply likeness, but immediate, apparent *tangibility*. However, it is a tangibility that has been transformed into a purely visual experience' (1990: 122–4; emphasis in the original). As Crary puts it, '[n]o other form of representation in the nineteenth century had so conflated the real with the optical' (1990: 124), a phrase that captures succinctly Hoffman's manipulation of reality, for whom 'matter was an optical toy', as Desiderio puts it (250).

By understanding how stereoscopic images are produced, we can better understand the politics of visuality presented in Carter's text. Firstly, the stereoscopic image cannot be seen in its totality and thus surveyed from a position of visual mastery. As Crary explains, the eyes 'never traverse the image in a full apprehension of the three-dimensionality of the entire field, but in terms of a localized experience of separate areas' (125). The stereoscopic eye-stalks of the peep-show do just this, preventing Desiderio from adopting a position of visual mastery.[16] This is in marked contrast with other visual devices, such as the daguerreotype, the photograph and the cinematograph, which give the impression at least of visual mastery as the spectator can survey the entire image at a glance. Secondly, the stereoscope spectator is an active participant, for the effect produced depends upon the physiology of the human eyes and brain. In Crary's words, such a spectator is a 'producer of forms of verisimilitude' (131). The peep-show not only works in this fashion but Carter in a way literalizes this notion of the spectator as a producer of images by having the very world that Desiderio travels through exist as an emanation of his (unconscious) desires. Lastly, it is not accidental that the stereoscopic peep-show displays pornographic images for as Crary points out, shortly after its popularization in the nineteenth century 'the stereoscope became increasingly synonymous with erotic and pornographic imagery' because the 'very effects of tangibility' sought by the inventors of the stereoscope could be 'quickly turned into a mass form of ocular possession' (127). Given that Albertina appears in the peep-show exhibit, this strengthens the idea of containment that I introduced at the beginning, for it is clear that Desiderio desires to possess her.

## Two scopic regimes

I want to turn now from an analysis of real optical devices like the kaleidoscope to a consideration of the one fictional, and arguably most important, optical instrument in the text: the desire machines. In particular, I want to ask whether or not this fictional optical device challenges what Martin Jay (1992) calls the dominant scopic regime of Western culture, a concept that I will briefly outline. I also want to look at the Minister's criticisms of Hoffman's proposal as well as his own opposing model of vision. I will conclude by briefly considering Desiderio's decision to destroy the desire machines and opt for the Minister's world view.

The first explicit outline of Hoffman's project as well as the Minister's opposing world view occurs in the discussions between the latter and Albertina. It quickly becomes apparent that Hoffman and the Minister hold opposing ideological beliefs, including differing views on the nature of vision. The Minister attacks Albertina over her father's destruction of his beloved cathedral, that 'masterpiece of sobriety' which was 'given the most vulgar funeral pyre' by being dissolved 'in a display of fireworks', an example of Carter's pyrotechnics at play (32). In a remark that indicates the kind of scopic regime that he subscribes to, the Minister adds that the cathedral was 'like the most conventional of stone angels' and that 'its symmetry expressed the symmetry of the society which had produced it' (33). By contrast, Hoffman's perspective is revealed by Albertina's linguistic playfulness when she completes the Minister's sentence 'It was an artifice-' with '-and so we burned it down with *feux d'artifice*-' (33).[17] Hoffman's actions here literalize Carter's observation in 'Notes for a Theory of Sixties Style' about the 1960s: '[i]n the pursuit of magnificence, nothing is sacred. Hitherto sacrosanct imagery is desecrated' ([1967] 2013: 134). Albertina and the Minister also argue directly over the metaphysics of the visual: in another clearly gendered example, the Minister likens Hoffman's mirages to the 'early days of cinema' because 'all the citizens are jumping through the screen to lay their hands on the naked lady in the bathtub!'[18] Albertina counters with the idea that 'their fingers [actually] touch flesh' (35). Whilst the Minister insists that these mirages are merely 'substantial shadow', Albertina retorts that this is instead 'a beautiful definition of flesh!' (35). The Minister nevertheless doggedly persists in his argument, likening Hoffman to a 'forger' who has palmed off 'an entire currency of counterfeit phenomena', but Albertina again responds pragmatically: 'You cannot destroy our imagery' (36). What this early discussion reveals is a disagreement about the relationship between social structures and the visual: whilst the Minister desires a society in which vision is clear and distinct, and both constitutes and reflects hierarchical order, Hoffman's project aims to disrupt this (visual) order by undoing social hierarchies in favour of greater democracy and individual freedom – his free-floating mirages are (or should be) in a sense a reflection of the free citizens.

I want to refer to this clash of world views between Hoffman and the Minister as a clash of two scopic regimes.[19] To better understand this, I want to briefly recount Jay's discussion of what he refers to as the dominant Western scopic regime and then examine two historical examples of challenges to this regime (1992). According to Jay, Western culture has tended to privilege a rational conception of sight in which the subject is able to survey the world from a safe distance. From the ancient Greek philosophers' conception of knowledge as the state of having seen to Rene Descartes' emphasis on clear and distinct ideas, the dominant conception of knowledge and truth is closely related to, if not premised on, a rational model of vision (see Jay 1992, 1994). This model of vision is also intimately tied up with forms of social control, as the work of Michel Foucault (1977), for example, has shown. From the Minister's remarks in the discussion cited above, it is clear that he adheres to the dominant Western model of vision. Later in the text, Desiderio hears a recording of the Minister in which the latter vociferously deplores the explosion of images created by the desire machines, referring to them as 'deceitful images' and likening Hoffman's transformation of the city to a plague. He affirms the association between vision and rationality when he tells his citizens that 'although unreason has run rampant through our streets' thanks to Hoffman's mirages, 'nevertheless, reason can – will – must! restore order in the end. For light to guide us, we have nothing but our reason' (246).[20] The Minister's adherence to this model of (visual) order is so strong that he employs extreme measures for trying to differentiate real objects and people from Hoffman's mirages: his fascist Determination Police round up suspicious objects or persons and incinerate them to test their reality status.[21] In order to maintain a world in which visual deception is impossible, the Minister is willing to destroy potentially real objects and people – no (visual) ambiguity or uncertainty can be tolerated.²²

Given that Hoffman's mirages are often indistinguishable from the real thing, and thus trouble the rational subject of vision, the Doctor's war of images can be read as challenging the dominant scopic regime of Western modernity. There are historical examples of just such a challenge. Jay draws on the work of Christine Buci-Glucksmann to argue that the baroque offered such a challenge by celebrating the 'disorienting, ecstatic, dazzling implications of the age's visual practices' (1994: 46). A much-cited example of this is Hans Holbein's *The Ambassadors* (1533), with its distorted skull which, Jay argues, functions as 'a reminder of an alternative visual order' (1994: 48). As he explains: 'By combining two visual orders in one planar space, Holbein subverted and decentered the unified subject of vision painstakingly constructed by the dominant scopic regime' (1994: 48). Hoffman's desire machines function in a similar way, challenging the visual order of the Minister's totalitarian-like city by unleashing phantoms and mirages drawn from the unconscious minds and memories of its citizens. Desiderio recounts that his city was filled with mirages of all kinds, from the resurrected dead to an 'Auditorium ... full of peacocks in full spread' (11). He goes on to explain that '[w]hether the apparitions were shades of the dead, synthetic reconstructions of the living or in no way replicas of anything we knew, they inhabited the same dimension as the living' (12). Like Holbein's painting, then, Hoffman has subverted and decentred the ordinary world of vision by overlaying an alternative visual order onto the dominant one – mirages and real people mingle freely in the same plane of reality, sometimes at odds with one another but also occasionally indistinguishable from the point of view of the subject.

Hoffman's new scopic regime can also be usefully read in the light of a significant historical transformation of vision, namely, that which occurred in the mid-nineteenth century. During this period, the 'ocularcentric spectacle of desire', writes Jay, 'was removed from the aristocratic court and given its bourgeois equivalent in the massive sheet glass windows displaying a wealth of commodities to be coveted', as well as the 'explosion of advertising images in newspapers and journals' (1994: 120). This age of mechanical reproduction of images, to use Benjamin's well-known phrase (1999), created two broad reactions. On the one hand, some commentators saw this flood of images as a form of 'visual pollution' and indeed the word 'kitsch' appeared around this time (1994: 122). One of the most significant new optical devices was the aforementioned daguerreotype, and as the market quickly became saturated with images, Baudelaire characterized this phenomenon as a 'cult of images' (cited in Jay 1994: 122). On the other hand, Jay suggests that this visual explosion could be 'interpreted as the democratization of visual experience, the extending down into the general population of those opportunities hitherto reserved for only the elite' (1994: 125). Indeed, by contrast with Baudelaire, the general reaction to this 'daguerreotype-mania' was 'overwhelmingly positive' (1994: 125).

Whilst this reading might suggest that Hoffman's aims are largely positive – a democratization of vision certainly sounds like an admirable political project – Desiderio eventually discovers that the Doctor betrayed the spirit of his endeavour by becoming a dictator of the visual. At the end of the text, Desiderio locates Hoffman in a 'Wagnerian castle' with stained glass windows that 'open eyes of many beautiful colours' (234). Appropriately, the Doctor's laboratory is described in cinematic terms – it is 'half Rottwang's laboratory in Lang's *Metropolis* but it was also the cabinet of Dr Caligari' – and Desiderio spots 'a curious collection of optical toys, a thaumatrope, a Chinese pacing horse lamp and several others, all of types which worked on the principle of persistence of vision' (245). As he leads Desiderio on a tour of the basement in which the desire machines are housed, the Doctor tells him that by bombarding the world with mirages, his new optical device will liberate 'man' by liberating his 'unconscious' (248–9). His ultimate aim, he explains, is to initiate the creation of 'autonomous, free-form, self-promulgation of concretized desires' (253). However, after encountering resistance from the Minister, Hoffman felt coerced into a 'military campaign' that he had 'certainly not bargained for' (252). As a result, 'an element of attrition entered the deployment of [his] imagery' and he began to 'control the evolution of the phantoms' (252–3). Like a communist dictator, then, Hoffman betrayed his own project of liberation by taking control of a process which he tells Desiderio should have been completely free-form and democratic. Rather than facilitating a world of autonomous images, Hoffman has bombarded the world with images directed by him in order to manipulate people's desires rather than setting those desires free.[23] After hearing Hoffman's confession, Desiderio opts for the Minister's world of reason and looks on the Doctor as a 'totalitarian' (247) and a 'hypocrite' for 'penn[ing] desire in a cage' while claiming to be a liberator of desire (248). While matter might be 'an optical toy' for Hoffman, Desiderio finds it hard to believe that he has any interest in liberation and assumes instead that the Doctor 'only wanted power' (250).

Desiderio decides to opt for the Minister's world of rational vision, but he confesses that his actions in stopping Hoffman are far from heroic and he often refers to his sense of passivity at the end of his narrative. Desiderio explains that he was placed in the 'unhappy position' of making the 'casting vote' between these two scopic regimes and only chose the 'barren yet harmonious calm' of the Minister's world out of a sense of disgust at the Doctor's scientific devices and anxiety concerning Albertina (247). Hoffman shows Desiderio the insides of the desire machines – a mixture of 'glowing screens', mirrors that cover every surface and caged lovers – and offers him a central role in his project as well as a 'night of perfect ecstasy' with Albertina in exchange for his freedom (251, 247). However, amidst the so-called 'love pens', which form 'a pictorial lexicon of all the things a man and a woman might do together within the confines of a bed', Desiderio declines the offer and murders both the Doctor and his daughter (255). Although momentarily tempted by the promise of a long-desired sexual union with the elusive Albertina, the idea of being a cog in the desire machines frightens him and he refers to her as his 'necessary extinction' (257). There are also hints that Desiderio feels his status as sovereign spectator threatened, as he notices in horror that the love slaves feeding the desire machines possess 'vacant eyes' (258) and, at the moment of Albertina's death, he says, almost reassuringly, that her eyes will now remain 'silent forever' (259).[24] Even the castle is described as 'clos[ing] its coloured eyes' as Desiderio turns his back on it and heads home (262). Finally, Desiderio concludes his narrative with the image of him 'clos[ing] [his] eyes' only to be greeted with Albertina's haunting image: '[u]nbidden, she comes' (265).

What is clear from these observations and remarks is that Desiderio, as detached and masterful spectator, feels threatened by Hoffman's reorganization of vision, embodied partly in the figure of Albertina, because his place as observer would necessarily change as a result. As both a typically male spectator within a patriarchal world and as an 'Inspector of Veracity' (30), Desiderio's position is threatened by Hoffman's new scopic regime because it would both trouble his ability to discern the real from the fantastic using the light of rational observation and undo the patriarchal construction of gendered vision which centres on an opposition between male spectator and female spectacle (and from which Desiderio benefits). Carter's frequent references to pre-cinematic devices embody this troubling and loosening of the conventional relationships between gender and visuality (and between desire and ways of seeing) because they gesture to a period in European culture when a historical transformation of vision, embodied in the production of a plethora of new optical devices, new media and ways of seeing, was contributing to a whole series of changes in society. Desiderio's decision to murder Hoffman and his daughter, and to destroy the desire machines, stems from both his rejection of the Doctor's totalitarianism and from his anxious reaction to Albertina as a troubling figure of femininity because they are two sides of the same coin: Albertina embodies Hoffman's reorganization of vision because the relationship between gender and the visual is one thing that would fundamentally change in this new scopic regime. Unlike the passive images of femininity produced for and consumed by male spectators, and the women who are treated as objects to be looked at, Albertina challenges Desiderio's masterful male gaze and has autonomy and agency. This is one reason that Desiderio associates her with so many optical devices that suggest multiple ways of seeing that trouble the sovereign spectator.[25] The novel's somewhat ambiguous conclusion suggests that challenges to the dominant scopic regime are likely to be either fought against by defenders of the status quo or will themselves devolve into reactionary and totalitarian forms that appear worse than the status quo. Furthermore, the text also makes clear that what is at stake in this is not technology per se; instead, it is desire, including the desire to see in its various forms (including scopophilia), which is the driving force behind both efforts to maintain the status quo and attempts to bring about radical change. As Carter makes clear in the title of this novel, optical devices are not just abstract ways of seeing but ways of desiring through seeing and seeing through desiring. The abundance of optical devices in Carter's text thus gestures towards the possibility of other ways of seeing-desiring, but without offering any guarantees of change to the dominant scopic regime of Western culture.

## Notes

1  As argued most famously by Laura Mulvey in 'Visual Pleasure and Narrative Cinema' and John Berger in *Ways of Seeing*.
2  For more on the connections between *Desire Machines* and Marcel Proust, see Tonkin (2012).
3  Although the daguerreotype employed a copper plate rather than an actual mirror, this plate was polished so that it functioned like a mirror.
4  Indeed, as he goes on to say, '[i]t seemed it would never change' (9). Desiderio's emphasis on stasis and the lack of change appears to locate the city in a kind of pre-modern or pre-industrial period. Hoffman's transformation of the city is akin to industrialization or perhaps better yet the culmination of industrialization in the early twentieth century – mechanical reproduction, technological spectacles and the like. This is not the only occasion on which Carter genders a city: in 'Envoi: Bloomsday', she writes 'Cities have sexes: London is a man, Paris a woman, and New York a well-adjusted transsexual' ([1982] 2013: 655).

5   Marina Warner has also written about the phantasmagoria in her book of the same name. There, she argues that Etienne-Gaspard Robertson's '[g]othic moving picture show […] turned any spectator from a cool observer into a willing, excitable victim' (2006:147–8).
6   Alternatively, Hoffman's phantasmagoric redefinition could be read in terms of Benjamin's analysis of nineteenth-century Paris as what he calls the capital of modernity.
7   Britzolakis argues that Carter's early novel *Love* makes a 'fetishized femininity serve as the figure for, and displacement of, socio-historical crisis, at the level both of figurative language and of narrative perspective' (47). My reading is similar to that of Britzolakis's insofar as I too see a close relationship between the female figure and the large socio-historical crisis in *The Infernal Desire Machines of Doctor Hoffman*.
8   These nightly apparitions bear a striking similarity to many of the most popular magic lantern shows which employed typical Gothic tropes such as ghosts and played on the macabre and the uncanny.
9   Despite this high level of ambiguity, Desiderio refers to Albertina in this guise as a man and uses the masculine pronoun.
10  In this essay ([1967] 2013), at least, Carter links the kaleidoscope with drag rather than with either a patriarchal version of femininity or an image of masculinity as in Baudelaire's use of the metaphor – modern man as a kaleidoscope gifted with consciousness.
11  Although these terms come from the work of Sigmund Freud, they were made more famous in academic discussions through Laura Mulvey's seminal essay 'Visual Pleasure and Narrative Cinema' (1975) which appears in the early 1970s.
12  On a related note, Lorna Sage once suggested that the plots of Carter's early texts move 'from one tableau to another, "still" after "still", quickened into movement by a kind of optical illusion – as in a flicker book, or of course a film' (1992:169).
13  There are also important allusions to cinema in this section of the text. As Susan Rubin Suleiman has observed, the chapter that introduces the peep-show as well as its proprietor is modelled on the German Expressionist film *The Cabinet of Dr Caligari* (1994: 115–32).
14  In Carter's short story entitled 'The Merchant of Shadows', the narrator describes the eyes of Americans as 'lenses on stalks that go flicker, flicker, and give you the truth twenty-four times a second' (1996: 364).
15  This is a distinctively Batallean image as in the overlapping and exchange of eyes and testicles in *The Story of the Eye* ([1928] 2001).
16  As Crary writes, the stereoscope 'require[s] the corporeal adjacency and immobility of the observer' (1990: 129). Cavallaro also notes the importance of the stereoscope for its commentary on Desiderio's position as a detached, controlling eye, writing

that 'in foregrounding the binocularity attendant upon her hero's perceptions [Carter] subtly refuses to pander to the myth of unitary vision which Western ocular centrism has so often and so uncritically espoused' (2011: 65).

17  For more on Carter's interest in fireworks, see her first collection of short stories, *Fireworks: Nine Profane Pieces* (1974), in particular 'A Souvenir of Japan', in which she explains how the Japanese call fireworks *hannabi*, meaning 'flower fire' (1996: 27).

18  This reference to early film spectators who were supposedly overwhelmed by the spectacle on screen and who responded to the image as if it were real suggests a more potent image of cinema than Desiderio's earlier reference to his life as a boring film. Here the film spectacle unsettles the spectator rather than provides pleasurable viewing at a safe distance.

19  David Punter has offered a different and equally interesting reading of this clash between Hoffman and the Minister, arguing that this novel can be read as 'a series of figures for the defeat of the political aspirations of the 1960s, and in particular of the father-figures of liberation, Reich and Marcuse' (1984: 211).

20  Hoffman's phantasmagoric redefinition of the Minister's city clearly subverts the power of reason. As Michael W. Jennings explains, for Benjamin 'the term "phantasmagoria" simply emphasizes the powerfully illusory quality of [the modern] environment, a quality that has a debilitating effect upon the human ability to come to rational decisions – and in fact to understand our own world' (2006: 14).

21  An alternative way to read this opposition would be along the lines of Foucault's discussion in *Discipline and Punish* of the contrast between what he calls the 'literary fiction of the festival', in which laws are suspended, prohibitions lifted and bodies mingle freely, and the 'political dream of the plague', which sees 'the penetration of regulation into even the smallest details of everyday life through the mediation of the complete hierarchy that assured the capillary functioning of power' (1977: 197–8). Carter herself drew on Foucault's work on vision and power in her novel *Nights at the Circus* (1984), and this connection has been examined by Joanne M. Gass (1994: 71–6).

22  Of course, there is a complex question here of the meaning of the term 'real' but this is the very point of disagreement between the Minister and Hoffman. While the former considers images to be unreal, the latter wants to collapse the distinction between object and image.

23  Seemingly, the only time when Hoffman is not in control of his mirages is after the peep-show samples, which are 'symbolic constituents of representations of the basic constituents of the universe' (109), are lost. As Albertina explains, '[a]ll hell has been let loose since we lost the set of samples' (160). Hoffman himself later confesses to Desiderio that 'once the set of samples was accidentally destroyed, my

calculations went awry' (253). Hoffman's control of his new visual order is only ever temporary.

24  For more on how Albertina's female gaze unsettles Desiderio's position as masterful, male spectator, see my chapter '"I resented it, it fascinated me": Carter's ambivalent cinematic fiction and the problem of proximity' (2019).

25  As he says towards the end of his narrative, 'I felt the uneasy sense of perfect freedom. Freedom, yes. I thought I was free of her, you see' (p. 260).

# Works cited

Bataille, G. ([1928] 2001), *The Story of the Eye*, London: Penguin.
Baudelaire, C. (1964), 'The Painter of Modern Life', in J. Mayne (ed. and trans.), *The Painter of Modern Life and Other Essays*, 1–40, London: Phaidon.
Benjamin, W. (1999), 'The Work of Art in the Age of Mechanical Reproduction', in H. Zorn (trans.), *Illuminations*, 211–44, London: Pimlico.
Benjamin, W. (2006), 'Paris, the Capital of the Nineteenth Century', in M. W. Jennings (ed), *The Writer of Modern Life: Essays on Charles Baudelaire*, 30–45, London: Belknap Press.
Berger, J. (1972), *Ways of Seeing*, London: Penguin.
Bowlby, R. (1997), *Feminist Destinations and Further Essays on Virginia Woolf*, Edinburgh: Edinburgh University Press.
Brooks, P. (1993), *Body Work: Objects of Desire in Modern Narrative*, Cambridge, MA: Harvard University Press.
Carter, A. ([1967] 2013), 'Notes for a Theory of Sixties Style', in J. Uglow (ed), *Shaking a Leg: Collected Journalism and Writings*, 131–5, London: Vintage.
Carter, A. ([1972] 2010), *The Infernal Desire Machines of Doctor Hoffman*, London: Penguin.
Carter, A. ([1978] 2013), 'Femmes Fatales', in J. Uglow (ed), *Shaking a Leg: Collected Journalism and Writings*, 427–32, London: Vintage.
Carter, A. ([1979] 2011), *The Sadeian Woman: An Exercise in Cultural History*, London: Virago.
Carter, A. ([1982] 2013), 'Envoi: Bloomsday', in J. Uglow (ed), *Shaking a Leg: Collected Journalism and Writings*, 536–41, London: Vintage.
Carter, A. ([1983] 2013), 'Notes from the Front Line', in J. Uglow (ed), *Shaking a Leg: Collected Journalism and Writings*, 45–53, London: Vintage.
Carter, A. (1996), *Burning Your Boats: Collected Short Stories*, London: Vintage.
Cavallaro, D. (2011), *The World of Angela Carter: A Critical Investigation*, Jefferson: McFarland & Company.
Crary, J. (1990), *Techniques of the Observer: On Vision and Modernity in the Nineteenth Century*, London and Cambridge, MA: MIT Press.

Crofts, C. (2003), *Anagrams of Desire: Angela Carter's Writing for Radio, Film and Television*, Manchester: Manchester University Press.

Foucault, M. (1977), *Discipline and Punish: The Birth of the Prison*, trans. A. Sheridan, London: Penguin.

Gamble, S. (2006), 'Something Sacred: Angela Carter, Jean-Luc Godard and the Sixties', in R. Munford (ed), *Re-visiting Angela Carter: Texts, Contexts, Intertexts*, 42–63, Basingstoke: Palgrave.

Garner, K. (2014), 'Blending the Pre-Raphaelite with the Surreal in Angela Carter's *Shadow Dance* (1966) and *Love* (1971)', in S. Andermahr and L. Phillips (eds), *Angela Carter: New Critical Readings*, London: Bloomsbury.

Gass, J. M. (1994), 'Panopticism in *Nights at the Circus*', *Review of Contemporary Fiction*, 14: 71–6.

Harvey, D. (1990), *The Condition of Postmodernity: An Enquiry into the Origins of Cultural Change*, Oxford: Blackwell.

Jay, M. (1992), 'Scopic Regimes of Modernity', in S. Lash and J. Friedman (ed), *Modernity and Identity*, 178–95, Oxford: Blackwell.

Jay, M. (1994), *Downcast Eyes: The Denigration of Vision in Twenty-Century French Thought*, Berkeley and Los Angeles: University of California Press.

Jennings, M. W. (ed) (2006), *The Writer of Modern Life: Essays on Charles Baudelaire*, London: Belknap Press.

Mulvey, L. (1975), 'Visual Pleasure and Narrative Cinema', *Screen*, 16 (3): 6–18.

Neumeier, B. (1996), 'Postmodern Gothic: Desire and Reality in Angela Carter's Writing', in V. Sage and A. Lloyd Smith (eds), *Modern Gothic: A Reader*, 141–51, Manchester: Manchester University Press.

Punter, D. (1984), 'Angela Carter: Supersessions of the Masculine', *Critique*, 25 (4): 209–22.

Sage, L. (1992), *Women in the House of Fiction*, Basingstoke: Macmillan.

Sivyer, C. (2019), '"I Resented it, it Fascinated Me": Carter's Ambivalent Cinematic Fiction and the Problem of Proximity', in M. Mulvey-Roberts (ed), *The Arts of Angela Carter: A Cabinet of Curiosities*, 223–45, Manchester: Manchester University Press.

Smith, A. (2010), 'Introduction', in A. Carter, *The Infernal Desire Machines of Doctor Hoffman*, vii–xii, London: Penguin.

Suleiman, S. R. (1994), 'The Fate of the Surrealist Imagination in the Society of the Spectacle', in L. Sage (ed), *Flesh and the Mirror: Essay on the Art of Angela Carter*, 115–32, London: Virago.

Tonkin, M. (2012), *Angela Carter and Decadence: Critical Fictions/Fictional Critiques*, Basingstoke: Palgrave Macmillan.

Warner, M. (2006), *Phantasmagoria: Spirit Visions, Metaphors, and Media into the Twenty-first Century*, Oxford: Oxford University Press.

Watz, A. (2017), *Angela Carter and Surrealism: A Feminist Libertarian Aesthetic*, Abingdon, Oxon: Routledge.

9

# 'The strangeness of the world made visible': Reading alignments between Angela Carter and Paula Rego

Béatrice Bijon

In the early summer of 1997, I was visiting Lorna Sage at her home in Florence. Inside the house overlooking the city, piles of papers and faxes covered several tables of the dining room. Sage was then collecting the chapters for *The Cambridge Guide to Women's Writing in English* which she was editing. As I was starting my PhD on Angela Carter, Sage seemed the perfect person to talk to. Amidst the many stories and anecdotes, Sage expatiated on her late friend's literary vigour and the sheer energy of her prose, in particular the multifarious references to contemporary and past writing and thinking that we find in Carter's work. The broad array of literary associations was both exciting and overwhelming. Indeed, it became apparent later when I was writing up my thesis that, to use Linda Hutcheon's phrase, the 'palimpsestuous intertextuality' (2006: 21) of Carter's texts does more than simply allude to other works of literature. The kinetic quality of Carter's writing allows texts to enter into dialogue with other texts to create a heightened resonance which fashions the whole reading process. Reading becomes an experience of friction, with texts 'rubbing' other texts so that, as Carter famously said, 'the reader [can] construct her own fiction for herself from the elements of [her] fiction [because] reading is just as creative an activity as writing' (1983: 69).

The reading creativity and practice that Carter called for is further enhanced by the visual fabric of her stories. I want to argue that the pictorial quality of the texts, the multiple examples of *ekphrasis* and the consistent summoning of paintings expand this reading space. By invoking Ensor, Gauguin, Moreau, Vallotton or Ernst, for instance, Carter creates a picture gallery that takes the reader out of the text. Or, more precisely, to take up Liliane Louvel's argument in *The Pictorial Third*, it creates an oscillation between text and image which calls for an 'intermedial' reading (2018). This oscillation between text and image was well illustrated by the curatorial choices of the exhibition Strange Worlds: The Vision of Angela Carter, held in Bristol from December 2016 to March 2017 (Mulvey-Roberts and Robinson 2016). On display were works by contemporary visual artists that echoed and responded explicitly to Carter in resonant and provocative ways (Ana Maria Pacheco, Di Oliver, Andrew Muñoz, Angela Lizon). Some other works had been selected by the curators for their implicit force of evocation and allusion (Marc Chagall, Paula Rego, Leonora Carrington). Whether the artworks were explicitly and specifically connected to her texts or not, the selection was a timely reminder of the explosive qualities of Carter's art. The invigorating experience of the exhibition truly propelled the readers of the texts and viewers of the artworks into an intermedial apprehension of and engagement with both arts.

To go back and pursue Carter's idea of creative reading, it seems apposite to push the boundaries and go beyond the painters and creators explicitly invoked by her texts. I am going to be looking at resonances between Carter and the painter Paula Rego, whose work, incidentally, I saw for the first time in reproduction in the cover of Lorna Sage's *Cambridge Guide to Women's Writing in English*. The painting chosen is *Prey* (1986), which features two young girls with plaited hair and nice dresses who could be straight out of fairy tales, were it not for details that give a sense of troubled disquiet. The girls are disproportionately large. One casts an eerie and menacing look back towards the viewer. There is a mallet ready to be used for some suspect purpose and a cat holding prey in its mouth. The scene is one of hidden secrets. The mood of disquiet is Carteresque, and so are the girls who present as aggressors or abusers. We know that Rego is fascinated by fairy tales and has read Carter's stories (Rego 2006), but there is, to my knowledge, no evidence that Carter admired or even saw any of Rego's paintings. Carter's texts and visual rhetoric correlate with Rego's paintings and narrative drive in a way that lends itself to a chiasmatic interpretation. Putting these two artists' works in conversation and getting both genres to 'rub' each other will allow a 'dialectic of mutual illumination and correction' (Gilman 1989: 12).

In her obituary of Angela Carter, Lorna Sage wrote that:

> her branching and many-layered narratives mirrored our shifting world of identities lost and found, insiders versus outsiders, alternative histories and utopias postponed… All of her writing was at odds with conventional realism,

yet she mapped with great precision the history and topography of our fantasies. She was miraculously 'at home' in this epoch where people and their 'images', facts and their shadows, co-exist so closely and menacingly.

(1992)

What Lorna Sage captures here is Carter's vigorous exercise at handling and devising paradoxes. Angela Carter revelled in them. The phrase 'at home' also strikes me as most interesting since its quotation marks seem to qualify its very meaning, even intimating unfamiliarity. A form of uncanny is expressed here, bringing familiarity with strangeness, which is one of the hallmarks of both Carter's and Rego's art.

Carter's texts steer a straight course, but one that requires readers to tack and swerve in order to read their way through paradoxes. This kind of shift in reading is epitomized in *The Passion of New Eve*. The narrator and central character's sexual (re)construction creates interpretative challenges which come into focus if a certain perspective is adopted. Similarly, the uncertain sexual identity of the transvestite Tristessa, as performed in the diegetic and enunciative scenes, requires readers to *accommodate* in the visual sense of the term, as described by Roland Barthes:

> When I read, I *accommodate*: not only the chrystalline humor of my eyes, but also that of my intellect, in order to reach the right level of signification… [E]ach of us *curbs* his mind, or *curves* it, like an eye, in order to grasp in the mass of the text *that certain intelligibility* he needs in order to know, to take pleasure, etc. In this, reading is a kind of work, a labor.
>
> (1977: 134, emphasis in the original)

Barthes' accommodating process is apposite to the reading of Carter's stories because her habitual literary gesture is one of dys-positioning.

Angela Carter took very little at face value. Her world is a world that subverts and outrages conventions, be they the conventions that define and represent femininity and masculinity or the conventions of storytelling. She endlessly plays with and upsets her readers' expectations. In her stories, masks and veils hide and reveal at the same time. When horror is seemingly concealed behind a mask, it is likely to be all the more exposed. Light humour vies with dark humour; a loud guffaw let loose is often the flipside of callous malice. The relationship between prey and predator is renegotiated. Little girls and women can be assaulted and abused, but they are also cruel and kill – and so do mothers and fathers.

Carter's visual language and imagery makes Roland Barthes' reflection on reading relevant. So does the power of the gaze, both as an embedded motif in the texts and as a defining literary and reading form. And this is precisely the pictorial quality of Carter's texts that steers us towards painting.

Paula Rego creates disturbing worlds similarly inhabited by animals and humans who bite and are bitten, who dominate and are dominated, who play and are played with. A contemporary of Carter, the British-Portuguese painter Paula Rego works through similar lines, and her mindscape resonates with that of Carter. Also venturing into the world of fairy tales and the classics of literature (nursery rhymes, *Jane Eyre*, operas, Peter Pan), Rego creates highly narrative paintings and works on paper. The self-described feminist painter delves into the abuse and cruelties of life. As forcefully as Carter, her work unleashes women's sexual power and self-empowerment. The association with Carter would not be complete if there was not also a twist or a slant to her work. Nothing is straightforward and, as is the case with the forests in fairy tales, nothing is ever as it seems. Violence and perversity are around the corner to unsettle vision and interpretation.

Many of Rego's paintings could relate to Carter very closely in their aesthetic, whether it be the experimental profusion of details and the surrealist tinge of the pre-1980s works or the many collages and paintings imbued with a sense of terror. But my interest is in her acrylic paintings of the mid-1980s and early 1990s, and her pastels of the mid-1990s. That is because Rego's works of this period steer me into another common theme in the Carter and Rego oeuvres: the grammar of the sexes within the family. The reader and the viewer are spared no torment in the exposition of domestic dramas – forced relationships, assaults, flawed love, inappropriate embraces that threaten to devour – and also pains and abuse untold, but implied through secrets and silences.

Beyond these two artists' irreverence is their preoccupation with the relationship between the sexes and scenarios of familial dysfunction. Families are sinister, relationships are violent and perverse, and incest, whether represented or suggested, is a presence. Both Carter and Rego challenge the models of the innocent little girl and the woman victim, undermining them by imagining especially disturbing alternatives.

To paraphrase Barthes in *Empire of Signs*, Carter's text does not 'gloss' Rego's images, which do not 'illustrate' the text (Barthes 1982: xi). The interlacing of Carter's and Rego's works creates an exchange and a circulation of signifiers. Putting both artists into alignment produces a disjointed complementarity. As Marina Warner asserts, discussing the alignment between Rego's work and

Bronte's *Jane Eyre*, 'Images and text combine and flow, like voices in a duet' (2003: 15). For instance, what happens in one field can account for what is happening in the other; or can be envisaged as the cause or the consequence of the other; or can provide another perspective; or else can fill up a blank left by the other; at any rate, it shapes a highly productive field of signification – a textual as well as a visual vacillation.

I propose in this chapter to expand further the accommodating process, to expand the 'curving and curbing of the mind' and suggest an *anamorphic* approach to understanding text and image. Introducing anamorphosis, a technique from the visual arts, is highly apposite to reading Carter's own work, so bent on visual gymnastics. Anamorphosis is the pictorial genre in which an object which appears distorted when seen frontally reveals its shape when seen laterally, typically from an oblique angle. This mode of perception is particularly fruitful and enlightening when creating a conversation between Carter and Rego. An anamorphic reading of Carter's and Rego's works hinges on a process of vacillation and a play with perspective. The sense of vacillation inherent to the notion is best exemplified if we make a little detour and consider Hans Holbein's well-known anamorphosis in the *The Ambassadors*, with its cunning play with perspective. Positioned in front of two learned men, the eponymous ambassadors, is a mangled shape, an object that is amorphous the first time it is seen. In order for the anamorphosis to reveal itself, the spectator needs to move aside to the right of the painting and look at it from another angle. The shape then comes to 'life', as it were, becoming recognizable as a human skull. I want to make three points: first, the process requires a physical movement on the part of the viewer; second, this results in the adoption of a new point of view or perspective; and finally, when the spectator comes back to the original frontal position, there is no way the newly formed shape can be forgotten. 'It is like something seen out of the corner of the eye, glimpsed at high speed or seen through a keyhole' (Collins 1992: 77) – an image that cannot be erased. Hence the vacillation of the gaze which endeavours to accommodate, but fails to return to the original image.

Much as the painter of an anamorphosis requires the viewer to move around the painting, engaging with Carter's and Rego's works necessitates that the gaze of viewers and readers to be thrown off-centre. Both artists take us to places where we do not want to be and tell us truths we are not keen to hear. To draw from John Berger, Carter and Rego have 'ways of witnessing' the disturbances of the world that are unsettling. I would argue that this is the dynamic process which is at play in the confrontation between Carter's and Rego's art, producing both playfulness and uncertainty, curiosity and discomfort. Understanding and interpreting then becomes a riddle, out of which meaning and subjectivity can emerge.

The cognate versions of the fairy tales Angela Carter reworked are grim and gruesome. But Carter plays with them so that, like the Beast in 'The Tiger's Bride', they become 'carnival figure[s] made of papier mâché' (Carter 1983b: 53). She stresses their oral quality to saturation, intersperses them with narratorial interventions and digressions, contrives jest and humour, thus creating distance with the seriously bleak content. It is noticeable that she heightened the playful side of the tales.

'The Tiger's Bride' and 'The Courtship of Mr Lyon' (Carter 1983a, 1983b) are telling examples. What are these two stories really about? They are the stories of a young girl who has been gambled and lost to a Beast by her father. I was intrigued to learn from a 1984 interview with Carter, broadcast on Australian radio, that when writing 'The Tiger's Bride' she had a painting by Edward Hicks in mind, titled *The Peaceful Kingdom*. She explained that she loved to see all the animals you can think of, together in the middle of the American wilderness, enjoying harmony with their own senses. She found it very moving that they were living at peace with their surroundings. Carter's association of this nineteenth-century painting with 'Courtship' is rather puzzling. It is true that the two new versions of 'Beauty and the Beast' and the treatment of monstrosity and humanity are rather benign and that the resolution of the two stories is quite harmonious and promising. The young girls submit to the fate carved out for them by their fathers, and stay and live with the beast. In one case, the Beast is not as beastly as he seems; in the other, the young girl becomes a tiger herself. She *has* turned things around.

In 'The Courtship of Mr Lyon', even if the narrative voice takes great care in asserting that the reader 'should not think that the young girl had no will of her own' (Carter 1983a: 45) and, therefore, made her own decision to stay when she could have gone; and even if it ends with a formulaic tongue-in-cheek happy ending, I feel it cannot elude a more serious reading. In 'The Tiger's Bride', similarly, the story remains somewhat open-ended, as it closes on the young girl turning into a tiger after having her skin licked off by the Beast. I would argue that the happy ending is so self-consciously clichéd and the cardboard carnival so overblown that these stories can but be read as forced distortion. I find that this seductive shape needs to be read obliquely from another angle. There appears, then, a much darker world that needs to be disclosed and gradually brought to life. 'The Courtship of Mr Lyon' and 'The Tiger's Bride' raise an array of questions about the daughters' itineraries, about their lineage and about their place in the family economy: What is it to be the daughter of a father who has gambled your life and left you as a token to a beast? What is it to be the daughter of a father whose behaviour has led to your mother's death? What is it to be the daughter of a mother who chose not to survive her child? And what is it to be a woman when you live with a man who is willing to precipitate your death?

Like the seductive shape at the front of Holbein's painting which gradually becomes decipherable when you move sideways, it is the watermark of these stories to invite the reader to displace reading. My personal reading experience is that, even in a textual environment that is deeply playful, teasing and happily subversive like Carter's, these profoundly serious issues evoked earlier, expressed laterally and emerging here, cannot be done away with once you have become aware of them. They have been dislodged and become frontal. Like an immaterial memory, they stay with the reader. This is one of the hallmarks of Carter's fiction; she manages to lay bare the demons in the psyche and let them roam, never completely staving off the horror.

Working also from a folkloric legacy, Paula Rego extends the same logic and proposes similar interrogations and concerns. The 'Girl and Dog' series (1986–7) illuminates Carter's reflection on girls and power in a way that is also both real and imagined. As John McEwen describes the series, 'the figurative narrative element is there but, at the same time, there is a sense of abstraction' (2006: 77). Each painting captures moments when a girl is handling a dog in various ways, each time exerting some form of control over it. In all the paintings of the series, the couple formed by the girl and the dog are rather disturbing and, as in most of Rego's paintings, cryptic and highly ambiguous. Does the dog stand for a baby, a partner, a brother, another kind of Beast or simply a dog? Or does it stand for all these things? These scenes are domestic interiors. The girl alternatively pampers, feeds, shaves and grooms the dog, until she gradually settles it in her lap, or rather between her legs in a dubious position. Rego challenges the model of the innocent little girl and undermines it by imagining especially disturbing alternatives: in *Girl Lifting Up Her Skirts to a Dog*, a tense, uninviting-looking girl seducing the dog (now motionless and completely passive) now lifts her skirt, no longer behind doors but outside, in the open. In *Looking Back*, it seems the three girls might have killed the dog, now reduced to a tiny toy. The sexual undertones and the triumphant, sly gazes of the girls are highly suspicious. Clearly, the trio has been up to some mischief. In *The Little Murderess*, a young woman in a nice Sunday dress is wielding a strip of fabric menacingly: is she about to strangle the dog? The white cloth or maybe a shirt on the left suggests that it might be a man she is about to murder; possibly the dog is now transformed into a human.

In this series, it is interesting how Rego affects our reading of Carter, in the way she explores straightforwardly what Carter left out, or rather left the reader to imagine. And similarly, although the paintings lend themselves to a narrative composition and interpretation, what precedes or has determined the scenes is outside the frame and left unknown, and needs to be imagined by the viewer. Carter and Rego are fellow travellers, but what is strikingly different is that Rego visualizes, or rather makes us visualize, portions of life that are not readily apprehended in Carter. As a matter of fact, Rego prompts more investment from the viewer for the characters, more appreciation of the human torments and transgressions that have caused miseries. What causes the viewer to deflect his or her gaze for a lateral interpretation is not tongue-in-cheek details or overblown humour as in Carter, but rather intense ambiguity arising from perverted relationships.

Other paintings introduce members of the family with similarly unsettling relationships: daughters, mothers, fathers and lovers. *The Family* is set in the intimacy of a bedroom in which the familial composition raises questions. At the centre, the father is being handled in a curious way: Is he being undressed? If so, the man's immobility, gaze and expression suggest terror and disempowerment. The girl in-between her father's legs seemed to have got her mother's approval for being there, despite the sexual inappropriateness of her position; and the girl's gaze is nothing short of menacing. Why is the father manhandled in this way? The little girl near the window, perversely relishing the scene, completes the picture. What is it that delights her? Very often in Rego's paintings, props are 'metaphoric counterpoints' (McEwen 2006: 157) or help invent a 'before' to the scene to construct the narrative. Here a jug, a rose and a shrine are props to prompt our imagination. Perhaps some of the answers to the many questions emerging from her painting are concealed in the recurring folds of fabric, in the trousers of a father, under the skirts of daughters, or in the convoluted folds of a long dress.

In these paintings as in many others, questions arise constantly. Paula Rego penetrates the world of childhood and gives girls agency; she pushes their empowerment to an extreme, as if daughters (and children) were answering back and gaining control over adults after the 'horrors of childhood [were] born by children in silence' (McEwen 2006: 35). She also portrays a form of equality in the wrongdoing. The grammar of the family is one that is based on perversion where the law that governs families (and places within the family) is twisted, distorted and perverted. *The Cadet and His Sister* for instance points to another twisted relationship. All the props point to a sexual relationship between these siblings, with the girl as the initiator: the traditional symbolism of the gloves; the red lining of the bag. The path receding into the distance forms a triangle that heightens the sexual nature of the relationship.

Carter's 'The Executioner's Beautiful Daughter' (1988), a story from *Fireworks*, takes us to similarly perverted and disturbing terrains. As is the case with many of Carter's stories, 'The Executioner's Beautiful Daughter' raises fundamental questions regarding reading. My argument is that this short story, as a *mise en abyme* of reading, exemplifies the argument developed so far regarding accommodative and anamorphic reading. Carter performs a *danse macabre* that seems to angle for an agile reader and viewer who is forced to consider how the text accommodates scenes of horror. What is one to do with the atrocities exhibited on the textual and visual scenes?

The story is set in a bleak fairy tale landscape in which a girl lifts her skirt to her father (an image that recalls Rego's *Girl Lifting Up Her Skirts to a Dog*). 'Gretchen', we are told, 'the only flower of the mountains, tucks up her white apron and waltzing gingham skirts so they will not crease or soil but, even in the last extremity of the act, her father does not remove his mask for who would recognize him without it?' (Carter 1988: 20). The short story is hinged on the decapitation of a young boy by his father who happens to be the village executioner. The 'dark spectacle' is witnessed by villagers ('the heroes of this spectacle') who are mesmerized by a staged scene:

> gloomily illuminated through unshed tears, the *tableau vivant* before us is suffused with the sepia tints of an old photograph and nothing within it moves. The intent immobility of the spectators, wholly absorbed as they are in the performance of their hieratic ritual, is scarcely that of living things and this *tableau vivant* might be better termed a *nature morte* for the mirthless carnival is a celebration of death.
> 
> (Carter 1988: 13–14, emphasis in the original)

The voice telling the story imbues the scene with dramatic details which turn it into a carefully staged performance, 'with light fall[ing] as if filtered through muslin' (Carter 1988: 13). The veiling of the show, as actualized by the teller's simile, seems to be justified by the hideous and grisly spectacle of the villagers: their bodies are deformed, men are 'monstrously hirsute' and 'all are filthy and verminous'. 'Clogged with lice and quiver[ing] with fleas', they are a 'museum of diseases' (Carter 1988: 18). No detail of the villagers' physical torments is spared. The primitive horde and the *Totem and Taboo* intertext are all too apparent. Their inner lives are equally tortuous with their 'inexhaustible capacity for sin' (Carter 1988: 19):

> Their days are shrouded troughs of manual toil and their nights wet, freezing, black palpitating clefts gravid with the grossest cravings, nights dedicated solely to the imaginings of unspeakable desires tortuously conceived in mortified sensibilities habitually gnawed to suppuration by the black rats of superstition whilst the needle teeth of frost corrode their bodies.
> 
> (Carter 1988: 18–19)

The Grand Guignol quality of this description can be said to act as a stylistic prop to deflect monstrosity.

Other structural elements of the 'The Executioner's Beautiful Daughter' extend the reflection on reading when an analogy is formed between the eyes of the villagers fixated on the execution and the eye of the reader. The counterpart to the grunts and squawks which is the only language known to the primitive villagers is their eyes: 'opaque fissures' which look with 'reptilian regard' (Carter 1988: 17). Similarly, the executioner's eyes are 'two narrow slits through which issue the twin regards of eyes as inexpressive as though they were part of the mask' (Carter 1988: 14). Transfixed as they are, the eyes are here reduced to the optic organs which actuate the scopic drive: they are fixed on the object, frontally, like a freeze frame, which is the very opposite of the kind of reading advocated in my argument.

The executioner and his mask exemplify the paradoxical principle of the anamorphosis, hiding and revealing at the same time. If the executioner is read as the primal father of the primitive horde, he is the one who lays down the law, but he is also the one who does not submit to it. He is his daughter's sexual abuser, while he is also the one who, in accordance with the law which forbids incest, beheads his own son for committing incest with his sister. Yet in a further perverse twist, we are told that the executioner is himself committing incest with his daughter. The perverted logic is inscribed in the signifier 'perpetrates' (Carter 1988: 20) whose etymology relates to the father (*pater*/father). The executioner's leather mask is worn like a second skin. But like the *maschera* which reveals and hides at the same time, the mask embodies and exhibits the law and hides its transgression concomitantly. The paradoxical nature of the mask is further amplified by its shape: it conceals the upper part of the face except for the two slits for the eyes and reveals only his blunt-lipped, dark-red mouth and the greyish flesh which surrounds it. Laid out in such an unnerving fashion, these portions of his meat in no way fulfil the expectations we derive from our common knowledge of faces. They have a quality of rawness as if, in some fashion, the lower face had been flayed. He, the butcher, might be displaying himself, as if he were his own meat.

(Carter 1988: 14–15)

Paradoxically again, it is not so much the mask and what it represents that creates horror but the bare part of the face, carved into a piece of meat displayed to his own eyes, 'as if, when he first put on the mask, he blotted out his own, original face and so defaced himself forever' (Carter 1988: 15). The executioner's raw face is a frontal spectacle of horror. And so is the decapitation of the twenty-year-old man by his father. The immobile spectators fix the block in silence: 'The axe falls. The flesh severs. The head rolls on. The cleft flesh spouts its fountains' (Carter 1988: 15).

The centrepiece of the short story, as the title suggests, is the executioner's 'tender-hearted daughter' (Carter 1988: 16), Gretchen, mentioned earlier. A Little Red Riding Hood figure, she goes every morning to collect eggs for her father who devours them, preferably when they are crunchy and ready to hatch. Contrary to all the other scenarios of torment, the father's incest is treated lightly, without the array of crude details that characterize the other monstrosities. The revelation of incest is delayed until the very end of the story, thus provoking unease for the reader who has read the story unaware. Equally disturbing is the way the narration bears no trace of a straight positioning regarding the treatment of perversity. Furthermore, the relationship between the sister and brother interrogates the reader. After her brother's head rolls away, she buries it. How are the metaphors of the 'bearded strawberry' and the 'precious fruit' (Carter 1988: 16) as a substitute for her brother's decapitated head to be interpreted? Should we surmise that her brother was more a fruit of delight than a forbidden one?

Beyond the multiple literal motifs suggesting anamorphic principles, an anamorphic reading reveals that something might be eluded: if one of the ways of reading the short story is as an exploration of the expression and the perversion of the law, when is the narrative voice conveying the expression of the law, that is the symbolic castration that forbids incest? Like the mesmerized villagers, is the unsettled reader condemned to face the text frontally, or does the enunciative architecture of the story provide space that allows a lateral reading? It is interesting that the voice framing the telling of the tale embeds the reader in a way meant to make him or her a participant in the performance: 'Here, we are high in the uplands' (Carter 1988: 13). The personal pronouns 'we' and 'us' interspersed through the text make the reader a visual and narrative companion to the anonymous spectator and teller of the story. But at the same time, the personal pronouns paradoxically create an enunciative space that permits some possibility of distance and sideways movement. It is also up to the reader's creativity to engage with hints offered by the text. The narrative voice is present through the multiplicity of 'as if' scenarios and through markers of subjectivity expressed by 'might' and 'must', which are spaces for the reader to accommodate his/her reading. We might also choose to hear the 'inadequacy' of the perverted family relationship and the expression of the law by displacement, unequivocally if modestly: 'An *inadequate* orifice in the flat roof puffs out a few scant breaths of domestic smoke and penetration inside is effected only with the utmost difficulty' (Carter 1988: 17, my emphasis).

Unease remains though, especially through the light-hearted treatment of Gretchen. Through a play with signifiers, the text humorously brings together the young girl with the chicks eaten by the father. 'The indifferent hens peck and cluck about her feet', 'peck' and 'cluck' turning into 'pluck' in a sort of portmanteau word. And 'her flaxen plaits bob above her breasts as she goes to pluck, from their nests, the budding eggs' (Carter 1988: 18) resonates like the traditional nursery rhyme:

> My old hen on a wall
> Pecks away and does not fall
> Peck, peck, peckety-peck,
> Flaps its tail and flies away.

The frivolous treatment of the perversity and the exhibition of torments are similarly unsettling.

'The Executioner's Beautiful Daughter' provides occasion to wonder about the spectacle of horrors and torments that Carter and Rego display. Both artists create enunciative, narrative and visual exits that are modes of *accommodation*. Unlike the villagers mesmerized by the block and the rolling head that is displayed before their eyes, readers and viewers are permitted to wander, roam, displace themselves. In Carter, black humour, wit and pervasive intertextuality, combined with horror, produce hiatuses and ruptures in reading. Laughter is a distraction – it entertains – but it also distracts us from what is expressed laterally. In Rego, the props within the paintings direct the gaze and interpretation out-of-frame, transporting the viewer to a moment beyond the scene that can only be imagined. When reading Carter, the eccentric position provided by Rego's painting enables us to alter perspective. The paintings reveal (in the photographic sense of the term) laterally what humour and laughter sought out to divert and tame in Carter's texts. At any rate, these are forms of evasion that alter meaning and produce distance with something irrepresentable, with that which might only be read or looked at laterally. Subsequently, as the reader/viewer takes back his or her frontal position, the glimpse or the flicker of that irrepresentable cannot be forgotten or eluded.

In her essay on Frida Kahlo, reflecting on the Mexican painter's art of self-portraiture and play with the gaze, Angela Carter wrote that 'when she was well enough, [Kahlo] painted the strangeness of the world made visible' (1989: 11). Making visible – if only through a glimpse – how inhabitable the world can be in its tormented and perverted humanity is the hallmark of Carter and Rego's art. Reflecting on her own painting, Paula Rego says as much when she explains that 'monsters are fear with no face… If I could give fear a face, it would be fine' (2006). The force of Carter's and Rego's art is that it manages to transport readers and viewers to an unsettling edge. These two artists use their pens and brushes to set the power of our imagination in motion and, in so doing, make the world more habitable and life more hospitable.

## Works cited

Barthes, R. (1977), *Roland Barthes by Roland Barthes*, trans. R. Howard, London and Basingstoke: Macmillan.
Barthes, R. (1982), *Empire of Signs*, trans. R. Howard, New York: Hill and Wang.
Carter, A. (1983), 'Notes from the Front Line', in M. Wandor (ed), *On Gender and Writing*, 69–77, London: Pandora.
Carter, A. (1983a), 'The Courtship of Mr Lyon', in *The Bloody Chamber*, 41–51, London: Virago.
Carter, A. (1983b), 'The Tiger's Bride', in *The Bloody Chamber*, 51–67, London: Virago.
Carter, A. (1988), 'The Executioner's Beautiful Daughter', in *Fireworks*, 13–21, London: Virago.
Carter, A. (1989), *Frida Kahlo*, London: Redstone.
Collins, D. (1992), 'Anamorphosis and the Eccentric Observer: Inverted Perspective and Construction of the Gaze', *Leonardo*, 25 (1): 72–82.
Gilman, E. (1989), 'Interart Studies and the "Imperialism" of Language', *Poetics Today*, 10 (1): 5–30.
Hutcheon, L. (2006), *A Theory of Adaptation*, New York and London: Routledge.

Louvel, L. (2018), *The Pictorial Third: An Essay into Intermedial Criticism*, New York and London: Routledge.
McEwen, J. (2006), *Paula Rego*, London: Phaidon.
Mulvey-Roberts, M. and F. Robinson (eds) (2016), *Strange Worlds: The Vision of Angela Carter*, Bristol: Sansom.
Rego, P. (2006), interview C. Courtney, 19 June, British Library sound collection, C466/238.
Sage, L. (1992), 'The Soaring Imagination', *Guardian*, 18 February. Available online: https://www.theguardian.com/books/1992/feb/17/fiction.angelacarter (accessed 5 May 2020).
Warner, M. (2003), 'Introduction', in P. Rego (ed), *Jane Eyre*, 7–17, London: Enitharmon Editions.

Part Four

# Material bodies

# 10

# Perceiving pleasures and appetites in *The Bloody Chamber*: 'Surprise me for dessert with every ice-cream in the ice box'

Maria José Pires

Angela Carter seemed to apprehend diverse pleasures and appetites in her short story collection *The Bloody Chamber* (1979), and this illustrates how she remained enquiring, controversial and fascinated by narrative risk at the end of the 1970s, though some of her readers were still caught by the entertaining surface of the texts published during that decade. She was indeed capable of calling attention to the most pointedly corporeal dimension of the fairy tale tradition, and hence 'shatter pure and evocative imagery with the crude' in a fireworksy manner. By bringing to mind that 'there's a materiality to symbols and a materiality to imaginative life which should be taken quite seriously' (Kenyon 1992: 33), Carter possibly tried to 'surprise me for dessert with every ice-cream in the ice box' (Carter 1979a: 23). This chapter seeks to outline how these pleasures and appetites were explored through interactive gastronomic experiences and the way they deal with the challenge of reading *The Bloody Chamber* and materializing such readings that pervade the field of multisensory perception (Spence 2014: 203) in a way that shows multilayered responses to Carter's short stories – from production and preparation/performance to consumption.

Almost forty years after the publication of *The Bloody Chamber*, Carter's 'Appetites beyond the grasp of imagination' were celebrated in two gastronomic experiences in 2017. Firstly, at the academic and cultural meeting *Receiving/Perceiving Angela Carter* (May) and secondly in the international conference *Experiencing Food: Designing Dialogues* (October), both conceived with students from the MSc Innovation in Culinary Arts and Sciences at the Estoril Higher Institute for Tourism and Hotel Studies (ESHTE), Portugal.[1] The former was a

Gothic-oriented interpretation of *The Bloody Chamber* at ESHTE's restaurant, in Estoril, whereas the latter revealed a more deconstructive one, along with Carter's explicit attentiveness to role-breaking and role-remaking and her studies of gender crossovers regarding passivity and aggression. These are predominantly strong in the two books published in 1979: *The Sadeian Woman* and *The Bloody Chamber*.[2] In her collection, the stories indicate a shift from a feminism that focuses on women's pain to a politics that stresses female pleasure – 'In making this shift, Carter eschews simple role reversal to create a synthesis between binarisms: masculine and feminine, predator and prey, consumer and consumed' (Parker 2000: 155).

These gastronomic experiences interpret the way Carter's fantasies persistently hold an anchoring in the actual, grounding escapism and the fairy tale tradition makes available what she needed – a strong reference point as the quintessential blend of reality and fantasy (Cavallaro 2011: 17). This pairs with Carter's definition of 'fairy tales' as 'stories from the oral tradition, [which] are all of them the most vital connection we have with the imagination of the ordinary men and women whose labour created our world' (Carter 1990: ix). Even though fairy tales transmit history, sociology and psychology, these are unofficial, according to Carter. Also, the efforts of the people mentioned by her continue over the centuries, but their identities are no more preserved in historiography than the names of those 'who first invented meatballs' (x).

In *The Bloody Chamber*, Carter argues that if women are to attain an independent existence, there is the need for a certain amount of tigerishness, 'if they are to avoid – at the extreme end of passivity – becoming meat' (Atwood 1994: 121). One way of looking at this collection is to read into its categories of meat-eater, given that the book is arranged in the following manner: three cat family stories in Atwoods' perspective – 'The Bloody Chamber', 'The Courtship of Mr Lyon' and 'The Tiger's Bride' – followed by a kind of comic coda – 'Puss-in-Boots' – three stories presenting ambiguous supernatural creatures – 'The Erl-King', 'The Snow-Child' and 'The Lady of the House of Love' – and three wolf family stories – 'The Werewolf', 'The Company of Wolves' and 'Wolf-Alice'.

As a revision of the Bluebeard narrative, the first story gives the reader two carnivores and two herbivores, each one composed of a male and a female (122). In this reworking, the Marquis typifies the cannibalistic appetite of previous male protagonists in Carter's writings. We witness a 'tenderness' which actually contradicts his efforts to 'tenderise' his bride, silencing her in a false secure world (Parker 2000: 155). After offering her the wedding dress, the Marquis' cannibalistic appetites are implied by the bride's feeling she was getting 'a

Christmas gift of crystallised fruit' – a comparison decisive to her acceptance of his proposal, possibly to 'banish the spectre of poverty from its habitual place at our [their] meagre table' (Carter 1979a: 7). Reference to Christmas usually implies an ephemeral blissful period, associated with such luxury food items as the gift of crystallized fruit, which compensates for material deprivations in her earlier life. Therefore, it turns into a way of bridging the deficiency in her life. Also, the next references to food – the 'box of marrons glacés' (8) which he offers her, the 'sticky liqueur chocolates' (16) brought in by the maid, or the 'silver bucket of iced champagne' (10) – denote high decadence and wealth, which contrasts with her relatively impoverished condition – 'in the salon of the princess where I'd first met him, among the tea-cups and the little cakes, I, the orphan, hired out of charity to give them their digestive of music' (13). At the October 2017 gastronomic event, the sensory food experience was accompanied by playing the piano pieces referred to in 'The Bloody Chamber' and every guest received a sealed letter beginning with 'Q. Why are you reading stories through a gastronomic experience?' 'A. Because all fiction should be open-ended'.

In the story, the dinner before the Marquis' departure from the castle is lavish. The main course is 'a Mexican dish of pheasant with hazelnuts and chocolate' (18), an exotic delicacy which uses mole, a traditional Mexican chocolate sauce originally used in Mesoamerica. The balance of a well-structured meal came with the 'salad', the 'white voluptuous cheese' (anticipating ample, unrestrained pleasure to the senses) and a 'sorbet of muscat grapes and Asti spumante' for dessert (19). The gastronomic aspect of the meal was carefully planned, since the dishes complemented each other, a balance and harmony that was achieved by avoiding repetitive colour, flavour, texture, or ingredients (even with the Italian Asti spumante and the muscat grapes).

An expensive and exclusive French Champagne accompanies the meal: 'A celebration of Krug exploded festively' (19). Beverages are invariably used to define the nature of an occasion and this choice reveals a discerning concern with taste and smell that one might expect from a gourmet: the complete barrel fermentation and much extended lees ageing account for the raciness and richness in palate of Krug wines, along with an oakiness, which combines a disgorgement freshness and oxidative maturity, on the nose. The reference to acrid black coffee served in the finest tableware perfectly complements Krug's characteristic dryness; the 'precious little cups so fine it shadowed the birds with which they were painted' (19) is indicative of the newly wedded feeling of being eclipsed by her husband – a feeling also present with other beverages. She has Cointreau, and he drinks cognac. Generally, there is a common distinction between 'masculine' and 'feminine' beverages – even where no other differentiation is found. Here, the versatility of the beverage imbibed by the narrator envisages her adaptability and resourcefulness, since Cointreau is usually used as an aperitif, but occasionally as a digestive, and it is considered to be either a triple sec or a unique category of liqueur, whereas cognac, the Marquis' choice, is a unique spirit in that it has been doubly distilled.

Since drinking constructs the social relationship between the drinkers, often dictating the interaction proper to the occasion, beverages were carefully chosen for both 2017 gastronomic experiences. For instance, national organic wine from a local producer was selected, who normally only exports his wines making it a relative rarity for consumption in Portugal. There are few, if any, alcoholic beverages termed 'socially neutral', and alcohol is normally studied as a symbolic vehicle for 'identifying, describing, constructing and manipulating cultural systems, values, interpersonal relationships, behavioural norms and expectations' (Social Issues Research Centre 1998: 31).

The newly wedded narrator in 'The Bloody Chamber' is not used to some of the eating rituals and confesses that her 'imagination, still that of a schoolgirl, ran riot' (Carter 1979a: 23). Her menu requests reflect a defiant exercise of free-will understandable for a newly empowered but rather clueless young lady: 'A fowl in cream – or should I anticipate Christmas with a varnished turkey? No; I have decided. Avocado and shrimp, lots of it, followed by no entrée at all. But surprise me for dessert with every ice-cream in the ice box' (ibid.). She replaces the meat course with seafood, neglects the expected entrée and asks for plenty of a sweet dessert in a way which is child-like. After eating the more adult and sophisticated palate-cleansing iced dessert of sorbet with the Marquis, she now changes to ice-cream, which contrasts with the denser and the intensely flavoured sorbet with its more fragile and ephemeral texture. Her choices perceptibly shock the housekeeper, who had previously ordered for the solitary bridal 'delicious' coffee and croissants and freshly squeezed 'aromatic juice from an orange into a chilled goblet' (22), with an emphasis on the sensory stimulus. But the narrator is celebrating her new personal and social status, lighting up the castle as a 'seaborne birthday cake' (24) reminiscent of a child's birthday party.

The essence of the second gastronomic moment in May 2017 ('Stripping the leaves off an artichoke') with a fresh tuna tartare, after a meat amuse-bouche, was subversive defiance. The cured egg-yolk (symbolizing birth, rebirth, but also something which was tampered) topped the fish and an opened artichoke brought to life the Marquis' cannibalistic desires, when the bride first perceived him studying her 'with the assessing eye of a connoisseur inspecting horseflesh, or even of a housewife in the market, inspecting cuts on the slab' (11), and when consummating their marriage, he stripped her like an artichoke: 'gourmand that he was, as if he were stripping the leaves off an Artichoke – but do not imagine much finesse about it; this artichoke was no particular treat for the diner [...]. He approached his familiar treat with a weary appetite', leaving her 'bare as a lamb chop' (15). The allusion to an artichoke anticipates their future, since this is a Mediterranean thistle-like plant widely cultivated for its large immature flower head, rather like her, known for its edible fleshy leaves and heart, which usually has to be cooked before eaten. Furthermore, apart from the English designation cautioning about the sharp-tipped bracts towards its innermost part, eating an artichoke is considered sensual, and by stripping her, the Marquis can be seen as curtailing her own mortality, for the artichoke was also a symbol of immortality in Greek mythology. There is a last reference to those cannibalistic desires, when the Marquis is about to kill his wife and declaims – 'Do you think I shall lose appetite for the meal if you are so long about serving it? No; I shall grow hungrier, more ravenous with each moment, more cruel!... I have a place prepared for your exquisite corpse in my display of flesh!' (39). Here Carter celebrates the power resulting from the destruction of a cannibalistic appetite when the heroine's mother usurps the traditional male role by blazing in to save her daughter.

At the October 2017 gastronomic experience, the menu included an appetizer of an open oyster ('Scene from a voluptuary's life'), a traditional aphrodisiac, tinted red in a bed of pebbles and seaweeds amidst which the guest could find a semi-hidden pearl of coated cooked meat. This moment portrayed a sexual tension in the dining experience, since the interpretation also encapsulates the heroine's status as a precious and beautiful object. Following this gastronomic moment, the entrée ('Sombre delirium, guilty joy') was then a mackerel bone fried on puffed rice in a bed of red algae covering a bare bone (on a Multiforma platter, designed by Mikaela Dörfel, Vista Alegre) to expose 'the full extent of the Marquis' perverse and murderous tendencies but also Carter's subversive spirit, as the murdered previous wives revealed the full pleasure in death' (Bonacho and Pires et al. 2018: 150).[3]

Considered Carter's second cat family fable in *The Bloody Chamber*, 'The Courtship of Mr Lyon' immediately transports us to 'the mean kitchen' where a girl waited for her father, who, meanwhile, was exhorted to eat and drink from silver tableware. The food offered indicates a carnivore host – 'sandwiches of thick-cut roast beef, still bloody... with some excellent mustard thoughtfully provided in a stoneware pot' – who considerately offers an alternative to the whisky in the decanter, soda. The mysterious Beast growls at the father to bring his daughter to dinner. As with the Marquis, the Beast's social status allows him to provide a luxurious environment – 'the dining room was Queen Anne, tapestried, a gem' – and exquisite food – 'an aromatic soup', 'bird', 'soufflé, cheese' (Carter 1979a: 45). However, unlike the Marquis, the Beast overtly acknowledges his otherness and refuses to participate in the meal, which is all cold, except for the soup, and admits disliking the presence of servants as these are a constant human presence which 'would remind him too bitterly of his otherness' (45). Indeed, the lack of other humans turns into an enigma, considering that the meals are always prepared while Beauty stays over – 'but the trays of food had arrived on a dumb waiter inside the mahogany cupboard in her parlour' (46). The service in both dining experiences in 2017 had analogous approaches, whereas the serving staff in the May gastronomic event became part of the setting through the use of elements related to the performance – like removing the feathered hat from the first amuse-bouche and wearing it back to the kitchen, balancing old keys while approaching the table for the 'The Bloody Chamber' inspired moment or letting a tarot card be perceptible in their black uniforms for the main course on 'The Lady of the House of Love' – in October the mirror-filled-room simultaneously multiplied the waiters and captivated their beings and images into the setting itself (at Palácio Foz, Lisbon).

In 'The Courtship of Mr Lyon', the Beast is changed by love from carnivore to herbivore (Atwood 1994: 124); since he 'had not the stomach to kill the gentle beasts' (Carter 1979a: 49), he could not eat during Beauty's absence and would only consider the possibility of eating some breakfast on her return. That triggered the last moment of the May 2017 dining experience: an all-edible garden in which guests would dig in (after the collapse of its four-wall isomalt-glass case engraved with 'A suspension of reality') and choose their preferred detail from the short stories: a rose, a diamond or ruby, a playing card, a key, pieces of mirror, bits of the forest or the 'Gobble you up!' sign. Accordingly, as Carter makes us believe in the unexpected, the pun here 'was to literally eat words and savour literature' (Bonacho and Pires et al. 2018: 149).

In the other Beauty and the Beast story, 'The Tiger's Bride', we are immediately presented with a reference to food while comparing the cold distant land Beauty and father came from with 'the lovely land where the lemon trees grow' and where 'the sun spills fruit for you' (Carter 1979a: 51), only now we find a different transformation. Here Beauty is determined not to give the 'cold, white meat of contract' of her body when isolated from her sense of self, but to give away her 'existence' (66). Food is again used to characterize the region that welcomes them with its 'poor food, pasta soaked in oil, boiled beef with sauce of bitter herbs' (53) and their economically deprived conditions by the reference to the potent pomace brandy grappa, which was originally made from leftovers at the end of the wine season. Like 'The Courtship of Mr Lyon', there are not many references to food, besides a sporadic allusion to the Beast's 'spurious Eden in which all the fruit was blighted by cold' (57) and to Beauty's changed circumstances as 'a frosted glass of sparkling wine [that] sat convenient to [her father's] hand beside an ice bucket' (65). Apart from these, the idea of being gobbled up ties in with nursery fears – 'if this young lady was not a good little girl and did not eat her boiled beetroot, then the tiger-man would…. GOBBLE YOU UP!' (56). This can be summarized as 'herbivore meets carnivore, meat meets teeth, at the most basic and primitive level' (Atwood 1994: 125). The emphasis on the sexual tension is apparent from our 'earliest and most archaic of fears, fear of devourment. The beast and his carnivorous bed of bone and I, white, shaking, raw, approaching him as if offering, in myself, the key to a peaceable kingdom in which his appetite need not be my extinction' (67). The culinary choice in October 2017 evoked the disruption of the lady lost at cards only to come to terms with her true nature with the beast ('If you are so careless of your treasures… ') through a rich fish soup, carefully arranged in the centre of a covered Marés plate (designed by Carsten Gollnick, Vista Alegre), which dissolved while a broth was poured over.

In Carter's radio play adaptation of Puss in Boots, she combines 'Perrault's great hero' with 'the Cat as Con Man', 'a Figaroesque valet – a servant so much the master already', in a version of the story which is 'a masterpiece of cynicism' (*Carter* 1998: 454). In Carter's short story 'Puss-in-Boots', the narrator Figaro uses food references in a wide variety of situations, as he lodges above a kitchen and helps his master to cheat at gambling to earn money and buy food. Indeed, their relationship is predicated on food, with the young master offering the cat a sandwich and a 'snifter of brandy' (Carter 1979a: 69), the first time he shows his 'habitual smile'. Puss knows how to appreciate not only the 'excellent beef sandwiches', given that he relished 'a lean slice of roast beef', but the beverage he was offered, for he had learned 'a taste for spirits, since I [he] started life as a wine-shop cat' (69). The world had sharpened his savouring ability, for he lives a carefree existence, 'lecherous as liquorice' (70). Food reflects moods and behaviours; the young man refuses to eat when faced with the impossibility of having the lady he has fallen in love with: 'I [Puss] brought him a fine pigeon from the inn kitchen, fresh off the spit, *parfumé avec* tarragon, but he wouldn't touch it so I crunched it up, bones and all' (72). Thus, Puss can be simultaneously sophisticated, by using French, and also primal, as when he crunches noisily. This crunching sound, the wooden barrel top for the wine reference and the feathered hat were part of the performance in the amuse-bouche of the May 2017 dining experience in which the food playfully deceived the guests: masquerading as traditional fried chicken legs, two similarly shaped coated legs, placed one on top of the other, one made from hare-meat, the other from vegetables. Twice conned, guests discovered the essence when they tasted it.

But Carter's 'ubiquitous Puss' evolved in such a way that the next time he mentions a meal it is 'one dinner honestly paid for, for a wonder' (79), and as the young fool is 'off his feed, again', the cat concludes, 'Satisfaction has not satisfied him; that soul they both saw in one another's bodies has such insatiable hunger no single meal could ever appease it' (79–80). Again, the reference could be 'lecherous as liquorice', but Puss had a new plan while being fed by the lady's kitty – 'she's saved me a pig's trotter, a whole entire pig's trotter the Missus smuggled to her with a wink. A feast! Masticating, I muse' (80). The sound unison of masticating and muse echoes an understandable harmony between the head and the stomach. The idea of feasting can also suggest that Puss' 'hitherto-untrammelled heart' had been wormed into, but the way his meals are presented mirrors his miserable life, in opposition to his intention to make the most of it and, as a result, this story proves to be a 'hymn to here-and-now common sensual pleasure, to ordinary human love, to slap-and-tickle delight, available to all. When compared to the three following stories, this one is "just a short entr'acte"' (Atwood 1994: 127), in the generally more Baroque context of *The Bloody Chamber*; so was the dish created in May 2017, 'Masticating, I muse'.

The first story of the middle group of *The Bloody Chamber* is 'The Erl-King', and the woods are described by a surprised wandering maiden on 'a cold day of late October, when the withered blackberries dangled like their own dour spooks on the discoloured brambles' (Carter 1979a: 84), by 'heavy bunches of red berries as ripe and delicious as goblin or enchanted fruit hung on the hawthorns' (85). Any of these various thorny shrubs impress and enthral her in a way that she is easily seduced by the sinister Erl-King, a seeming personification of the forest itself. The references to food in this story are both literal and metaphoric. The maiden is clearly warned that 'there are some eyes [that] can eat you [*sic*]' (86) – later she observes that his are 'eyes green as apples. Green as dead sea fruit' (89) – but she is interested in his way of life and mainly in what he eats:

> Why, the bounty of the woodland! Stewed nettles; savoury messes of chickweed sprinkled with nutmeg; he cooks the foliage of shepherd's purse as if it were

cabbage. He knows which of the frilled, blotched, rotted fungi are fit to eat; he understands their eldritch ways, how they spring up overnight in lightless places and thrive on dead things. Even the homely wood blewits, that you cook like tripe, with milk and onions, and the egg-yolk yellow chanterelle with its fan-vaulting and faint scent of apricots, all spring up overnight like bubbles of earth, unsustained by nature, existing in a void. And I could believe that it has been the same with him; he came alive from the desire of the woods.

(86)

Taking bounty as a reward, an inducement or payment, especially one that is given for acts deemed beneficial to the woodland helps introduce and better understand the Erl-king. The bounty described above is prepared by him, which allows us to acknowledge his human-like needs as when he is stewing nettles, seasoning herbs with spices to make these more flavoursome. At the same time, he is a supernatural creature with magical powers. His knowledge and diet hint of his own self-sufficiency, and cooking skills with these edible agarics, whose fragrance and geometric design are described. The choice of a tree bark to contain the dessert conceived in May 2017 was an interpretation of this relation with the bio-system.

The description of the Erl-king's diet is rather long and includes his gathering and delicate handling of unnatural treasures, along with the preparation of nature's gifts: 'a soup or stew, seasoned with wild garlic' from a trapped rabbit, or 'soft cheese that has a unique, rank, amniotic taste' (86). The uniqueness of his cheese's taste and the use of wild garlic to season meat, with its pungent onion odour, reveal his preferences for certain tastes and smells. Another sense of sound is indulged by the birdsong of the girls turned into birds and imprisoned in cages. Even the 'musical and aromatic' kitchen cannot distract the reader from recognizing his almost carnivorous carnality, for as the maiden comments: 'He is the tender butcher who showed me how the price of flesh is love; skin the rabbit, he says! Off come all my clothes' (87).

Despite returning to him ('Eat me, drink me; thirsty, cankered, goblin-ridden'),[4] the maiden finally understood his intentions, and the similarity between his feeding the trapped birds and her own consumption becomes apparent – 'he spreads out a goblin feast of fruit for me, such appalling succulence' (89). If she became entirely a part of nature, her human self-consciousness would vanish, leaving her bound to nature's cycle. She did not want to be defined absolutely by the Erl-King's seductive but obliterating sexuality. In this match of inequalities, it was her freedom against his, and she chose hers and that of other girls, by opening 'all the cages' (Atwood 1994: 127). This moment was portrayed in May 2017 by the sound from the popcorn ice-cream created for the dessert mentioned above; at the same time, the hidden soft red-fruit coulis was deliberately hidden between the innocence-like white ice-cream and the all-organic dark tree bark. Similar to this interpretation, in October there were two desserts: a watermelon carpaccio brushed with wild cherry and dried fruit granola disguised as meat ('A haunting sense of the imminent cessation of being') and an olive cake with preserved orange, egg cream and honey pollen ('We must learn to cope with the world before we can interpret it').[5]

The brief fable 'Snow Child', in which the Count's desire for a 'perfect' virginal girl-child as a sexual object materialized into a snow-child, has no reference to food. However, it became transversal to the October gastronomic experience as a whole, through the choice of exclusively white dishware for the meal; black bread spread throughout the table; the palate-cleansing mint meringue infused with broom on white rose petals, over which guests were invited to leave drops of red juice using a pipette (on an O!Moon Eclipse plate by designer Santos Bregaña, Vista Alegre); and a final red bonbon that intentionally tainted the mouth, which guests were made aware of through the use of a hand-mirror.

In contrast, the 'The Lady of the House of Love' story, based upon the BBC Radio 4 radio play 'Vampirella', first broadcast in 1976 (1992), has various references to food and the idea of feeding. It illustrates the possibility of reversing the gender polarities of the lion and tiger stories, since 'the carnivore here is a female vampire' (Carter 1979a: 128), who survives by enticing young men into her bedroom and feeding on them, in a family tradition. Thus, from the beginning not only are her guests seen as food/nourishment but she is also compared to food itself (94). Terms like 'voracious' and 'gorge' contrast with 'the ghastliness of her condition, nothing'. Even if the Countess always wants 'fresh meat' because 'hunger always overcomes her', she loathes the food she eats and would rather be the provider, as she demonstrates to unwise young men while serving them 'coffee in tiny cracked, precious cups, and little sugar cakes' (96).

This recurring situation is only altered by a virginal English soldier. She is warned of his arrival through the famous two verses: 'Be he alive or be he dead/I'll grind his bones to make my bread' (96). Again, the temptation is through food, with the Countess's housekeeper's invitation to supper. For a second time, we are reminded of the enticing role of food, but in more detail: 'while he bemusedly drank his wine, she disappeared but soon returned bearing a steaming platter of the local spiced meat stew with dumplings, and a shank of black bread' (99–100). The homely peasant fare contrasts with the delicacy of how the

Countess welcomes him with coffee 'patiently filtering her fragrant brew' herself, since the housekeeper has left a 'silver spirit kettle, a silver coffee pot, cream jug, sugar basin, cups ready on a silver tray'. This was the theme for the decoration of the room and side table in May 2017.

In 'The Lady of the House of Love' the comparison between the 'strange touch of elegance, even if discoloured' (101), hints at the possibility of change, albeit the vampire's automatic behaviour. Yet, after the coffee is drunk, the sugar biscuits eaten, this sinister 'Sleeping Beauty' only knows of 'one kind of consummation' (103). Her intentions to feed on the young soldier, supported by the portraits on the walls clanging 'Dinnertime, dinnertime', are motivated by 'a ghastly hunger', which gnaws her entrails. However, the somnambulist maiden is dead by the following morning and her keeper has no bones to bury under her roses – 'The food her roses feed on gives them their rich colour, their swooning odour, that breathes lasciviously of forbidden' (105). Similarly to the previous story, 'The Snow-Child', a fanged rose is all that is left, the rose of death. Roses also played a relevant role in May 2017 gastronomic experience, when guests were blindfolded and felt the rose-scented atmosphere, listened to the broadcast of 'Vampirella', while two pig heads were placed centrally on base of dirt (concocted of blood and activated charcoal) surrounded by red roses, for the remaining of the dinner, and the main course of pork was plated on a tombstone engraved with 'Angela Carter 1940–1992'.[6] In addition to these roses and the ones from the edible garden, guests were offered a red-sugared one to keep.

As already mentioned, *The Bloody Chamber* concludes with three wolf stories. The first, 'The Werewolf', retells 'Little Red Riding Hood', but here the wolf turns out to have been the grandmother herself. This short story presents a cold northern country and in the first half mentions its fears and superstitions where food is an important ingredient – 'the leg of a pig hung up to cure, [and] a string of drying mushrooms', and in these upland woodsmen's graveyards, instead of flowers, they 'put out small, votive offerings, little loaves, sometimes a cake' but, yet, it is common knowledge among them that the Devil 'holds picnics in the graveyards and invites the witches; then, they dig up fresh corpses, and eat them' (108). These references were echoed in the main course just described (May 2017).

In the second half of 'The Werewolf', we realize that women can also be werewolves and not necessarily victims. At the end of the 1970s, Carter returned to her demanding 'cold country' Sheffield and similarly to the good child in this story, she recognized more than ever the need to be a competent child, 'to know how to recognize danger but to avoid being paralyzed by fear, to know how to use your father's hunting knife to defend yourself against those who also hunt' (Atwood 1994: 129–30). The 'The Company of Wolves', which may be read as a variation on 'The Tiger's Bride', presents a virginal, innocent but strong Little Red Riding Hood, who makes her way through the forest. The wolf, a 'carnivore incarnate', who having once had 'a taste of flesh then nothing else will do', easily identifies 'our smell of meat' (Carter 1979a: 110). The introduction mainly portrays the wolf's irrationality and effectiveness as a hunter ('for if you stray from the path for one instant, the wolves will eat you'). It is famine and irrationality that also justify the actions described, but the wolf still mourns for its own, 'irremediable appetites' (112). A long introduction to the wolf's condition leads to what sounds like the original story of Red Riding Hood; however, as a 'well-warned [girl], she carried a carving knife in the basket prepared by her mother to take to her grandmother' (112–13). Analogously, a wooden-handle knife was used for the main course in October 2017, even if the interpretation was on 'Wolf-Alice'.

The basket she carries is packed with cheeses, 'a bottle of harsh liquor distilled from brambles; a batch of flat oatcakes baked on the hearthstone; a pot or two of jam' (113). All these products actually result from transforming nature's offerings, and concerning the brambles, whose fruit includes the blackberry and raspberry, there are many types with recurved thorns that dig into clothing and flesh when the victim tries to pull away from them and, therefore, the thorny varieties are sometimes grown for game cover, and occasionally for protection. Hence, this is not such an artless basket of food as it may seem, and the carving knife is evidence of a well-equipped girl in addition to the brambles reference, which suggests a maturing and defensive girl. In such a way, Carter splashes our imagination and that became the pre-dessert motto in May 2017: 'an exotic feeling given by the spices, as ginger, cardamom; different textures, as soft, creamy, crumble, velvet and the breaking of the sphere; and the red fruits represent the fruits from the basket' (Bonacho and Pires et al. 2018: 149).

She later laughs at the wolf confidently when he says: 'All the better to eat you with' (Carter 1979a: 118), realizing she has to rescue herself. The girl then 'freely' gives the kiss she owes him for their bet, because she knows she is 'nobody's meat', and then climbs into bed with the wolf, who by the following morning has become 'tender'. Atwood's conclusion clearly expresses this perception:

> As with all of Carter's would-be steaks and chops, this 'wise child' wins the herbivore-carnivore contest by refusing fear, by taking matters into her own hands, by refusing to allow herself to be defined as somebody's meat, and by 'freely' learning to – if not run with the tigers – at least lie down with them.

Whether she has become more wolf-like or he has become more human is anybody's guess, but in this story each participant appears to retain his or her own nature. A consolatory nonsense… that tries for the kind of synthesis Carter suggested in *The Sadeian Woman*: 'neither submissive nor aggressive'.

(Atwood 1994: 130)

This is a clear example of Carter's position revealing how the 1970s was a turning point in her writing career. What Carter had learnt by then complies with running with tigers or lying down with them; she had seen what it takes to become a wise child.

The last story, 'Wolf-Alice', the most grotesque of the last group, depicts a strange alliance between two oddities, a feral female child who was raised as a wolf and an undead ghoulish werewolf, a Duke, who casts no reflection in mirrors and feeds on corpses. Accordingly, both these characters are the carnivore in its least attractive form, and the story explores the journey towards subjectivity and self-awareness from the perspective of the child – as he gradually comes to realize her own identity as a young woman.

The Duke is, like the wolf, 'carnivore incarnate'; even his bedroom 'is compared to a place where animals are slaughtered and dressed for food or market', 'like the interior of an Iberian butcher's shop'; and at night 'his eyes see only appetite' (Carter 1979a: 120). The image created by the 'rusted wash of pain' implies the declining of a lifetime that simultaneously brought and caused pain. To a certain extent, he is portrayed as such an oddity that nothing seems to deter him from his 'menus': 'If you stuff a corpse with garlic, why, he only slavers at the treat: cadavre provençale' (121). The reference to this French cookery term lends the description a sharper and intelligent twist. In such a state of affairs only someone 'who is not wolf or woman' seems able to escape his walk of life. Which is why, having been raised with flesh-eaters, and hence lacking human consciousness, the sight of the Count in the kitchen with a man's leg slung over his shoulder does not trouble her – 'in her absolute and verminous innocence' (123). Her innocence is characterized as supreme, unconditional and infested with, or suggestive of, vermin. Thus, she is portrayed as being in-between stages and that makes her preferences unique.

From the narrator's standpoint, the ending is neither hallucinating happy nor unhappy: the girl has grown up and got what she wanted; although she has played both lamb and tiger, yet she is neither, only a grown-up woman. This ending also reveals Carter's easiness with her own experiences before travelling to Japan, in Japan and on her return, 'because now she knew how to wear clothes and so had put on the visible sign of her difference from them [wolves]' and, for that reason, she is aware that, similarly to this self-aware woman, 'her footprints on damp earth are beautiful and menacing as those Man Friday left' (125). Such a self-awareness and the link to the Count inspired the main course in the October 2017 dining experience: fragrances of the woods, cubed pork-belly, layers and textures of caramelized cabbage as her rough skin, and a pea flower (in a sexual inference) were organized on one side of the plate, coupled with a pork spare rib and a jus of dark-green coriander oil on the other.[7]

Understanding the manner of food for the modern subject implies knowing himself or herself, as a self-reflective, self-regulating individual. Today moderation is invoked to limit pleasure, and, in the contemporary forms of the technologies of the self, there is a desire to discover one's *true* self. In order to decipher its truth, there is a need to separate it from that which may obscure or alienate it (Foucault 1986: 362). Carter's answering back to de Sade and to Bluebeard-like characters is recreated by Atwood as follows: '*You see* – she [Carter] appears to be saying [to them] – *you didn't have to confine yourself to those mechanistic stage sets, those mechanical rituals. It wasn't just eat or be eaten. You could have been human!*' (1994: 132). Actually, *The Bloody Chamber* reminds us that there is no such thing as a free lunch, since every moment of anarchic pleasure and apparently unlimited freedom should be understood as moments, not permanent achievements (Cavallaro 2011: 118).

As people persist in constructing meanings around food (by developing taxonomies, expressing satisfaction or dissatisfaction with food or refusing to accept advertising or medical messages), they have agency and issues of power cannot be ignored but can be defied, or accepted, which is apparent in diverse ways on the subject of food. Carter's writing evidences such constructions of meanings around food. This desire to discover one's true self is patent in Carter's writing in the 1970s, and what seems strange or frightening becomes perfectly rational when set in context. Since the sharing of food within distinct food cultures remains the focus of food in literature, the October 2017 gastronomic experience had forty guests, representing the four decades since Carter visited Portugal with Shirley Cameron and Roland Miller – an experience she expected to be 'something gripping, twelve days of exhibitions, debates, films, performances and God knows what else besides' (Carter 1998: 219). These were mainly paying guests (120€ each unlike the non-paying May guests) from the *Experience Food, Designing Dialogues* conference who did not know Carter's work and who had only heard about the May experience during this conference on food design and food studies. For this reason, every guest was presented with a locked wooden box (scented with white lilies as in 'The Bloody Chamber') containing menu cards that presented each story of the collection, which they could only access after finding the key under their plates. Subsequently, most of the guests went on to read Carter's texts following the gastronomic experience.[8]

The distinct readings of Carter's texts by different MSc students in both May and October resulted in diverse approaches and moments. The guests were equally distinct. In contrast to the October event, most of the twenty-five guests in May were familiar with Carter's *Bloody Chamber*, since the experience followed the academic event *Receiving | Perceiving Angela Carter*, which included the exhibition 'Designing Perspectives. Challenging Boundaries' with readings from Design and Multimedia Design students. They mainly expected a surprising deconstruction of Carter's complexity at an aesthetic and gastronomic level which would mirror the dialogical essences in her work, according to their recorded expectations.[9] In fact, the exhibition opened the appetite of those not so familiar with Carter's work to surprise, controversy and the challenge of transforming texts into a meal – the expressions used ranged from 'fleshy', 'dark', 'bloody', 'pleasure' and 'woman'. Similarly, the recorded reactions to the experience focused on the ambience created from the moment every guest was led, one at a time, to the dining room following a waiter with a candle through a dark red maze. The main course on the tombstone was frequently mentioned in feedback, as well as the overall experience in terms of sensory diversity, which Carter would have appreciated in a witty way. Participants appreciated finding Carter in the depths of the mysterious complexities of humanity, reality and circumstances mirrored in the food and the environment created, but mostly enjoyed being presented a world that was simultaneously familiar and completely unknown, turning it into an experience of discovery which matched the critical and questioning spirit of the author. The ambience and the performance translated some of the different levels of a literary work as an immersive experience that went beyond both literature and gastronomy.[10]

By using a distinctive discourse, Carter reinforced the tradition of the fairy tale as a semiotic event and a dramatic structure – 'she adopts these ingredients, alongside many related staples and condiments of standard fairy tale fare, in the preparation of her bountiful narrative repast' (Cavallaro 2011: 107). 'We must learn to cope with the world before we can interpret it', declared Carter, who appreciated Perrault's ability to transform the moral of each tale in 'little parables of experience', to read and interpret her stories through food became a pyrotechnic experience.

## Notes

1. There were the following menu moments in May – 'Masticating, I muse'; 'Stripping the leaves off an artichoke'; 'All claws and teeth, she strikes, she gorges'; 'Irremediable appetites; The bounty of the woodland'; and 'A suspension of reality'. See video documenting details of the preparation by the ESHTE MSc students, the guests' expectations and reactions to the gastronomic experience in May (Bonachoricardo 2017), a news report that aired on national TV on the 24 May 2017, 8pm (TVI24, 2017) and further documentation on the *Receiving|Perceiving English Literature in the Digital Age* website, which includes pictures of the dishes (RP|LE 2017a). The menu moments in October were as follows – 'Scene from a voluptuary's life'; 'Sombre delirium, guilty joy'; 'If you are so careless of your treasures'; 'The voices of my brothers, darling'; 'I love the company of wolves'; 'I wish I had a girl as white as snow'; 'A haunting sense of the imminent cessation of being'; and 'We must learn to cope with the world before we can interpret it'. For documentation, see Coelho (2017), RP|LE (2017b) and Público (2017a, 2017b, 2017c).
2. Besides these two publications, Carter's interest in food writing in the 1970s includes her journalism pieces published in *New Society* (Carter 1998, 56–91), where she discusses the power dynamics of food and openly reflects upon her anorexia nervosa (56) when reviewing Mara Selvini Palazzoli's 'Self-Starvation'.
3. These two moments from the October event are documented in Coelho (2017) and Público (2017a).
4. In Christina Rossetti's *Goblin Market* (1862), the irregular and songlike rhythm describes the sisters Lizzie and Laura listening and reacting to the tempting calls of goblins selling delicious fruit. In both this long narrative poem and Carter's *The Bloody Chamber*, words appear to be unstable and ripe to enchant and then unsettle us in terms of the objectification of women.
5. Documentation of these two moments from the October experience is available in Coelho (2017) and Público (2017c).
6. In the film adaptation *The Company of Wolves* (1984), a witch turns the whole wedding party into wolves, making the guests' outsides match their insides as these debased, primal forms mock their aristocratic finery. The metamorphoses of the decadent feast were also implied in the multi-sensorial May 2017 gastronomic experience (Bonacho and Pires et al. 2018) as documented in the middle part of the video documentation (Bonachoricardo 2017).
7. The main course of the October event is documented by Coelho (2017) and Público (2017b).
8. Martin Hablesreiter and Sonja Stummerer commented: 'We have loved the Angela Carter dinner, it was the first "eat art" dinner which made sense for us – ever' (2017).
9. The guests were interviewed on video both before and after the gastronomic experience in May (Bonachoricardo 2017).

10   Quoting some of the reactions to the experience from two Carter scholars: 'I feel I just had dinner with Angela Carter! … I could absolutely see how *The Bloody Chamber* had fueled the conception of this whole meal' (Anna Watz); 'It was an extraordinary experience to have this Angela Carter banquet, a real tribute to her memory and to actually have eaten the main course off a tombstone of Angela Carter was amazing! The food was extraordinary and it really fitted with the themes of her fiction and I was absolutely overwhelmed by the standard of the cooking, the quality and just how extraordinary the whole experience was: with the dry-ice, the roses, eating bones. Absolutely amazing! Thank you so much for this incredible experience, It truly was entering a bloody chamber and eating a bloody chamber' (Marie Mulvey-Roberts), as documented by Bonachoricardo (2017).

# Works cited

Atwood, M. (1994), 'Running with the Tigers', in L. Sage (ed), *Flesh and the Mirror: Essays on the Art of Angela Carter*, 117–35, London: Virago Press.

Bonacho, R., M. Pires, C. Viegas, A. Coelho and A. Sousa (2018), 'Angela Carter: Receiving Literature through Food & Design', in R. Bonacho, A. C. De Sousa, C. Viegas, J. P. Martins, M. J. Pires, S. Velez Estêvão et al. (eds), *Experiencing Food, Designing Dialogues*, 147–51, London: CRC Press, Taylor & Francis.

Bonachoricardo (2017), 'Angela Carter. Appetites beyond the grasp of imagination Part I', YouTube Available at: https://www.youtube.com/watch?v=Kga6DT_v560 (accessed 30 April 2021).

Carter, A. (1976), *Vampirella*, G. Dearman (dir), BBC Radio 4 to Radio 3, 15 November.

Carter, A. (1979a), *The Bloody Chamber*, London: Victor Gollancz.

Carter, A. (1979b), *The Sadeian Woman: An Exercise in Cultural History*, London: Virago Press.

Carter, A. (1984), *The Company of Wolves*, N. Jordan (dir.), Palace/ITC Entertainment.

Carter, A. (1990), 'Introduction', in A. Carter (ed), *The Virago Book of Fairy Tales*, ix–xxii, London: Virago Press.

Carter, A. (1998), *Shaking a Leg: Collected Journalism and Writings*, J. Uglow (ed), London: Vintage.

Cavallaro, D. (2011), *The World of Angela Carter: A Critical Investigation*, Jefferson, North Carolina/London: McFarland & Company.

Coelho, A. P. (2017), 'A virgem, o marquês sádico e um crime à mesa', *O Público* Available at: https://www.publico.pt/2017/10/29/sociedade/noticia/a-virgem-o-marques-sadico-e-um-crime-a-mesa-1790014 (assessed 10 February 2011).

*The Company of Wolves* (1984) [Film] Dir. Neil Jordan, UK: Palace/ITC Entertainment.

Foucault, M. (1986), 'On the Genealogy of Ethics: An Overview of Work in Progress', in P. Rabinow (ed), *The Foucault Reader*, 340–72, New York: Vintage.

Hablesreiter, M. and S. Stummerer (2017), Personal Email, 23 October.

Kenyon, O. (1992), 'Angela Carter', in *The Writer's Imagination: Interviews with Major International Women Novelists*, 23–33, Bradford: University of Bradford Print Unit.

Parker, E. (2000), 'The Consumption of Angela Carter: Women, Food, and Power', *Ariel: A Review of International English*, 31 (3): 141–69.

Pires, M. J. (2017), 'The Bloody Chamber – A Taste of Angela Carter' presented at the Fireworks: the Visual Imagination of Angela Carter Conference (UWE Bristol). *Receiving | Perceiving English Literature in the Digital Age*. Available at: https://receivingperceiving.wordpress.com/angela-carter/the-bloody-chamber-a-taste-of-angela-carter/ (accessed 30 April 2021).

Público (2017a), 'À mesa com Angela Carter: as entradas' Vimeo. Available at: https://vimeo.com/240131664 (accessed 30 April 2021).

Público (2017b), 'À mesa com Angela Carter: os pratos principais' Vimeo. Available at: https://vimeo.com/240179319 (accessed 30 April 2021).

Público (2017c), 'À mesa com Angela Carter: as sobremesas' Vimeo. Available at: https://vimeo.com/240216992 (accessed 30 April 2021).

RP|EL (2017a), 'Angela Carter. Appetites beyond the Grasp of Imagination. Part I', *Receiving | Perceiving English Literature in the Digital Age*. Available at: https://receivingperceiving.wordpress.com/angela-carter/angela-carter-appetites-beyond-the-grasp-of-imagination/ (accessed 30 April 2021).

RP|EL (2017b), 'Angela Carter. Appetites beyond the Grasp of Imagination. Part II', *Receiving | Perceiving English Literature in the Digital Age*. Available at: https://receivingperceiving.wordpress.com/angela-carter/angela-carter-appetites-beyond-the-grasp-of-imagination-part-ii/.

Rossetti, C. G. ([1862] 1995), 'Goblin Market' in A. Leighton and M. Reynolds (eds), *Victorian Women Poets: An Anthology*, 378–90, Cambridge: Blackwell Publishers Ltd.

Social Issues Research Centre (1998), *Social and Cultural Aspects of Drinking* (A report to the European Commission), Oxford: Social Issues Research Centre. Available at: http://www.sirc.org/publik/drinking1.html (accessed 10 February 2011).

Spence, C., Piqueras-Fiszman, B. (2014), *The Perfect Meal. The Multisensory Science of Food and Dining*, Oxford: Wiley Blackwell.

TVI24 (2017), 'Um Jantar Inspirado em Contos Sombrios', TVI24 News, 24 May. Available at: https://tvi24.iol.pt/videos/sociedade/um-jantar-inspirado-em-contos-sombrios/5925deed0cf2004cbd40d4bf (accessed 30 April 2021).

# 11

# The skin that holds you in: States of dress and undress in Angela Carter's animal/human transformation stories

Carys Crossen

## Introduction

Angela Carter's interest in fashion,[1] according to her biographer, was an inheritance from her mother. Carter viewed her mother's mode of dress – which embraced beautiful dresses and stylish hats – as one that represented a desire for more than the life of a conventional suburban housewife. Carter herself believed that 'clothes are the visible woman – the detachable skin which expresses inner aspirations, dreams and fantasies' (Gordon 2016: 11). Accordingly a recurring theme in Carter's fiction is the uses of and symbolism of clothes and fashion. Melanie's theft of her mother's wedding dress in *The Magic Toyshop* is the cataclysmic act that is echoed in the death of her parents and her family's removal to the sinister toyshop of the title. The hapless bride in 'The Bloody Chamber' is transformed from poor music student to stunning chatelaine by a new, expensive wardrobe. Fashion does serve as a mode of self-expression in Carter's fiction, with characters ranging from the lecherous Grand Duke in *Nights at the Circus* to the stolid Emily in *Shadow Dance* (in sturdy red-and-green shoes and red-and-white-striped jumper) using fashion to display their wealth, backgrounds or their outlook on life. Conversely, clothing can be used to constrict or impose an unwanted identity on Carter's fictional beings, particularly in instances where men select clothing for women. And the absence of clothing and nakedness is invested with especial significance in Carter's work, particularly when the genitals are displayed. The naked girl raised by wolves in 'Peter and the Wolf' opens up her lips (both of them) and offers him a disconcerting view of her vagina, described as 'a set of Chinese boxes of whorled flesh… his first, devastating, vertiginous intimation of infinity' (Carter 1996d: 287). The mystery displayed before the village boy Peter is one he attempts to resolve with conventional religion. However, as he leaves the village for training in a seminary, he once again encounters the wolf girl, living wild in the forest. Peter undergoes an epiphany, desiring to join the wolf girl, but he frightens her away. Nonetheless, having 'experienced the vertigo of freedom' (291), he leaves behind both his tiny village and his desire to become a priest, striking out into an unknown world.

Carter's use of and interest in fashion encompasses both masculine and feminine attire. For instance, she examines the subversive potential of the male dandy in her essay 'Notes for a Theory of Sixties Style' (1967). Catherine Spooner argues that the male dandy, through his mode of dress, rebels against the establishment (2019: 167), yet experiences a simultaneous disastrous dissolution of his subjectivity owing to the importance of the gaze of others to his mode of dress. He is there to be looked at (rather like any beautiful woman). Nonetheless, this process is not to be deplored, as it permits new ways of thinking about the self and the possibility of different, more fluid modes of identity.

The precise opposite is expressed through masculine garments such as the beautifully cut green smoking jacket worn by the lecherous Grand Duke in *Nights at the Circus* or the glossy black bowtie worn by the domineering Uncle Philip in *The Magic Toyshop* during a puppet show in which he acts as puppet-master. Both are very much part of the dominant patriarchal order and their clothing signifies this. The former identifies the wearer as a louche, wealthy aristocrat, the latter marks Uncle Philip as the stage magician and performer controlling the action of his puppets – and by extension, his niece, Melanie. Not coincidentally, both pose a threat to the respective heroines Fevvers and Melanie, despite the undoubted courage of the former and resilience of the latter. In 'Notes on a Theory of Sixties Style', Carter makes the interesting observation that people dress to express their environment, something that has different connotations for the masculine examples cited here (2013: 131). These men are in control of their environments: their dress is both an expression of their surroundings and the image they wish to present. Her women, by contrast, seldom have such power over their circumstances – their modes of dress (and undress) are dictated by the environment they find themselves in. Carter's Red Riding Hood figure is obliged to strip for the wolf in 'The Company of Wolves', while another dutiful granddaughter wraps herself up in sheepskin to keep out the cold in 'The Werewolf'. In stories such as 'Peter and the Wolf', the wolf-girl, despite never changing physical forms, lives among wolves and so is completely naked throughout the story. This article will argue that ultimately, despite the potential of clothing to assert the wearer's identity, Carter's humans, animals and animal-human hybrids dress to mirror their environment, whether they find themselves amongst high society or living in the midst of a dark forest amongst wolves.

There are some differences between how masculine and feminine fashion are presented in Carter's animal stories. There is an emphasis on practical uses for masculine clothing in the short stories examined in this chapter, such as when the soldier of 'Puss-in-Boots' pawns his underwear for survival. Fashion for women in Carter's tales, by contrast, is rarely without some relation to the female character's identity, her desires or the role she is sublimated into within her story. Even the sheepskin-clad granddaughter in 'The Werewolf' is no sacrificial lamb, the coat intended as misdirection. Feminine fashion can be used as a mode of expression but is equally likely to be used to constrain or suppress a woman's desires and ambitions. The heroine of the short story 'Puss-in-Boots' is shrouded top-to-toe whenever she ventures into the city streets, while Aunt Margaret in *The Magic Toyshop* wears a featureless grey dress and a silver collar made by her husband as the Sunday best of a respectable housewife. The attire of both women clearly symbolizes their imprisonment in unhappy marriages and their casting it off represents a new freedom. The downtrodden Aunt Margaret wears a green dress (a nod to her Irish heritage) and pearls borrowed from her niece when she finally defies her tyrannical husband Philip, while the mistress of 'Puss-in-Boots' strips naked for a wild bout of sex on the bedroom floor with her virile lover (her dead husband is occupying the bed).

Although Carter's interest in fashion surfaces in all her writings, clothing is endowed with even greater significance in her animal-human short stories, which play with the boundaries between humans and beasts, wilderness and civilization. At its most basic level, clothing is a marker of humanity – animals do not wear dresses or robes. However, Carter is rarely so straightforward as simply to assign clothing to humans and nakedness to animals. The titular hero of 'Puss-in-Boots' is never anything other than a cat, who delights in hunting rats and licks himself clean, but who is seldom without his fine, shining boots. The Wolf-Girl of 'Peter and the Wolf' never wears a scrap of clothing in the story, though her claim to humanity is a tenuous one at best, as shall be argued later. It should also be remembered that Carter's short fiction featuring human-animal transformations and talking, walking beasts are re-workings of famous European fairy tales, which possess a long tradition of significant items of clothing. Cinderella's glass slipper, Puss's boots, Red Riding Hood's scarlet cape, the ragged animal pelt in 'Donkeyskin' are but a few of the garments that possess magical power, or which distinguish the wearer in their fairy story. The list of notable fashion articles in fairy tales is far too long to be listed in entirety here, but clothing, particularly shoes or boots, is frequently invested with magical properties in the fairy tale. Clothing that is able to literally transform the wearer appears often: Cinderella is turned into a princess, the brothers in 'The Wild Swans' are transformed from swans into men in just two instances. Clothes therefore take on an even more important role in Carter's animal-human stories, where animals can turn into humans ('The Courtship of Mr Lyon') or humans into animals ('The Tiger's Bride').

This chapter will focus on Carter's animal-human stories: specifically, the stories to feature wolves and cats (large and small) in *The Bloody Chamber* (1979) and the short story 'Peter and the Wolf', first published in 1985 as part of the collection *Black Venus*. The former, arguably Carter's best-known work, represented a daring engagement with the fairy tale form and a new, potentially feminist appropriation of their tropes and conventions (Sauvage 2019: 58). The chapter will examine the role clothing plays in Carter's re-workings of fairy tales, how clothing is used in forming and performing identity in her works and how it is subject to the environment the wearer finds themselves in, with the characters' surroundings proving the most influential factor in their states of dress and undress, irrespective of whether the wearer is a man, a woman or even a wolf or a lion.

## Carter's theatrical animals: Gender, clothing and performance

Carter's choice of animals to feature in her work is democratic. Lions, tigers and wolves populate Carter's short fiction alongside lapdogs and hearthside cats. Even some humans run about on all fours, naked and hairy. There is some correlation between the settings of her reworked fairy tales and the animals that appear in them: 'The Courtship of Mr Lyon' is set in a 'perfect miniature Palladian house' (1996c: 144) and besides the titular Mr Lyon features a curiously ladylike spaniel. The eponymous Puss in Boots wanders the streets and gaming salons of an unnamed Italian city, while Carter's wolves and werewolves stalk the forests and mountainsides of her imaginary landscapes. Clothing in these tales tends to be tailored to suit the wearer's environment. In 'The Werewolf', the granddaughter off to visit her grandmother wears a sheepskin coat to ward off cold, while the heroine of 'The Courtship of Mr Lyon' wears furs, evening gowns and elaborate jewellery during her sojourn in London, where she attends parties and the theatre. Modes of dress in these stories enable Carter's characters, both human and animal, to move and function in the social strata they find themselves in – I hesitate to use the term 'belong'. Mr Lyon, a literal talking lion, and the nameless Master of 'The Tiger's Bride' clearly do not belong amongst the wealthy human nobility their money and property places them on a par with. Nonetheless, Mr Lyon's elegant apparel clearly signifies his status as a wealthy country gentleman, an eligible suitor for the poor but genteel heroine. Likewise, the Master's kid gloves, powdered wig and liveried servant indicate his status as a member of the nobility, irrespective of the fact that he is a tiger and his servant a talking monkey. The iconic red hood worn by the heroine of 'The Company of Wolves' is symbolic on several levels, evoking the traditional fairy tale and serving as an emblem for the menstruation that has just commenced for her. The two garments mentioned in connection with Wolf-Alice are a shift the nuns coax her into wearing (for the sake of modesty rather than comfort) and a wedding dress she finds amongst the detritus left by the grave-robbing Duke in whose household she resides in the latter part of the tale. The wedding dress is transformed into a plaything for Wolf-Alice, who adores the feel of it against her skin – a subversion of its typical purpose as an emblem of a woman's purity. Wolf-Alice's animal upbringing and identity ensure she perceives garments differently from humans, either not seeing the need for them (she hates the shift) or turning them into a source of amusement rather than an emblem of what society deems the most important day in a woman's life.

Nonetheless, practical or otherwise, clothing and shoes in Carter's animal-human stories usually serve as signifiers of a character's gender, social class, origins and their intent within their stories. The obvious critical theory with which to frame the use of clothing and fashion in Carter's work is Judith Butler's concept of gender as performance (2006: xv). In her work *Gender Trouble*, Butler defines gender as repeated actions: 'a re-enactment and re-experience of a set of meanings already socially established' (2006: 191). Butler decries the possibility of gender as something that is natural or innate to humans, instead arguing that gender is wholly constructed through signs and gestures to which our cultural history has ascribed a gendered meaning. Butler elaborates:

> Acts, gestures, enactments, generally construed, are *performative* in the sense that the essence or identity that they otherwise purport to express are *fabrications* manufactured and sustained through corporeal signs and other discursive means.
>
> (2006: 185)

Butler emphasizes the contradictory aspects of gender as performance, observing that the acts and gestures incorporated in such a performance imply an internal, natural 'core' or identity, yet this is enacted on the surface of the body. Although Butler does not specify clothing as comprising part of this performance, its position on the surface of the body, visible to all, ensures its importance when enacting gender. Clothing in Carter's short fiction serves the same purpose: acting as a costume, enabling the performance of gender.

Butler's theory of gender as performance is a popular one in analyses of Carter's texts, with critics such as Paulina Palmer and Lorna Sage using the concept of performativity to examine Carter's depiction of gender in her major novels (Palmer 1997: 24–42) and in her reworked fairy tales (Sage 2001: 65–82). There is certainly enough material in Carter's texts to support an interpretation of Carter's characters as performing gender, especially given her abiding interest in fashion and the theatrical. For instance, when confronted with a life-size marionette of herself, the heroine of 'The Tiger's Bride' decides to let the puppet take her place in society: 'I will dress her in my own clothes, wind her up, send her back to perform the part of my father's daughter' (1996c: 167). Performance will be enhanced with the correct costume, but what is interesting about the conclusion to this fairy tale is that the daughter's role is reduced to nothing more than her mode of dress. A similar scenario is enacted in Leonora Carrington's short story 'The Debutante', first published in 1937, which Carter included in her anthology *Wicked Girls and Wayward Women* (1986).[2] In Carrington's tale, the eponymous (nameless) debutante swaps places with a hyena to avoid attending a ball. Dressed up in gown, gloves and high-heeled shoes and wearing the face she has chewed off an unlucky servant, the only thing that distinguishes the hyena from the girl is her strong, animalistic scent. Similarly, the tiger of 'The Tiger's Bride' has an overpowering smell of 'purplish civet' that leads the narrator to speculate on what kind of stench he is trying to mask (1996c: 155).

Although the clothes are not described in detail, the derisory manner in which the part of the father's daughter is depicted confirms that for a Russian noblewoman identity consists solely of what exists on the surface. Immediately afterwards, the tale's narrator is shown stripping naked, and what's more, having the skin ripped from her to reveal the fur underneath, in yet another echoing of Carrington's story, in which the disguised hyena tears off her borrowed human visage and devours it. Both for the hyena and the tigress, their abandonment of all gestures, rituals and performance ought to negate all human identity if their status as a woman/girl is entirely constructed.

However, both Carrington and Carter are ambiguous in this regard. The hyena in Carrington's story is gifted with human speech no matter what she wears. An initial reading of 'The Tiger's Bride' appears to support a Butlerian interpretation of identity: by disrobing, rendering herself naked and finally being flayed alive – the ultimate shedding of her former self – the heroine abandons a human/female identity and adopts a tigerish one. To become a tigress, she must discard all her clothing and appear in nothing but her skin to the Beast. An animal identity precludes the possibility of dress, in 'The Tiger's Bride' and other stories such as 'Peter and the Wolf', in which the nameless wolf-girl never dons clothing and instead grows a hairy pelt. This constructivist concept of gendered identity dovetails with Butler's theories. But Carter, a maverick who challenged all dominant discourses, is never this straightforward to analyse. The heroine, even after she has disrobed and left human society behind, still has a human identity that must be discarded if she is to become an animal, which is only achieved after literally changing her physical form. Likewise, in 'The Tiger's Bride' and 'Puss-in-Boots', the felines featured may adopt human dress but are essentially unchanged by it. The tiger remains a tiger, and Puss remains a cat – albeit a talking one with a penchant for natty footwear.

But crucially, both the tiger and Puss are allowed entry into the world of humans and to participate in it owing to their human garb. Though Puss is not the only cat in his story, he is the only one to talk with humans and to adopt disguises as required. Tabby, his romantic interest, is a much more traditional cat who lives by the hearth and only talks to Puss, who by contrast quite literally serves as the voice of reason when his Master needs assistance. Mr Lyon, another gigantic talking feline, is clearly a wealthy country gentleman despite his leonine appearance, as indicated by his manners and his mode of dress. Although he lives the life of a recluse and thus does not participate in human society in any meaningful sense, he possesses all the power and influence of a rich man, as indicated by his skilful lawyers who do much to restore the fortunes of the heroine's family. Clothes do not quite make the man in this example, but they hint at Mr Lyon's true place in the world. Fittingly, he is transformed into a human and an appropriate match for the heroine by the close of the tale.

There is never any doubt that these beasts are masculine creatures. The seductive woodsman and werewolf in 'The Company of Wolves' is clearly male, if not always a man, while the femaleness of Wolf-Alice and the wolf-girl of 'Peter and the Wolf' is never in question. As the quote used at the start of this chapter indicates, the wolf-girl's femaleness is an essential part of the story, while the onset of Wolf-Alice's menstruation is an important event in her tale. Unlike in many of Carter's novels, drag is conspicuous by its absence in the stories examined here. At no point in the tales does a man perform a female identity, or vice versa. Although Puss and his Master take on the roles of ratcatchers and doctors in order for the Master to woo the woman he loves, they presumably do not impersonate female tradespeople. Marina Warner, in an examination of Carter's use of cross-dressing as a form of rebellion, observes that 'it is interesting, in the context of fairy tale narrators' masquerades, that Carter was also deeply fascinated with female impersonation as a literary device, as a social instrument of disruption and as an erotic provocation' (2016). The fairy tale masquerades referred briefly to by Warner are numerous and diverse: the fairy tales 'The Little Mermaid', 'Donkeyskin' and 'Cap O'Rushes' all feature women in disguise for one reason or another. And yet cross-dressing – men dressing as women, or women dressing as men – does not appear in Carter's reworked fairy tales. A partial explanation may be that it is rarer for men to adopt disguises in fairy tales, but it is safe to assume Carter's maverick tendencies would have overcome any scruples in this regard. I would argue, however, that Carter is simply more interested in how women, old and young, those raised as noblewomen and those raised by wolves, perform their femininity or else disavow it. And crucially, going clothed or naked is an important element in both the construction and deconstruction of identity in Carter's fairy tales – one that allows her protagonists to perform not only gender, but humanity or beastliness as desired.

## Performing identity in the fairy tale

As observed earlier, clothing in Carter's short fiction can be used to signify social status or as a form of misdirection. The role of clothing in Carter's short fiction is also enhanced owing to its fairy tale inheritance. Dani Cavallaro observes that

> Clothes and accessories feature prominently in fairy tales as major personality markers and as talismanic agencies capable of investing their wearers with more or less temporary preternatural powers: invisibility cloaks, metamorphic ball gowns and seven-league boots exemplify this proposition.
>
> (2011: 27)

Perhaps curiously, none of the garments depicted in Carter's short fiction possess any magical properties (except the sables that transform into a pack of rats in 'The Tiger's Bride'), despite their transformative potential. Even shoes, which are endowed with special power in many fairy tales, do not possess any particular magic. Although Puss wears his boots proudly, they are not supernatural. In the original fairy tale 'Puss in Boots... acquires a human appearance to help his master. His boots [are a] caricature of high social status' (Papachristophorou 2008: 858). Carter's Puss does not require a human appearance to assist his Master, so his boots are pure affectation, a marker of Puss' exceptional cunning and wits.

Nonetheless, one form of fairy tale masquerade that does appear numerous times in Carter's fairy tales is a human being turned into an animal, or an animal becoming human. Clothing is typically shed or put on during these scenes – though Carter is never so simplistic as to just depict her humans dressed and her animals naked. The fairy tale transformation between human and animal is another method in which Carter subverts essentialist notions of identity. Jessica Tiffin, in an analysis of Carter and the fairy tale form, asserts that Carter assumes a basic sexual identity that exists prior to the one acquired during the process of gender acquisition. However, she also points out that Carter's animal-human transformations become a method of questioning and subverting essentialist notions of identity (2009: 75). Wolf-Alice, despite being a wholly human girl in appearance, naked or otherwise, is not described as human by Carter. 'Nothing about her is human except that she is *not* a wolf', Carter offers (1996c: 221). Some characters quite literally acquire fur, others shed it, others run around naked on all fours but clothes do not necessarily make the man (or woman) in Carter's fiction, and neither does the surface of the body, despite all that is enacted upon it. Carter refuses to allow even her beasts to be entirely wild or completely domestic, not allowing them to completely fulfil the roles human society has allocated them. The feline scoundrel Puss-in-Boots settles down with a tabby and produces several kittens by the close of his tale, while the prim spaniel belonging to Mr Lyon is reduced to a scruffy stray during the story: 'this one's fringed ears were matted with mud, her coat was dusty and snarled' (1996c: 151). Even the potentially rapacious werewolf in 'The Company of Wolves' becomes a 'tender wolf' (1996c: 220) during his encounter with Red Riding Hood.

In regard to constructing identity, the importance of Carter's structure and narrative in her short fiction – most particularly her re-imaginings of the fairy tale that lend greater power and agency to the women they feature – has been examined by several critics. For Jessica Tiffin, gender identity is not only performed via dress, gesture and speech but the inhabitants of fairy tales follow a script laid out for them by the traditional fairy tale narrative. She explains that

> In *The Bloody Chamber* the 'trick' of both gender and structure is recognized and examined by female characters who reflect on their artificially structured entrapment within the roles set out for them by fairy tale traditions, and the limitations placed on their sexual identity by those roles and predetermined narrative outcomes. The often-experimental performance of roles embedded in fairy tale becomes a performance of structure, one which, through irony, exaggeration, and parody, insists on the artificiality of the system.
>
> (2009: 73–4)

By allowing her characters to self-reflectively examine their assigned roles and methods of averting or subverting them, often through self-transformation, Carter exposes both the artificiality of the stories her characters are caught up in and the construction of identity, gendered and otherwise. Some critics argue that Carter's re-workings of fairy tales are no less restrictive in terms of gender roles. Patricia Duncker argues that Carter re-wrote her fairy tales 'within the strait-jacket of their original structures' (1996: 6), and Avis Lawallen, in her examination of female sexuality in *The Bloody Chamber*, perceives female identity as reduced to a handful of stereotypes (1998: 157). Interestingly, Lawallen refers to the style of Carter's writing as a type of performance, remarking on its 'gloss and shimmer' (1998: 144) implying that her style acts a disguise for the standard patriarchal oppression contained in the stories. Carter's proclivity for purple prose is evident, and even Carter herself remarked upon it.[3] The vividness, the dramatic impact and the undeniable skill of her prose are pyrotechnic, a spectacular display of ostentatious performance. Likewise, both her masculine and feminine characters perform the roles society expects of them with the aid of elaborate, showy clothing in stories such as 'The Tiger's Bride' and 'The Courtship of Mr Lyon', which feature dutiful daughters and wealthy, aristocratic gentlemen (albeit ones with fur and claws). The tiger of 'The Tiger's Bride' wears a wig and kid gloves; the daughter who goes to live with Mr Lyon wears evening gowns and furs when her father's fortune is restored. The latter again implies patriarchal power, with the fancy clothes a double gift – from a doting father to his daughter, and from Mr Lyon, whose assistance in some unspecified legal matter has provided the wealth for such indulgence.

That patriarchal oppression is *depicted* in Carter's work is inarguable; whether her work upholds it is another matter. However, the critics cited above continue to examine identity in Carter's work through the prism of gender. This makes sense given the late-twentieth-century reclamation of Carter as a feminist writer, as observed by Trevenna; critics argue either that Carter upholds patriarchal, oppressive structures of identity or that she undermines them (2002: 286). But examining Carter's treatment of identity predominantly using gender theories does not address Carter's subversions of and reimagining of identity through her breaking down of the human-animal binary in her fairy tales. Carter's subverting of gender assumptions is apparent in her presentation of beasts in her stories; the animals are mostly, but not always male. Whilst male capacity for beastliness in popular culture is almost taken for granted, the notion of women somehow being closer to nature, less civilized than men is also one that is deeply ingrained in Western culture. Tanya Krzywinska notes of the Ancient Greeks that their 'philosophers were preoccupied with explaining the difference between man and animals (they were not that bothered about women)' (2006: 142). In Carter's egalitarian take on the fairy tale, males and females are equally likely to be bestial, savage and vicious. Few remain polite and civilized, because, after all, where is the fun in that?

But as with traditional fairy tales the transformative potential of the body in Carter's work is tremendous. Humans turn into animals, animals into humans, animals don clothes and perform humanity and other humans run about naked and assume an animal identity, on which more shortly. As demonstrated, clothing can be used to assist in these transformations; when the seductive werewolf approaches Red Riding Hood in 'The Company of Wolves', he is wearing a green coat and stylish hat that immediately distinguish him from the village boys the heroine is familiar with. His mode of dress is evidently alluring, as it helps convince the heroine to linger and engage in the 'commonplaces of a rustic seduction' (216). The film *The Company of Wolves* (Jordan 1984), based on Carter's wolf stories, presents the wolf in an elegant, embroidered coat and tricorn hat, suggestive of an eighteenth-century gentleman (although his eyebrows still meet in the middle as a visible marker of his inner beastliness).

The contrast between the (apparently) wealthy, upper-class huntsman and the peasant boys the heroine is used to, made visible by the former's ornately embroidered coat and the rough homespun garments belonging to the latter, also indicates the numerous human identities clothing makes it possible to adopt. Human identity is marked by social class, as well as gender. By donning the guise of a wealthy man, the werewolf increases his allurement. He can offer the heroine wealth and status, in addition to his sexual attentions. Of course, the huntsman's human appearance is strictly performative, concealing his wolfish self and serving his purpose of securing the heroine's interest. In Carter's short story, his language and voice also form aspects of performativity: he mimics Red Riding Hood's voice to deceive her grandmother, in an echo of the original fairy tale. By adopting a 'high soprano' (217) the huntsman tricks the old woman into granting him entry, exposing the performative nature of gender and the gendered body, as according to Butler's theory. That the gendered body, according to Butler, 'is performative suggests that it has no ontological status apart from the various acts that constitute its reality' (185). The huntsman's successful impersonation of a young girl, although brief, reinforces this supposition. He also successfully impersonates a *human* for a far greater length of time, although signs of his wolfish identity (such as snacking on the dead birds he is draped with) emerge when he is alone with no audience to perform for. But his performance is unmistakably that of a human *man*: Butler also argues gender overlaps race, class, sexuality and nationality in forming identities (6), whether it is performative or not. This is arguably borne out in the stories of *The Bloody Chamber* – none of the characters ever attempt to change their gender through dress, and only the huntsman's brief mimicking of a female voice indicates adopting another gender through language.

However, *human* identity is by no means a fixed construct in Carter's short fiction, with numerous characters altering different aspects of their identities through dress. Class and occupation in particular are shown to be performative: the penniless soldier in 'Puss-in-Boots' adopts numerous disguises (including a sawbones and a ratcatcher) in order to woo his love. Even Carter's short stories that do not feature human-animal transformation often feature humans adopting numerous identities through changing their mode of dress, such as the narrator of 'The Bloody Chamber', a penniless music student who marries a stupendously wealthy nobleman. She is transformed into a chatelaine through an expensive wardrobe and jewellery, though she confesses she is more comfortable in her shabby old skirt and blouse, the 'costume of a student' (126). It is notable that all these instances of changing dress include an element of performance: Puss's master acts a part to gain access to the heroine's bedroom, while the narrator of 'The Bloody Chamber' plays at being the lady of the manor in her fancy new wardrobe. Later, after she has discovered her new husband murdered his previous three wives, she invokes the transformative power of her performance at the piano, telling herself that if she plays all of Bach's equations without error, she will become a virgin again (134).

Conversely, Carter also acknowledges the restrictive potential of clothing in relation to the body in 'The Company of Wolves', relating a tale about how to repel a werewolf: 'so old wives hereabouts think it some protection to throw a hat or an apron at the werewolf, as if clothes made the man' (214). Clothing in 'The Company of Wolves' apparently carries the risk of locking an individual into a particular identity. Carter elucidates: 'before he can become a wolf, the lycanthrope strips stark naked' (214). There is a lengthy history in werewolf fiction of a werewolf being unable to transform back to human unless he is in possession of human garments; Marie de France's *Bisclavret* (probably composed in the late twelfth century) is one of the most prominent examples with an unfortunate knight forced to assume the shape of a wolf until his clothes are restored to him. If a character is forced to don clothing, in Carter's work, it has the potential to overwhelm them and fix them in the role society has ordained for them, society dictating style. I have already explored the example of the protagonist of 'The Tiger's Bride'. There is also the example of Carter's werewolves who might be rendered human by an apron flung in the face and even the 'Missus' of 'Puss-in-Boots' is kept shrouded in a veil by her tyrannical husband, as a method of marking her as his property.

The fairy tale costumes in *The Bloody Chamber* are invested with so much history and meaning that it is impossible to completely remake them and invest them with a totally new connotation. Their location on the surface of the body, where identity is constructed and acted out, is another reason for this tremendous power wielded by garments. Clothing and costume are a double-edged sword in Carter's fiction. So, what happens when it is shed, and humans and animals appear naked in her works?

## Her bold nakedness: Nudity in Carter's animal-human tales

As previously observed, Carter does not simply assign clothing to humans and nakedness to animals. However, as Rebecca-Anne C. Do Rozario argues, 'for Carter, clothing is absolutely the raiment of human culture, staving off sex' (107). It is undeniable that in the stories explored in this chapter, human clothing permits animals to interact with and move amidst human society, while humans shedding clothing is frequently (though not always) an indicator of sexual desire. Cats don boots, lions wear smoking jackets and humans strip off at the slightest provocation – usually for a bout of bed-thumping sex. It is nearly always women who appear nude in Carter's stories, and their removal of clothing is often portrayed as a liberating act. In 'Puss-in-Boots', the Missus achieves sexual satisfaction, and, it is strongly implied, loses her virginity, after divesting herself of her garments and veil. Red Riding Hood casts her clothes into the fire at the behest of the wolf, but it is suggested that she sidesteps her usual role of victim in 'The Company of Wolves' when the conclusion depicts her sleeping safely in bed with a gentle wolf. Nudity in Carter's tales reveals the body and divests it of the roles enacted upon it. And yet there is a performative element to being naked in some of Carter's texts: the protagonist of 'The Tiger's Bride' reveals her extreme discomfort at the thought of exposing herself to the Beast: 'but it is not natural for humankind to go naked, not since we hid our loins with fig leaves. He had demanded the abominable' (168). The suggestion that clothing is natural for humans, and that nudity is an assumed, abnormal state of being, is at odds with the assumption that clothing is an aspect of performing identity. Nonetheless, within Carter's fiction (and non-fiction) the human body and sex exist within an ideological system, one in which sex is irretrievably intertwined with power. Within 'The Tiger's Bride', the masculine desire of the Beast, irrespective of species, is perceived as a humiliation by the protagonist as his desire is not to pay her for sex – which would at least be an honest transaction – but to glimpse a fair virgin form that no man has ever seen before. The Beast's desire is for *performance*; not for nothing does the heroine liken herself to a 'ballet girl' (163). Only when he reveals himself naked to her does she respond in kind. However, the tale still closes with an act of erotic flaying as she sheds her skin and becomes an animal. Finally, the heroine can leave behind all modes of performance should she desire to do so.

The only way in which Carter's characters can fully escape the necessity of performing identity is to leave humanity behind altogether. The wolf-girl of 'Peter and the Wolf' is ostensibly human; no physical transformation into a wolf takes place in the story. And yet Carter is careful to establish the difference between her and the eponymous Peter, who espies her on the mountainside. Carter writes that

> Her face itself was the mirror of a different kind of consciousness than ours is, just as her nakedness, without innocence or display, was that of our first parents, before the Fall.
>
> (290)

The description of the wolf-girl's nudity as 'without innocence or display' is in contrast to the deeply significant disrobing of 'The Tiger's Bride' or even the human nakedness of 'Puss-in-Boots' or 'The Company of Wolves', in which lack of clothing is always sexualized – or at the very least, a necessity for sexual intercourse. While nudity offers the potential for transformation to Carter's lycanthropes, or to enact a different type of identity to that which people perform when clothed – the dutiful wife turns into an adulteress, the man into a wolf – only animals can exist without performing identity. The body, with all clothes and costumes removed, is still loaded with significance in the context of human society. As Jessica Tiffin observes, 'Carter offers bodily, sexual identity as simply one more of the constructions of self' (2009: 75).

The wolf-girl, counter to this construction of self, resists all human attempts to claim her – as a girl and as a granddaughter – and returns to the wolves who raised her. Her final appearance suggests a creature far more wolfish than human, with Carter describing her as 'hairy as Magdalen in the wilderness' (290). Her very hairiness is a marker of her wildness: as Marina Warner comments, 'hairiness indicates animal nature: it is the distinctive sign of the wilderness and its inhabitants' (1995: 359). It also represents the closest Carter comes to introducing cross-dressing in the short fiction analysed here. None of her male characters ever don a dress, or other female garments, nor do any of her women, even those in the wilderness who presumably would prefer practical dress, wear men's clothing. But the wolf-girl's hairiness, for a Western audience reading in the late twentieth or early twenty-first centuries, indicates an undesirable masculine characteristic. As Karín Lesnik-Oberstein comments, hirsute women 'are monstrous in being like men, or masculine' (2007: 2). The potential for a gendered identity is present even in the wildest of Carter's characters, one who does not have the slightest conception of what humanity is or that she may be considered as human. Yet Carter sidesteps this denouement by having Peter, the man who espies the wolf-girl and perceives her hairiness, long to run off and join her. He actually attempts to do so, but his noisy blundering frightens her off.

Carter describes Peter as desiring the wolf-girl's 'marvellous and private grace' (290) but also includes a crucial explanation of why Peter – and his family, who attempt to claim her as a granddaughter – cannot impose an identity on the wolf-girl. 'Language crumbled into dust under the weight of her speechlessness' (290), as Carter observes. 'Speechlessness' used in this context does not simply mean the wolf-girl does not know human speech. Neither does Carter's other wolf-girl, Wolf-Alice. Yet by learning to recognize herself in the mirror, Wolf-Alice acquires a specifically human concept of self. As Joel Dor posits in an examination of Lacanian theory, 'the child's primary identification with this image [the reflection] promotes the structuring of the "I" and puts an end to that singular aspect of psychic experience that Lacan calls *the fantasy of the fragmented body*' (1998: 95). Dor explains how the child initially perceives the image in the mirror as another being, and gradually learns to recognize themselves in the mirror, thus gaining knowledge of themselves as a unified whole. From being fragmented, they become an 'I'. This Lacanian acquisition of identity is arguably enacted by Wolf-Alice's eventual recognition of herself in a looking glass. However, Carter's child gazing into the mirror is female, unlike the child at the centre of Lacan's mirror-theory. Lacan, in his essay 'Some Reflections on the Ego' published in 1953 refers to the child as 'he' throughout his analysis of the child encountering the mirror and his reflection. Carter's re-gendering of this gradual process of self-recognition leaves out the recognition of an Ideal-I, the image of perfection the child initially perceives in the mirror.[4] Kimberly J. Lau, in her analysis of this scene, argues that Wolf-Alice recognizes herself in the mirror not as the Ideal-I, the coherent self of Lacan's mirror stage (for Lacan, a misrecognition) but rather as shadow, as reflection, and it is this different recognition that keeps her from entering into the Symbolic Order, keeps her outside of language (2015: 140).

In perceiving a shadow rather than the Ideal-I, Wolf-Alice is unburdened of striving to attain the perfection of the Ideal-I and suggests what Lau terms 'an outside to the Symbolic Order' (58). Moreover, in eliminating the Ideal-I, Carter offers an implicit critique of what Lau terms 'the primacy of the phallus, the primacy of the Law of the Father' (58). To comprehensively examine the Lacanian theory of the phallus and the 'phallocentric logic that undergirds Western culture' (Lau, 58) would take more space than is available here. Nonetheless, Carter criticized the psychoanalytic myths underpinning Western culture (notably the concept of the female as castrated) in texts such as *The Sadeian Woman* (1979). She referred to 'the social fiction of the female wound, the bleeding scar left by her castration' which she refers to as an 'imaginary fact… that transforms women from human beings into wounded creatures who were born to bleed' (2000: 22). In perceiving a fellow wolf, a potential playmate in the mirror and later comprehending it as her reflection, Wolf-Alice ensures she will never be fully human, never be admitted to the Symbolic Order.

However, this is not necessarily presented as a negative within the context of the story. Female identity in Western society is predicated on a lack, on a wound according to psychoanalytic theory – the wound left by castration, the absence of the penis. In failing to recognize the (implicitly male) Ideal-I, Wolf-Alice may never acquire a fully human identity, but although her position in the world is a lonely one, it spares her the subordinate status afforded women in a patriarchal society. Although she learns to recognize herself in the mirror as any human child would, she has no comprehension of any deficiencies in herself. It is her remaining outside the Symbolic Order that grants her power in the story. When garbed in a wedding dress she finds in the attic and playing in the graveyard, she is mistaken for the vengeful ghost of a recently deceased bride by terrified villagers hunting the Duke. The villagers flee in horror, with Wolf-Alice inadvertently saving the Duke's life.

The wedding dress is the only garment worn willingly by Wolf-Alice within the story, and it is divested of all its traditional symbolism by both Wolf-Alice (who views it as a plaything) and the villagers (who perceive it as a shroud). However, it is worth noting that it is only after Wolf-Alice achieves an identification of herself in the mirror – albeit not a traditionally human one – that she voluntarily begins to don clothing. But the wolf-girl of 'Peter and the Wolf' never achieves even a vague human conception of self. Carter even includes an opportunity for her to view her reflection in a river, but 'she could never have acknowledged that the reflection beneath her in the river was that of herself. She did not know she had a face' (290).

The wolf-girl not only fails to acknowledge that the reflection in the river is herself but her lack of interest in it prevents her from identifying both the Ideal-I and another human/wolf in the water. The mirror-theory does not apply to the wolf-girl, meaning she will remain forever outside the Symbolic Order, never learn language, never be human. Her lack of a human conception of herself ensures it is impossible for Peter to impose an identity on her. Carter, whose stories often feature bawdy, sexualized elements, makes no attempt to eroticize the wolf-girl's nakedness. She is not an object of sexual desire, nor does she have any human relationships that can categorize her as granddaughter, cousin and so forth – the humans have cast her out. The wolf-girl has no self, no identity and it is precisely for this reason that she alone is completely without artifice. Crucially, unlike Wolf-Alice, she lives in the forest, away from all human paraphernalia, whereas Wolf-Alice lives in a castle surrounded by mirrors, wedding gowns, carpets and other accoutrements. The wolf-girl has no identity to perform, gendered or otherwise. But all Carter's other characters, human and beast, male and female, clothed or naked, perform their identities at some point in their stories – and both clothes and a lack of clothes are essential in this performance.

## Conclusion

That gender is performed in Carter's work is inarguable; also, clothes form an essential component of this performance. Clothes are a vital ingredient in making the man (or woman) in Carter's work, regardless of who or what wears them. Male, female, human or animal – donning human dress allows a character to perform a human identity. Likewise, stripping naked and standing only in fur or skin offers the prospect of leaving behind an old or unwanted identity and the chance to remake or renew the self.

Catherine Spooner observes that in Carter's fiction, fancy dress in particular offers freedom from societal strictures, allowing characters to discover new aspects of themselves (2004: 141). Her argument is lent credence by the suffusion of theatricals throughout Carter's novels and short fiction. The theatre, music halls, cinema, puppet shows and con artistry are all gloried in throughout Carter's texts, with her characters donning elaborate costumes and using props to depict themselves as innocent virgins, clowns, rapacious swans and numerous other alter egos. Yet, despite Carter's obvious affection for and interest in the theatre, professional performances are conspicuous by their absence in the short stories examined in this chapter. Save for an evening's busking in 'Puss-in-Boots', there are no professional actors, performers, musicians or con artists in Carter's animal-human short stories. I argue that in Carter's short fiction, being human is the true performance. Clothes are always fancy dress; they do not indicate who is human and who is animal, as the abundance of costumed animals in her fiction suggests. But they become an essential prop when a character wishes to perform a human identity, regardless of what species they are underneath their wigs and gowns. They allow a limited transformation to take place, in fairy tale tradition. But Carter never invests her shoes and dresses with the power of Cinderella's slipper or the animal pelt of 'Donkeyskin'. The Beast of 'The Tiger's Bride' cannot alter his tigerish nature, no matter what finery he dons. And even if a man or woman runs about completely naked, once they are among humans their body carries significance, thrusting them into a role to be performed. But crucially, the absence or presence of clothing allows the wearer or non-wearer to reflect their environment and perform their role accordingly. A human running naked in the forest becomes an animal: a beast in a smoking jacket and living in a grand house becomes a gentleman to whom society permits certain eccentricities.

As this essay has argued, the only way to escape the necessity of having to perform a human identity is to leave all humanity behind. Human identity in Carter's texts is the true performance, and it is dictated by the environment her characters – human, animal or both – find themselves in. Of course, there are always exceptions in Carter's work, as with the mischievous, deceptive Puss-in-Boots, who is never anything other than a cat, despite his boots. But his footwear allows him to move through the human world with impunity, speaking in Italian (and French) and arranging matters to his satisfaction. As with everything in Carter's work, an object or a character is never entirely one thing or the other. There is always an ambiguity to her works, and only the identity chosen by or for her characters to be enacted can offer any certainties in her tumultuous, disturbing fairy tale worlds.

## Notes

1. One of Carter's most interesting essays on the rebellious potential of fashion is 'Notes on Theory of Sixties Style', which I examine in this chapter.
2. Although it is impossible to ascertain if Carrington's short story influenced the 'The Tiger's Bride', the fact that Carter was aware of the story – and admired it sufficiently to include it in the anthology – suggests the possibility.
3. One of Carter's most famous comments on her style of writing was given in 1992 during an interview for the BBC2 programme *Angela Carter's Curious Room*: 'so I write overblown, self-indulgent, purple prose. So fucking what?'
4. There are three separate stages in Lacan's mirror-theory: firstly, the child perceives another being in the mirror, the Ideal-I, an image of perfection which the child then spends its entire life trying to attain. Secondly, the child realizes what it is seeing is an image, rather than another human. Thirdly, the child learns to recognize itself in the mirror. For a more detailed explanation, see Dor (95–7).

## Works cited

Butler, J. (2006), *Gender Trouble: Feminism and the Subversion of Identity*, London and New York: Routledge.
Carrington, L. (2016), 'The Débutante', in A. Carter (ed), *Wayward Girls and Wicked Women*, 25–8, London: Virago.
Carter, A. (1996a), 'The Bloody Chamber', in A. Carter, *Burning Your Boats: Collected Short Stories*, 111–43, London, Vintage.
Carter, A. (1996b), 'The Company of Wolves', in A. Carter, *Burning Your Boats: Collected Short Stories*, 212–20, London: Vintage.
Carter, A. (1996c), 'The Courtship of Mr Lyon', in A. Carter, *Burning Your Boats: Collected Short Stories*, 144–53, London: Vintage.
Carter, A. (1996d) 'Peter and the Wolf', in A. Carter, *Burning Your Boats: Collected Short Stories*, 284–91, London: Vintage.
Carter, A. (1996e), 'Puss-in-Boots', in A. Carter, *Burning Your Boats: Collected Short Stories*, 170–85, London: Vintage.
Carter, A. (1996f), 'The Tiger's Bride', in A. Carter, *Burning Your Boats: Collected Short Stories*, 154–69, London: Vintage.
Carter, A. (1996g), 'Wolf-Alice', in A. Carter, *Burning Your Boats: Collected Short Stories*, 221–8, London: Vintage.

Carter, A. (2000), *The Sadeian Woman: An Exercise in Cultural History*, London: Virago.
Carter, A. (2013), 'Notes For a Theory of Sixties Style', in A. Carter, *Shaking a Leg: Collected Journalism and Writings*, 131–5, London: Vintage.
Cavallaro, D. (2011), *The World of Angela Carter: A Critical Investigation*, Jefferson, NC: McFarland & Company Inc.
*The Company of Wolves* (1984) [Film] Dir. Neil Jordan: UK, Palace/ITC Entertainment.
Do Rozario, R. C. (2018), *Fashion in the Fairy Tale Tradition: What Cinderella Wore*, Cham, Switzerland: Palgrave Macmillan.
Dor, J. (1998), *Introduction to the Reading of Lacan: The Unconscious Structured Like a Language*, New York: Other Press.
Duncker, P. (1996), 'Re-imagining the fairy tales: Angela Carter's Bloody Chambers', *Literature and History*, 10 (1): 3–14.
Gordon, E. (2016), *The Invention of Angela Carter*, London: Chatto & Windus.
Jordan, Neil (1984), *The Company of Wolves*, Cannon Film Distributors.
Krzywinska, T. (2006), *Sex and the Cinema*, London: Wallflower.
Lacan, J. (1953), 'Some Reflections on the Ego', *The International Journal of Psycho-Analysis*, 34 (1): 11–7.
Lau, Kimberly J. (2015), *Erotic Infidelities: Love and Enchantment in Angela Carter's The Bloody Chamber*, Detroit, MI: Wayne State University Press.
Lesnik-Oberstein, K. (2007), 'The Last Taboo: Women, Body Hair and Feminism', in K. Lesnik-Oberstein (ed), *The Last Taboo: Women and Body Hair*, 1–17, Manchester: Manchester University Press.
Lewallen, A. (1998), 'Wayward Girls but Wicked Women? Female Sexuality in Angela Carter's *The Bloody Chamber*', in G. Day, and C. Bloom (eds), *Perspectives on Pornography: Sexuality in Film and Literature*, 144–57, New York: St. Martin's.
Palmer, P. (1997), 'Gender as Performance in the Fiction of Angela Carter and Margaret Atwood', in J. Bristow and T. Lynn Bristow (eds), *The Infernal Desires of Angela Carter: Fiction, Femininity, Feminism*, 24–42, Harlow, Essex and New York: Longman.
Papachristophorou, M. (2008), 'Shoe', in D. Haase (ed), *The Greenwood Encyclopaedia of Folktales and Fairy Tales Volume 3: Q to Z*, 861–2, Wesport CT and London: Greenwood.
Sage, L. (2001), 'Angela Carter: The Fairy Tale', in D. M. Roemer and C. Bacchilega (eds), *Angela Carter and the Fairy Tale*, 65–82, Detroit MI: Wayne State University Press.
Sauvage, J. (2019), 'Bloody Chamber Melodies: Painting and Music in *The Bloody Chamber*', in M. Mulvey-Roberts (ed), *The Arts of Angela Carter: A Cabinet of Curiosities*, 58–79, Manchester: Manchester University Press.
Spooner, C. (2004), *Fashioning Gothic Bodies*, Manchester: Manchester University Press.
Spooner, C. (2019), '"Clothes Are Our Weapons": Dandyism, Fashion and Subcultural Style in Angela Carter's Fiction of the 1960s', in M. Mulvey-Roberts (ed), *The Arts of*

*Angela Carter: A Cabinet of Curiosities*, 166–82, Manchester: Manchester University Press.

Tiffin, J. (2009), *Marvellous Geometry: Narrative and Metafiction in the Modern Fairy Tale*, Detroit MI: Wayne State University Press.

Trevenna, J. (2002), 'Gender as Performance: Questioning the "Butlerification" of Angela Carter's Fiction', *Journal of Gender Studies*, 11 (3): 267–76.

Warner, M. (1995), *From the Beast to the Blonde: On Fairy Tales and Their Tellers*, London: Vintage.

Warner, M. (2016), 'Angela Carter: Fairy Tales, Cross-dressing and the Mercurial Slipperiness of Identity', *The British Library*, 25 May. Available online: https://www.bl.uk/20th-century-literature/articles/angela-carter-fairy tales-cross-dressing-and-the-mercurial-slipperiness-of-identity (accessed 20 September 2017).

12

# Angela Carter's questioning of 'age-appropriate' appearance and behaviour in *Wise Children*

Zoe Brennan

Older female characters appear on the margins of many of Angela Carter's narratives: from the ancient waitresses populating Bristol's coffee bars in her first novel *Shadow Dance* (1966) through to the wolfish grandmothers found in the fairy tale reworkings of *The Bloody Chamber* (1979). But they finally take centre stage in Carter's last novel *Wise Children* (1991), where the narrator Dora Chance reflects on her life with her twin Nora and their career as self-professed 'hoofers'. As this description suggests, Dora's is an irreverent account framed by a day in the present: the twins' seventy-fifth birthday, a date they share with their father Sir Melchior Hazard and his twin brother Perry. The novel finishes with the older generation's centenary celebrations, providing the backdrop for a night of revelations and the flouting of conventions including those that frame old age and gender. In this chapter, I explore Carter's suggestions about contemporary attitudes towards ageing and age-appropriate behaviour. I begin by reading the more obvious ways that the sisters refuse to conform and then go on to consider those discourses that more subtly try to manipulate them into behaving 'as they should', focusing on appearance and issues of visibility and invisibility. Bringing gerontological theory to bear upon the portrayal of the 'Lucky Chances' and the other older characters, like Lady A., allows me to suggest that Carter's career-long interest in the social construction of gender in this novel is joined by an age-sensitive portrayal of her protagonists' identities. In doing so I argue that she, like her characters, challenges dominant ageist prejudices by telling stories that move beyond youth and middle-age.

Critical responses to *Wise Children* have tended to focus on its sustained engagement with the Shakespearean canon. In an interview with Lorna Sage, Carter explained that when writing the novel she had wanted to explore

'Shakespeare as a cultural ideology' (cited in Gamble 2001: 166). In the first chapter, Dora explains how her paternal grandfather, Ranulph Hazard, one of the 'great, roaring, actor-managers' (14), was evangelical about taking Shakespeare to all corners of the world, allowing Carter to present the intimate connections between 'Shakespeare's cultural domination and British imperialism' (Gamble 2001: 169). Performing *King Lear*, Shakespeare's tragedy about, amongst other subjects, old age, Ranulph marries the considerably younger actress who plays Cordelia: an exploit repeated a generation later by his son, Melchior, which prompts Dora to wryly remark that it is 'evidently something of a Hazard family tradition' (37). As this intergenerational marriage suggests, it is not only the more highbrow aspects of the Shakespearean legacy that Carter celebrates but also its bawdier elements; Shakespeare as a 'writer of earthy comedy which challenges all notions of respectability and propriety' (Gamble 2001: 168). The dissolution of the boundary between low and high culture contributes to the carnivalesque tone of the novel and forms another focus for critical discussion.[1] A large part of the carnival's disruptive power lies in its defiance of established hierarchies, and it is the distinction between the illegitimate and legitimate that Carter most often challenges, as *Wise Children's* opening foregrounds: 'My name Is Dora Chance. Welcome to the wrong side of the tracks' (1). Carter undoubtedly 'celebrates wrong-side-of-the trackness' in this 'paean to bastardy' and the Chance's refusal to adopt 'legitimate' ways of ageing forms another strong illustration of the carnival's ability to question and undermine social respectability (Rushdie 1992: 5).

Despite mentions of ageing, *King Lear* and patriarchy, writings on *Wise Children* do not offer sustained analysis of the interaction between age and gender.[2] Partly, this is because literary theory on ageing is at a relatively fledgling state compared to those studies driven by an interest in other aspects of identity such as gender, race and sexuality. Texts like Barbara Frey Waxman's *From the Hearth to the Open Road*, Mike Hepworth's *Stories of Ageing* and Zoe Brennan's *The Older Woman in Recent Fiction* offer age-sensitive readings of fiction centred on older characters and contribute to this developing field. However, taking into account the fact of an ageing population, it is reasonable to expect more debate than is currently evident.[3] One explanation for this reticence is that it is symptomatic of, what Simone de Beauvoir calls in *The Coming of Age*, the 'conspiracy of silence' which positions the old as 'outcasts' (1996: 2). Betty Friedan takes this up as a starting point in *The Fountain of Age*, where she correctly claims that a dread of senescence results in society adopting the twin reactions of '*an increasing obsession with the problem of age*' and its 'outright denial – as early and as long as possible' (1994: 3). This has led to the language of deterioration and loss of youth dominating rhetoric and to the absence of cultural representations of the aged. Friedan focuses on the media and I have argued elsewhere that a similar pattern of marginalizing older women is noticeable in literature.[4] Returning to Shakespeare, in terms of older protagonists there are, for instance, Lear and Falstaff, to whom Carter explicitly compares the larger-than-life Perry, but no female equivalents.

Whilst a disheartening situation, helping to contest this invisibility and 'age as decline' narrative are the baby boomers who have now reached retirement age and older.[5] Carter explored their reframing of what it meant to be a teenager and young adult in the 1960s in her first three novels *Shadow Dance* (1966), *Several Perceptions* (1968) and *Love* (1971), subsequently labelled 'the Bristol trilogy' because of their setting, the city in which Carter lived for over a decade.[6] Featuring beatniks and hippies, they chart particular moments 'within the wider history of the counterculture' (O'Day 1994: 28). Fifty years on and baby boomers are now questioning the options they find themselves being offered as older individuals and are equally dismissive of the status quo. Carter lies just outside this demographic being born in 1940 (whereas it is generally agreed that baby boomers are a post-Second World War generation). However, she can be categorized as part of the politically outspoken second wave of feminists, who, heeding the rallying cry 'the personal is political', are now turning their insightful gaze onto the ways in which ageing intersects with gender. Friedan falls into this category as does Germaine Greer with the polemical *The Change* (1991) and, more recently, Lynne Segal with *Out of Time* (2012).

Despite this activism, the 1990s London of *Wise Children* had certainly not benefited from dissent against ageist and patriarchal paradigms. Although pejorative stereotypes of ageing are often implicit in the text, even a brief appraisal of the sisters' conduct rapidly illuminates the ways in which they refuse to be pigeonholed by indulging in behaviour that the mainstream would label 'age-inappropriate'. Considering that their youthful exploits as 'teenage sexpots' (94) were equally indecorous, it is of little surprise that in their seventies the twins still spontaneously burst into song on the street. The refrain 'What a joy it is to dance and sing!' appears as a chorus throughout the novel and forms its final line. It captures both a sense of 'joie de vivre' and a gratitude for the life-affirming experiences that they can continue to share.

Focusing on three of the most evident ways that Nora and Dora do not abide by the unwritten 'rules' of the septuagenarian allows for a glimpse of the sorts of ideologies that underpin an ageist culture. With this aim in mind, I want to briefly consider: their continued visibility in public spaces, Dora's active sexuality and their newfound maternal role.[7]

Firstly, the book begins with a description of the geographical location of the Chance's house in Brixton, London, and although it quickly moves on to its interior, it does not remain there. Instead the narrative wanders between countries, residences, theatres and film sets. The sisters in the present continue to roam the streets, shop at markets and drink in their 'local' pub. They refuse to be domesticated or confined to the private sphere, but instead are boisterous and annoy the neighbours: 'The window on the second-floor front window of 41 Bard Road went up, a head came out… "You two, again," he said' and adds '"Well, you just watch it, in case a squad car comes by"' (231). Their behaviour is effectively policed here in a cultural as well as criminal framework. In a different context, Dora challenges the erasure of the aged by continuing to make her voice heard. She may no longer be on the stage but Dora's voice refuses to remain within the four walls of her home. She warns the listener/reader:

> Well, you might have known what you were about to let yourself in for when you let Dora Chance in her ratty old fur and poster paint, her orange (Persian Melon) toenails sticking out of her snakeskin peep-toes, reeking of liquor, accost you in the Coach and Horses and let her tell you a tale.
>
> (227)

Just as her unorthodox dress demands to be acknowledged so too does her drunken story. While she recognizes that perhaps she should be silent, it is clearly not imperative enough a feeling to make her stop bearing witness to her life.

One of the advantages of a memoir that looks beyond the aged present and back to a younger self is that it allows the narrator to reveal how identity changes over the course of a lifetime. In *Wise Children*, Carter dramatizes how 'women throughout their lives are defined by their physical appearance and sexuality' (Browne 1998: 4) and there are two quite distinct stages in this process. Julia Twigg, in *Fashion and Age*, notes that the invisibility of the aged female body is in direct opposition to the culturally 'hypervisibility' of their 'idealized' youthful bodies (2013: 41). Subjected not only to the traditional male gaze of patriarchy but also to 'the additional gaze of youth', the older physique is described in terms of lack (Twigg 2013: 41). The adolescent Dora's approach towards her grandmother's nudity neatly demonstrates this. She recalls a meeting in the bathroom: 'There we both were, captured in the mirror, me young and slim and trim and tender, she vast sagging, wrinkled, quivering. I couldn't help but giggle'

(94). Dora's reaction is prompted by discourses which posit the 'normal' body as youthful. In her old age, she is sorry: 'I see it, now, as a defeat that we, her beloved grandchildren inflicted upon her out of heedlessness and vanity and youth' (94).

Connected to, but distinct from, appearance is the second obvious way that Dora subverts expectations and that is through the expression of her sexuality. In representing her as desiring and desirable, Carter counters the usual side-lining of post-menopausal body that takes place in a heteronormative society. Susan Sontag focuses on this relegation in her seminal essay 'The Double Standard of Ageing' about the gendering of the ageing process:

> For most women, ageing means a humiliating process of gradual sexual disqualification. Since women are considered maximally eligible in early youth, after which their sexual value drops steadily… They are old as soon as they are no longer very young.
>
> (1972: 32)

Dora refuses to buy into this 'disqualification' and accept enforced celibacy. She instigates sex with her Uncle Perry at the party, an act with such transgressive potential that Carter describes it as almost bringing 'the house down' (220). There is a lack of shame which permeates many representations of aged sexuality. It is noisy and emphatically not secretive; Nora tells Dora later that there was 'one ecstatic moment… when she thought the grand bouncing on the bed upstairs… would bring down that chandelier' (220). There is also a lack of authorial airbrushing insofar as Carter does not make it a disembodied occurrence but an embodied event, as Nora's comments suggest and Dora's description of a post-coital adjustment: 'I tucked my tits away neatly into my lynx-print top' (223). Coyness is kept at bay in favour of a realism that refuses to stigmatize the event or excuse it as a purely sentimental exercise.

Thirdly, the Chances refuse to be marginalized within their own family, adopting their nephew's two illegitimate children at the end of the novel and ensuring their continuing place as important members of the Chance/Hazard dynasty. In manufacturing a non-biological maternal role with this decision, they mirror the actions of their guardian Grandma Chance who brings them up after their mother's death. Portrayed as an ardent naturist, vegetarian and lover of crème de menthe, Grandma is said to be 'reminiscent of Carter's description of her own maternal grandmother' (Gamble 1997: 180) to whom she said she owed her 'core of iron' (Obituary 1992). There has been much critical interest in the novel's playfulness with beliefs about parentage, and it has been framed as part of Carter's attempt to 'subvert traditional notions of marriage and family as idealized in western culture' (Katsavos 1997: 27).[8] The narrative is fascinated by complex 'ideas of paternity' as Carter herself explained (cited in Gamble 1997: 164), leading to pithy comments such as 'a mother is a biological fact, whilst a father is a moveable feast' (216). Perry later undercuts this perceived wisdom by questioning whether Dora knows who her biological mother is, offering his aphorism 'Mother is as mother does…' (223). It is clear in *Wise Children* that Carter 'redefines "mother" as a performative term', allowing the older female characters a great freedom as they avoid the restraints of the biological clock and are permitted to finally fulfil a maternal role despite being post-menopausal (Simon 2004: 203). Thinking about Grandma Chance, Dora admits that 'the older we [The Chances] grow, the more like her we become' (28), the three of them sharing a derisive attitude towards social norms and inventing a family through 'sheer force of personality' (35).

Carter's entertaining portrait of the raucous and self-sustaining Chance women, her blurring of the boundaries between conduct conventionally framed as youthful and that framed as suitable for the old, adds to *Wise Children*'s carnival atmosphere. However, although not specifically centred on its engagement with ageing, there is debate about whether the novel is essentially optimistic or pessimistic.[9] For example, whilst framing the carnivalesque elements of the novel as a disruptive force Carter simultaneously questions their ability to offer a sustained challenge to the status quo. She underlines their limitations at several points, including after Dora's sexual encounter with Perry. He says, '"Life's a carnival"' to which the narrator responds, '"The carnival's got to stop, some time"' (222). A tension between the carnival and the prosaic, the comic and the tragic runs throughout text. Simon points out that for a book that rejoices in life and renewal in the shape of numerous birthdays and an ever-growing family tree, death lurks around the corner (for instance with the demise of the twins mother and later Grandma Chance). Indeed, Simon compares Dora to Scheherazade, the young bride in *Arabian Nights* who keeps death at bay by spinning her stories (242). Further, whereas Dora expresses approval for the narrator of *Mansfield Park*'s dismissive: 'Let other pens dwell on guilt and misery'; Carter is unafraid to include these more problematic sides of life (163).

With this darker aspect of the narrative in mind, it is unsurprising that, alongside Carter's celebratory framing of rebellious septuagenarian life, there is also a consideration of those unable to escape the damaging effects of ageist attitudes. This is most apparent in her portrayal of Lady Atlanta Hazard. Once independently wealthy and lauded as a great beauty, Lady A. is abandoned by her husband Melchior, who goes on to serially marry ever younger women. Her daughters are similarly fickle, casting her out of the family home when they reach adulthood. Carter even leaves open the possibility that they pushed her down the stairs, causing her paralysis and confinement to a wheelchair (hence her occasional nickname of 'Wheelchair'). It is their lack of filial decency that has led critics to refer to them as 'Goneril-and-Regan-like', referencing King Lear's famously disloyal daughters (Katsavos 1997: 34). Whilst Melchior is often textually connected to the Lear role, Lady A. in many ways plays it more fully as she is effectively banished from her former life and sources of power and dignity. Woven throughout the text, Lear's story offers a sombre counter-narrative to the sort of ageing allowed the Chances and complements its more troubling undercurrents.

Whilst the Chances' care for Lady A. is laudable, and despite Dora's increased self-awareness, she, to a certain extent, perpetuates the ageist attitudes that led to the youthful mockery of her grandma's nakedness. Dora's explanation that they've 'been storing Wheelchair in the basement for well-nigh thirty years' taps into all sorts of pejorative ideologies (7). Most notably, the moniker 'Wheelchair' works to erase her humanity by reducing her to an object, and Dora's use of the word 'storing' is equally telling. It chimes with the language sometimes used to describe caring for the old which is based around the concepts of 'warehousing' and 'quarantine'. Friedan points out that this response is driven by an irrational fear that the old, given the opportunity, could 'contaminate, in mind or body, the rest of society' (Friedan: 1994, 16). This urge for 'containment' results in the senescent being pushed to the social margins and slowly losing the cultural and economic benefits that accrue to adulthood. Those in the fourth age, the most ancient and physically decrepit, are frequently offensively envisaged as experiencing a second childhood which effectively discounts their adult experiences and achievements. Carter nods to this in Dora's half-affectionate and half-dismissive comment to Nora that 'Wheelchair' is like their 'geriatric little girl' as they 'bathe her, feed her, change her nappies, even' (189). Dora goes on to further describe their daily relationship: 'Sometimes she goes on a bit, on and on, on and on and bloody on… until you want to throw a blanket over her, like you do to shut up a parrot' (7). Lady A. is compared to a pet, furthermore one sometimes perceived as an annoyance. Her speeches are characterized as repetitive and of so little interest that Dora would rather she was silent. The stigmatization of the aged by the aged is common and a result of the internalization of prevailing norms. 'Wheelchair' acts as a discomfiting portrait of what-may-be and a reminder that old age is the 'fourth guest' at the Chance's table (189). Ultimately, although Dora's response sometimes echoes that of mainstream society, her actions reflect her belief in Lady A.'s continuing humanity as she is a central, and beloved, part of the household at Bard Road. Further, the narrator consistently uses humour to help deal with many of the more challenging aspects of her life. For example, Lady A.'s comparison to an unruly parrot illustrates how the use of comedy can lighten a situation that at times is psychologically and physically demanding.

Dora and Nora's knowledge of ageist dominant discourses helps to explain the pains they take with their appearance. Despite their bravado, they can neither ignore nor fully escape the limitations of age. The narrator offers the readers several detailed explanations about how they carefully manufacture an exterior to present to the world. She says, for example, of their morning make-up routine that they use: 'The Max Factor Pan-Stik, the false eyelashes with the three coats of mascara, everything', adding that they 'always make an effort. We paint an inch thick. We put on our faces before we come down to breakfast'(6). Carter emphasizes that there is little natural about the 'faces' they create. The constructed quality of their appearance can be read as a dramatization of the performance of identity discussed by, for instance, Judith Butler. Her anti-essentialist explanation, which appears in *Gender Trouble* (1990), describes masculinity and femininity as formed by a 'stylized repetition of acts' that helps to 'constitute the illusion of an abiding gendered self' (Butler 140). The 'illusion' that the Chance's create is not solely to do with appearing female but also youthful, emphasizing the similarities between the discursive production of both gender and age.

From a gerontological perspective, their conduct can be interpreted via a phenomenon known as the 'mask of ageing'. This paradigm focuses on ageing identity and is introduced by Mike Featherstone and Mike Hepworth in their influential essay 'The Mask of Ageing and the Postmodern Life Course' (1991). They suggest that since the Second World War, 'postmodern change' has led 'to some blurring of what appeared previously to be relatively clearly marked stages [of life] and the experiences and characteristic behaviour which were associated with those stages' (372). However, a crucial part of their argument is that this is only an emergent trend, tallying with my earlier point that whilst baby boomers are beginning to transform the current landscape of ageing much of it remains intact. Featherstone and Hepworth assert that when it comes to old age (particularly what they call 'deep old age'), the individual remains bound by largely restrictive 'stereotypes of age appropriate behaviour' (373). The resulting 'stigmatization' of the old body is one of the barriers preventing older people from accepting the ageing process. There arises a disparity between the age an individual appears, and how they are consequently treated, and the age they feel on the inside: what gerontologists differentiate as a 'look age' and a 'feel age' (Featherstone and Hepworth 1991: 381). As a result, a mature face is felt to be 'a mask which conceals the essential identity of the person beneath', a 'disguise concealing the essentially youthful self' (379). Dora refers to this sensation when reunited with Perry at Melchior's party: 'he saw the girls we always would be under the scrawny, wizened carapace that time had forced on us' (208). Her subjective sense of identity does not chime with her exterior – a disjunction between mind and body that has led gerontologists to point out that masking can lead to the body being pathologized and experienced as 'abnormal'.

One response to the mask is for individuals to resort to what Featherstone and Hepworth refer to as 'camouflage' and other gerontologists, borrowing the term from discussions of race and sexuality, describe as 'passing'. Individuals attempt to lessen the perceived gap between 'look' and 'feel' age and present a more youthful appearance to the world, a process Dora captures when she comments: 'we painted the faces we always used to have on to the faces we have now' (192). Trying to distance oneself from negative social reactions by stylizing one's exterior clearly poses problems, primarily that if the facade ever drops you are 'exposed' as trying to present yourself as something you are not. The twins' actions could thus be framed as a potentially harmful form of age denial, particularly because as the years pass there are 'limitations to the plasticity of the body and its capacity to perform youthfulness' (Twigg 2013: 49).

However, Twigg has pointed out the more recalcitrant aspect of women who refuse to adopt a self-effacing and approved appearance (although still noting resistance is 'fraught with ambiguity') (49). Carter certainly picks out the more subversive aspects of the twins' efforts. Dora states, 'We're stuck in the period at which we peaked, of course. All women do. We'd feel mutilated if you made us wipe off our Joan Crawford mouths' (5–6). However, the twins, attached as they are to their make-up, are not concerned about 'passing' as younger because they are under no illusion that anyone will be 'fooled' by it. Nora recognizes this sense of masquerade in a comment: 'It's every woman's tragedy... that, after a certain age, she looks like a female impersonator' (192). Dora laughingly responds: 'Mind you, we've known some lovely female impersonators', puncturing the tragic aspect of their camouflaging strategies.[10] Carter frames their habit of applying 'warpaint' as rebellious rather than a shamed reaction to an ageist society, as illustrated by a reference Dora makes to Dylan Thomas' oft-quoted 1947 poem 'Do Not Go Gentle into That Good Night' (Thomas 1995). Thomas' speaker urges readers not to allow death to steal them quietly away, with the famous opening lines: 'Do not go gentle into that good night, / Old age should burn and rave at close of day' (128). Dora gestures to this call-to-arms when, directly after the detailing of their morning routine, she states: 'Nobody could say the Chance girls were going gently into that good night' (6). The faces they create contest the limiting bounds of good taste and are part of their strategy to avoid fading peacefully into the background.

It is not just their faces that the sisters manipulate but also their garments, which Dora cheerfully admits are 'sixty years too young' for them (197). Twigg's reading of fashion helps to place this individual decision within a wider context:

> Dress… has a significant part to play in the process of being visible, of occupying social and cultural space… This is particularly significant in the context of old age where older women can find themselves becoming invisible culturally, no longer seen or noticed.
>
> (2013: 4)

Carter has Dora address this fact when, waiting patiently in line to greet their father at his party, she observes: 'even dressed up like fourpenny ham-bones, our age and gender still rendered us invisible' (199). Twigg also points out that fashion is 'age-ordered', that there is a 'systematic patterning of cultural expression with regard to dress according to an ordered and hierarchically arranged concept of life' (3). Styles of dress that are deemed appropriate for older women, and to a lesser extent men, suggest that they should cover more of their flesh and wear more sober styles then when they were younger. Women who refuse these 'rules' leave themselves open to accusations that they are 'mutton dressed as lamb'. Featherstone and Hepworth clarify the source of such condemnation: 'Clothes… transmit age-related messages, and when men or women do not dress to their age, society may be offended. The source of the offence or deviation here is not the fact of being old but the refusal to accept the state' (Featherstone and Hepworth 1991: 380). With this statement in mind, the Chance sisters wearing outfits that are too young for them can be interpreted as a rejection of the construction of normative mature femininity.

The twins play with the possibilities of fashion helping them to retain their visibility, even at the expense of social approval. Dora describes 'the customary nasty shock' when they spot their reflection in the big gilt mirror: 'two funny old girls, paint an inch thick' with 'stars on their stockings and little wee skirts skimming their buttocks' (197). Once again, a potentially embarrassing situation is laid to rest by the next lines spoken by Nora:

> 'Oooer, Dor', she said. 'We've gone and overdone it'.
> 
> We couldn't help it, we had to laugh at the spectacle we'd made of ourselves and, fortified by sisterly affection, strutted our stuff boldly into the ballroom. We could still show them a thing or two, even if they couldn't stand the sight.
> 
> (198)

Temporarily disconcerted, they quickly embrace the fact that they appear a spectacle and are emboldened rather than cowed by their appearance. Carter had an abiding interest in the semiotics of fashion and, in an essay about 1960s style, wrote that clothes are 'our weapons, our challenges, our visible insults' (1998b: 105). This certainly captures the nature of the sisters' outfits, chosen as they are to create an aura of confidence the pair do not necessarily feel and challenge the supercilious complacency of the 'legitimate' side of the family. Carter also considered the more pleasurable side of fashion: 'women *do* love to dress up, and also to dress down: we dress to cheer ourselves up, to reward ourselves, to transform ourselves' (1998a: 138). Dora's reminiscences are threaded through with details about dressing up; from the dying of her hair 'Spanish Ebony' when fifteen to make her 'stand out' (79) through the listing of 'sumptuous' costumes worn on stage (90) to minutiae about the designer-wear she sported 'Schiaparelli, I kid you not – charcoal wool, fox wrap collar and cuffs' (112). Throughout Dora's life, fashion acts a source of both transformation and aesthetic satisfaction and Carter does not deny her this pleasure just because she has reached the third age.

Before moving on to the conclusion, I want to briefly turn to Carter's take on male ageing with a consideration of Melchior and Perry. They provide a contrast to Dora and Nora, whose victories, in terms of their continuing agency, are particularly impressive when considered against the fact that 'many of the issues women face in their younger years become crystallized disadvantages with age': issues such as 'unequal pay, segregated employment opportunities' and 'unpaid caregiving duties' (Browne 1998: xvii–xviii). Similarly, the brothers inherit an old age moulded by their earlier lives but, in this case, have managed to retain some of the privileges held by younger men in a patriarchal society. Carter depicts them as possessing a sanctioned visibility and power denied their female counterparts. Melchior is still very much the patriarch, able at his late stage of life to grant his daughters the approval they have spent a lifetime craving. Further, his party is a media event, due to his status as a 'national treasure', at which he appears dressed in his father's Lear costume complete with battered crown.

When his twin Perry arrives, Dora sees him as physically unchanged, 'still the size of a warehouse' with 'hair red as paprika – not one speck of grey, evidently untouched one jot by age' (207). Much of his apparent immunity to the physical effects of time can be explained through Dora's adoring gaze. Worldly wise she may be aware of their many faults, but both brothers are viewed through a lens distorted by Dora's sentiments.

However, the depiction of the brothers as somehow less damaged by pejorative stereotyping can also be interpreted as a reflection of how men are culturally '"allowed" to age without penalty' in 'ways that women are not' (Sontag 1972: 29). Sontag's observation is largely based around judgements about attractiveness and sexuality. As mentioned earlier in this chapter, society values youthful female bodies and ignores older female bodies in ways which are not equivalent for men. Alternatively, Sontag suggests that the male 'ageing crisis is linked to that terrible pressure on men to be "successful"' in their chosen careers and economically', a reminder that class also intersects with gender and age throughout the life course (Sontag 1972: 31). The Hazard brothers are wealthy enough to maintain their cultural currency. Additionally, Carter even allows them their continued virility, which is one of the key markers of youthful masculinity and so, overall, they seem comparatively unscathed by age. As a caveat to this fictional picture of 'easy' male ageing, I want to mention that the direction of the gerontological gaze has shifted over the last few decades to no longer treat male experience as universal. This benefits not only older women but also men because as a result more attention is being paid to, for instance, why women tend to have a longer life expectancy than their male counterparts.[11]

## Conclusion

At the start of this chapter about *Wise Children* and its representation of the aged, I stated my interest in exploring the non-conformist behaviours and attitudes of the Chance sisters. Throughout the novel we see them contesting, with various degrees of success, the intertwining forces of ageism and sexism. Focusing initially on three aspects of their characterization which blatantly showed their resilience and refusal to 'behave' has allowed me to highlight some of the implicit ideologies that underpin a contemporary experience of female ageing. Bringing in Lady A.'s more prosaic and disengaged life acts as a counterbalance to the more successful ageing represented by the twins. Yet, Dora's internalization of many ageist discourses in her descriptions of 'Wheelchair' acts as a sombre reminder about the insidious nature of the stereotyping of old age as something to be dreaded. When taken together, these different stories of ageing help create a more nuanced view of the topic than is sometimes observed in discussions of the novel and beyond.

I focused on Dora and Nora's appearance partly because Carter makes much of it but also because society, as discussed earlier, still defines women in terms of their bodies, although, in old age, it works to desexualize and nullify them. The model of the mask of ageing, which I initially used to analyse their actions, points out the discrepancies that many individuals feel between the cultural construction of the aged body and a subjective sense of self. The hope is that one day this paradigm will become outdated when society constructs old age in more positive terms. In the meantime, Featherstone and Hepworth remind us: 'The individual struggle to maintain a balance between the external stereotypes of age-appropriate behaviour and the subjective experience of the self requires considerable energy, tenacity and other resources' (1991: 378). The Chance sisters possess the necessary obstinacy and manage to resist many restrictions, particularly regarding dress, which reflects their refusal to disappear. Moving away from the mask and applying Twigg's work allowed for this more subversive reading of their fashion choices and reclamation of the visibility that being 'mutton dressed as lamb' can bring. As Carter wrote: 'Clothes are so many things at once', and in this novel, they work simultaneously as a reminder of ageist discourses but also a way to challenge them (1998b: 105).

In a discussion of ageing and *Wise Children*, it is difficult to ignore the fact that Carter was diagnosed with the cancer that would eventually kill her when writing this book.[12] In several interviews she mentions that the Chances' story is a re-imagining of an aunt's life who had been persuaded to give up her dream of going on the stage and instead became a clerk (cited in Gamble 1997: 164–5). Perhaps, in Dora, it is not too far-fetched to sense Carter's hopeful imagining of a boisterous old age and a vision of a time when, like her fictional counterpart, she too would still be cornering people and spinning them tales.

On a less speculative note, it is worth emphasizing that simply by placing a variety of older characters at the centre of the book Carter does not follow in the footsteps of the wider society by marginalizing their lives and experiences. Instead she opens alternative vistas and points to ways in which old age could be constructed differently. Salman Rushdie wrote of her that she 'loved nothing so much as cussed – but also blithe – nonconformity' and this is the tone of the *Wise Children* (1992: 5). Not only does she make Dora and Nora memorably visible but by creating an old age full of song and dance, sex and sisterhood she resists those portraits of ageing that would banish these pleasures and label them either inappropriate or out-of-reach.

## Notes

1. See Day chapter 7, Gamble, *Angela Carter*, Webb and Gamble *Fiction* 163–85 for a summary of several critics' views on the role of carnival in the novel.
2. See Simon 189–249. She offers some insight into the ageing female body but focuses on Carter's depiction of death rather than old age.
3. See Browne, especially the 'Introduction', for an extended discussion of how both feminism and gerontology have tended to ignore the older woman.
4. On the comparative paucity of novels that focus on older female characters, see Brennan, *The Older Woman*, especially chapter 1.
5. See Friedan for further discussion of contemporary challenges to established models of old age.
6. See Brennan, 'Angela Carter' for a discussion of the 1960s counterculture.
7. Each of these experiences could be examined in more depth but for the purposes of my argument a 'snapshot' will suffice to highlight attitudes towards the old.
8. For further discussion of the maternal and paternal, see Day chapter 7, Gamble *Fiction* 163–85, and Katsavos and Simon 189–213 for an especially insightful discussion of maternity.
9. Both Simon 243 and Gamble, *Fiction* 163–85 summarize this issue.
10. Once again, we return to Butler as she invokes the drag queen as an example of gender performance in action. See Brennan, *The Older Woman*, chapter 3, for further discussion of this topic in relation to the ageing face.
11. Friedan discusses life expectancy and gender in chapter 4 titled 'Why Do Women Age Longer and Better than Men?' Explanations for this phenomenon include that conventionally women are encouraged to invest in friendships, and this intimacy helps to create support networks – a fair description of the Chances and the various connections they maintain.
12. Lorna Sage explains that the plot had been decided by the time of Carter's diagnosis (Sage, cited in 'Obituary'). I am not suggesting that the structure changed; rather, the novel's portrait of the sisters might have been affected.

## Works cited

Brennan, Z. (2005), *The Older Woman in Recent Fiction*, Jefferson: McFarland and Co.

Brennan, Z. (2015), 'Angela Carter's Bristol Trilogy: A Gothic Perspective on Bristol's 1960's Counterculture', in M. Mulvey-Roberts (ed), *Literary Bristol: Writers and the City*, 162–82, Bristol: Redcliffe Press.
Browne, C. V. (1998), *Women, Feminism and Ageing*, New York: Springer.
Butler, J. (1990), *Gender Trouble*, New York: Routledge.
Carter, A. (1998a). 'Elizabeth Wilson: Adorned in Dreams', in J. Uglow (ed), *Shaking a Leg: Collected Journalism and Writings*, 138–41, London: Vintage.
Carter, A. (1998b), 'Notes for a Theory of Sixties Style', in J. Uglow (ed), *Shaking a Leg: Collected Journalism and Writings*, 105–9, London: Vintage.
Carter, A. ([1991] 2006), *Wise Children*, London: Vintage Books.
Day, A. (1998), *Angela Carter: The Rational Glass*, Manchester: Manchester University Press.
De Beauvoir, S. (1996), *The Coming of Age*, trans. Patrick O' Brian, New York: Norton.
Featherstone, M. and M. Hepworth (1991), 'The Mask of Ageing and the Postmodern Life Course', in M. Featherstone, M. Hepworth and B. S. Turner (eds), *The Body: Social Process and Cultural Theory*, 37–389, London: Sage.
Friedan, B. (1994), *The Fountain of Age*, London: Vintage.
Gamble, S. (1997), *Angela Carter: Writing From the Frontline*, Edinburgh: Edinburgh University Press.
Gamble, S. (2001) (ed), *The Fiction of Angela Carter: A Reader's Guide to Essential Criticism*, London: Palgrave Macmillan.
Greer, G. (1991), *The Change: Women, Ageing and the Menopause*, Harmondsworth: Penguin.
Hepworth, M. (2000), *Stories of Ageing*, Oxford: Oxford University Press.
Katsavos, A. (1997), 'Using the Fantastic to Disrupt the Domestic: An Examination of Marriage and Family in Angela Carter's *Nights at the Circus* and *Wise Children*', in M. A. Morrison (ed), *Trajectories of the Fantastic*, 27–38, Westport: Greenwood.
'Obituary: Angela Carter' (1992), *The Daily Telegraph*, 17 February. http://www.telegraph.co.uk/news/obituaries/5899665/Angela-Carter.html (accessed 6 July 2017).
O'Day, M. (1994), 'Mutability Is Having a Field Day': The Sixties Aura of Angela Carter's Bristol Trilogy', in L. Sage (ed), *Flesh and the Mirror: Essays on the Art of Angela Carter*, 24–59, London: Virago.
Rushdie, S. (1992), 'Angela Carter, 1940–92: A Very Good Wizard, a Very Dear Friend', *The New York Times Book Review*, 8: 5.
Segal, L. (2013), *Out of Time: The Pleasures and Perils of Ageing*, London: Verso.
Simon, J. (2004), *Rewriting the Body: Desire, Gender and Power in Selected Novels by Angela Carter*, London: Peter Lang.
Sontag, S. (1972), 'The Double Standard of Ageing', *The Saturday Review*, 23: 29–38.
Thomas, D. (1995), 'Do Not Go Gentle into That Good Night', in *The Dylan Thomas Omnibus*, 128–9, London: Phoenix.
Twigg, J. (2013), *Fashion and Age: Dress, the Body and Later Life*, London: Bloomsbury.
Waxman, B. F. (1990), *From the Hearth to the Open Road: A Feminist Study of Ageing in Contemporary Literature*, New York: Greenwood.
Webb, K. (1994), 'Seriously Funny: *Wise Children*', in L. Sage (ed), *Flesh and the Mirror: Essays on the Art of Angela Carter*, 279–307, London: Virago.

# Index

Académie Française, La 80
Adam 143, 149, 150 n.7
adaptation 2, 6–7, 30, 71, 82, 115–25, 127–8, 131–7, 145, 185, 195, 204 n.6
Agamben, G. (2005)
  *State of Exception* 66–7
ageing 9, 229–31, 223–7, 239–43
ageism 240
Amos, Tori 118
anamorphosis 177, 181–3, 185
Angela Carter, compiled list of her library, University of East Anglia archives 29n.2
Angela Carter Society, The
Angry Brigade, The 145
anorexia nervosa 204 n.2
anthropology 91 n.2, 143
Anzieu, Didier
  *Psychic Envelopes* 37, 39
apocalypse 140–9, 150 n.2, 151–2
*Arabian Nights*, The 234
Araki, Sozo 3, 6, 15
  *Seduced by Japan: A Memoir of the Days Spent with Angela Carter* 17, 29 n.1, 30
Armageddon 141
Arp, Jean 71
Atwood, Margaret
  'Running with the Tigers' 190, 200, 202, 205
Aulnoy, Madame de 76
Austen, Jane
  *Mansfield Park* 234

'Babes in the Wood' (folk song) 57–9
Bacchilega, C.
  *Postmodern Fairy Tales: Gender and Narrative Strategies* 106, 110
  'Sex Slaves and Saints? Resisting Masochism in Angela Carter's "The Bloody Chamber"', 99, 102, 110

Badham, Van
  *The Bloody Chamber* (playscript) 116, 119–20
ballads 45, 57, 68–9, 91 n.7
Ballard, J. G.
  *The Drowned World* 141–2, 144, 150
Balodis, Janis
  *The Practice of Adaptation: Turning Fact and Fiction into Theatre* 121, 126, 136
Barchilon, J.
  *Le Conte merveilleux français de 1690 à 1790* 73
  'Remembering Angela Carter' 73, 92
baroque 122, 164, 196
Barthes, Roland
  *Empire of Signs* 19–20, 29 n.2, 30, 176
  *Roland Barthes by Roland Barthes* 175–6, 185
Bartók, Béla
  *Bluebeard's Castle* (opera) 119–20
*Basile*, Giambattista
  *The Pentamerone* 91 n.7
Bastille Day (France, July 14) 2
Bat for Lashes 53
Bataille, Georges
  *The Story of the Eye* 168
Baudelaire, Charles 11, 71, 99–100, 154–5, 165, 168 n.10, 170–1
  'Les Bijoux' in *Les Fleurs du mal.* 99, 110 n.2
Beardsley, Aubrey
  *How Sir Tristram Drank of the Love Drink* 101–2, 107
*Beaumont*, Jeanne-Marie Leprince de
  'Beauty and the Beast' 89
Beauvoir, Simone de
  *The Coming of Age* 230, 243
Bedford, Les 145
Bell, Ronald
  *The Japan Experience* 18

Benjamin, Walter
   'Paris, the Capital of the Nineteenth Century' 157, 168 n.6, 169 n.20, 170
   'The Work of Art in the Age of Mechanical Reproduction' 139, 150, 164, 170
Benson, Susan
   'Inscriptions of the Self: Reflections Contemporary Euro-America' 25, 30 on Tattooing and Piercing in
Berger, John
   *Ways of Seeing* 167 n.1, 170, 177
*Bibliothèque Bleue* ("Blue Library") 76, 91 n.3
Bijon, Beatrice 8
Björk 12, 53
Black September 145
Blake, William 4, 14, 35
   *The Great Red Dragon and the Woman Clothed with the Sun* 35
   *The Marriage of Heaven and Hell* 4
   *The Bloody Chamber* dir. Matthew Lutton (theatrical adaptation) 115–37
Bluebeard 72, 74, 77, 82, 87–9, 96–7, 99–100, 102, 111, 120, 125, 129–31, 134–5, 190, 202
Boccaccio, Giovanni
   'Griselda' 75–7, 80, 82, 89, 91
Boileau, Nicolas 76, 80–1, 83
   'Satire X' 80
Bonacho and Pires et al.
   'Angela Carter: Receiving Literature through Food & Design' 193–4, 200, 204 n.6, 205
Bonachoricardo 204 n.1, n.6, n.7, 205 n.10
Bonfire Night (UK, November 5) 2
Bottigheimer, R.
   'Before *Contes du Temps Passé* (1697): Charles Perrault's "Grisélidis" (1691), "Souhaits d'Asne" (1694)' 80, 90 n.1
   Ridicules (1693), and "Peau" 91 n.3, 92
Bowen, Elizabeth
   *The House in Paris* 31, 39
Bowlby, Rachel
   *Feminist Destinations and Further on Virginia Woolf* 155, 170
Boyes, Georgina

   *The Imagined Village: Culture, Ideology and the English Folk Revival* 54, 67
Brennan, Zoe
   'Angela Carter's Bristol Trilogy: A 1960's Counterculture' 243
   Gothic Perspective on Bristol's *The Older Woman in Recent Fiction* 230, 242 n.4, n.6, n.10
Breton, André
   *The Manifesto of Surrealism* 4–5, 11
Briggs, Anne 52
Bristol 2, 10, 12, 15, 44–5, 116, 174, 229, 231
*Bristol Post*
   'Angela Carter Show' 136
Bristol University 43
Britanje, Thomas von
   *Roman de Tristan* 96
British Library, The 151, 186
British Museum, The 75
British New Wave, The 146
Britzolakis, Christina 157, 168 n.7
Broadwood, Lucy 54
Brontë, Charlotte
   *Jane Eyre* 177
Brooks, Peter 158, 170
The Brothers Grimm, Jacob Ludwig and Wilhelm Carl 76, 112, 90 n.2
   *Kinder- und Hausmärchen* 90 n.2
Browne, C. V.
   *Women, Feminism and Aging* 232, 239, 242 n.3, 243
Buci-Glucksmann, Christine 164
*Bunraku* (Japanese puppetry) 6, 17, 19–21, 27
Burd Ellen 92
Burnett, J.
   'More Stories Emerge of Rapes in Post-Katrina Chaos' 66–7
Burroughs, William S. 148
Busoni, Ferruccio 107
Butler, Judith 9, 13, 227
   *Gender Trouble: Feminism and the Subversion of Identity* 11, 108, 110, 211–13, 218, 225, 236, 242 n.10, 243

*The Cabinet of Dr Caligari* 165, 168 n.13
Cameron, Shirley 202
Campaign for Nuclear Disarmament, The
Campbell, Marion May

*Poetic Revolutionaries: Intertextuality and Subversion* 64, 67
cannibalism 190, 192–3
(CND) 140
'Cap O' Rushes' (fairy tale) 214
Caravaggio, Michelangelo Merisi Da 34
Carrington, Leonora 174
  'The Debutante' 212–13, 225 n.2
Carter, Angela *See also* Angela Stalker
  *Adam and Eve at the End of the World* (unused book title) 105 n.7
  'Addenda: to [sic] The Story That Needs Re-writing' (unpublished) 148
  'The Alchemy of the Word' 5, 140
  'Alison's Giggle' 44
  *And Tomorrow's Doomsday* (unwritten) 140
  *Angela Carter's Book of Wayward Girls and Wicked Women* (ed.) 111, 212, 225–6
  *Angela Carter's Curious Room* (BBC 2 programme) 11, 225 n.3
  'Anger in a Black Landscape' 139–40
  'Ashputtle, *or* The Mother's Ghost: Three Versions of One Story' 110 n.6, 112
  'The Better to Eat You With' 73, 79, 93
  *Black Venus* 9, 210
    'Overture and Incidental Music for A Midsummer Night's Dream' 69
    'Peter and the Wolf' 9, 207–10, 213, 220–1, 223, 225
  *The Bloody Chamber and Other Stories* 4, 7–9, 11–12, 70, 72, 74, 76, 78, 83, 88–92, 95–8, 102, 104–6, 109–11, 116, 189–90, 193, 196, 199, 202–5, 204 n.4, 210, 216, 218–19, 226, 229
    'The Bloody Chamber' 7, 77, 84, 86–8, 92, 96–103, 106, 110–11, 116, 123, 130–1, 134, 190–2, 194, 203, 218, 225–6 (*see also The Bloody Chamber* (theatrical adaptation))
    'The Company of Wolves' 7, 96, 102–3, 190, 200, 205, 208, 211–13, 215, 217–20, 225 (*see also The Company of Wolves* (film))
    'The Courtship of Mr Lyon' 8, 178, 185, 190, 193–5, 210–11, 213, 215–16, 225
    'The Erl-King' 7, 57, 60, 62, 64–6, 68, 190, 196–7
    'The Lady of the House of Love' 7, 190, 194, 198–9 (*see also The Lady of the House of Love* (theatrical adaptation))
    'Puss-in-Boots' 74, 116, 190, 195–6, 209–10, 213–15, 218–20, 224–5 (*see also Puss-in-Boots* (radio adaptation by Angela Carter))
    'The Snow Child' 190, 198–9
    'The Tiger's Bride' 7–9, 83, 89, 92, 178, 185, 190, 194, 200, 210–14, 216, 219–20, 224–5
    'The Werewolf' 110 n.3, 190, 199, 208–10
    'Wolf-Alice' 7, 96, 98, 100, 102–6, 190, 200–1, 211, 213, 215, 221–3, 225
  Bristol Trilogy, The 29, 231, 243
  *Burning your Boats* 11–12, 15, 68–70, 136, 170, 225
  *The Curious Room: Collected Dramatic Works*, ed. Mark Bell 12, 69
  'Envoi: Bloomsday' 167 n.4, 170
  'The Events of a Night' (unpublished) 79
  *The Fairy Tales of Charles Perrault* (trans) 6, 74, 79, 91 n.4
  'Fictions Written in a Certain City' 13
  *Fireworks: Nine Profane Pieces* 1, 3–5, 11–12, 30, 93, 169
    'Afterword' 3, 44, 68
    'Elegy for a Freelance' 3
    'The Executioner's Beautiful Daughter' 8, 181–5
    'Flesh and the Mirror' 22, 94, 171, 205, 243
    *The Great Hermaphrodite* (unused title) 5, 148
    'The Loves of Lady Purple' 4, 21
    'Penetrating to the Heart of the Forest' 59, 68
    'A Souvenir of Japan' 1, 18, 21, 27, 68, 169
  'Fred Jordan-singer' 51, 68
  Frida Kahlo 185 *The Gates of Paradise* (unused book Title) 149

'The Patience of Grizelda' (unpublished translation) 7, 74, 79, 87, 91
*Heroes and Villains* 25, 30, 139, 142–51
*The Infernal Desire Machines of Doctor Hoffman* 5, 8, 10–11, 139, 146–51, 153–71
'Introduction', in A. Carter (ed.), *The Virago Book of Fairy Tales* 44, 53, 68–9, 205
Journals 1–2, 8, 11, 18, 30, 48, 57, 65, 68, 71, 90 n.2, 92, 139–40, 144–5, 148–9, 151, 164
  1960 90 n.2, 92, 151
  1961 2, 11, 48, 68
  1962–3 57, 68
  1963–4 65, 68
  1969 1, 11
*Love* 6, 11, 31–9, 149, 151, 168, 171, 231
*The Magic Toyshop* 2, 8, 11, 68, 142, 149, 150 n.1, 151, 207–9
*The Manifesto for Year One* 8, 139, 148, 150
'The Merchant of Shadows' 168 n.14
'Misery City' (unpublished) 79
'Mishima's Toy Sword' 23–4
'New Mother Goose tales' 78
*Nights at the Circus* 7, 8, 11, 116, 137, 139, 143, 149, 169 n.21, 171, 207–8, 243
'Notes for a Theory of Sixties Style' 162, 170, 225–6, 243
'Notes from the Front Line' 3, 110
'Now is the Time for Singing' 68
*Orlando: The Enigma of the Sexes* (libretto) 115
*The Passion of New Eve* 5, 8, 11, 139, 146–9, 151, 175
'People as Pictures' 26
'Poor Butterfly' 22
*Puss-in-Boots* (radio adaptation) 195
'The Quilt Maker' 5, 11
*The Sadeian Woman: An Exercise in Cultural History* 38–9, 62, 74, 88, 93, 96, 111, 170, 190, 20, 205, 222, 226
*Several Perceptions* 29, 39, 68, 231
*Shadow Dance* 29, 39, 56, 61–2, 68, 142, 151, 171, 207, 229, 231
*Shaking a Leg: Collected Journalism and Writings* 4, 12, 15, 30, 68, 93, 110, 151, 170, 205, 226, 243

'That Arizona Home' 147
'Vampirella' (radio play) 198–9, 205
*Wise Children* 7, 9, 11, 56, 61, 69, 116, 229–43
Carter, A. and Carter, P.
  *Paul and Angela Carter's Folk Music Archive* 9, 45–8, 69
Carter, Paul 2, 7, 43, 45–8, 69
'Catskin, or the Wandering Gentlewoman' 91
Cavallaro, Dani
  *The World of Angela Carter: A Critical Investigation* 168–9 n.16, 170, 190, 202–3, 205, 214, 226
Chagall, Marc 71
Chaucer, Geoffrey
  'The Miller's Tale' 74
Chisholm, David 120, 125
Child, F. J. 58, 63, 65, 69
'Cinderella' 72, 76, 78, 82, 209–10, 224, 226
Cixous, Hélène
  'Le Rire de la Méduse' 100, 102
Clapp, Susannah
  'Introduction', in A. Carter, *The Curious Room: Plays, Film Scripts and an Opera* 43, 69
Clark, R.
  'Angela Carter's Desire Machine' 96, 110
Clarke, Sonny 128, 136
clothing 207–25
Cobain, I. and J. Ball
  'New Light Shed on US Government's Extraordinary Rendition Programme' 66, 69
Coelho, A. P.
  'A virgem, o marquês sádico e um crime à mesa' 204–5
Colarelli, Sandro 17–136
Collins, D.
  'Anamorphosis and the Eccentric Observer: Inverted Perspective and Construction of the Gaze' 177, 185
Collins, Shirley 54
Communist Party, The 145
'The Company of Wolves' (dir. Neil Jordan) 204–5, 217, 226
Cordlingley, Anna 129
'The Cottage in the Wood' 48
Cox, Harry 52
Crary, Jonathan

*Techniques of the Observer: On Vision and Modernity in the Nineteenth Century* 156, 161–2, 168 n.16, 170
Crawford, Joan 237
Crofts, Charlotte 10, 93
  *Anagrams of Desire: Angela Carter's Writing for Radio, Film and Television* 10, 12, 43–4, 69, 115, 136, 153, 171
  *Pyrotechnics: A Union of Contraries* (ed.) 10
Crossen, Carys 9

'Dada and Surrealism Reviewed' (exhibit) 140
dadaism 140
Daguerreotype 153, 155–6, 161, 164–5, 167 n.3
Dalí, Salvador
  *Christ of St John of the Cross* 35
Daniel (Old Testament) 141
Daverio, J.
  '*Tristan und Isolde*: Essence and Appearance' 97, 108, 110
Day, A.
  *Angela Carter: The Rational Glass* 136, 243
Deathridge, J.
  'Public and Private Life: On the Genesis of *Tristan und Isolde* and the *Wesendonck Lieder*' 97, 110
Debussy, Claude 123
deconstruction 120, 127, 133, 149, 203, 214
Derrida, Jacques
  'No Apocalypse. Not Now,' 142, 151
Descartes, Rene 163
Deulin, Charles
  *Contes de Ma Mère l'Oye avant Charles Perrault* 75
Diefenbach, Jacob 118, 124
  'The Place of Annihilation' 124
  'Racing into Springtime' 131
  'Too many roses growing on the vine' 127
Dimovitz, Scott 8, 10
  *Angela Carter: Surrealist, Psychologist, Moral Pornographer* 3, 12, 92–3, 145, 151
Donne, John
  'The Relic' 39
Dor, J.
  *Introduction to the Reading of Lacan: The Unconscious Structured Like a Language* 221, 226
Duchamp, Marcel
  *Etant donne* 160
Duncker, Patricia
  'Re-Imagining the Fairy Tales: Angela Carter's Bloody Chambers' 96, 110, 216, 226
Dworkin, A.
  *Pornography: Men Possessing Women* 96, 111
  'The Sexual Politics of Fear and Courage' 96, 111

Edo government of Japan 29 n.3
*Ekphrasis* 173
English folk revival, The 44, 49, 53–6, 67
Enlightenment, The 76, 90, 91 n.3
Ennis, Seamus 52
Ensor, Baron J. S. E. 173
Ernst, Max
  *The Antipope* 33
  *The Robing of the Bride* 33
eroticism 7, 105, 108–9, 135
Estate of Angela Carter, The 16, 90
Estoril Higher Institute for Tourism and Hotel Studies
  *Receiving/Perceiving Angela Carter* (academic event) 189–90
  *Experiencing Food: Designing Dialogues* (conference) 189
ethnomusicology 44, 54
Evans, Daniel
  *The Lady of the House of Love* (playscript) 116, 118–19, 121–2, 124–5, 127, 131, 135–6
'The Everlasting Circle' (folk song) 46, 48, 70

fairy tales *See also* folk tales 5–10, 43–4, 53, 68–76, 94–7, 100, 104–12, 115, 127, 131–4, 174, 176, 178, 181, 189–90, 203, 205, 209–19, 224–9
Falstaff, Sir John 231
fantasy 21, 28–9, 33, 54, 67, 69, 131, 142, 190, 221
fashion 9, 30, 75, 158, 207–12, 225–6, 232, 238–9, 241, 243

Featherstone, Mike and Mike Hepworth
'The Mask of Ageing and the Postmodern Life Course' 236–8, 241, 243
Feinauer, I and A. Lorens
'The Loyalty of the Literary Reviser: Author, Source Text, Target Text or Reader?' 129, 136
femininity 10–11, 14, 20–4, 27–8, 154, 155–6, 159, 167–8, 175, 214, 226, 236, 238
feminism 6–7, 10–11, 13, 20, 29, 49, 72–3, 77–9, 87–90, 94, 96, 100, 102, 107, 109–12, 131, 135, 137, 146, 150–2, 170–1, 176, 190, 210, 216, 225–6, 231, 242–3
femme fatale 100, 102, 106–7, 158, 170
Fenton, David 116, 118, 121–2, 125, 127–8, 131, 133–4, 136
fetishes 33–4
film 2, 10, 12, 17, 23, 44, 61, 69, 72, 111, 115–16, 128, 136–7, 145, 153, 157, 168–9, 171, 202, 205, 226, 232
fireworks 1–4, 10–12, 71, 162, 169 n.17, 189
'Fireworks: The Visual Imagination of Angela Carter' (conference) 10, 206
'The Flower of Sweet Strabane' (folk song) 68
folk music *See also* music 6–7, 10, 12, 43–70
folklore, folk tales *See also* fairy tales 6, 38, 53, 72–8, 88, 91, 131, 179, 226
Fontaine, Jean de La 75–7
*Le Pouvoir des Fables* 81
Foucault, M.
*Discipline and Punish: The Birth of the Prison* 163, 169 n.21, 171
'On the Genealogy of Ethics: An Overview of Work in Progress' 171, 202, 205
'The Fox' (folk song) 55
France, Marie de
*Bisclavret* 219
Frankenstein's monster 118
Frayling, Christopher 54, 70
Freud, Sigmund 83, 139, 145, 157, 168
'Screen Memories' 35, 39
*Totem and Taboo* 182

Friedan, B.
*The Fountain of Age* 230–1, 235, 242 n.5, 242 n.11, 243
Frye, Northrop
*The Anatomy of Criticism: Four Essays* 57, 69

Gamble, Sarah
*Angela Carter: A Literary Life* 145, 151
*Angela Carter: Writing from the Front Line* 115, 131, 137, 149, 151, 230, 233–4, 241–3
'Something Sacred: Angela Carter, Jean-Luc Godard and the Sixties' 153, 171
*The Fiction of Angela Carter: A Reader's Guide to Essential Criticism* 230, 242–3
Garner, Katie
'Blending the Pre-Raphaelite with the Surreal in Angela Carter's *Shadow Dance* (1966) and *Love* (1971) 142, 151, 153, 171
Garrett, G.
'Technics and Pyrotechnics' 4, 12
Gass, Joanne M.
'Panopticism in *Nights at the Circus*' 169 n.21, 171
Gauguin, Paul 173
*geisha* 18–9
gender 5–13, 19–20, 30, 82, 96, 103, 106–11, 117, 133–6, 140, 144–5, 156–9, 162, 166–7, 185, 198, 211–18, 221–7, 229–31, 233, 236, 238, 240, 242–3
gender crossover 190
Genesis, Book of 143
gerontology 242
Get Angela Carter, http://getangelacarter.com, curated by C. Crofts and M. Mulvey-Roberts 12, 93
Ghost Dance movement, The 147
Gilman, E.
'Interart Studies and the "Imperialism" of Language' 174, 185
Glass, Frank
*The Fertilizing Seed: Wagner's Concept of the Poetic Intent?* 110 n.5, 111
Goethe, Johann Wolfgang von
'Erlkönig' 64

Goldberg, Rube 142
Goldsworthy, K.
　'Angela Carter' 108, 111
Gollancz, Victor 72
Gordon, Edmund
　*The Invention of Angela Carter* 2, 5, 12,
　　17, 19, 30, 44–5, 53, 69, 72, 93, 140,
　　144–5, 149–51, 207, 226
Gothic, The 30, 92, 129–31, 133
　　168 n.8, 171, 190, 226, 243
Grainger, Percy 54
Greenwood, the 7, 53, 56–67, 226, 243
Greer, Germaine
　*The Change: Women, Ageing and
　　Menopause* 231, 243
Grey, T. S.
　'In the Realm of the Senses: Sight,
　　Sound and the Music of Desire in
　　*Tristan und Isolde*' 111
Groos, A.
　'Between Memory and Desire: Wagner's
　　Libretto and Late Romantic
　　Subjectivity' 106, 108, 111
Grünewald, Matthias
　*Grünewald Crucifixion, The* 61
Gruss, S.
　'Angela Carter's Excessive Stagings of
　　the Canon: Psychoanalytic Closets,
　　Hermaphroditic Dreams and
　　Jacobean Westerns' 115, 137
Gunpowder Plot (1605) 2
Guy Fawkes 3

Haffenden, John
　'Angela Carter' in
　　*Novelists in Interview* 92 n.9, 93, 143–4,
　　148, 151
Hall, Reg 55, 70
*hanabi* (Japanese for 'fireworks') 3, 71
*hara-kiri* 23
Harker, Dave
　*Fakesong: The Manufacture of British
　　'folksong' 1700 to the present day*
　　54, 69
Harker, J. (2016)
　'Stop Calling the Calais Refugee Camp
　　the "Jungle"' 66, 69
Harman, G.
　*Towards Speculative Realism: Essays
　　and Lectures* 32, 39

*Harper's and Queen* 140
Harrison, M. John
　*Light* 33, 39
Harvey, David
　*The Condition of Postmodernity: An
　　Enquiry into the Origins of Cultural
　　Change* 157, 171
Harvey, P. J. 53
Hayward Gallery, The 140
Heaney, Joe 52
Hennard Dutheil de la Rochère, Martine
　'Angela Carter's *objets trouvés* in
　　Translation: From Baudelaire
　　to *Black Venus*' 71, 93
　'From the Bloody Chamber to the
　　*Cabinet de Curiosités*: Angela
　　Carter's curious Alices through
　　The Looking-Glass of Languages'
　　71, 93
　'Modelling for Bluebeard: Visual and
　　Narrative Art in Angela Carter's
　　"The Bloody Chamber"' 95, 99, 111
　'"Morning Glories of the Night":
　　Angela Carter's Translational
　　Poetics in *Fireworks*' (forthcoming)
　　11 n.1, 12, 72, 93
　*Reading, Translating, Rewriting:
　　Angela Carter's Translational
　　Poetics* 71–2, 90 n.2, 92 n.12, 93,
　　103, 110–11
Hepworth, Mike
　*Stories of Ageing* 230
*Herald Sun, The* 132
Herbert, Kate 132, 137
Hicks, Edward
　*The Peaceful Kingdom* 178
'Higher Germany' (folk song) 46–7, 70
Hogg, Mrs 54
Holbein, Hans
　*The Ambassadors* 164, 77, 179
Hollywood 153
*honne* (Japanese for 'true feelings') 19
Huebner, S.
　'*Tristan*'s traces' 96, 102, 107, 111
humour 38, 73, 79, 90 n.1, 91 n.3, 140,
　　175, 178, 180, 184–5, 236
Hunt, Stephen
　*Angela Carter's 'Provincial Bohemia':
　　The Counterculture in 1960s and
　　1970s Bristol and Bath* 10, 12

Hutcheon, Linda
    *A Theory of Adaptation* 120, 173, 185

Ikoma, Natsumi 6, 12, 27, 29–30 n.3, 30 n.4, 30
incest 176
Independence Day (USA, July 4) 2
Ingham, M. A. 125
interdisciplinarity 9, 10, 115–16
intertextuality 6–7, 10, 12, 67, 72, 79, 88, 91 n.5, 115–16, 127, 171, 173, 182, 184
*Irezumi* (Japanese tatoos) 6, 17, 24, 26–7, 30
irony 72–3, 79, 140, 216
Isaiah (Old Testament) 141

Jackson, R.
    *Fantasy: The Literature of Subversion* 67, 69
Jacobs, Joseph
    *English Fairy Tales* 90 n.2
James, Garry 51
Japan and the foreign woman 21, 27–9
Japan Society for the Promotion of Science (JSPS), The 29
Japanese culture, society 6, 17–19, 21–3, 26
Japanese men 18, 22, 24
Jay, Martin
    *Downcast Eyes: The Denigration of Vision in Twenty-Century French Thought*
    'Scopic regimes of modernity' 162–5, 171
Jennings, Hope
    'Dystopian Matriarchies: Deconstructing the Womb in Angela Carter's *Heroes and Villains* and *The Passion of New Eve*' 150–1
Jennings, Michael W.
    (ed.) *The Writer of Modern Life: Essays on Charles Baudelaire* 169 n.20, 171
John of Patmos (The Book of Revelation) 141
Jones, C. A.
    *Mother Goose Refigured: A Critical Translation of Charles Perrault's Fairy Tales* 81, 91 n.3, 93
    'The Juniper Tree' 65

*Kabuki* (Japanese theatre) 17, 20, 22–3, 27, 29–30
kaleidoscopes 8, 11, 153–6, 158, 160, 162, 168 n.10

Kappeler, S.
    *The Pornography of Representation* 96, 111
Karpinski, Eva
    'Signifying Passions: Angela Carter's *Heroes and Villains* as a Dystopian Romance' 150 n.4, 151
Katsavos, Anna
    'A Conversation with Angela Carter' 89, 92 n.13, 93
    'Using the Fantastic to Disrupt the Domestic: An Examination of Marriage and Family in Angela Carter's *Nights at the Circus* and *Wise Children*' 234–5, 242 n.8, 243
Keats, John
    'On First Looking into Chapman's Homer' 8, 150 n.1, 151
Keenan, S.
    'Angela Carter's *The Sadeian Woman*: Feminism as Treason' 108, 111
Kellaway, K.
    'Interview Emma Rice: "I don't know how I got to be so controversial"' 116, 137
Kenyon, O.
    'Angela Carter', in *The Writer's Imagination: Interviews with Major International Women Novelists* 189, 206
Kerman, J.
    'The Prelude and the Play' 97, 111
Kerrigan, Catherine
    'Introduction', in C. Kerrigan (ed.), *An Anthology of Scottish Women Poets* 55, 69
Kidson, Frank 54
Killen, Louis 49, 52, 68
*Kimono* 19
King Lear 92 n.7, 230
Klein, Melanie
    *Love, Guilt and Reparation and Other Works 1921–1945* 37, 39
Kneehigh Theatre Company
    *Nights at the Circus* (theatrical adaptation) 116, 137
Kramer, Lawrence
    *Music as Cultural Practice, 1800–1900* 107, 111

Krzywinska, Tanya
 *Sex and the Cinema* 217, 226

La Fontaine, Jean de 75–7, 81
Lacan, Jacques 62, 70, 221–2, 226
'Lady Isobel and the Elf-Knight' (folk song) 57, 59, 63–4, 70
*The Lady of the House of Love* dir. David Fenton (theatrical adaptation) 116–37
Lang, Fritz
 *Metropolis* 165
Larner, Sam 52
Lau, K. J.
 'Erotic Infidelities: Angela Carter's Wolf Trilogy' 102, 106, 111, 222, 226
Lauman, Shelly 132
Lawrence, David Herbert
 *Apocalypse* 150–1
Lee, A.
 *Angela Carter* 115, 137
Leech, Geoffrey
 'Music in Metre: Sprung Rhyme in Victorian Poetry' 57, 69
Lesnik-Oberstein, Karín
 *The Last Taboo: Women and Body Hair* 221, 226
Lessing, Doris
 *The Golden Notebook* 74
Lévi-Strauss, Claude 143
Lewallen, Avis
 '"Wayward Girls but Wicked Women?" Female Sexuality in Angela Carter's *The Bloody Chamber*' 96, 111, 226
Lewis, C. S.
 *The Discarded Image* 66, 69
*Liebestod* (German for 'love-death') 98–100, 103, 107
Lilac Fairy, The 78
'The Little Mermaid' (fairy tale) 214
'Little Red Riding Hood' 74, 76–7, 96, 103, 183, 199–200, 208–9, 215, 217, 219
Lizon, Angela 174
Lloyd, A. L. 44, 52–3, 69
Lloyd, A. L. and Ralph Vaughan Williams
 *The Penguin Book of English Folk Songs* 46, 69
Lloyd, Bert 65
Locke, Belinda 78, 136–7

Lomax, Alan 45
Louis XIV 80–1, 83, 86
Louvel, Liliane
 *The Pictorial Third: An Essay into Intermedial Criticism* 174, 186
Lucretia 81
'Lucy Wan' (folk song) 46–7
Lutton, Matthew 116, 119–25, 128–32, 134, 137

McClary, S.
 *Feminine Endings: Music, Gender and Sexuality* 107, 111
MacColl, Ewan 52
McEwen, John
 *Paula Rego* 179–80, 186
McIntosh, Josh 125
Maehder, J.
 'A Mantle of Sound for the Night: Timbre in Wagner's *Tristan und Isolde*' 97–8, 106, 111
*The Magic Toyshop* (film, dir. David Wheatley) 13
Makem, Sarah 52
Makinen, Merja 4, 12
male gaze, The 8, 22, 99–100, 106, 153, 155–6, 158–60, 167, 176, 232
Malthouse Theatre, Melbourne
 *The Bloody Chamber* (theatrical adaptation) 116, 119, 124, 132, 135
Marcuse, Herbert 169 n.19
Mari Lwyd, The 33
martyrs, martyrdom 87–8, 91 n.3, 99, 102, 105, 109
marxism 147–8, 157
masculinity 8, 20, 23–4, 26–8, 80, 104, 106, 133–4, 146, 155–7, 168 n.9, 168 n.10, 171, 175, 190, 192, 208–9, 213, 216, 220–1, 236, 240
masochism 26–8, 88, 110
maternity 9, 112, 232–4, 242
Matheson, Richard
 *I Am Legend* 145
Matthew 9:17 49
Meaney, Geraldine
 'History and Women's Time: *Heroes and Villains*,' 150 n.5, 151
medieval, medievalism 49, 68, 71, 74, 80
Medusa, the 100, 102

melody 57, 67, 104, 124
melos 57
Metro Arts, Brisbane 116, 118, 135
Meyer, L.
  *Style and Music: Theory, History and Ideology* 97, 111
Michael, M. C.
  *Feminism and the Postmodern Impulse: Post-World War II Fiction* 131, 137
Miller, Roland 202
Milton, John
  *Paradise Lost* 149
Minier, Márta
  'Definitions, Dyads, Triads and Other Points of Connection' 129–30, 137
mirrors 19, 29, 36, 99, 105–6, 128, 156–7, 159–61, 166, 167 n.3, 174, 194, 198, 201, 203, 209, 220–3, 225 n.4, 232–3, 238
Mishima, Yokio 6, 17, 23–4
  'Onnagata' 23, 30
misogyny 20–1, 23, 79–80, 83, 86
'Mr Fox' 65
Molan, Christine 45–8
  'Angela Carter' 65
  'Authentic Magic: Angela, Folksong and Bristol' 58, 69
Moorcock, Michael 142
Moreau, Gustave 173
Morris, Tom 116
Mother Goose 78
Motherwell, W.
  *Minstrelsy Ancient and Modern* 54, 70
Mulvey, Laura
  'Visual Pleasure and Narrative Cinema' 167 n.1, 168 n.11, 171
Mulvey-Roberts, Marie 10, 174, 205 n.10
  *The Arts of Angela Carter: A Cabinet of Curiosities* (ed.) 10, 12
  *Pyrotechnics: A Union of Contraries* (ed.) 10
  *Strange Worlds: The Vision of Angela Carter* (ed.) 186
Munford, Rebecca
  *Decadent Daughters and Monstrous Mothers: Angela Carter and European Gothic* 21, 30
  *Re-visiting Angela Carter: Texts, Contexts, Intertexts* 10, 12

Muñoz, Andrew 174
Murphy, V.
  'Building Block Four: Choose an Evocative Stageable Image' 128, 137
music *See also* folk music 72, 95, 97–109, 111, 117–30, 135, 191, 197, 207, 218, 224, 226
musicality 6
mutability 97, 107, 148, 158, 243
myth 7, 32, 38, 72, 78

nakedness, nudity 27, 92, 163, 207, 209–10, 212–15, 217, 219–20, 223–4, 232, 235
Nattiez, J.-J.
  *Wagner androgyne: Essai sur l'interprétation* 98, 104, 107, 112
Neumeier, Beate
  'Postmodern Gothic: Desire and Reality in Angela Carter's Writing' 159, 171
New Jerusalem 141
*New Society* 68, 204 n.2
*New Worlds* 142
Nietzsche, Friedrich
  *On the Genealogy of Morality* 150 n.2, 151
1960s counterculture 10, 12, 231, 242 n.6, 243
nuclear war 8, 139, 140, 142–4, 146–8

Oberge, Eilhart von
  *Tristrant und Isolde* 96
*Observer, The* 116, 137
O'Day, M.
  '"Mutability is Having a Field Day": The Sixties Aura of Angela Carter's Bristol Trilogy' 243
Oliver, Di 174
*Omega Man* (dir. Boris Segal) 145
Opie, Iona and Peter
  *The Classic Fairy Tales* 73
otherness 1, 22, 194
Owen T. M.
  *Welsh Folk Customs* 33, 39

Pacheco, Ana Maria 171
Pagels, E. *Revelations: Visions, Prophecy, & Politics in the Book of Revelation* 141, 152

Palazzoli, Mara Selvini
 'Self-Starvation' 204 n.2
Palmer, Paulina
 'Gender as performance in the Fiction of Angela Carter and Margaret Atwood' 212, 226
Papachristophorou, M.
 'Shoe' 226
Parker, E.
 'The Consumption of Angela Carter: Women, Food, and Power' 190, 206
parody 36, 72, 100, 157, 216
patriarchy 6, 8, 20–1, 38, 44, 54–5, 79, 82, 88–9, 140, 143, 145, 147–9, 154, 166, 168 n.10, 208, 216, 222, 230–2, 239
Paulusma, Polly 6–7, 12, 54
 *Invisible Music: Folksongs That Influenced Angela Carter (CD)* 10, 55
Peach, L.
 *Angela Carter* 115, 137
peep-shows 159–62, 168 n.13, 169 n.23
*Penguin Book of English Folk Songs, The* 46, 49
performance 3–4, 8–10, 13, 19–24, 29, 49, 55, 67, 100, 108–9, 115–12, 124–8, 130–6, 156, 158, 181, 184, 189, 194, 196, 202–3, 211–12, 216, 218, 220, 223–4, 226–7, 236, 242 n.10
performativity 6, 22, 29, 108, 212, 217
Perrault, Charles 75
 *L'Apologie des femmes* 81
 *Le Cabinet des fées*, ed. Charles-Joseph de Mayer 73, 76, 78
 *Contes des fées* (ed. Lamy) 73, 81, 94
 *The Fairy Tales of Charles Perrault* (trans. A. Carter) 76–9, 93
 *Griselidis, Nouvelle, avec le conte de Peau d'Âne et celui des Souhaits ridicules* 80, 91 n.3
 'La Marquise de Salusses ou La Patience de Griselidis' ('The Patience of Grizelda') 73, 75–6, 79–82, 85, 87–9, 92–4
 'Peau d'Âne' ('Donkey-Skin') 73–4, 76–8, 81–2, 89, 91–2 n.7, 92, 210, 214, 224
 'Les Souhaits ridicules' ('The Foolish Wishes') 73, 92
 *Histoires ou Contes du temps passé (Histories or Tales of Past Times)*, aka *Contes de ma mère l'Oye* 73–4, 92
 'La Barbe bleue' ('Bluebeard') 88
 'La Belle au Bois dormant' ('The Sleeping Beauty in the Wood') 84, 76
 'Cendrillon ou la Petite Pantoufle de verre' ('Cinderella : or, The Little Glass Slipper') 76
 'Le Petit Poucet' ('Hop 'o my thumb') 76
 Barchilon edition 73, 92
 Collinet edition 92 n.10, 93
 *Perrault's Popular Tales* (ed. Andrew Lang) 73–5, 78, 93
 *Le Siècle de Louis Le Grand* 80–1
Peter Pan 176
Petrarch, Francesco
 *Historia Griseldis* 80, 82, 91 n.3
phantasmagoria 8, 156–8, 168 n.5, 168 n.6 169 n.20, 171
Pierpont Morgan Library, The 73
Pireddu, N.
 'CaRterbury Tales: Romances of Disenchantment in Geoffrey Chaucer and Angela Carter' 91 n.5, 94
Pires, Maria José 9, 193–4, 200, 204–6
Pitt Rivers Museum, The 36
Pollock, Mary S.
 'Angela Carter's Animal Tales: Constructing the Non-Human' 66, 70
Pollock's Toy Shop 58
pornography 44, 96, 111, 148, 153, 159, 226
Portman, Emily 53
postmodernism 6, 29, 110, 131, 133, 136–7, 140–1, 152, 157, 171, 236, 243
Powell, Enoch 23
Preetorius, Emil 106
Pre-Raphaelite Brotherhood, The 151, 153, 171
'Procrustean bed', The 18
Proust, Marcel 154–5, 167 n.2
Provisional IRA, The 145
psychoanalysis 140, 226
Punter, David 6

'Angela Carter: Supersessions of the
    Masculine' 169 n.19, 171
*Pyr* (Greek for 'fire') 1
pyrotechnics 3–4, 10, 12, 17, 71, 162

'Quarrel About Women' *See also* Boileau
    80–1
'Quarrel between the Ancients and the
    Moderns' *See also* Boileau 80
Queensland Cabaret Festival 117
queer theory 104, 108–9

radio 4, 10, 12, 43–4, 69, 115, 136, 171,
    178, 198, 205
Rainbow Fairy Books 74–5
    *The Blue Fairy Book* 75
rape 56, 62, 66–7, 79, 135, 143, 145
'Reading the Fantastic: Tales beyond
    Borders' (conference) 110 n.1
Red Riding Hood 74, 76–7, 96, 103, 183,
    199–200, 208–9, 215, 217, 219
Reed, Lou
    'Some Kinds of Love' (song) 39
Reeves, Jim
    *The Everlasting Circle* 9, 46, 48, 70
religion 84, 147, 208
Renato's Theatre Company 13, 116
Rego, Paula 8, 174–81, 184–6
    *The Cadet and His Sister* 181
    *The Family* 180
    'Girl and Dog' series 179
    *Girl Lifting up Her Skirts to a Dog* 179,
        181
    *The Little Murderess* 179
    *Looking back* 179
    *Prey* 174
Reich, Wilhelm 169 n.19
repression 19–20, 25–9, 74
'Reynardine' (folk song) 65–6, 70
Rhys, Jean 74
rhythm 7, 53, 56–63, 67, 141, 204 n.4
Rice, Emma 116, 137
Riggs, Ashley 7, 110 n.1, 110 n.6, 112
Robertson, Etienne-Gaspard 168 n.5
Robinson, Fiona and Marie Mulvey-
    Roberts, *Strange Worlds: The Vision
    of Angela Carter* (ed.) 186
Roffe, Carole 145
Roman Empire 141
Rosen, Elizabeth

*Apocalyptic Transformation: Apocalypse
    and the Postmodern Imagination*
    141, 152
Rosenthal, H. and J. Warrack
    *The Concise Oxford Dictionary of
    Opera*, 2nd edn 96, 112
Rossetti, Christina
    '*Goblin Market*' 204 n.4
Rousseau, Jean-Jacques 143–4, 150 n.4
Rushdie, Salman
    'Angela Carter, 1940–92: A Very Good
        Wizard, a Very Dear Friend' 10, 13,
        230, 241, 243
    'Introduction', in A. Carter, *Burning Your
        Boats: Collected Stories* 43
    *Shame* 38–9

Sade, Donatien Alphonse François,
    Marquis de 21, 70, 87, 96–7, 105,
    108, 202
sadism 27–8, 83, 145
Sage, Lorna 149, 173, 229
    '*Angela Carter*' 152
    'Angela Carter: The Fairy Tale' 212,
        226
    *The Cambridge Guide to Women's
        Writing in English* (ed.) 174
    *Flesh and the Mirror: Essays on the Art
        of Angela Carter* (ed.) 94, 171, 205,
        243
    'The Soaring Imagination' (Angela
        Carter obituary) 174–5, 186, 242 n.12
    *Women in the House of Fiction* 168 n.
        12, 171
Saint Cecilia 88
'St Mary's/Church Street Medley' (folk
    song) 68
*Samurai* 18–19, 23–4
Sauvage, J.
    'Bloody Chamber Melodies: Painting
        and Music in *The Bloody Chamber*'
        210, 226
Saxton, Josephine 146, 148
Scheherazade 234
Schiaparelli 239
Schopenhauer, Arthur 97
science fiction 141, 146, 148
Scott, Sir Walter 54
Seeger, Peggy 49, 51–2, 68, 70
Segal, Lynne

*Out of Time: The Pleasures and Perils of Ageing* 231
Sermain, Jean-Paul 90 n.1
   *Le Conte de fées du classicisme aux Lumières* 94
   '*Griselidis* de Perrault: l'anti-Baudelaire' 91 n.3, 94
   'Perrault, conteur en vers' 91 n.3, 94
sex, sexuality 3, 8–9, 22, 44, 60, 64, 66, 71, 74, 78–9, 86, 88–9, 96–7, 102–3, 105, 107–11, 115, 148–9, 158, 160, 166–7, 175–6, 179–82, 193, 195, 197–8, 202, 209, 215–23, 226, 230–4, 237, 240–1
sexism 240
Shakespeare, William
   *King Lear* 92 n.7
Sharp, Cecil 54–6
   'Common People' 54
   *English Folk Song: Some Conclusions* 70, 56
   *English Folk Songs from the Southern Appalachians* 46
Shaw, George Bernard 107
Sheffield 199
Simon, J.
   *Rewriting the Body: Desire, Gender and Power in Selected Novels by Angela Carter* 234, 242 n.2, 242 n.8, 242 n.9, 243
Sinfield, A.
   *Faultlines: Cultural Materialism and the Politics of Dissident Reading* 108, 112
Sivyer, Caleb 8, 171
*The Sleeping Beauty* 72, 74, 76, 118, 127, 199
Snaith, Helen
   'Fictions written in a Certain City' 2–4, 13
Smith, A. C. H. and Christopher Northam
   *Pussy: An Angela Carter Musical Extravaganza* dir. Tony Rowlands (musical adaptation) 13, 116
   *The Ruby Choker* dir. Tony Rowlands (musical adaptation) 13, 116
Smith, Ali
   'Introduction', in A. Carter, *The Infernal Desire Machines of Doctor Hoffman* 159, 171

Smith, Phoëbe 46
*Social and Cultural Aspects of Drinking* (A report to the European Commission) 206
Sontag, Susan
   'The Double Standard of Aging' 233, 240, 243
Spencer, S.
   'Staging *Tristan und Isolde*' 106, 112
Spooner, Catherine
   '"Clothes Are Our Weapons": Dandyism, Fashion and Subcultural Style in Angela Carter's Fiction of the 1960s' 208, 226
   *Fashioning Gothic Bodies* 224, 226
Stalker, Angela *See also* Angela Carter
   'Come in, take a chair, lean on it, and sing' 49–51, 70
Stead, Christina 4
stereoscopes 161
Stevenson, R. L.
   'On Some Technical Elements of Style in Literature' 57, 70
Stoddart, H.
   *Angela Carter's Nights at the Circus* 115, 137
*Strange Worlds: The Vision of Angela Carter*, eds. Marie Mulvey-Robert and Fiona Robinson (exhibition) xii, xv, 174
Straparola, Giovanni Francesco 76
Strassburg, Gottfried von
   *Tristan* 96
stress (metrical) 57
subversion 11, 67, 69, 110, 211, 217, 225
Suleiman, Susan Rubin
   'The Fate of the Surrealist Imagination in the Society of the Spectacle' 160, 168 n.13, 171
Summer of Love, The 39
surrealism 5, 11, 94, 140, 145–6, 150, 152–3, 171
Swan and Sugar Loaf, The 51
symbolism 8, 128, 144, 181, 207, 223
Szymanowski, Karol
   *Efebos* 107

Tamlane 91–2
*Tatemae* (Japanese for 'public behaviour, opinions') 19

tattoos (Western) 6, 24–7, 30 n.5, 30, 34–5, 143
Taylor, T.
   *Nights at the Circus Teacher's Resource Pack* 116, 137
*Techne* (Greek for 'art') 1
theatricality 115–16
Thomas, Dylan
   'Do Not Go Gentle into That Good Night' 238, 243
Tiainen, Milla
   'Corporeal Voices, Sexual Differentiations: New Materialist Perspectives on Music, Singing and Subjectivity' 52, 70
Tiffin, Jessica
   *Marvellous Geometry: Narrative and Metafiction in the Modern Fairy Tale* 215, 221, 227
Tolkien, J. R. R.
   *On Fairy-Stories* 63, 70
Tonkin, Maggie
   *Angela Carter and Decadence: Critical Fictions/Fictional Critiques* 158, 167 n.2, 171
   'The Rough and the Holy: Angela Carter's Marionette Theatre' 115, 137
transformation 7, 9, 61–2, 66, 91 n.7, 100, 106, 108–9, 122, 125, 140–1, 145, 147–8, 152, 157, 161, 163–4, 166, 167 n.4, 194, 209, 215–18, 220, 224, 239
translation 6–7, 10, 12, 18, 20, 71–4, 77–9, 82–3, 86, 89, 90 n.2, 91 n.3, 91 n.4, 91 n.10, 93, 96, 104, 107, 111–12, 129, 137
transmutation 34
Trevenna, Joanna
   'Gender as Performance: Questioning the 'Butlerification' of Angela Carter's Fiction' 9, 13, 216, 227
'"Truly It Felt Like Year One" A Tour of Angela Carter's 1960s Bristol' 12
Turner, K. and P. Greenhill, eds (2012), *Transgressive Tales: Queering the Grimms* 108, 112
'The Twa Corbies' (folk song) 48
'The Twa sisters' (folk song) 45, 65

Twigg, Julia
   *Fashion and Age: The Body in Later Life* 232, 237, 241, 243

'The Unquiet Grave' (folk song) 48

Vallotton, Félix 173
*Verklärung* (German for 'transfiguration') 7
Virgin Mary, The 130
voyeurism 84, 88, 155, 157, 160

Wagner, Wilhelm Richard 6, 97–8, 103–4, 106–9, 110 n.5, 111, 165
   *My Life* 97, 112
   *Opera and Drama* 104
   *Tristan und Isolde* 7, 95–8, 102, 105, 107–12
*The Walking Dead* 137
Ware, Martin 72
Warner, Marina
   'Angela Carter: Bottle Blonde, Double Drag' 92 n.8, 94
   'Angela Carter: Fairy Tales, Cross-dressing and the Mercurial Slipperiness of Identity' 214, 227
   'Chamber of Secrets: The Sorcery of Angela Carter' 95, 106, 112
   *From the Beast to the Blonde: On Fairy Tales and Their Tellers* 221, 227
   'Introduction', in A. Carter (ed.), *The Second Virago Book of Fairy Tales* 43, 70
   'Introduction', in P. Rego, *Jane Eyre* 176–7, 186
   *Once Upon A Time: A Short History of Fairy Tale* 72, 94
   *Phantasmagoria: Spirit Visions, Metaphors, and Media into the Twenty-first Century* 168 n.5, 171
   'Why Angela Carter's *The Bloody Chamber* Still Bites' 43, 70
Watz, Anna
   *Angela Carter and Surrealism: 'A Feminist Libertarian Aesthetic'* 71, 94, 142, 150 n.6, 152–3, 171, 205 n.10
Waxman, B. F.
   *From the Hearth to the Open Road* 230, 243
Webb, K.

'Seriously Funny: *Wise Children*' 242 n.1, 243
Wedekind, Benjamin Franklin
   *Lulu* 115
Wesendonck, Otto 97, 110
Whyte, Alison 119–20, 123–5, 129–30, 132, 134–5
'The Wild Swans' (fairy tale) 210
Willett, Tom 55
Winick, S.
   'A. L. Lloyd and Reynardine: Authenticity and Authorship in the Afterlife of a British Broadside Ballad' 70
Winter, Trish and S. Keegan-Phipps
   *Performing Englishness: Identity and Politics in a Contemporary Folk Resurgence* 54, 70
Wise Children (theatre company) 116
Wolf Alice 53
Woodward, Jethro 125

*Yakuza* (member of Japanese organized crime syndicate) 26, 30 n.5
Yeandle, Heidi
   *Angela Carter and Western Philosophy* 150 n.3, 150 n.4, 152

Žižek, Slavoj
   'Kant with Sade: The Ideal Couple' 70

www.ingramcontent.com/pod-product-compliance
Lightning Source LLC
Chambersburg PA
CBHW062123300426
44115CB00012BA/1787